Sound for Film and Television

2nd Edition
Tomlinson Holman

**Focal
Press**

Boston Oxford Auckland Johannesburg Melbourne New Delhi

Focal Press in an imprint of Butterworth-Heinemann.

 A member of the Reed Elsevier group

ISBN: 0-240-80453-8

The publisher offers special discounts on bulk orders of this book.
For information, please contact:
Manager of Special Sales
Butterworth-Heinemann
225 Wildwood Avenue
Woburn, MA 01801-2041
Tel: 781-904-2500
Fax: 781-904-2620

For information on all Focal Press publications, contact our World Wide Web home page at:
http://www.focalpress.com

10 9 8 7 6 5 4 3 2 1

Printed in the United States of America

Table of Contents

Preface to the First Edition

This book is an introduction to the art and technique of sound for film and television. The focus in writing the book has been to span the gulf between typical film and television production textbooks with perhaps too little emphasis on underlying principles, and design engineering books that have few practical applications, especially to the film and television world. The guiding principle for inclusion in the text is the usefulness of the topic to film or video makers.

The first three chapters provide background principles of use to anyone dealing with sound, especially sound accompanying a picture, and, by way of examples, demonstrate the utility of the principles put into practice. The rest of the book walks through the course of a production, from the pickup of sound by microphones on the set, to the reproduction of sound in cinemas and homes at the end of the chain. For the sake of completeness, some information has been included that may be tangential to end users. This information has been made separate from the main text by being indented and of smaller type.

No study of film and television sound would be complete without listening to a lot of film and television shows. This is practical today in classrooms and at home because with a decent home theater sound system, available for a few thousand dollars, the principles given in the text can be demonstrated. Here are some film examples that are especially useful.

- *Citizen Kane*, the scene in the living room at Xanadu where Kane and his love interest interact, photographed with the great depth of field that was the innovation of Greg Toland for the picture. The sound in this scene can be contrasted with that in the next scene of Kane and his girl friend in the back seat of a car. In the first scene, the sound is very reverberant, emphasizing the separation of the characters. In the second, the sound is very intimate, emphasizing the change of scene that has taken place. Orson Welles brought the techniques he had learned in radio to films. This is used to illustrate Chapter 1, Objective Sound, and the difference that attention to such factors can make.

- *Days of Heaven,* reel 1 from opening to arrival of the train at the destination. After an opening still photo montage accompanied by music, we come in on an industrial steel mill where the sound of the machinery is so loud we often cannot hear the characters. A fight ensues between a worker and his boss, and the content of the argument is actually made stronger by the fact of our not being able to discern it. This illustrates frequency masking, a topic in Chapter 2. A train leaves for the country then, accompanied by music, and the question posed is: Do we hear the train or not and what does it matter if we do or don't? A voice over narration illustrates the speech mode of perception, when it abruptly enters and demands our attention. The lyrical music accompanied by the train motion is a strong contrast with the sound that has come before, and is used in the vaudeville sense of "a little traveling music, please"—making it an effective montage. At the end of the scene there is a crossfade between the music and the reality sound that puts an end to the montage, punctuating the change in mood.

- *Das Boot,* reel 1 from the entrance of the officers into the submarine compound until the first shot of the submarine on the open ocean illustrates many things. At first the submarine repair station interior is very noisy, and the actors have to raise their voices to be heard. Actually, the scene was almost certainly looped, therefore it was the direction to the actors that caused their voices to be raised, not the conditions in which they were recorded. Next, the officers come upon their boat, and despite the fact they are still in a space contiguous with the very noisy space, the noisy background gives way to a relatively quiet one, illustrating a subjective rather than totally objective

view. Then the submarine leaves the dock, accompanied by a brass band playing along in sync (an example of pre-recorded, or at least post synced, sound). The interior of the boat is established through the medium of telling a visitor where everything is. Sound is used to help establish each space in the interior: noise for the men's quarters, and a little music for the officer's, Morse code for the radio room, and mechanical noise for the control room. Next we come upon a door from whence we hear a loud sound, then going through the door, we find it is the engine room with the very noisy engine causing the actors to speak loudly once again. The whole reel, up to the going to sea shot, is useful in the ways that sound is used to tell the story.

- *Cabaret* is used for two principal purposes. The first is to show a scene that involved extensive pre-production preparation of a music recording, then filming, then using the pre-recorded and possibly post-recorded materials after the picture was edited to synchronize to the perspective of the picture. The scene is of the Nazi boy singing "The sun on the meadow is summery warm . . ." until the main characters leave with the question, "Do you still think you will be able to control them?" What is illustrated here is very well controlled filmmaking, for we always hear what we expect to, that is, sound matched to picture, but over a bed of sound that stays more constant with the picture cuts. The second point of using *Cabaret* is that filmmaking is a powerful, but neutral, tool, that can help move people to heights of folly. Whether the techniques taught here are used for good or ill is in the hands of the filmmaker.

- *Platoon* demonstrates a number of sound ideas in the final battle scene. Despite the fact that it is difficult to understand the characters while they are under fire, the effect of their utterances is bone chilling nevertheless. The absolutely essential lines needed for exposition are clearly exposed, with practically no competition from sound effects or music. On the other hand, there is one line that can only be understood by lip reading, since it is covered by an explosion. Still, the meaning is clear and the "dialog" can be understood since the words spoken are so right in the context of the scene.

A list of other films that I have found to be of enduring interest are listed in the Filmography at the end of the book.

Acknowledgments

Ken Miura, associate dean at USC Cinema-Television, read the first drafts of the text and provided valuable input, as well as ongoing encouragement over a period of years. Clay Westervelt, as a second year graduate student read the text and contributed much to its readability by laymen. The discussion of the Gestalt psychologists and psychoacoustics in Chapter 2 owes a great deal to Dr. Brian C. J. Moore's book *An Introduction to the Psychology of Hearing*, referenced in the bibliography. Bill Hogan provided input on time code. The illustrations were composed by Lowell Schwartz. The editor was Marie Lee, and the production editor Maura Kelly.

Ben Burtt, Gary Summers, Gary Rydstrom, Randy Thom, Laurel Ladevich, and others provided the reason for me to do this book through their dedicated work in the sound art. Virtually all of the stories in this book are a result of their work, not mine, but I repeat them here for a wider audience than just lunches at Lucasfilm.

I interviewed a number of people on video for a possible future extension of this book to a more interactive domain. These included Andy Davis (director of *The Fugitive* and *Under Siege*); Jeff Wexler (production sound recordist for *Independence Day* as well as many other pictures since I was his boom operator on what was for both of us our first Hollywood movie, *Cool Breeze*, produced by Gene Corman in 1972, and photographed by Andy Davis); Richard Anderson (sound designer of many, many pictures); and Steve Quale (who learned film sound formats at USC so well he got hired by Lightstorm Entertainment, where he was responsible for the development of their screening room and was second unit director on *Titanic*).

Colophon

The text is set in Sabon and the headings in Univers. J. D. Colley specified the type, but the author is responsible for the design.

Dedication

This work is dedicated to M. L. H. and F. P. C. K.

Preface to the Second Edition

This edition has been largely modified from the first because of the changes that have rapidly engulfed the film and television industries in just a few short years. Today it is unlikely to see physical editing equipment supplying rows upon rows of film playback devices called dubbers. Digital nonlinear editing and mixing have come of age, and rapidly. The film and television sound industry now chases such statistics as the 60% per year increase in recorded density on hard disks that has gone on for the 10 years from 1991 to 2001, with little end in sight.

Thanks are due to a number of people who helped with this second edition, as well as those who are recognized for their help with the first edition in the previous preface. Elliott H. Berger provided valuable new input on hearing loss. My colleagues in the Sound Department of the University of Southern California School of Cinema-Television read Chapters 6–8 of the manuscript and contributed to them, especially Midge Costin, Don Hall, and Tim Maloney. Once again Bill Hogan has provided feedback on time code and synchronization issues.

Dedication
This edition is dedicated to Henry Kloss, who showed me the way.

"Talkies, squeakies, moanies, songies, and squawkies . . . but whatever you call them, I'm absolutely serious in what I have to say about them. Just give them 10 years to develop and you're going to see the greatest artistic medium the world has known."

D. W. Griffith

Introduction

Sound for film and television defined

Sound for film and television is an aural experience constructed to support the story of a narrative, documentary, or commercial film or television program. Sound may tell the story directly, or it may be used indirectly to enhance the story. Although there are separate perceptual mechanisms for sound and picture, the sound may be integrated by the audience along with the picture into a complete whole, without differentiation. In such a state, the sound and picture together can become greater than the sum of the parts.

In most instances, film and television sound for entertainment and documentary programming is constructed in post production by professionals utilizing many pieces of sound mixed seamlessly together to create a complete whole. The sources for the sound used include recordings made during *principal photography* on sets or on location, sound effects libraries and customized recordings, and music, both that composed for the film and from pre-existing sources. Sound for film and television is thus a thoroughly constructed experience, usually meant to seamlessly integrate many elements together and not draw specific attention to itself.

The relative roles of picture and sound can change with regard to storytelling from scene to scene and moment to moment. A straight narrative picture will likely have dialog accompanying it, whereas a picture montage will often be accompanied by music, or at least manipulated sound effects, as the filmmaker varies the method of storytelling from time to time to add interest to the film, and provide a moment for audiences to soak up the action, make scene transitions, and so forth.

Nearly everyone involved in production of a film or television program affects, and is affected by, sound. Writers use sound elements in their storytelling, with suggestions in the script for what may be heard. Location scouts should note bad noise conditions at potential shooting sites because while the camera can "pan off" an offending sign, there is no such effective way to eliminate airplanes flying over from the sound track—the "edges" of a sound frame are not hard like those of a picture frame. Directors need to be keenly aware of the potential for sound, for what they are getting on location and what can be substituted in post production, as sound is "50% of the experience" according to a leading filmmaker. Cinematographers can plan lighting so that a sound boom is usable, with the result being potentially far better sound. Costumers can supply pouches built into clothing that can conceal microphones, and can supply booties so that actors can wear them for low noise when their feet don't show. Grips, gaffers, and set dressers can make the set quiet and make operable items work silently.

Roles of sound

Many kinds of sound have a direct storytelling role in filmmaking.[1] Dialog and narration tell the story, and narrative sound effects can be used in such a capacity too, for example, to draw the attention of the characters to an off-screen event. Such direct narrative sound effects are often written into the script, since their use can influence when and where actors have to take some corresponding action.

Sound also has a subliminal role, working on its audience unconsciously. While all viewers can tell apart the various objects in a picture—an actor, a table, the walls of a room—listeners barely ever perceive sound so analytically. They tend to take sound in as a whole, despite its actually being deliberately constructed from many pieces. Herein lies the key to an important storytelling power of sound: the inability of listeners to separate sound into ingredient parts can easily produce "a willing suspension of disbelief" in the audience, since they cannot separately discern the function of the various sound elements. This fact can be manipulated by filmmakers to produce a route to emotional involvement in the material by the audience. The most direct example of this effect is often the film score. Heard in isolation, film scores[2] often don't make much musical sense; the music is deliberately written to enhance the mood of a scene and to underscore the action, not as a foreground activity, but a background one. The function of the music is to "tell" the audience how to feel, from moment to moment: soaring strings mean one thing, a single snare drum, another.

Another example of this kind of thing is the emotional sound equation that says that low frequencies represent a threat. Possibly this association has deep primordial roots, but if not, exposure to film sound certainly teaches listeners this lesson quickly. A distant thunderstorm played underneath an otherwise sunny scene indicates a sense of foreboding, or doom, as told by this equation. An interesting parallel is that the shark in *Jaws* is introduced by four low notes on an otherwise calm ocean, and there are many other such examples.

Sound plays a grammatical role in the process of filmmaking too. For instance, if sound remains constant before and after a picture cut, the indication being made to the audience is that while the point of view may have changed, the scene has not shifted—we are in the same space as before. So sound provides a form of continuity or connective tissue for films. In particular, one type of sound represented several ways plays this part. *Presence* and *ambience* help to "sell" the continuity of a scene to the audience.

Sound is often "hyper-real"

Sound recordings for film and television are often an exaggeration of reality. One reason for this is that there is typically so much competing sound at any given moment that each sound that is recorded and must be heard has to be rather overemphatically stated, just to "read" through the clutter. Heard

---

1. This term is used instead of the clumsier, but more universal, "program making." What is meant here and henceforth when terms such as this are used is the general range of activities required to make a film, video, or television program.

2. The actual score played with the film, not the corresponding music-only CD release.

in isolation, the recordings seem silly, over-hyped, but heard in context, they assume a more natural balance. The elements that often best illustrate this effect are called *Foley* sound effects. These are effects recorded while watching a picture such as footsteps, and are often exaggerated from how they would be in reality, both in loudness and in intimacy. While some of this exaggeration is due to the experience of practitioners finding that average sound playback systems obscure details, a good deal of the exaggeration still is desirable under the best playback conditions, simply because of the competition from other kinds of sound.

Sound and picture

Sound often has an influence on picture, and vice versa. For instance, making picture edits along with downbeats in a musical score often makes the picture cuts seem very right. In *The Wonderful Horrible Life of Leni Riefenstahl* we see Hitler's favorite filmmaker tell us this lesson, for she cut the waving flags in the Nuremberg Nazi rally in *Triumph of the Will* into sync with the music, increasing the power of the scene to move people.

Scenes are different depending on how sound plays out in them. For example, "pre-lapping" a sound edit before a scene changing picture edit[3] simply feels different than cutting both sound and picture simultaneously. The sense is heightened that the outgoing scene is over, and the story is driven ahead. Such a decision is not one taken at the end of the process in post production by a sound editor typically, but more often by the picture editor and director working together, since it has such a profound impact on storytelling. Thus involvement with sound is not only important to those who are labeled with sound-oriented credits, but to the entire filmmaking process represented by directing and editing the film.

Sound personnel

Sound specific personnel on a given film or television job may range from one person,

---

3. By cutting to the sound for the incoming scene before the outgoing picture changes.

that being the camera-person on a low-budget documentary with little post production, to quite large and differentiated crews as seen in the credits of theatrical motion pictures. In typical feature film production, a production sound recordist serves as head of a crew which may add one or more boom operators and cable persons as needed to capture all the sound present. On television programs shot in the multi-camera format "filmed in Hollywood before a live studio audience," an even larger crew may be used to control multiple boom microphones, to plant microphones on the set, and to place radio microphones on actors, then mix these sounds to a multi-track tape recorder. Either of these situations is called production sound recording.

Following in post production, picture editors cut the production sound track along with the picture, so that the story can be told throughout a film. They may add some additional sound in the way of principal sound effects and music, producing, often with the help of sound specific editors, up to "temp mixes" of use in evaluating the current state of a film or video in post production. Without such sound, audiences, including even sophisticated professional ones, cannot adequately judge the program content as they are distracted by such things as cutting to silence. By stimulating two senses, program material is subject to a heightened sensation on the part of the viewer/listener which would not occur if either the picture or sound stood alone. A case in point is one of an observer looking at an action scene silently, then with ever increasing complexity of sound by adding each of the edited sound sources in turn. The universal perception of observers under these conditions is that the picture appears to run faster with more complex sound, despite the fact that precisely the same time elapses for the silent and the sound presentations: the sound has had a profound influence on the perception of the picture.

When the picture has been edited, sound post production begins in earnest. Transfer operators take the production sound recordings and transfer them to an editable format such as mag film or into a digital audio workstation. Sound editors pick and place sound, drawing on production sound, sound effects libraries, and specially recorded effects, which are also all transferred to an editable format. From the edited sound tracks, various mixes are made by re-recording mixers (called dubbing mixers in England). Mixing may be accomplished in one or more steps, more generations becoming necessary as the number of cut sound tracks increases to such large numbers that all tracks cannot be handled at one time. The last stage of post production mixing prepares masters in a format compatible with the delivery medium, such as optical sound on film, or video tape.

The technical vs. the aesthetic

While it has a technical side, in the final analysis what is most important for film and television sound is what the listener hears, that is, what choices have been made throughout production and post production by the filmmakers. Often, thoughts are heard from producers and others such as, "can't you just improve the sound by making it all digital?" In fact, this is a naive point of view, since for instance what is more important to production sound is what the microphone technique is, rather than the method of tape recording. Unwanted noise on the set is not reduced by digital recording, and often causes problems, despite what method to record the production sound may be in use.

When film sound started in the late 1920s, the processes to produce the sound track were very difficult. Camera movement was restricted by large housings holding both the camera and the cameraman so that noise did not intrude into the set. Optical sound tracks were recorded simultaneously with the picture on a separate sound camera, and could not be played back until the film was processed and printed. Microphones were insensitive so actors had to speak loudly and clearly. Silent movie actor's careers were on the line, as it was discovered by audiences that many of them had foreign accents or high, squeaky voices.

Today, the technical impediments of early sound recording have been removed. Acting styles are much more natural, with it more likely that an actor will "underplay" a scene due to the intimacy of the camera than "overplay" it. Yet the quality achieved in production sound is still subject to such issues as whether the set has been made quiet, and whether the actor enunciates or mumbles his lines. Many directors pass all problems in speech intelligibility to the sound "technician," who, after all, is supposed to be able to make a high-quality recording even if the director can't hear the actor on the set!

The dimensions of a sound track

The "dimensions" of a sound track may be broken down for discussion into frequency range, dynamic range, the spatial dimension, and the temporal dimension. A major factor in the history of sound accompanying pictures is the growth in the capabilities associated with these dimensions as time has gone by, and the profound influence this growth has had on the aesthetics of, for example, motion-picture sound tracks. Whereas early sound films only had a frequency range capability (bandwidth) about that of a telephone, steady growth in this area has produced modern sound track capabilities well matched to the frequency range of human hearing. Dynamic range capability improvements have meant both louder and softer sounds are capable of being reproduced and heard without audible distortion or masking. Stereophonic sound added literally new dimensions to film sound tracks, first rather tentatively in the 1950s with magnetic sound release prints, and then firmly with optical stereo prints in the 1970s, which have continued improvement ever since. Still, even the monophonic movies of the 1930s benefited from one spatial dimension: adding reverberation to sound tracks helped place the actors in a scene and to differentiate among narration, on-screen dialog, off-screen sound effects, and music.

Chapter 1: Objective Sound

An old story

A tree falls over in a wood. Does it make a sound? From one point of view, the answer is that it must make a sound, since the physical requirements for there to be sound have been met. An alternate view is that without any consciousness to "hear" the sound, there in fact is no sound. This dichotomy demonstrates the difference between this chapter and the next. A physicist has a ready answer—to her, of course, there is a great crashing noise. On the other hand, a humanist philosopher thinks consciousness may well be required for there to be a sound.

The dichotomy observed is that between objective physical sound and subjective psychoacoustics. Any sound undergoes two principal processes for us to "hear" it. First, it is generated and the objective world acts on it, and then that world is represented inside our minds by the processes of hearing and perception. This chapter concentrates on the first part of this process—the generation and propagation of physical sound—while

Chapter 2 discusses how the physical sound is represented inside our heads.

The reason the distinction between the objective and subjective parts of sound perception is so important is that in finding cause and effect in sound, it is very important to know the likely source of a problem: Is there a real physical problem to be solved with a physical solution, or does the problem require an adjustment to accommodate human listening? Any given problem can have its roots in either domain, and is often best solved in its own dominion. On the other hand, there are times when we can provide a psychoacoustical solution to what is a actually an acoustical problem.

An example of this is that often people think that there is an equipment solution to what is in fact an acoustical problem. High background noise level of a location cannot be solved with digital recording, for instance, although some producers wonder whether this might not be true.

Properties of physical sound

There are several distinguishing characteristics of sound, partly arising from the nature of the source of the sound (Is it big or small?; Does it radiate sound equally in all directions, or does it have a directional preference?), and partly from the prevailing conditions between the point of origin and the point of observation (Is there any barrier or direct line of sight?). Sound propagates through a medium such as air at a specific speed and is acted on by the physical environment.

Fig. 1.1 The waves resulting from a stone dropping into a pond radiate outward, as does sound from a point source in air.

Propagation

Sound travels from one observation point to another by a means that is analogous to the way that waves ripple outwards from where a stone has been dropped into a pond. Each molecule of the water interacts with the other molecules around it in a particular orderly way. A given volume of water receives energy from the direction of the source of the disturbance and passes it on to other water that is more distant from the source, causing a circular spreading of the wave. Unless the stone is large and the water splashes, the water molecules are only disturbed about their nominal positions, but eventually they occupy about the same position as they had before the disturbance.

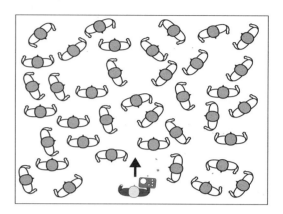

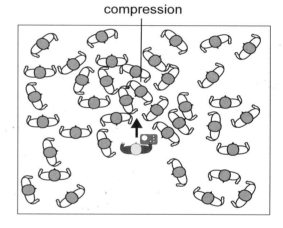

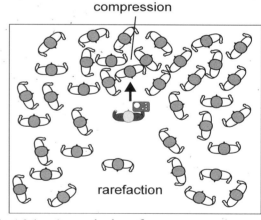

Fig. 1.2 A waiter on the dance floor compresses dancers in front of him, and leaves a rarefied space behind him.

Consider sound in air for a moment. It differs from other air movement, like wind or drafts, by the fact that, on the whole, the molecules in motion will return to practically the same position they had before the disturbance. Although sound is molecules in motion, there is no *net* motion of the air molecules, just a passing disturbance.

Another way to look at how sound propagates from point to point is to visualize it as a disturbance at a dance. Let's say that we are looking down on a crowded dance floor. With contemporary dancing, there isn't much organization to the picture from above—the motion is random. A waiter, carrying a large tray, enters the dance floor. The dancers closest to the waiter have to move a lot to get out of his way, and when they then start to bump into their neighbors, the neighbors move away, etc. The disturbance may be very small by the time it reaches the other side of the dance floor, but the action of the waiter has disturbed the whole crowd, more or less. If the waiter were to step in, then out, of the crowd, people would first be compressed together, then spread apart, perhaps further than they ever had been while dancing. The waiter in effect leaves a vacuum behind, which people rush in to fill. The two components of the disturbance are called *compression*, when the crowd is forced together more closely than normal, and *rarefaction*, when the spacing between the people is more than it is normally.

The tines of a tuning fork work like the waiter on the dance floor, only the dancers are replaced by the air molecules around the tuning fork. As the tines move away from the center of the fork, they compress the outside air molecules, and as they reverse direction and move towards one another, the air becomes rarefied (Fig. 1.3). Continuous, cyclical compression and rarefaction form the steady tone that is the recognized sound of a tuning fork.

Our analogy to water ripples can be carried further. In a large, flat pond, the height of the waves gets smaller as we go further from the origin, because the same amount of energy is spread out over a larger area. Sound is like this too, only the process is three dimensional, so that by spreading out over an expand-

ing surface, like blowing up a balloon, the energy further from the source is even less. The "law" or rule that describes the amplitude of the sound waves falling off with distance is called the *inverse square law*. This law states that when the distance to a sound source doubles, the size of the disturbance diminishes to one quarter of its original size.

Strength of sound at a distant point = original strength/distance^2

Track 2 of the CD illustrates the inverse square law effect of level vs. distance.

The inverse square law describes the fall off

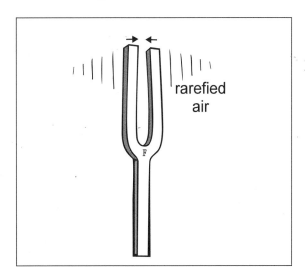

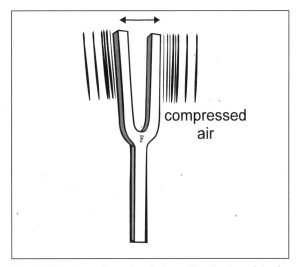

Fig. 1.3 The tines of a tuning fork oscillate back and forth, causing the nearby air to be alternately rarefied and compressed.

of sound energy from a *point source*, radiating into free space. A point source is a source that is infinitesimal and shows no directional preference.

In actual cases, most sources occupy some area and may show a directional preference, and most environments contain one or more reflecting surfaces, which conspire to make the real world more complex than this simple model.

> One of the main deviations from this model comes when a source is large, say, a newspaper press. Then it is difficult to get far enough away to consider this to be a point source, so the fall off with distance will typically be less than expected. This causes problems for narrative filmmakers trying to work in a press room because not only is the press noisy, but the falloff of the noise with distance is small.

Another example is an explosion occurring in a mineshaft. Within the shaft, sound will not fall off according to the inverse square law because the walls prevent the sound pressure from spreading. Therefore, even if the sound of the explosion is a great distance away, it can be nearly as loud as it is near its source, and quite dangerous to the documentary film crew members who think that they are sufficiently far away from the blast to avoid danger.

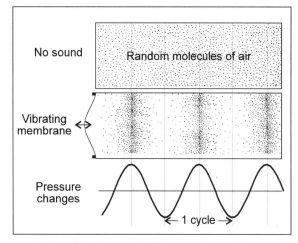

Fig. 1.4 Sound is the organized pressure changes above and below ambient pressure caused by a stimulating vibration, such as a loudspeaker.

The water analogy we used earlier falls apart

when we get more specific. Ripples in water are perpendicular to the direction of propagation, that is, ripples in a pond are up and down. These are called transversal waves. Sound waves, on the other hand, are longitudinal; that is, they are in the direction of travel of the wave. Visualize a balloon blowing up with a constant rate of inflation equal to the speed of sound, while its surface is oscillating in and out, and you have a good view of sound propagation.

A medium is required

Sound requires a medium. There is no medium in the vacuum of outer space, as Boyle discovered in 1660 by putting an alarm clock suspended by a string inside a well-sealed glass jar. When the air was pumped out of the jar to cause a vacuum and the alarm clock went off, there was no sound; but when air was let back in, sound was heard. This makes sense in light of our earlier discussion of propagation: If the waiter doesn't have anything to disturb on the dance floor, he can hardly propagate a disturbance.

For physicists, the famous opening scene of *Star Wars* makes no sense, with its spaceship rumbles arriving over one's head, first of the little ship and then the massive Star Destroyer. No doubt the rumble is effective, but it's certain that somewhere a physicist groaned about how little filmmakers understand about nature. Here is an example of where the limitations of physics must succumb to storytelling. Note that although radio signals and light also use wave principles for propagation, no medium is required: These electromagnetic waves travel through a vacuum unimpeded.

Speed of sound

The speed of sound propagation is quite finite. Although it is far faster than the speed of waves in water caused by a stone dropping, it is still incredibly slower than the speed of light. You can easily observe the difference between light and sound speeds in many daily activities. Watch someone hammer a nail or kick a soccer ball at a distance, and you can easily see and hear that the sound comes later than the light—reality is out of sync! Filmmakers deal with this problem all the time, often forcing into sync sounds that in reality would be late, in time. This is another example of film reality being different from actual reality. Perhaps due to all of the training that we have received subliminally by watching thousands of hours of film and television, reality for viewers has been modified: *Sound should be in hard sync with the picture,* deliberately neglecting the effects of the speed of sound, unless a story point sets up in advance the disparity between the arrival time for light and sound.

The speed of sound is dependent on the medium in which the sound occurs. Sound travels faster in denser media, and so is faster in water than in air, and faster in steel than in water. The black-hatted cowboy puts his ear to the rail in order to hear the train coming sooner than he can through the air, partly due to the faster speed of sound in the material and partly due to the fact that the rail "contains" it, with only a little sound escaping to the air per unit of length.

Sound travels 1130 ft/sec in air at room temperature. This is equal to about 47 ft. of travel per frame of film at 24 frames per second. Unfortunately, viewers are very good at seeing whether or not sound is in sync with the picture. Practically everyone is able to tell if the sync is off by two frames, and many viewers are able to notice when the sound is one frame out of sync!

> Because sound is so slow relative to light, it is conventional lab practice to pull up the sound on motion picture release prints one extra frame, printing the sound "early," and thus producing exact picture-sound sync 47 ft. from the screen. (Picture and sound are also displaced on prints for other reasons; the one frame is added to the other requirements, as described in Chapter 9.) In very large houses, such as Radio City Music Hall or the Hollywood Bowl, it is common practice to "pull up" the sound even more, putting it into sync at the center of the space. Still, the sound is quite noticeably out of sync in many seats, being too early for the close seats, and too late for the distant ones. Luckily, this problem is mostly noticeable today only in those few cases where the auditoriums are much larger than the average theater. Because of

the one-frame pull up built into all prints, in order for a listener to be two frames out of sync, the listener would have to be three frames away from the screen, or about 150 ft. The Hollywood Bowl measures 400 ft. from the stage to the back row, so the sync problems there are quite large, and are only made tolerable by the small size of lips when seen from such a large distance. The speed of sound is fairly strongly influenced by temperature (see *Speed of sound* in the Glossary), so calculations of it yield different results in the morning than on a warm afternoon, when the speed of sound is faster.

Amplitude

The "size" of a sound wave is called by many names: volume, level, amplitude, loudness, sound pressure, velocity, or intensity. In professional sound circles, this effect is usually given the name *level*. A director says to a mixer "turn up the level," not "turn up the volume," if he wants to be taken seriously.

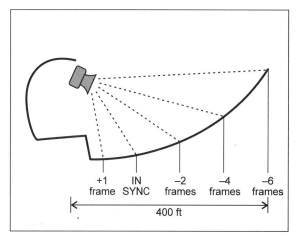

Fig. 1.5 The Hollywood Bowl is over 400 ft long, and sound from the front of the house is significantly out of sync by the time it reaches the back.

The size of a sound disturbance can be measured in a number of ways. In the case of water ripples, we could put a ruler into the pond, perpendicular to the surface, and note how large the waves are, from their peak to their trough, as first one then the other passes by the ruler. This measurement is one of amplitude.

> When reading the amplitude of a wave, it is customary to call the measurement just defined peak-to-peak amplitude, although what is being meant is the distance from the peak to trough.

Confusion occurs when trying to decide which dimension to measure. If asked to measure the peak-to-peak amplitude of a wave, you might think that you should measure from one peak to the next peak occurring along the length of the wave, but that would give you the wavelength measurement, which is discussed in the next section, not peak-to-peak amplitude.

In sound, since it is more easily measured than amplitude directly, what is actually measured is *sound pressure level,* often abbreviated SPL. *Sound pressure* is the relative change above and below atmospheric pressure caused by the presence of the sound.

Atmospheric pressure is the same as barometric pressure as read on a barometer. It is a measure of the force exerted on an object in a room by the "weight" of the atmosphere above it, about 15 lbs./sq. in. The atmosphere exerts a steady force measured in pounds per square inch on everything. Sound pressure adds (compression) and subtracts (rarefaction) to and from the static atmospheric pressure, moment by moment. The changes caused by sound pressure during compression and rarefaction are usually quite small compared with barometric pressure, but they can nonetheless be readily measured with microphones.

> Although measuring sound pressure is by far the most common method of measurement, alternative techniques are available that may yield additional information. For our purposes, we can say that all measures of size of the waveform—including amplitude, sound pressure level, sound velocity, and sound intensity—are members of the same family, and so we will henceforth use *sound pressure level* as the measure because it is the most commonly used.

> Sound intensity, in particular, provides more information than sound pressure because it is a more complex measure, containing information about both the amplitude of the wave and its direction of propagation. Thus, sound intensity measurements are very useful for finding the source of a noise. Sound intensity measures are rarely used in the film and television industries, though, due to the complexity and cost of instrumentation..

Wavelength and frequency
Wavelength
Another measure of water waves or sound

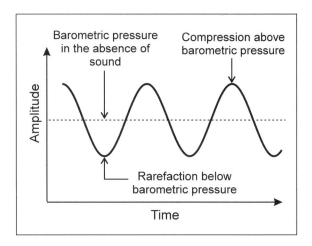

Fig. 1.6 Sound pressure adds (compression) and subtracts (rarefaction) to and from the static atmospheric pressure.

waves we have yet to discuss is the distance from one peak, past one trough, to the next peak along the length, called the *wavelength*. Note that wavelength is perpendicular to the amplitude dimension, so the two have little or nothing to do with each other. One can have a small, long wave or a large, short one (a tsunami!). The range of wavelengths of audible sound is extremely large, spanning from 56 ft. (17 m) to $^3/_4$ in. (1.9 cm) long in air.

> Notice how our purist discussion of objective sound has already been circumscribed by psychoacoustics. We just mentioned the *audible* frequency range, but what about the inaudible parts? Wavelengths longer than about 56 ft. or shorter than about $^3/_4$ in. still result in sound, but they are inaudible and will be covered later. The wavelength range for visible light, another wave phenomenon, covers less than a 2:1 ratio of wavelengths from the shortest to the longest visible wavelength, representing the spectrum from blue through red. Compared to this, the audible sound range of 1000:1 is thus truly impressive.

Track 3 of the CD contains tones at 100 Hz, 1 kHz, and 10 kHz, having a wavelength in air of 11' 3" (3.4 m), 13 $^1/_2$" (34.4 cm), and 1 $^3/_8$" (34.4 mm) respectively.

Frequency
Wavelength is directly related to one of the most important concepts in sound, *frequency*. Frequency is the number of occurrences

of a wave per second. The unit for frequency is Hertz (abbreviated Hz, also used with the "k" operator for "kilo" to indicate thousands of Hz: 20 kHz is shorthand for 20,000 Hz).

Wavelength and frequency are related reciprocally to the speed of sound such that, as the wavelength gets shorter, the frequency gets higher. The frequency is equal to the speed of sound divided by the wavelength:

$$f = \frac{c}{\lambda}$$

where f is the frequency in Hz (cycles per second), c is the speed of sound in the medium, and λ is the wavelength. Note that the units for speed of sound and wavelength may be metric or English, but must match each other.

Thus the frequency range that corresponds to the wavelength range given earlier is from 20 Hz to 20 kHz, which is generally considered to be the audible frequency range. Within this range the complete expressive capability that we know as sound exists. The frequency range in which a sound primarily lies has a strong storytelling impact. For example, in the natural world low frequencies are associated with storms (distant thunder), earthquakes, and other natural catastrophes.

When used in film, low-frequency rumble often denotes a threat is present. This idea extends from sound effects to music. An example is the theme music for the shark in *Jaws*. Those four low notes that begin the shark theme indicate that danger lurks on an otherwise pleasant day on the ocean. Alternatively, the quiet, high-frequency sound of a corn field rustling in *Field of Dreams* lets us know that we can be at peace, that there is no threat, despite its connection to another world.

Infrasonic frequencies

The frequency region below about 20 Hz is called the *infrasonic* (or, more old fashioned,

the *subsonic*) range, although the lowest note on the largest pipe organs corresponds to a frequency of 16 Hz, and this is still usually considered audible sound, not infrasonics.[1] This region is little exploited deliberately in film and television production, although problems can arise on sets when there is a very large amount of infrasonic noise, a not uncommon finding in industrial settings. The infrasonic sound level can be so

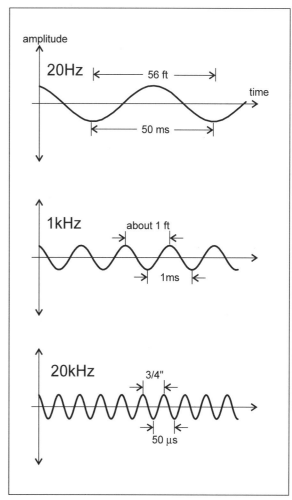

Fig. 1.7 Wavelength and frequency of sound in air over the audible frequency range.

---

1. You can see that the 20 Hz low-frequency limit is a little "fuzzy."

high that it modulates voices, that is, it "roughens" their sound, making them sound as though spoken with a gurgle.

The frequency range around 12 Hz, when present at very high amplitude, may cause another problem—nausea. It has been found that people working in buildings with large amounts of structure-borne noise at 12 Hz may become ill from the high level of vibration, and the consequent infrasonic sound. Fortunately, in most cases this effect has yet to be exploited by filmmakers.

There was a sound enhancement system used on several pictures called Sensurround™, that employed large amounts of low-frequency energy to cause a "rumble" effect, useful to simulate ground movement during the film *Earthquake* (1974) and for the aircraft carrier takeoffs and landings in the film *Midway* (1976). The frequency range of the loudspeakers was from 15 to 100 Hz, so the system probably did not have enough energy as low as 12 Hz to stimulate this effect. On the other hand, Sensurround pointed the way to the expressive capability of very low-frequency sound, which was followed up over the years by the addition of subwoofers in theaters and separate sound tracks prepared for them.

Filmmakers exploit the lack of audibility of infrasonic sound on sets sometimes. "Thumpers" are used that put out very low frequency sound to cue actors in dance numbers, for instance. Subsequent post production practice can filter[2] out such low-frequency sound, retaining the actor's vocal performance.

Ultrasonic frequencies

The frequency region beyond 20 kHz is called *ultrasonic*. (The word supersonic is generally relegated to speed of aircraft, not sound.) Although some people can hear high-level sounds out to as much as 24 kHz, most sound devices use 20 kHz as the limit of their range, focusing on the huge importance of sound below this frequency compared with the very minimal effects above it.

2. See Chapter 10.

There are several types of devices that employ frequencies above the audible range, but they are of little common interest to filmmakers.

They include acoustical burglar alarms (although many that claim to be ultrasonic actually operate around 17 kHz and can be heard, and perhaps worse recorded, on location at times), some television remote controls, and specially built miniature loudspeakers made for acoustical testing of models.

One common problem in recording *stages* (the film term for recording spaces, different from the music term *studio*) is the use of conventional television monitors. U.S. color television uses a horizontal sweep rate of 15,734 Hz, well within the audible range. Many video monitors emit strong acoustic energy at this frequency, and must either be acoustically shielded from microphones, or else a filter must be employed to avoid recording this audible sound.

Importance of sine waves

So far what we have been considering are waves that have two dimensions, amplitude and wavelength. We have not yet considered the shape that the wave takes, the waveform.

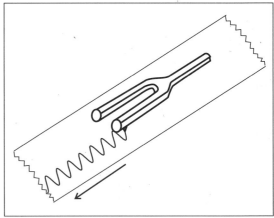

Fig. 1.8 One tine of a tuning fork moving traces out a sine wave as time goes by. The shape of the wave vs. time is called the waveform.

For simple sources, like a tuning fork, in which the motion of the tines oscillates back and forth like the swing of a pendulum, the waveform traced out over one cycle is a *sine wave*. More complex sources than a simple tuning fork emit more complex waveforms than a sine wave because the motion that produces their sound is more complicated. A violin string playing a note is a good example. The string exhibits complex motion, with parts of it moving in one direction and adjacent parts moving in the opposite direction at the same instant, in a complex manner. In 1801, a French mathematician, Jean Baptiste Fourier, made a very important theoretical breakthrough. He found that complex systems, such as a moving violin string, could be broken down into a number of basic ingredients, which, when added together, summed to describe the whole complex motion of the string. Fourier found that all complex motion, including sound, could be described as a summation of multiple sine waves.

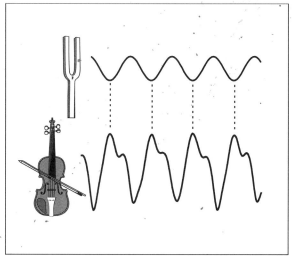

Fig. 1.9 While a tuning fork produces a sine wave, more complex motion, such as of a violin string, results in a more complex waveform, due to the addition of harmonics to the fundamental.

A waveform may change rapidly in time, as it does when a violinist goes from note to note, and even within one note when vibrato[3] is applied, but for each point in time *spectrum analysis* (also called *frequency analysis*) can be performed to tell us what underlying sine waves are being added together to produce the final complex composite waveform. Fourier found that not only were the constituent, fundamental parts of a complex waveform multiple sine waves, but

---

3. A moment-by-moment frequency variation that adds interest to the sound of many instruments.

also that the sine waves were, for many sounds, related to one another in a specific way—harmonically. This means that a waveform can be broken down into a *fundamental frequency* and a series of *harmonics*. The harmonics lie at two times, three times, etc. the fundamental frequency. For example, a violin playing middle "A" has a fundamental frequency of 440 Hz, and it also has harmonics at 880, 1320, 1760 Hz, etc.

You can better understand how such complex motion can arise by thinking about the motion of a guitar string, tied at the two ends and plucked in the center. The fundamental frequency corresponds to the whole length of the string involved in one motion, up and down, with the amplitude varying from greatest at the center to nonexistent at the clamped ends.

The string can also vibrate simultaneously at harmonic frequencies. In one instance, one half of the string moves up, while the other half moves down, relative to the fundamental. The string acts for this harmonic as though it is clamped at the two ends, just like the fundamental, but also as if it is clamped in the middle. This *harmonic* radiates sound at twice the fundamental frequency, because each half of the string vibrates separately, at twice the rate of the fundamental. This is called the second harmonic.

> Do not be confused by the fact that this frequency is actually the first *harmonic* found. It's still called the second harmonic because it is at twice the fundamental frequency.

This process also occurs at three, four, and more times the fundamental frequency, leading to multiple harmonics. A string can vibrate in more than one mode at one time, moving both at the fundamental frequency and harmonic frequencies, leading to a complex motion in which the constituent parts may not be readily apparent. For any given point along the length, the shape of the curve traced out over time results from adding together the effect of the fundamental frequency and the harmonics.

One of the most important techniques to

identify different sources of sound involves using their pattern of harmonics. The relative strength of harmonics plays a large role in determining the different sounds of various instruments playing the same note. A violin has a structure of harmonics that typically is not very extended and in which the harmonics are not as strong as that of a trumpet. A trumpet is thus called *brighter* than a violin. Spectrum analysis of a trumpet versus a violin shows a more extended and stronger set of harmonics for the trumpet than for the violin.

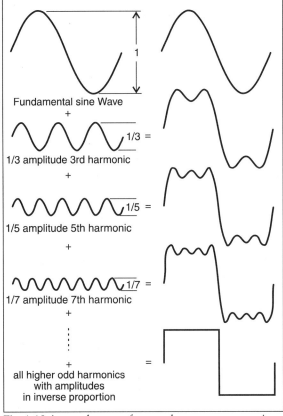

Fundamental sine Wave
+
1/3 amplitude 3rd harmonic
+
1/5 amplitude 5th harmonic
+
1/7 amplitude 7th harmonic
+
⋮
+
all higher odd harmonics
with amplitudes
in inverse proportion

Fig. 1.10 A complex waveform such as a square wave is built up from the summation of harmonics—the square wave includes the 3rd harmonic at 1/3 the amplitude of the fundamental, the 5th harmonic at 1/5 amplitude, and so forth.

Alternative names for harmonics are *overtones* and *partials*. Despite this relatively straightforward definition of harmonics, real-world instruments are more complex than this simplified discussion. They may radiate sound at other frequencies as well as at the fundamental and harmonics.

Track 4 of the CD contains various wave-

form signals at the same frequency and amplitude, illustrating some of the differences that waveshape makes.

While the generation of harmonics for tonal sounds such as produced by notes played on an instrument should now be clear, what about sounds which have no explicit pitch, such as speech or waves heard at a beach? Do they have harmonics? Although less evident, perhaps, speech too consists of fundamental frequencies with harmonics, although both change rapidly in time. It is more difficult to assign a fundamental frequency to speech than to singing (which, if the singer is in tune, is the note written), but a fundamental frequency is nevertheless present.

Waveforms that have a clear fundamental frequency are generally called *tonal* by acousticians, while those for which the fundamental frequency is less clear may be called noise-like. *Noise* has several definitions. In the most common popular usage, noise means unwanted sound. An acoustician, on the other hand, would call the sound of surf a noise-like signal, because it is impossible to extract a fundamental frequency from it, despite the fact that the surf "noise" may be a desirable or undesirable sound, depending on your point of view at the time. Noisy sounds, like surf, consist of a great many simultaneous sinusoidal frequencies. The difficulty with separating the frequencies into fundamental and harmonics is that there are so many frequencies present at the same time that no particular order can be determined, either using an instrument, or the human ear.

The discussion of fundamental frequency and harmonics can be extended to *sub-harmonics*. Some devices and instruments can radiate sound at one-half, one-quarter, etc. times the typical fundamental frequency, especially at high levels. In an instrument, this can add a desirable feeling of "weight."

In these cases, determining which is the fundamental and which are subharmonics is usually done by spectrum analysis; the strongest of the multiple frequencies is usually the fundamental.

Sub-harmonics can be synthesized by a device in film production and their addition adds body to the recorded sound. The voice of Jabba the Hutt in *Return of the Jedi* for instance was processed by having sub-harmonics added to it. While the technical addition of sub-harmonics was important, the primary consideration was casting.

Sympathetic vibration and resonance

If one tuning fork that has been struck is brought nearby a second one that is at rest and tuned to the same frequency, the second will receive enough stimulus that it too will begin to vibrate. This *sympathetic vibration* can occur not just in deliberately tuned devices such as tuning forks, but also in structural parts of buildings, and can cause problems with room acoustics. An example is a room in which all the surfaces are covered in 4×8 ft. sheets of $\frac{1}{4}$ in. plywood nailed to studs only at their perimeter. This room acts like a set of drum heads, all resonant at the same frequency. The frequency at which they resonate is determined by the surface density of the sheets of plywood and the air space behind the plywood. Any sound at a particular frequency radiating in the space will cause the surfaces to respond with sympathetic vibration; the surfaces are said to be *in resonance*. There will be an abrupt change in the room acoustics at that frequency, producing a great potential for audible rattles.

Sympathetic vibration can create a major problem in the room acoustics of motion-picture theaters. This is because the sound pressure levels achieved by sound tracks are quite high at low frequencies in movie theaters, more so than in other public spaces. In some cases, the sound system may be capable of producing sufficient output at the resonant frequency of building elements that very audible rattles occur, distracting the audience at the very least.

Phase

We have already described two main properties of a waveform, amplitude and wavelength. These two properties together are enough to completely specify one sine wave, but they are inadequate to describe everything going on in a complex wave, which includes a fundamental and its harmonics. To do this we need one more concept before we have a complete description of any wave—phase.

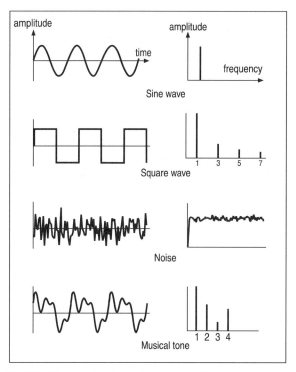

Fig. 1.11 The amplitude vs. time curves of some common signals and the corresponding spectrum analysis for each.

In our example of a string vibrating in different modes, there was one thing in common among all of the modes, that is, all motion ceased at the two ends of the string, by definition, where the string was attached. But not all generators of sound have such fixed end points, for instance, an organ pipe has one open end, and the harmonics may not have zero amplitude at the open end.

Phase is a way to describe the differences in the starting points on the waveform of the various harmonics relative to the fundamental. Because one sine wave cycle is described mathematically as occupying 360° around a circle, phase is given in degrees of shift, comparing the phase of each of the harmonics to that of the fundamental.

The reference for phase is not usually the peak of compression or the trough of rarefaction, but rather the point at which the waveform goes through zero, heading positive. If the second harmonic is at the crest of its compression at the moment that the fundamental is heading through zero on its way positive, we say that the second harmonic is shifted by 90° phase leading. Conversely, if it is in its trough at the same point, we say it is shifted by 90° phase lagging. In 1877, Helmholtz, based on some experiments he conducted, thought that phase shift

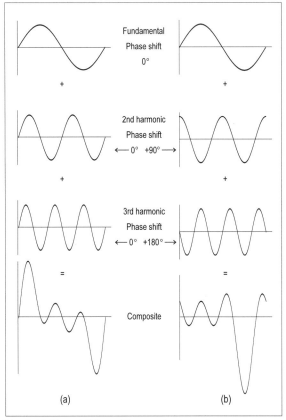

Fundamental
Phase shift
0°

2nd harmonic
Phase shift
←— 0° +90° —→

3rd harmonic
Phase shift
←— 0° +180° —→

Composite

(a)　　　　　　　　(b)

Fig. 1.12 The addition of harmonics in various phases changes the overall waveform. In this example, harmonics of the same number and amplitude have been added together to make up two different composite waveforms. The only difference between examples (a) and (b) is the phase shift applied to each of the harmonics relative to the fundamental. Although the resulting waveform is quite different, it may sound only slightly different, if at all, due to the relative difficulty of hearing phase effects.

was inaudible, and his finding dominated thinking for a long time. Later research has shown situations where it is audible. Added phase shift between a fundamental and its harmonics, which is caused by microphones, electronics, recorders, and loudspeakers, may be audible in certain circumstances. Another way to look at phase shift is called *group delay*. Group delay expresses the fact that leading or lagging phase can be converted to time differences between the fundamental and its harmonics. The time difference is only relative—there is no way to "beat the clock" and make sound arrive earlier than it went into a system in the case of a leading phase shift—what happens is that the fundamental is more delayed than the higher frequency in this case.

Let us say that a recording system is so bad that it delays the 10th harmonic by one second relative to the fundamental. This amount of delay

distortion is obviously audible since the fundamental may stop and the 10th harmonic play on for a second. So it is not the audibility of such effects that is in question, but rather the amount of delay that it takes to make the phase shift audible.

The concept of phase shift has been used incorrectly to describe all that is done well or poorly by a recording system but which remains a mystery. Phase shift is audible in large amounts, which result in time delays in one part of the frequency range compared with another above an audible threshold, but not so much as to make it a kind of magic ingredient that can be hypothetically adjusted to make everything perfect.

Influences on sound propagation

Up until now we've been discussing pretty abstract cases of sound propagation, with point sources and strings radiating into a "free field," that is, without encountering any objects. In the real world, sources are more complicated than this, and a number of influences affect the sound before it may be received by a listener or a microphone. These include absorption, reflection, diffraction, refraction, constructive and destructive interference, and Doppler shift. Most of these play some part in the overall sound of a film or television show.

Source radiation pattern

The first of these is due to the complexity of the source itself and is called its *radiation intensity*. Most sources do not radiate sound equally in all directions but instead have a preferred direction, which often changes in a complex way with frequency. The fundamental may be radiated most strongly in one direction, but one harmonic may radiate mostly in a different direction, and another harmonic in yet a third direction. This is critically important to understand because if sources have priority for certain frequency ranges in certain directions, where is one to place a microphone to "capture" the sound of the source—which position is "right"? Inevitably one shows a preference for one frequency range or another by the forced choice of microphone position.

So let us say we don't have to be practical and instead of one microphone we can use a whole array of microphones located equally spaced all over a sphere surrounding the source. We connect these to a multitrack recorder and record each microphone signal on a separate track. Then we arrange a whole array of loudspeakers, connected to the tracks, in accordance with the microphone positions, and radiating sound outwards from the recorded source. With such a system, we have a means to capture all of the relevant details of the sound field produced by the source, especially the complex way in which it radiates sound directionally into the world. Let us say that we have just described how to capture the sound of a clarinet completely. We've got one instrument of an imaginary orchestra finished, and now let us start on instrument no. 2, a flute.... You can see how quickly such a system, meant to be absolute in its ability to actually reproduce an audible event, falls apart. Thousands of microphones, recorder tracks, and loudspeakers later, we can reproduce the compete sound of an orchestra with great fidelity, but that is so impractical that no one has ever tried it.

So there is a fundamental theoretical problem with recording sound—no practical system can be completely said to "capture" the sound of most real sources in all their spatial complexity. What production sound recordists, boom operators, and recording engineers become highly proficient at is choosing one, or a few, microphone positions that instead *represent* the sound of the source, without making a valid claim to actually *reproduce* the source completely. This idea is commonly used on motion-picture and television sets, although it is probably expressed here in a different manner than is used by practitioners. What has been developed over time is microphone technique that permits adequate capture of sound for representation purposes. We take up microphone technique in Chapter 4. Here, what is important to understand is that the choice of microphone technique is highly dictated by the requirements of the source, especially its radiation intensity.

Of course, in movies and television perhaps the most important source much of the time is a human speaking voice. Talkers radiate different frequency ranges preferentially in different directions, similar to orchestra instruments. Thus exactly the same microphone, at the same distance, will "sound" different when recording a voice as it is moved around the talker. The practical direction that is preferred for the largest number of cases is overhead, in front of the talker, about 45° above the horizon, in the "boom mike" position, which was named for the device that holds it up, not for the microphone itself. In many cases, this positioning stimulates debate on the set over the relative merits of different microphone positions, with the camera department holding out for placements of hidden microphones on set pieces and underneath the frame line, all in an effort to avoid the dreaded boom shadow. The experience of the sound department, on the other hand, shows that the overhead microphone position "sounds" more like the person talking naturally than other positions. For example, with a position that is located below the frame line, the microphone is pointed at the mouth but is closer to the chest of the talker than when in the overhead position, and the recording is often found to be "boomy," or "chesty" in this position compared with the overhead mike. This difficulty is caused by the radiation pattern of the voice.

Another difficulty occurs when the actor or subject is capable of moving. If we use a microphone to one side of the frame, this may sound all right in a static situation, but when the actor turns his head to face the other side of the frame from the microphone, he goes noticeably "off mike." Thus the more neutral overhead mike position is better in the case where the actor may turn his head.

Track 5 of the CD illustrates recording a voice from various angles, demonstrating the radiation pattern of the voice.

Absorption

Sound may be absorbed by its interaction with boundaries of spaces, by absorptive devices such as curtains, or even by propagation through air. Absorption is caused by sound interacting with materials through which it passes in such a way that the sound energy is turned into heat.

The atmosphere absorbs sound preferentially, absorbing short wavelengths more than long ones (and thus absorbing high frequencies more than low ones). Thus, at greater distances from the source, the sound will be increasingly "bassy." While this effect is not usually noticeable when listening to sound in rooms, it is prominent out of doors. It is atmospheric absorption that causes distant gunfire sound to have no treble content but a lot of bass. This effect is used very well in the jungle scene in *Apocalypse Now*. Among the sounds that we hear in the jungle is a very low-frequency rumble, which we have come to associate through exposition earlier in the film with B52 strikes occurring at a distance:

```
EXT. BOAT — DAY
A loud, low-frequency rumble is
heard.
                    CHEF
          Hey, what's that?

CAPT. WILLARD (in a normal voice)
          Arc Light.


              ANOTHER MAN
              What's up?


            CAPT. WILLARD
            B52 strike.


            SOMEONE ELSE
               Man.


            BOAT CAPTAIN
            What's that?


       CAPT. WILLARD (louder)
            Arc Light.


              FIRST MAN
I hate that—every time I hear that
    somethin' terrible happens.
```

The later jungle scene has a sense of foreboding that is heightened by hearing, even more distant than in the exposition scene, another B52 strike.

The effect that the atmosphere produces on

sound is also frequently simulated by sound effects editors and/or mixers. In a long shot showing the Imperial Snow Walkers in *The Empire Strikes Back*, the footfalls of the walkers are very bassy. As the scene shifts to a closer shot, with a foot falling in the foreground, the sound takes on a more immediate quality—it is not only louder, but also brighter, that is, it contains more treble. In this case, the increased brightness was created by literally adding an extra sound at the same time as the footfall, the sound of a bicycle chain dropping onto concrete. Mixed together with the bassy part of the footfall, the treble part supplied by the bicycle chain makes it seem as though we have gotten closer to the object, since our whole experience with sound out of doors tells us that distantly originating sound sources sound duller (less bright) than closely originating sources. Thus, in this case the filmmaker has indicated the distance to the object subliminally, when, in fact, no such object ever existed. The sound is animated, in a sense, like the corresponding picture that uses models. A principle of physics has been mimicked in order to make an unreal event seem real.

The surfaces of room boundaries (walls, ceiling, and floor), as well as other objects in a room, also absorb sound and contribute to room acoustics that are discussed later. Many materials are deliberately made to absorb sound, while other materials, not specifically designed for this purpose, nevertheless do absorb sound more or less. Some rules of thumb regarding absorption are as follows:

- Thick, fuzzy materials absorb more lower frequency sound than similar thin materials.

- Adding a few inches of spacing off the surfaces of the room to the absorption greatly improves its low-frequency absorption.

- Placement of absorption in a room is often important.

- Absorption is rated on a scale of 0 to 1, with 0 being no absorption, a perfectly reflective surface, and 1 being 100%

absorption, equal to an open window through which sound leaks, never to return.

- Absorption changes with frequency, yielding the 0 to 1 rating that is given in tables as a function of frequency.

Quite commonly on motion-picture location sets "sound blankets" are hung around the space, in order to reduce reverberation. The area available for absorption is made most effective by using thick absorption mounted a few inches from the wall or ceiling—a thinly stretched sound blanket doesn't do as much good.

Reflection

Sound interacts with nonabsorbent surfaces in a manner that depends on the shape of the surface. Large, flat, hard surfaces reflect sound in much the same way that a pool ball is reflected off the edges of a pool table. Such "specular" reflection works like light bouncing off a flat mirror, that is, the angle of incidence equals the angle of reflection, or the angle incoming is equal to the angle outgoing, bisected by a line perpendicular to the reflector.

Parabolic reflectors concentrate incoming sound from along the axis of the parabola to its focal point. Parabolic reflection is used for specialized microphones that are intended to pick up sound preferentially in one direction. By placing a microphone at the focal point of a parabola, the whole "dish" concentrates sound waves that are parallel to the axis of the parabola on the microphone. The problem with parabolic reflectors is that due to the wide wavelength range of sound, they are effective only at high frequencies unless the reflector is very large.

There are two prominent uses of parabolic microphones in film and video production. One is by nature filmmakers, who must capture bird song at a distance without distracting the birds; because the bird chirps are high frequencies, the dish size does not cause a limitation. The second is in sports broadcasts, where the super directionality of a parabolic mike can pick up football huddle and scrimmage high-frequency sounds and add

immediacy to the experience. (The bass is supplied by other microphones mixed with the parabolic mike.) The parabolic mike supplies a close up of the action, whereas other microphones supply wide-frequency-range crowd effects, etc. Notice that this corresponds to the finding that greater amounts of high-frequency sound make the scene seem closer, as in *The Empire Strikes Back.*

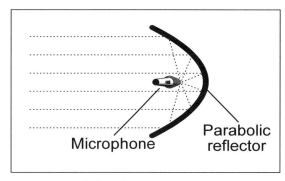

Fig. 1.13 A parabolic reflector concentrates incoming waves on a microphone. The combination is called a parabolic microphone.

Elliptical reflectors are used in "whispering galleries," usually located at museums. Here a person whispering at one focal point of an elliptical reflector can be heard clearly by a listener positioned at the second focal point of the ellipse, despite the remote spacing of the two foci, such that others standing away from either focal point cannot hear the conversation. This results from the large area available to gather sound from one focal point of the ellipse and deliver to it to the second focal point of the ellipse, yet outsiders do not hear the effect of the concentration of sound energy.

An architectural feature found in some auditoriums is a spherical or elliptical shaped dome. A great difficulty with these shapes is that they tend to gather sound energy and concentrate it on parts of the audience. A whispering-gallery effect is quite common in domed spaces—you can hear other members of the audience under the dome, even if they are whispering. The only solution to this problem is to make the domed surface quite absorptive, or to make the focus of the dome well away from listening areas.

An inside view of a parabola or an ellipse shows sound waves converging on focal points. What about the outside of such surfaces? Sound impinging on such "bumpy" surfaces is scattered, spreading out more rapidly than if reflected from a flat surface.

Such surfaces are called *diffusers*, and play an important role in room acoustics, which are discussed in the next section.

Diffraction

One of the most profound differences between seeing and hearing is that sound is heard around corners, whereas sight stops at an opaque object. Diffraction occurs when waves interact with objects; the sound "flows" around corners in much the same way as in-coming parallel water waves interact with an opening in a breakwater. Going past the gap the waves are seen spreading out in circles. A second generation of waves occurs too when a set of sound waves encounters the edge of a barrier. While the sound in the *acoustic shadow* may not be as distinct as sound with a direct, undiffracted path, it is nevertheless very audible.

Sound diffraction, and especially the everyday experience we have with it, has strong effects on how sound is used in movies. While the frame line of the picture is practically always an absolute hard line, there is no such boundary for sound. We expect to hear sound from around corners, that is, from off screen as well as on. Screenwriters often refer to off-screen action in scripts, with the attention of actors being drawn outside the frame line, and the easiest way to indicate this to an audience is with sound. With picture, the way to accomplish this is with a cut away, a shot that literally shows us the object that is to draw the attention of the actors. This may often seem clumsy because it is too literal, whereas off-screen sound can seem quite natural because it is part of our everyday experience.

The situation in media is parallel to what occurs in life: Seeing is limited to the front hemisphere view, but sound can be heard from all around. In order to make use of this fact of life, which is based on the diffraction of sound waves about the head to reach the ears, the film industry has been developing *surround sound* for more than 25 years, a great expressive medium that is underutilized, but growing, in television. Surround sound is based on the differences between viewing and hearing caused by diffraction. Not surprisingly perhaps, some of the best surround sound on television is heard in certain commercials.

Refraction

In addition to complete reflection, sound waves can also be bent by changes in the density of the atmosphere. Following the same principle by which lenses bend light waves, sound is refracted when stratification occurs in the atmosphere due to differing temperatures (and thus densities) in different layers. Be careful here to distinguish the terms *refraction* (bending) and *rarefaction* (opposite of compression), as they mean quite different things.

Constructive and destructive interference and beating

Sound waves interact not only with objects in the room but also with one another. For example, one wave having a sinusoidal waveform with a specific wavelength and amplitude is flowing from left to right and is joined by a second wave, having the same wavelength and amplitude, but flowing from right to left. The result at any observation point will depend on the moment-by-moment addition of the two. Even in this simple case, there is a wide range of possible outcomes. This is because although we specified the wavelengths and amplitudes as equal, we failed to specify the difference in phase between the two waves. If the two waves have identical phase, that is, if their compression and rarefaction cycles occur at the same time, then the two waves are said to be *in phase*, and the result is addition of the two waves, resulting in doubling of the amplitude.

In the opposite case, if the two waves are completely *out of phase* with each other, with the peak of one wave's compression cycle occurring at the same time as the trough

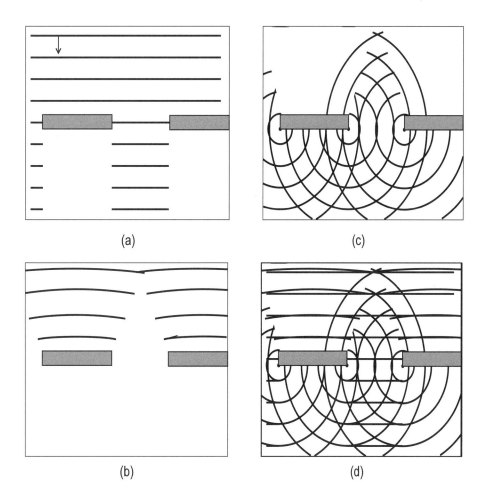

(a)

(c)

(b)

(d)

Fig. 1.14 The four frames show various effects of waves interacting with barriers. In (a) the incoming wave is shown, and it passes through the barrier unimpeded, corresponding to the *direct sound*. In (b), the waves reflected from the barriers are shown. In (c), the *diffraction* off the edges of the barrier is shown. In (d), the combination of the three sets of waves is shown, those due to direct waves, reflected waves, and diffracted waves.

of the other wave, then the result is subtraction of the two waves. Since the two are now equal but opposite, the outcome is zero, which is called a *null*. So the range over which two simple waves can interact is from double the amplitude of one of the waves, to complete cancellation! The first case is called *constructive interference,* while the latter is called *destructive interference*. Between these two extremes the results change smoothly. This represents the condition, more common in actuality, in which the waves are not quite in- nor out-of-phase, but rather have some phase difference between them. We will see how this affects recording in the section on room acoustics.

If instead of the two waves having an identical wavelength, they have slightly different wavelengths, then the result is that at some points in time the waves add, and at a slightly later time they cancel, with the difference in the times being equal to the difference in the frequencies of the waves. For example, if waves at 1000 Hz and 1001 Hz are mixed together, what one observes is a variation in the level of the sum at a rate of 1 Hz. This effect is called *beating*. It is what is often heard in out-of-tune pianos when playing only one note and is caused by the piano using multiple strings for one key, which may not be tuned to exactly the same frequency.

Film sound designers make use of beating in making certain sound effects. By manipulating various sound tracks, for example, slowing them down slightly and mixing the slowed version with itself, the kind of "waa-aaah, waaaaah, waaaaah" effect heard opening the ark in *Raiders of the Lost Ark* is produced. This is far more interesting than the simpler low-frequency rumble that might have been used in the same film had it been made 10 years earlier.

Doppler shift

In 1842 an Austrian physicist, Christian Johann Doppler, published a paper describing an effect he thought must exist but had yet to be demonstrated, Doppler shift. Given that the speed of sound is fairly slow, Doppler questioned what would happen to sound generators in motion. As they approach a point of observation, the sound waves should be "crowded together" by the velocity of the source, and likewise, should spread apart while receding into the distance. This "crowding" results in a shorter wavelength on the approach, and thus a higher frequency, and a corresponding lowering of the observed frequency as the object recedes.

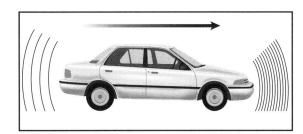

Fig. 1.15 The sound waves emitted by a race car are affected by its speed, being crowded together in front of the car, and spread apart behind it, leading to the characteristic change in pitch as a moving object passes a listener.

Three years after Doppler's paper was published, his theory was put to the test. A train was loaded with 15 trumpeters who played the same note continuously while the train approached, passed, and then pulled away from a train station. Sure enough, while listeners on the train heard a constant pitch, those in the train station heard the pitch being raised, and then lowered as the train passed the station.

Filmmakers fake this effect to simulate ob-

jects in motion, and sometimes exaggerate for emphasis. In the Philip Kaufman version of *Invasion of the Body Snatchers* (1978), when two characters are riding in a car just before a man is struck and killed by a car (the man being the star of the earlier version of the movie, a kind of tongue-in-cheek homage), we hear cars pass us on a busy San Francisco street. The exaggeration is in the amount of pitch shift used: those cars would have to be traveling in excess of 90 m.p.h. to produce that effect!

A more complex example is heard near the end of *Indiana Jones and the Temple of Doom,* when Indy has made it across to the far side of a chasm but is being chased by the bad guys, with arrows being shot at him. The challenge was to simulate an arrow sound throughout its flight, as it is exceedingly difficult to attach a microphone and recorder to an in-flight arrow. The steps that the sound designer took were as follows:

- A recording was made of an arrow passing by a microphone. The first attempts were futile, since good arrows make very little sound. So the arrow's tail feathers were ruffled and a new, more useful "take" was made.

- Of course, this recording was far too short to simulate a full flight, being just a "zip" past the microphone. So the recording was transferred to a digital audio sampler, and "looped" to extend it to the length of the flight.

- The recording was processed by a digital pitch shifter, which increased the frequency at the beginning of the flight and decreased it towards the end, producing a fake Doppler shift.

- During mixing, the arrows were panned so that their flight moved across the screen to match the action.

Doppler shift is also very commonly used for simulating transportation devices in motion. There are several types of sound effects that an effects recordist can make to "cover the bases" so that all uses of a device in a film can be covered by the smallest number of effects. For an automobile, such as the title-maker in the movie *Tucker*, a recordist will record at least:

- Engine idling

- Acceleration from stop

- Braking to a stop

- A *pass by* in which the microphone is at a fixed location and the car moves by it

- A *steady* in which the microphone moves with the car using an exterior perspective

- An interior steady

With these in hand, a sound effects editor can make up a trip of nearly any length by methods to be described later, blending them together to make a functionally single-sounding whole. The greatest challenge in this list is simulating a realistic pass by, because there could be a great many of them possible in a film, at various speeds. It is possible to turn the steady into a pass by using a faked Doppler shift as a primary processing tool to make it sound realistic. Since the speed of the pass by is controlled by a knob in post production, one steady can be adequate to produce a large number of pass bys.

Doppler shift is demonstrated on Track 6 of the CD.

Room acoustics

The acoustics of interior spaces are extremely important to filmmakers since so many of them are involved sequentially in the final perception of the sound of a film or video. There are the acoustics of the live action shooting environment; those of various post-production studios, including recording and monitoring stages; and those of the theater or viewing room.

The classic art forms of theater and music obviously depend on the room acoustics of the spaces in which they are performed, as is well known. Cinema and video depend on room acoustics as well, but, as we shall see, film and video producers seek to control what is heard through recording and reproducing under very specific conditions so that the sound of their productions translates

from one environment to another. This is a fundamental concept behind recorded media: The performance is captured in time, for future display in many venues and at different times. This concept depends on the ability of the display venues to deliver the performance, ideally free of alteration, to the listener.

The modern story of room acoustics starts in 1885 with a junior assistant professor of physics at Harvard, Wallace Clement Sabine. Sabine was given a job that no one else wanted, to solve the problem of speech intelligibility in the newly built Fogg Art Museum lecture theater in Cambridge. Students had complained that they couldn't hear the lecturers in the theater. Sabine conducted an experiment to answer the question, How long does it take sound to die away to inaudibility after the source is abruptly stopped? To avoid contaminating the measure-ment by his presence, Sabine built a wooden box with a hole in the top of it for his neck, so that his body was essentially not present in the room, acoustically speaking. Then he used organ pipes with valves so that their own sound stopped very quickly when cut off to make sound in the room. What he heard after the organ pipe stopped was the reverberation of the room. He used a stop watch to determine how long it took the sound to die out audibly and called this the *reverberation time*.[4]

The time was rather long, on the order of seconds. Apparently realizing that when speech was heard in the room each syllable stimulated its own *reverberant tail,* Sabine found that these reverberant tails overlapped with new syllables uttered, causing the intelligibility problem. In order to test his hypothesis, Sabine added units of absorption to the room that would soak up the reverberation. For Sabine, one unit of absorption was one Sanders Theater seat cushion, borrowed at night from the venue across the

---

4. This was later codified to be the length of time required for the sound to decay by 60 dB in level, a factor of 1000 in sound pressure level. See the end of this chapter for more information.

street. With the added absorption, in various amounts, Sabine found a curve of reverberation time versus absorption in the room, which is still used today to predict the reverberation time of rooms before they are built and furnished.

In addition to the mathematical prediction capability of Sabine's reverberation time, it was also his understanding of the damage that reverberation does to speech intelligibility that is used widely in the film industry today. We make motion picture theaters "dead" acoustically, for the same reasons that Sabine found absorption useful. By the way, using the knowledge he gained starting with the experiment just described, Sabine went on to design Symphony Hall in Boston, widely considered to be one of the best sounding concert halls in the world.

> Sabine's equation, while still used today, was modified to cover a wider range of conditions by later acousticians. In particular, Eyring found in the 1930s that Sabine's work did not predict the reverberation times of rather dead spaces well, and found a better equation to describe such spaces. It is interesting to note that Eyring was working on the problem of spaces coupled by recording, in particular, motion-picture shooting stages and theaters, when he added new information to the entire field of acoustics.

Sound fields in rooms
Direct sound
In all practical rooms, there are three sound fields to consider. The first is *direct sound,* which is sound radiated in a straight line between the source and receiver, that arrives at the receiver first, before any reflected sound. If the observer is far enough away that the source can be considered a point, the direct sound follows the inverse square law falloff in level versus distance.

> Note that in certain circumstances, such as when sitting behind a column in a theater, there may in fact be no direct sound. This is one of the reasons (in addition to visual impairment) that such seats are undesirable.

Discrete reflections
The second sound field consists of discrete reflections. Reflections are first produced from one "hit" off surfaces or objects in the room, such as off the floor in front of the listener at home, or the side wall of a theater. Over time, later and later first reflections from more distant surfaces are produced and are joined by second-order reflections, which involve two hits, and so forth. The first, second, and higher order reflections are all considered discrete reflections, until there are so many reflections that they merge into reverberation, which is discussed in the next section.

The audible significance of discrete reflections varies, depending on their time of arrival and direction, their relative strength compared with direct sound, and their relative strength compared with the third sound field to be discussed, the reverberant field. Early discrete reflections may cause audible changes to direct sound, but not usually in such a manner that they can be distinguished from the direct sound. Instead, they change the sound by adding *spaciousness,* one sense of being in a room; they may affect localization; and they may *color* the direct sound by changing its timbre, to be defined in the next chapter. The direction of the reflections matters as well, with reflections having nearly the same angle as the source being less audible than reflections at great angles to the source.

Adding artificial "reflections" by use of digital delay in post production can change the character of a sound. Darth Vader's voice is processed by adding an apparent reflection 10 ms after the direct sound (about 1/4 of a frame) about equal in amplitude to the direct sound. This gives the voice the "sound in a barrel" quality that makes it sound mechanical.

Later arriving discrete reflections may potentially form echoes if they arrive late enough and are strong enough relative to the direct sound. Even without hearing obvious echoes, they may also color the sound field.

Track 7 of the CD shows the effect of adding one strong early reflection (at 10 ms, about $^1/_4$ frame of film) to the voice.

Reverberation

The third sound field in a room is the reverberant field. Reverberation occurs after there have been enough discrete reflections for no one reflection to be distinguishable from the others. Instead a "cloud" of energy, generally having no apparent direction, fills the room. What is usually desired for good acoustics is a smooth, diffuse decay of sound, having no particular signature or pattern. There are a variety of deviations from this ideal, with potentially damaging results.

> For example, flat, hard, parallel walls lead to *flutter echoes,* a particular pattern of reflections in which a "ta-ta-ta-ta-ta" effect is heard in larger spaces, and a kind of "sizzle" is heard in smaller spaces.

Reverberation time in a room was defined by Sabine as the time that it takes an abruptly terminated sound to die away to inaudibility. Sabine found that there were only two factors involved in computing the reverberation time: the volume of the room and the absorption of the surface area in the room, including the walls, ceiling, floor, and objects in the room. The *room volume* is the height times length times width, in units such as cubic feet. The *absorption* is expressed as the surface area times the average absorption, on a scale from 0 to 1, of each of the surfaces in the room.

> Note that the placement of absorptive materials for Sabine's equation does not matter, however, it does matter in lower reverberation time rooms where placement certainly affects discrete reflections, at the least, and possibly the reverberation time as well.

Reverberation time must be evaluated across a range of frequencies. This is because most room surface treatments do not absorb sound equally well at all frequencies, and often have less absorption at low frequencies than at high ones.

In addition, air absorption enters the evaluation at high frequencies in larger rooms.

This usually leads to a characteristic reverberation time curve versus frequency that has longer times at low frequencies, and shorter times at high frequencies, than in the

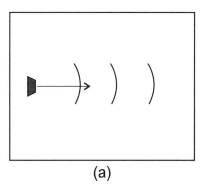

(a)

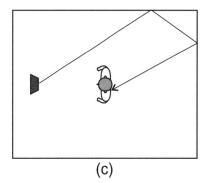

(b)

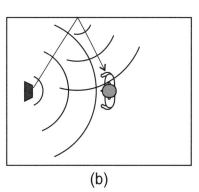

(c)

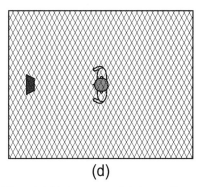

(d)

Fig. 1.16 Sound fields in a room: (a) shows direct sound, (b) 1st-order reflected sound, (c) higher-order reflected sound, and (d) a reverberant field where there are so many reflections per unit of time that each becomes indistinguishable from its peers.

middle frequency range. This can be important to filmmakers, since it can change the perception of certain effects dramatically. In the film *2010*, a loud, low-frequency rumble was used for the spaceship interior, and silence was used for the vacuum of space (physicists take note: a filmmaker followed physical law this time). Abrupt cuts between an interior shot and an exterior shot thus call for a loud, low-frequency sound to cease abruptly. At the Coronet theater in San Francisco where I heard the film, the approximately 5 second(!) reverberation time at very low frequencies caused the cut to seem, well, silly—the rumble just floated away slowly, negating the desired effect. Room acoustics conspired against the filmmakers in this case, even though they had followed the requirements of physics closely.

A headline in the *San Francisco Chronicle* some years ago highlighted how little is known among laymen about acoustics. The headline read "Six second echo in largest church rivals Grand Canyon." The article went on to describe how the church of St. John the Divine in New York has a 6 second "echo," and that is how long it takes sound to cross the Grand Canyon and return. The problem is that St. John the Divine does not have a 6 second echo; it has a 6 second reverberation time. A 6 second echo (that is, organized, intelligible sound arriving 6 seconds after the direct sound) does not sound at all similar to a reverberant decay that requires 6 seconds to die away to inaudibility.

> Most books treat room acoustics as having three sound fields: the direct sound, the *early reflections,* and the reverberant field. Unfortunately, in the room acoustics of motion-picture theaters, which are relatively dead, that is, have both a low reverberation time and a low level of reverberation, discrete reflections may occur at any time, early or late, and still be detectable, by ear or by instrument. In many large rooms, like concert halls, discrete reflections become covered up with reverberation fairly quickly over time. This does not happen in cinemas, where even the effect of the port glass for the projector in an otherwise absorptive back wall of a theater may cause a delayed reflection to the front seats in the auditorium that is large enough to be audible!

Track 8 of the CD illustrates reverberation effects.

Sum of effects

So the actual sound heard in a room is a sum of the effects we have been discussing. First the source radiates sound, probably with a preference for one or more directions, and the straight-line path to the observer contains the direct sound. Discrete reflections start to arrive and then reverberation builds up, as time goes by. While discrete reflections may arrive at any time after the direct sound, they may be blended into reverberation or not, depending on how late they arrive, and how strong they are compared to the prevailing reverberation. The sum of these effects is extremely complicated, but there are some interesting examples of methods that have evolved, especially in the motion-picture industry, to achieve reasonable overall results. They also illustrate an adaptive industry that has changed over time.

In the late 1920s the introduction of sync sound to movies was mostly done in converted vaudeville theaters, because specifically designed and built cinemas had yet to come into being. Many theaters had a live show and then a film. Over time, live stage show venues had reached a compromise on reverberation time between desirably low times for good intelligibility and higher times, which were basically cheaper.

Live stage actors changed their performance to accommodate the acoustics of the space, slowing down and enunciating as necessary to be heard. Since absorptive materials were fewer in type and quality at that time than today, most auditoriums were fairly live, that is, reverberant, and treatments were minimal, using only drapery to make speech intelligible, if not optimum. This resulted in fairly long reverberation times in the venues where movies were first shown with sync sound. It was known in Hollywood at the time that if reverberation was also recorded on the sound track, the combination of recorded plus live reverberation put intelligibility over the edge. For this reason, shooting stages were virtually *anechoic,* that is, were practically 100% absorptive, with thick mineral wool covering the walls and ceiling, held in place with acoustically transparent cloth or wire. Thus, one heard only one reverberation time in the final auditorium screening, because the recorded reverberation was so small as to be negligible.

This empirically derived method of working with reverberation from the 1930s has been completely reversed in recent years. Instead of live theaters and dead shooting stages, we now have dead theaters and permit relatively more lively shooting conditions. The reasons for this quantum shift are several:

- If the listening space always adds its own reverberation to everything that is heard in it, it is difficult to "transport" an audience from the acoustic sound of the back seat of a car to a gymnasium on a picture cut between the two. It is better for the listening room to be relatively dead and then use recorded reverberation to move the audience from scene to scene. This idea is greatly enhanced in the stereophonic era since reverberation is, by definition, a spatial event, and stereophonic systems can reproduce spatial effects, whereas a monophonic system cannot.

- Today we have far better means to add controlled reverberation in post production than in earlier times. This means that recording in a dead studio, and playing back in a dead auditorium, can be enhanced by deliberately added high-quality and flexible reverberation, which is one of the primary processes done during post production in order to provide good continuity from shot to shot, and to "place" the sound, that is, make a space for it to live in.

- The cost of production on sets in Hollywood studios has become prohibitively high, so the trend has been to shoot on location. Locations are almost never as dead as Hollywood shooting stages, so we live with increased reverberation in recordings, even if the microphone technique is identical in the studio and on location.

- Sometimes the tolerance for reverberation recorded on location is taken too far. In *Midnight in the Garden of Good and Evil* for instance, the large, live rooms portrayed in Georgia mansions look good, but sound too lively.

Another effect of summing the direct, reflected, and reverberant sound fields is seen when listening at the source and then moving away from it, along the direction of preferred radiation. When the observation point is near the source, we say it is *in the direct field,* or is *direct-field dominated.* For small sources measured nearby, the drop off in sound level as we move away from the source follows the inverse square law, as long as we remain direct-field dominated. Far away from the source in a very reverberant room, we are *in the reverberant field,* or *diffuse-field dominated.* Despite moving the point of observation around in the reverberant field, the level does not change. This is because one part of the definition of a reverberant sound field is "everywhere the same," so the rules are obeyed and we find no difference in level.

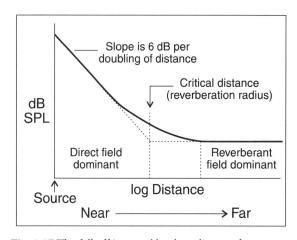

Fig. 1.17 The fall off in sound level vs. distance from a point sound source in a very reverberant room. Near the source, the sound level drops off at 6 dB per doubling of distance (see the end of this chapter for a definition of dB), and far away from the source the level is constant. The distance from the source along the line of principal radiation where the level of the direct sound and reverberant sound is equal is called the critical distance. The critical distance is made longer by a more directional source, or a less reverberant room (one having a lower reverberation time) and vice versa.

In between the region where the level falls off as an inverse square with distance and where the level is constant with distance, there is an elbow in the curve of level versus distance. The midpoint of this elbow is the place where the direct sound field and the reverberant sound field levels are equal, called the *critical distance* from the source. All other things being equal, the critical distance varies in the following ways:

- As a room becomes more reverberant, for example by removing absorption, the critical distance gets shorter (since there will be more reverberation).

- As a source becomes more directional in the direction we are measuring, the critical distance increases (since this tends to increase the direct field compared with the reverberant field at our measurement point).

For rooms that have more ordinary reverberation time than the example of Fig. 1.17, such as say a living room, the fall off of sound level vs. distance is likely to be closer to a straight line on the graph.

This discussion may seem fairly abstract in light of the day-to-day concerns of filmmakers, but it has a profound effect on the perception of film and video sound, due to the differences in the venues in which the programs are heard. Today, with films destined for multiple lives, first as theatrical releases, and then as home video, the problems associated with transfer of the experience from theaters to homes has received greater attention.

> In motion-picture dubbing stages and first-rate theaters, the primary listening locations are direct-field dominated, because the reverberation times are low for the room volume and the speakers are directional. In homes, however, listening rooms are typically more reverberant for their room volume than theaters, and speakers are less directional. Therefore, listening at home is reverberant-field dominated, and the viewer frequently asks, "What did he say?" A frequent comment from video viewers of film material is that the dialog is not as intelligible as it should be, and this is one of the reasons—the acoustical conditions are very different.

Another feature of this discussion that is important to filmmakers is the relatively low reverberation times present in theaters today, creating a strong propensity for uneven sound coverage. The sound level near the screen can be very high compared with the back of the room; after all, the inverse square law is working in the direct field, and we are direct-field dominated in a low-reverb-time space. While this is true, theater sound system design has found a way out of this dilemma. Film screen loudspeakers are located and aimed in such a way that they deliberately send less sound in the direction of the front rows and more towards the back rows, overcoming, to a large degree, the falloff from front to back that occurs along the axis of radiation. In other words, the sound system is aimed over the heads of the audience to promote uniformity from front to back.

Standing waves

So far what we have been discussing involves waves moving from point to point, and the effects on them. These moving waves are called *progressive waves*, but there is another kind of wave, called a *standing wave*. The lowest frequency standing waves occur when a wave is propagated within a room and the wavelength being radiated "fits" precisely into the dimensions of the room. The longest wavelength of sound that fits this requirement is *twice* the distance between the two walls (because there needs to be a full wavelength, including a compression and a rarefaction to complete the wave). What occurs is that the reflection of the wave reinforces the incoming wave, and the pattern generated seems to "stand still." This process goes on and on, with reflection after reflection contributing to the standing wave pattern. It also occurs at higher harmonics of this fundamental such that more than one wavelength "just fits" into the room dimensions. Standing waves, also called *room modes*, occur between two parallel walls, as described, and there are higher orders of standing waves that involve two and three pairs of surfaces as well. Simple, parallel-wall standing waves are called *axial*, while those involving two pairs of surfaces are called *tangential*, and those involving three pairs are called *oblique*. It is usually the axial modes that show the strongest effects.

The consequence of standing waves is exaggeration or diminution of certain low frequencies at one particular point in the space, and strong variation in these perturbations as you move around the space. This problem is worse in smaller rooms and at lower frequencies. When sitting in one position in a small room one hears one thing, but when sitting in another position there may be a quite different impression, caused by the pattern of standing waves in the room.

For production sound, the consequences can be a boomy quality to a sound recording, such that male voices sound like they have an exaggerated "uh-uh" quality to everything said, usually made increasingly worse with increasingly smaller and more live (less absorptive) rooms. In addition to reverberation, this is the reason that men like to sing in the shower—it gives bass boost to their voices. However, the same phenomena is very troubling for production sound and would call for a great deal of treatment in post production to make a recording from a lively shower useful (as well as to reduce the noise).

One principle that applies is that all of the sound pressure "piles up" at the frequencies of the standing waves at the boundaries and intersections of the room. The bass is thus stronger at the walls, stronger still in the corner of two walls, and strongest at the joint of two walls and the floor or ceiling. To filmmakers, this has the following two consequences:

- Most producers sit at the back wall in dubbing stages, where they can talk on the phone while a mix is in progress. Unfortunately, this is just where the bass is exaggerated in the room, so they receive a bass-heavy impression of the mix.

- The effectiveness of low-frequency absorption varies depending on its placement.

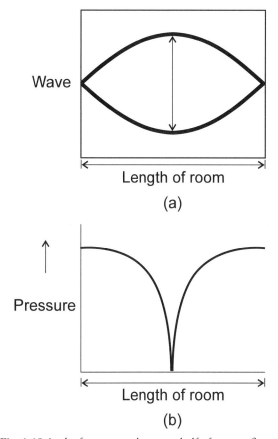

Fig. 1.18 At the frequency where one-half of a wave fits precisely the room dimensions, a standing wave is formed. At this frequency, the pressure is high at the two walls, and low in the center of the room.

Noise

We've used one technical definition of noise already—noise as a sound without tonality, such as a waterfall. The more popular definition of noise is unwanted sound, which of course varies from time to time and from person to person. Thus, no strict definition of noise is possible.

Unwanted sound is a problem for filmmakers at many times and places. In production sound, it can have a strong effect on budgets, since shooting in a noisy location may well mean the actors need to return for an ADR[5] session (also called looping) so that their voices can be re-recorded. In theaters, background noise may be so loud that it obscures the quieter passages of a sound track.

_____
5. Automated dialog replacement.

Noise reaches listeners and microphones by two possible paths. Either it is airborne or it is structure borne, which then radiates from the room surfaces to become airborne. In more serious cases, it may even generate sufficient vibration such that the noise becomes noticeable not because of its audibility but because it directly shakes the listener. Airborne noise leaking directly into a set is prevented by having an air seal all around the space. This especially means providing a method to get cables in and out of the space through some kind of air lock, otherwise, the shooting space is in direct contact with the noisy outside world.

Airborne noise sources include transportation noise, air handlers, and many other parts of everyday life. These sources are an extra problem for modern-day shooting, where the full expressive range of acting is expected to be captured by the production sound crew, with no technical limitation. In the 1930s actors were expected to speak loudly and clearly, and for several years after the introduction of sound there was a sound director in charge of the movie's sound, including the voices of the actors. The sound director was even known to fire actors for their inability to speak clearly. Some careers of silent film stars were ruined by the transition to the talkies because the actors did not sound like what the audience expected. Today, if an actor can't be understood it is routinely thought to be a technical fault, no matter how much of a mumbler the actor is. These problems are made only worse by intrusive noise on location.

One of the first applications of the new science of room acoustics, and particularly noise control, was the building of MGM studios by Louis B. Mayer. During planning it was realized that on one stage there could be a quiet love scene being shot, while on the next stage over a battle was to be raging. A proposition was made to MGM that a wire grid be strung up between the stages to ensure noise control. Luckily, someone at the studio saw through this poppycock and went looking for a scientist willing to tackle the problem (which was by no means small).

They found a UCLA physicist, Vern O. Knudsen, to help them out, who proposed massive walls and huge, solid doors for noise control. This led to the problem of heat. Because the shooting stage was a sealed box, combined with the extensive lighting needed for the slow film speeds of the day, actors were strongly affected by the temperature. The first air-conditioning noise control system was invented by Knudsen on a cross-country train trip to see the vendor so that he could meet the simultaneous needs of keeping the actors cool and keeping the noise low enough that production sound could be recorded at MGM.

Structure-borne noise is often even more insidious than airborne noise, and harder to solve since the whole room may be moving from the vibration. Let us say that there is a subway close to a cinema. The subway in operation puts vibration into the ground, and, in turn, the walls of the theater move in response to the vibration, creating sound emitted in the theater. The only possible fix is to break the connection with the ground and suspend the theater on vibration-isolating mounting, which can be done, but the expense is enormous. This problem affects the Astor Plaza theater in New York city, for example.

Filmmakers working on location can usually do nothing about structure-borne noise, except to be aware of its effects and to use special microphone mounting devices, called *vibration isolators* or *suspensions* to avoid conducting vibration directly to the microphone. Airborne noise, on the other hand, can be treated to some extent by sealing the environment away from the noisy world. Producers should also be aware that shooting in pretty but noisy locations will increase post production costs, because more treatment of the sound will be required, perhaps including the need for actors to loop their performances.

Scaling the dimensions
Frequency range
We already know that the frequency range of audible sound is large. In order to de-

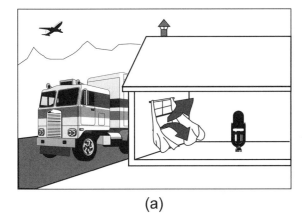

(a)

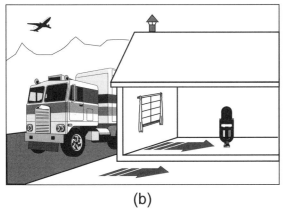

(b)

Fig. 1.19 The two principal noise sources are (a) airborne and (b) structure borne.

scribe the range, we could use a linear scale from 20 Hz to 20 kHz, but we would then devote one half of the scale to the range from 10 kHz and 20 kHz. In this high-frequency region, only the high harmonics of some instruments and sounds are found, and the region is less important than what lies below it. For this reason, and for others we will see in Chapter 2, it is more common to think of the frequency scale as being composed of octaves, that is, of having equal increments along a scale of 2:1 units of fre-quency. One such scale is given in Table 1.1. Audible sound thus covers 10 octaves of frequency (whereas visible light ranges from 400 to 700 nm, a range of less than one octave).

Track 9 of the CD illustrates the audible frequency range, with a "boink" in each octave from 31.5 Hz to 16 kHz, covering a wide part, but not all, of the audible frequency range.

Amplitude range

We have left the scaling of amplitude range until last in this chapter because it forms a bridge to psychoacoustics. We've already seen how human hearing has influenced the way in which we view the frequency range of sound, despite the fact that there may well be sound outside the audible frequency range. What about an amplitude scale?

Normal sounds encountered in the world cover an enormous range of amplitudes, with a range of about 1:1,000,000 in the sound pressure level difference from the softest sound we can hear to the loudest we can normally stand. In order to represent this world conveniently, it is commonplace to use a logarithmic scale, in which equal increments along the scale are given in powers of 10 as 1, 10, 100, ... This log scale is used principally for convenience in representing the extreme range of amplitude encountered in real life. With some mathematical manipulation, the log scale is represented in the unit deciBel (dB) and this is the most widely used unit for noting the amplitude of physical and recorded sound.

The term dB always refers only to a ratio of amplitudes. Although very often lost, a reference is always at least implied if not stated. In the case of physical sound, the deciBel scale for sound pressure level (SPL) has its reference at 0 dB SPL, roughly equal to the threshold of hearing, the softest sound one can hear. Quiet background sound such as that found standing in a still field at night is about 30 dB, face-to-face speech averages 65 dB, typical film dialog around 75 dB, and the loudest sounds in theatrical films are up to 115 dB, all in dB SPL.

The deciBel scale for sound pressure level for audible and tolerable sound runs from 0 dB to 120 dB SPL (Table 1.2). Of course, there are sounds louder than we can tolerate as listeners, and sounds softer than we can hear, so this scale can be carried to both lower and higher levels, but thankfully such ranges do not typically apply to film or television production. The reference is approximately the threshold of hearing, 0 dB SPL, which is a pressure of 2×10^{-5} Newtons/m^2.

Along a deciBel scale, 3 dB is twice the power and 6 dB is twice the voltage, but it takes about 10 dB to sound twice as loud. Thus stereo salesmen who claim that a 60 watt receiver plays much louder than a 50 watt receiver are wrong—the difference is only 0.8 dB, and the loudness difference is very small!

Table 1.1: Octave Band Center Frequencies for the Audible Frequency Range

1	2	3	4	5	6	7	8	9	10
31 Hz	63 Hz	125 Hz	250 Hz	500 Hz	1 kHz	2 kHz	4 kHz	8 kHz	16 kHz

Table 1.2: Typical Sound Pressure Levels Relative to 0 dB SPL

120 dB	Threshold of sensation "tickle" in the ear
118 dB	Loudest sound peaks in digital theatrical films[1]
90~95 dB	Loudest sound peaks in 35mm analog theatrical films[2]
80~90 dB	Typical loudest sounds from television
75 dB	Average level of dialog in films
65 dB	Average level of face-to-face speech
50 dB	City background noise (but varies greatly)
30 dB	Quiet countryside
20 dB	Panavision camera running with film measured at 1 m
0 dB	Threshold of hearing in silence

1 In digitally equipped theaters playing at the standardized volume control ("fader") setting, measured with a wideband, peak reading, sound pressure level meter. This combination of ingredients leads to the highest possible reading, but one that does *not* represent the noise exposure of an audience to sound level. This is because a movie has constantly changing level, with rare peak moments at such a high level. See Chapter 2 for more information on the loudness level of movies.
2 Measured as above.

Track 10 of the CD illustrates a good part of the audible dynamic range, with a special noise signal recorded in 10 dB steps.

Chapter 2: Psychoacoustics

Introduction

Many issues in human perception of sound are a direct result of the physical acoustics of the head, outer ears, ear canal, and so forth interacting with sound fields. While not strictly in the realm of psychoacoustics, this kind of physical acoustics only occurs because a person is present in a sound field, so we will take it up here. The head is a rather large object, acoustically speaking, so there are many interactions between the head and a sound field. A sound wave arriving from the front must "spread around" the head from the front to the sides through diffraction, interact with the outer ear structure principally through reflection, progress down the resonant ear canal to the ear drum, and so forth. This interaction between the sound field and the object observing the sound field is fundamentally different than with, say, a tiny measurement microphone. The small size of such microphones is specified by the need to measure the sound field with only minimal disturbance, almost as if the microphone were not there.

The placement of the head in a sound field also matters. As children, we first hear reflections off the ground shortly after direct sound, because we are close to the ground. As we grow taller, the reflection is heard later than the direct sound. The difference between these conditions is a result of the physical acoustic differences of the conditions; nevertheless, we incorporate them into "perception." We are, after all, continuously training our perception because we use it to function in the world all the time. We learn that a certain pattern of reflections represents our bodies standing in the real world. Let us look at those parts of perception that are most influenced by physical acoustics first, and then examine the more psychological aspects.

The physical ear

The first part to consider in talking about "the ear" is actually the human body, especially the head. As stated earlier, incoming sound waves interact with the head as a physical object, with sound waves "flowing" around the head via diffraction. (A relatively minor effect even results from sound reflecting off the shoulder.) The interaction differs for various incoming angles of incidence, making the level and time of arrival of the sound wave at the two ears different.

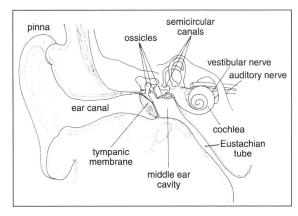

Fig. 2.1 A cutaway drawing of the ear showing the primary parts described in the text.

After reaching the outer ear structure, called the *pinna*, various reflections and resonances occur due to the structure of the outer ear convolutions. Older treatments on how this worked concentrated on the pinna's hornlike quality, its ability to gather sound from many directions and deliver it to the ear canal. In the past 25 years, the detailed role of the pattern of reflections and resonances caused by the pinna has come to be better understood. The details of the pinna structure play an important role in localizing sound because the pattern differs for sound arriving from different directions. We come to learn these patterns and rely on them for finding direction.

After interaction with the head and pinna, sound waves enter the ear canal. The length and diameter of the ear canal tube cause it to be tuned, like a whistle, to the mid-high frequency range. This ear canal resonance increases the sensitivity of hearing in the frequency range to which the canal is tuned by a factor of about three. An increase in sensitivity in the middle high frequencies proves highly useful in survival, since it is the range in which many threatening forces might make noise, such as the sound of a snapping twig behind us or the sound of lions moving through tall grass.

At the end of the ear canal lies the eardrum, which stretches across the end of the canal and seals it. This tympanic membrane vibrates in response to incident sound. Sound is airborne up until it strikes the eardrum; thenceforth sound is represented as vibration of the structures further inside the ear, although for convenience it is often still called *sound* (to distinguish it from *vibration* which is felt by structures other than the ear). The inside cavity beyond the eardrum is called the *middle ear*, and is supplied with air by way of the Eustachian tube, which exits into the throat. The purpose of the Eustachian tube is to keep the eardrum from being pushed to the limits of its travel by pressure changes in the atmosphere. The Eustachian tube equalizes the ambient pressure on the two sides of the eardrum, thus letting the eardrum come to rest at the center of its possible range of displacement, rather than becoming "stuck" to one side. It is these tubes that become clogged when you have a cold. Without being able to equalize pressure on both sides of the eardrum, it is pushed all the way to its limit of travel, and hearing suffers greatly. It may be dangerous to our hearing, or at least very painful, to fly with a cold and go through the air pressure changes involved in air travel, first to lower pressure while ascending and then to a higher pressure while descending. During such airplane flights, or even while going up or down in an elevator, it is a good idea to try to get your eardrums to "pop" to relieve the pressure before it reaches an extreme by moving your jaw around, chewing gum, or holding your nose shut while attempting to blow air out it gently, thus forcing air up through the tubes into your middle ear.

Inside the middle ear, the eardrum is connected to three tiny moving bones, called ossicles, organized in sequence. These three bones form a mechanical lever that magnifies the motion of the eardrum by a second factor of three before delivering it to the inner ear. Attached to these bones are two small muscles, whose contraction and relaxation are affected by the sound level. A loud sound causes the muscles to tighten, producing the *aural reflex*. Tightening the muscles reduces the transmission between the eardrum and the inner ear. The aural reflex is most active with intermittent, intense impulses of sound, but it does take time to act. For these reasons, the first burst of gunfire in an otherwise quiet sequence sounds loud, and later bursts may sound softer as the aural reflex begins to act. Filmmakers often ignore the fact that continuous loud sound is no longer perceived as loud by the audience because the aural reflex "turns down the volume," making the scene less effective than expected. Many contemporary action-adventure films clearly suffer from this problem providing no time for the audience to relax the aural reflex before another loud sound is presented.

The inner ear, or cochlea, has several roles. It is the organ that converts the vibrations received from the middle ear bones into nerve impulses destined for perception by the brain, and it also has an important role in maintaining physical balance. The cochlea is a small, snail-shell shaped organ with a "window" at one end to which the last bone in series in the middle ear is attached. The length of the cochlea is bisected by a stretched *basilar membrane*, on either side of which are fluids. About 30,000 hair cells are present along this basilar membrane and are attached to nerve cells. It is the motions of the hair cells that get converted to nerve impulses that register with the brain as sound.

Sound waves are magnified by ear canal resonance, which is converted into mechanical vibration by the motion of the eardrum, and is magnified again by the lever action of the middle ear, producing a combined nine times gain in amplitude. The inner ear selectively converts this mechanical motion into electrical signals via the aural nerves that correspond to the hair cells.

Specific sounds are destined to stimulate specific nerves because the basilar membrane is stretched stiffly suspended at the entrance for sound and is loosely stretched at the far end. Like tuning a drum, the tighter the drum is stretched, the higher the pitch is when the drum head is struck. The membrane in the cochlea acts like a continuous series of drum heads, each tuned to a progressively lower frequency as the distance from the input increases. Thus if the incoming vibrations are relatively fast, corresponding to a high frequency, they cause the greatest stimulus where the membrane is stiffly suspended, near the entrance. A lower note causes more movement where the membrane is more loosely suspended, further from the entrance. The hair cells that move the most put out the largest number of nerve firings and thus indicate to the brain that a particular frequency range is strong in the sound signal. The cochlea is thus basically a frequency analyzer, that breaks down the audio spectrum and represents it as level versus frequency, rather like Fourier frequency analysis but with important differences that we will consider later.

Hearing conservation

Evolution recessed the eardrum in order to protect it from damage and increase the sensitivity to important sounds. The cochlea is in one of the most protected regions of the body, inside the skull. These are examples of the importance nature placed on hearing. Two main factors cause hearing to deteriorate: aging, and exposure to high sound levels.

Hearing deteriorates naturally with age, which has been found even in quiet, primitive societies. Hearing loss with age primarily affects high frequency sensitivity, and there are statistically significant differences between men and women, with women faring better with age. It is not known whether this is an innate biological difference or is caused by more men than women working in noisier industrial environments and having noisier hobbies.

The fine hairs of the inner ear can be permanently damaged by one very loud sound; even the U.S. Army does not allow recruits to be exposed to sound pressure levels over 140 dB, even briefly. Gunfire close at hand is the most likely source of sound that may

31

cause a permanent loss with as little as one exposure. Luckily, film and television sound systems cannot play loudly enough to cause this kind of near-instantaneous damage. On the other hand, lower levels of sound, when accumulated over time, may lead to hearing loss. An engineer working for a chain of theaters throughout England found in the 1960s that the volume control was set higher, on average, in movie theaters in the north of England than in the south. The audience in the north consisted largely of textile mill workers, still working with noisy 19th-century machinery. The average hearing loss of the population was greater in the north than the south of England, due to occupational noise exposure.

Noise induced hearing loss begins to occur when the sound level is above a certain threshold, set by standards to typically 80 dB,[1] called the *threshold level*. Exposure to sound below this level is ignored as not playing a significant rôle in sound-induced hearing loss. Above the threshold there is a trade off: *louder* sound is permitted, but only for a *shorter* time. A *criteria level* of 85 dB may be allowed for 8 hours, 88 dB for 4 hours, and so forth. This is called a 3 dB (level vs. time) trading rule. Thus continuous noise sources of many industrial machines can be ranked for how much exposure is created by them, and a program of abatement of the noise source, or wearing required hearing protection, can be put into place.

Listening to movies and television shows makes life more complicated than simple continuous industrial noise since they have constantly varying level. A method of averaging the level over time is required, and one widely used one is called L_{eq}. Using the concepts of threshold and criteria levels, the trading rule, and L_{eq} together results in a percentage value called a *daily noise dose*. Going to the movies in theaters that play them at their original post production levels

(note: many theaters turn the sound down from the original level), results in noise doses of between 2% on a dialogue driven picture with one loudish scene (*Tea with Mussolini*) and 55% for a space adventure (*Episode I: The Phantom Menace*); thus going to the movies, even daily, does not expose one to enough sound to cause any statistically significant greater hearing loss than normal aging.

Conversely, working on films and television shows for long hours at a time, especially dubbing loud action features, may well produce noise doses that are over the amount that will cause sound induced hearing loss greater than aging. Professionals who work on loud films may find themselves confronted with the dilemma of working now vs. working over a long career. Some mixers have resorted to wearing hearing protection on the dubbing stage, because their exposure to the loud passages of a movie are so much greater than that of their ultimate audience, given the hundreds of times they may listen to a loud passage.

There are undoubtedly sound professionals who have suffered different degrees of hearing loss in the pursuit of their professional duties, although the evidence for this comes mainly from music recording, not film and television work. In rock music recording, an average monitor sound level may be 10 dB higher than it is for film dubbing and, without controls over that level, can go much higher.[2] Television mixing is, in turn, done at a level typically 5 to 7 dB lower than film dubbing, so the potential for hearing loss is certainly less for film and television mixers than for rock music mixers.

Avoid attending live amplified concerts without wearing hearing protection. The sound pressure level of these concerts is routinely more than 10 dB louder than the loudest sound possible in a film, and this level is sustained for much longer times.

---

1. This number is measured with an *A weighting* curve that emphasizes middle high-frequency range sound over low and high frequency sound, to better match human susceptibility to sound levels.

---

2. Film dubbing is done at a standardized "volume control" setting, but music mixing generally uses no such standard.

Each person varies in his or her susceptibility to hearing damage. One person at a specific rock concert may lose a significant amount of hearing permanently, while another person sitting next to him may be affected only short term. There is no way to know in advance whether you are a particularly susceptible person.

One indication that you are exposed to too much sound level over time is if you experience tinnitus after the event. Tinnitus may variably be described as an internal whistling, ringing, buzzing, hissing, or humming heard when you are in a quiet environment.

Certain drugs, such as some of the most powerful antibiotics, may have negative effects on hearing, and their use is restricted to life-threatening cases and is accompanied by monitoring of hearing. Even aspirin may affect tinnitus, with the onset of hearing the effect indicating too large a dose. High-impact aerobics, professional volleyball, and high-mileage running have been implicated in high-frequency hearing loss and balance problems for some fraction of the participants in these sports.

Auditory sensitivity vs. frequency

Threshold value—the minimum audible field

Human hearing does not respond equally well to all frequencies in the audible range. This is because evolution has caused our sensitivity to be increased in frequency ranges at which threats and voices might be most easily perceived, while being relatively less sensitive at other frequencies. As a broad statement, humans are most sensitive around the middle to high frequency ranges, with the worst sensitivity at the low and more extreme high frequencies. Scientists can measure the threshold of perception versus frequency with relative ease because it is largely a matter of finding a space quiet enough to be able to hear the softest sounds, and then presenting calibrated sound-pressure-level sine waves at various frequencies to large numbers of listeners (usually headphones are used to eliminate the effects of room acoustics, which otherwise must be accounted for). By averaging a large number of observations, individual variations disappear, leaving a curve of auditory sensitivity

versus frequency, the *minimum audible field*. The reason that this is a straightforward psychoacoustic experiment is that we ask the subjects whether or not they hear something. An experiment involving scaling loudness is much more difficult, because it is a lot harder to get common agreement on what is twice as loud, when comparing one sound to another, than to determine whether a subject hears any sound at all. *Hearing loss* of an individual is rated in terms of the increase in hearing threshold for various frequencies compared with the standard minimum audible field.

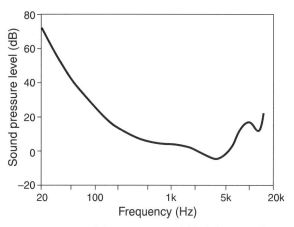

Fig. 2.2 A curve of the minimum audible field versus frequency, showing the greatest sensitivity for human hearing in the 2–4 kHz range, and greatly diminished sensitivity at higher, and especially lower, frequencies.

Of course, such average curves do not characterize any one individual, but they are accepted in international standards as being representative of the population as a whole. The standard deviation on these experiments is on the order of ±5 dB, that is, 67% of the normal population will lie within ±5 dB, and 90% within ±10 dB, of the average curves. The greatest sensitivity corresponds to the bottom of the curve in Figure 2.2 because that is where the smallest possible sound level can be detected. Note that 0 dB SPL is roughly the bottom of the curve (constructed such that the numbers will almost always come out positive), but the minimum audible field does go below zero in the most sensitive range, at around 3 kHz.

In light, if we are properly dark adapted, we can see one photon, the minimum divisible packet of light energy. In sound, we can hear displacements of molecules in air that are smaller than the size of the orbit of the sole electron spinning about the hydrogen atom. Perception is so finely tuned to the environment that any further development would not be very useful. For example, the minimum audible field has a higher threshold at lower frequencies than at midrange frequencies, as shown in Figure 2.2. This is thought to provide the evolutionary advantage of helping humans to sleep soundly. If we had greater sensitivity at low frequencies, we would spend excessive time listening to internal bodily functions such as breathing.

Equal-loudness curves

At levels higher than threshold, perceptual scientists ask another question of large numbers of people, and get good results. The question is, How strong must each frequency be to sound as loud as the same sound pressure level at, say, 1 kHz? That is, how does loudness vary with frequency? The outcome of such an experiment produces curves of equal loudness.

You can think of them in this way. The background "grid" on the graph is the physical world, while the lines on the graph are the psychoacoustic representations of that world. For instance, take a sine-wave tone at 1 kHz and 20 dB SPL. This is a clear, although soft, tone. Now change the frequency to 100 Hz. What we see is that at 100 Hz we have now dropped below the threshold of hearing and no sound is perceived at all, simply by a change in frequency. So the frequency of a tone affects loudness, as does its sound pressure level.

Another finding has to do with the shape of the curves. Notice that at no level is hearing flat with frequency. Since we perceive the whole world in this manner, we do not find this unnatural, but it does have some serious consequences for film sound. For example, all of the curves go up at low frequencies.

This means that more energy is required at low frequencies to sound equally as loud as

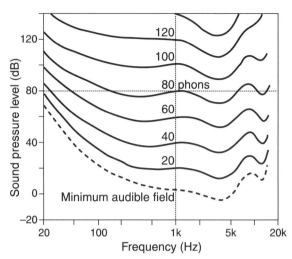

Fig. 2.3 The curves of equal loudness vs. frequency. The background grid represents the objective world, and the curves represent the response of an average human listener to that world in loudness. The contours are labeled in *phons*, one unit of subjective loudness, which is equal to the sound pressure level at 1 kHz. Taking the point 80 dB at 1 kHz as a reference, and following the 80 phon contour down to 20 Hz, shows that about 110 dB sound pressure level is needed to sound equally as loud as an 80 dB SPL 1 kHz tone. Human response to sound pressure level does not stop abruptly at high frequencies as shown, but this is the limit of experimental data.

midrange sounds. Recently designed film sound systems are constructed with this in mind, with much greater level playing capacity in the low bass than in the midrange in order to account for this psychoacoustic effect.

Yet there are plenty of places in audio recording and reproduction where this lesson has not been applied, such as analog optical sound tracks. For example, *Return of the Jedi's* optical track reveals that Jabba the Hut's basso profundo voice uses up practically all of the available area of the sound track[3] yet is not very loud. The reason for this is that the technique used by the sound designer made Jabba's voice very bassy, and thus bigger and more threatening sounding (remember *Jaws*). In order to sound even normally loud, the level of Jabba's voice had to be adjusted upwards, which used up practically all of the available area of the sound track. Conventional optical sound tracks have a maximum capability that is flat with frequency, whereas hearing requires more low frequencies than high frequencies to sound equally loud. A direc-

---

3. The recorded width of the optical sound track corresponds to the amplitude of the waveform.

tor who demands "more bass" is, of course, right, because that is what he or she thinks necessary to make the point, but getting what a director wants may be limited by the capability of the medium in which he or she is working.

Another effect occurs because the equal-loudness curves of perception converge at low frequencies, which is called the *loudness effect*. This occurs when sounds are reproduced at a level higher or lower than the original sound. At a lower level, sound seems to lack bass when compared with playing it at its original level. This is often a problem in film production in which music, faded underneath dialog, becomes thin sounding, that is, lacking in bass. A post production mixer can make up for this effect by adding bass as the level is turned down, and this is exactly what the loudness control or switch on a consumer receiver is designed to accomplish: Activating the switch turns the volume control into a loudness control. (Unfortunately, many of these on consumer receivers are poorly designed and so bass is overemphasized upon turning the level down.) Track 11 of the CD illustrates the loudness effect.

What's wrong with the deciBel— magnitude scaling

While a logarithmic scale serves well to "compress" the range of the real world into manageable numbers, the relationship between a strict log scale such as deciBels and hearing perception is not simple. Research studies have not settled on one single amplitude scale because experimental results are affected by the method used to obtain them. After all, we are dealing with human perception; we cannot hook up a loudness meter inside a brain to measure the sensation level but must rely on listener reports, such as "This sound is twice as loud as that sound." Depending on the experiment, "twice as loud" falls along the deciBel scale between 6 and 10 dB, tending toward the higher value more often. So for everyday purposes, we say that 10 dB is twice as loud.

> Once again, note that twice as much power is 3 dB, twice as much voltage is 6 dB, and twice as loud is 10 dB. This means that to play music twice as loud without distortion as, say, a

50 watt receiver requires a 500 watt receiver!

The minimum difference in level that is detectable on program material is usually said to be 1 dB; however, this is a number for untrained laymen. Trained sound mixers can set sound levels so they match to within $\frac{1}{2}$ dB.

Loudness vs. time

The foregoing discussion regarding loudness concentrated on more or less continuous sounds, such as that of a kitchen fan. While ranking constant sources for perceived loudness is certainly important, it is also useful to know how loudness changes over time for more rapidly changing sounds.

This factor is called the *integration time* of hearing, because it takes a finite amount of time for loudness to grow to its full value. A high-level sound presented only briefly, say, for less than one frame, will not achieve the full loudness as a sound having the same level that is sustained for about one third of a second. There are many variations in the types of experiments that have been done in this area, including center frequency of the phenomena, number of occurrences within a period of time, etc., and consequently a large range of results can be obtained for the "time constant" of hearing. The range of time for a high level but brief sound to reach nearly its full loudness is between 35 and 300 ms (1 to 8 frames at 24 fps). Track 12 of the CD illustrates loudness vs. time.

Spectrum of a sound
Critical bands of hearing

Across the audible frequency range there are about 24 frequency regions, called *critical bands*, each representing about 0.05 in. in length along the basilar membrane and encompassing about 1300 nerve receptors. The frequency width of the critical bands varies, being wider in the bass than the mid-range and treble, but typically they are about one third of an octave wide.

When two tones of equal amplitude that lie within one critical band are added together, the result is an increase in loudness. If the same amplitude tones are further than one critical band apart, the result is an even greater increase in loudness. A typical meter displaying the amplitude will have the same reading in either case, but in the second case, we perceive a louder sound. So the loudness of sound depends not only on the level measured, but also on the *spectrum* of the sound. The spectrum is a plot of level versus frequency, for example, showing all the harmonics of a sound.

> Note that the critical bands are not fixed at rigid frequency boundaries but rather "slide" to fit the stimulus. The critical band concept thus involves the selectivity of the ear, that is, how narrow a frequency band the effect covers, not the absolute frequency limits.

In general, the more spectrum a sound takes up, the louder the sound will be. For a low-frequency rumble to sound louder, it is useful to add other higher frequency components to the sound, such as adding the sound of gravel being poured from a dump truck to the sound of a bassier rumble. So, to maximize loudness, frequency components spanning a wide range are used, usually by the addition of added sound layers editorially.

Frequency masking

Louder sounds cover up softer ones, especially those that are nearby in frequency, which is called *frequency masking*. The idea of masking is a major plot point in Alfred Hitchcock's *The Man Who Knew Too Much*. Assassins plan to shoot an ambassador during a concert in London's Royal Albert Hall. The chief plotter uses a phonograph record of the music to be played at the concert to train the assassin when he can shoot and not be heard by firing the gun simultaneously with a big cymbal crash. The record is played several times to get the point across. Whether masking would in fact work in this context is a matter of some conjecture and depends on many factors, but it certainly works in this movie, which has a twelve minute section with no dialogue surrounding the shooting. In the end, Doris Day screams in the silence just before the cymbal is to crash and distracts the assassin just enough that his aim is spoiled and the ambassador is only wounded instead of killed.

To make the maximum number of different sounds audible at one time, it is useful for them to be spread out across frequency in order to minimize the masking of one sound by another. Editors and composers employ a strategy of choosing different frequency ranges for a variety of effects and music, just to minimize the masking of one sound by another.

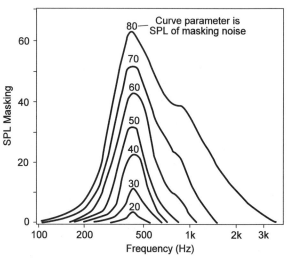

Fig. 2.4 Frequency masking: a narrow frequency band of noise centered near 400 Hz masks sound at nearby frequencies, and the effect grows to cover a greater frequency range, especially towards the higher frequencies, as the level increases. The curves are numbered with the sound pressure level of the masking noise, and show the level versus frequency which is masked. In other words, any frequency components lying below the curves are masked when a band of noise at 400 Hz and the stated SPL is present. Adapted from Egan, J. P. and Hake, H. W., "On the masking pattern of a simple auditory stimulus," *J. Acoust. Soc. Am.* 22, 622–630.

At low levels, frequency masking effects are contained in a relatively narrow frequency range about the masker (the louder sound which does the masking). As the level increases, the masker becomes more effective at masking than just a level change would predict, and this effect is greater towards higher frequencies than towards lower ones, as shown in Fig. 2.4. Thus, there is an upwards spread of masking with increases in level, and more of a masking effect at higher levels. Frequency masking is routinely used in another way by sound editors.

Let us say that we have a production sound track recording of a scene that is reasonably good, containing fine performances by the actors, etc., but there is a flaw: the background noise changes from shot to shot within the scene in a noticeable manner. This could easily arise if the scene was shot out of order over the course of a day and the noise level at the location changed over time. The background noise difference might not have been noticeable at the time of shooting, but when the shot made in the morning is cut together with that made in the afternoon, the change is heard at the edits. The abrupt changes in room tone, as the background noise is called, distract from the feeling that the scene is one continuous whole. Various processes are used in post production to clean up this background noise, but there may still be a residual change at the edits.

To prevent the audience from hearing small background level changes at edits a second track is provided, running in parallel with the first and containing an ambience appropriate to the setting, and it is mixed together with the production sound. The continuous nature of the ambience, and its use in masking the actual recorded background noise produce smooth-sounding edits and good continuity.

Track 13 of the CD demonstrates frequen cy masking.

Temporal masking

A loud sound can mask a soft sound that does not occur at precisely the same moment. This seems clear from the example of, say, a gunshot covering up a soft sound for a time after the shot, and is called post or forward masking. A higher level masker (such as our gunshot) extends the time of masking further than a lower level one, as might be expected.

One of the most astonishing findings of psychoacousticians that, at first glance, confounds a scientific mind is that temporal masking works in the other direction as well. What is amazing is that the same gunshot covers up sound momentarily even before the shot! This occurs because the louder sound is perceived more quickly by the brain than the softer one, and is called premasking

or backward masking. The extent of this effect is not very large, with most of its utility occurring within 10 ms, or one perforation of 35mm film at 24 fps. Nevertheless, sound editors use backward masking frequently to cover up discontinuities at edits. A sound editor will edit music "on the beat" by cutting just before a loud cymbal crash is to occur. The cymbal crash then covers up the fact that there may be a momentary discontinuity at the actual edit point, using premasking.

Track 14 of the CD illustrates temporal masking.

> Knowledge of the details of frequency and temporal masking has been fundamental to the development of a relatively new branch of audio, low bit-rate digital coding, which is discussed in Chapter 11. The basic idea behind this technology is that there are sounds that are inaudible to human listeners because they would be masked, and thus there is no need to store and transmit such sounds. This topic is controversial, as are many in which psychoacoustics are used, since agreement among a great many listeners must be reached to say what is truly inaudible.

Pitch

The subjective sensation of pitch is often thought of as being interchangeable with the fundamental frequency of a note, but there are several factors on which pitch depends other than frequency. No instrument can measure whether a musician is in fact playing in tune or not, since pitch depends not only on fundamental frequency but also less strongly on level and possibly other factors, so expert listeners must determine whether or not a musician is playing in tune.

Another example of the difference between the objective measure of frequency and the subjective measure of pitch occurs if a recording is made and the fundamental is removed. Perception will recognize a "missing" fundamental in the pattern of harmonics and will supply it. Subjectively one hears the missing fundamental, even if it is not present, and associates it with a pitch (of a nonexistent frequency in the sound). Naturally the idea of pitch applies to musical notes, but what about voice or other sounds? The speaking voice is also said to have pitch, despite the fact that it is not singing. Raising the pitch will make voices seem more feminine, and it is likely that films that use men in drag also alter their spoken voice by deliberate upwards pitch shifting in post production.

> Another example of pitch being associated with nonmusical sounds is *repetition pitch*. In 1693, the French astronomer Christiann Huygens, standing near a staircase, was struck by how the sound of a fountain nearby seemed to contain a pitch sensation. Repetition pitch occurs when direct sound is heard along with a pattern of reflections. The fact that the reflections are evenly spaced in time reinforces certain frequencies, while partially canceling others, due to constructive and destructive interference. Because the steps are a regular structure, so is the pattern of reflections, and their effect on the direct sound is also patterned in such a way that we hear the effect.

An example of pitch shift causing changes in a filmmaker's work occurs routinely with transfers of films to the PAL system of video used in Europe and elsewhere. PAL video uses 25 fps, not 24, so theatrical film is sped up by $\frac{25}{24}$ths, or about 4%, for transfer to European videos. Increasing the speed of playback raises the frequency of sound, and thus the pitch. For example, Darth Vader in *Star Wars* takes on a less menacing quality as James Earl Jones' voice is misrepresented by being pitch raised. Some films are transferred through a compensating pitch-shift device to remove this error, but this compensation regrettably is used infrequently.

Spatial perception

Spatial perception is one of the areas where technology and art are most interrelated. Perceiving the sonic world in three dimensions is something we are accustomed to doing every day, and film and television sound systems are designed to provide the means to reproduce the most salient directional characteristics of the real world, with an ability to place sound around you. The aesthetic difficulty comes in choosing what sounds to represent where, because the picture has boundaries, but the sound is unbounded in the same sense. We take this idea up later, but first let us examine the underlying psy-

choacoustics to see how it has an impact on film.

Transients and the precedence effect

Localization is best for transient sounds. A *transient* is a brief sound such as fingers snapping or a drum hit. It is worst for relatively steady-state sounds such as pipe organ notes. Striking a piano note first produces an onset transient, which then tends toward steady state sound over time. Nevertheless, the brief transient attack at the beginning of the note gives us enough information to localize it, even in the presence of a lot of reflections and reverberation. This attention to the first-arriving sound is called the *precedence effect*. The precedence effect says that we will locate a sound in the direction of the first-arriving wavefront, unless later arriving sound is even higher in level than the direct sound. The effect is quite strong and has obvious utility in survival, because locating the tiger early is critical in avoiding him.

Influence of sight on sound localization

Vision is obviously also important for localization and can overwhelm aural impression. Sight dominates sound for localization. Nevertheless, mismatches between the position of a sound source visually and aurally do cause cognitive dissonance, which tends toward limiting the suspension of disbelief usually sought. Here, professionals and laymen differ on their level of perception and the annoyance experienced from mismatches. For professionals, just a 4° mismatch in the horizontal plane between the position of visual and aural images is noticeable, whereas it takes a 15° mismatch to annoy average laymen.

An example of vision dominating sound in film is the "Exit Sign" effect. In *Top Gun*, when jets fly left to right across the screen and then exit screen right, what may be perceived aurally is the jet flying off screen as well, right into the exit sign. In fact, the film sound system does not have the capability to accomplish this effect technically, but it is nonetheless perceived due to vision overwhelming auditory spatialization.

Localization in three dimensions: horizontal, vertical, and depth

Human localization is best in the horizontal plane because our ears are located on the sides of our heads, not the top and bottom, and, crudely speaking, triangulation works. The reason for this evolutionary adaptation is obvious: threats in our primeval environment most often came in the horizontal plane and so needed to be localized well, and quickly! The triangulation idea of using both ears for direction finding is a crude one because what actually occurs is considerably more complex. Conventional triangulation would rely on two spaced pickup points "seeing" the whole sound field, unobstructed. Instead, there is a large object in the way—the head. Let us think about the head as a simple hard sphere, with pickup points for sound located where ear holes would be.

Even in this simple model, sound waves impinging on the head from a direction of, say, right front in the horizontal plane reach the right ear hole first. Slightly delayed, sound reaches the left ear hole by diffraction about the head, with the delay being caused by the extra time it takes for sound from the right to wrap around the head, plus the "as the crow flies"[4] time.

> Human perceptual capability is so good that JNDs (just noticeable differences) of the time difference between ears in the most tightly controlled experiments are on the order of 10 microseconds! Four thousand of these time intervals pass by in one frame of time at 24 fps. That is, moving a source in the horizontal plane so that it arrives 1/100,000 of a second earlier at one ear than the other, compared with the reverse, can be apparent under the most sensitive experimental conditions. This is an astonishingly fast speed, much faster than brain transmission processes, but note that it is not absolute time that is being measured but the match between two paths from the two ears, which must match within the brain remarkably well.

For this sound field coming from right front, we say the left ear hole is *in the acoustic shadow* of the head. The shadow effect var-

---

4. An English idiom that means "by the most direct path."

ies with frequency and reduces the level at the left ear relative to the right. At low frequencies, sound diffracts around the head easily, so the level is nearly the same at the two ears, but for high frequencies the head appears to be a larger object due to the shorter wavelengths of high frequencies, so the level is substantially reduced at the left ear.

So there is both a time difference arising out of the geometry and a level difference due to the shadowing effect. The time difference is used primarily as the localization strategy up to about 1 kHz, and the level difference is used from about 4 kHz up. This leaves a hole between the two strategies, which might suggest poor localization performance in this range, and that is the experimental finding.

For the model just described, we used a sphere of average head dimensions with ear holes as pickup points for illustration, and its use demonstrated amplitude and time differences well. In fact, such a sphere with embedded microphones in the positions of two ear holes is on the market as a stereophonic microphone, which is claimed to be capable of reproducing the level and time differences of hearing. The pinna were left out of our model but play a part in localization as well. As stated earlier, the convolutions of the pinna cause different interactions with sound waves, depending on their direction of incidence. Although there are a variety of effects, the main one is the difference caused by reflections off the *concha*, the principal cavity leading to the ear canal, combining with the direct (or diffracted) sound. The combination of the direct sound with a reflection causes construc-tive and destructive interference at the entrance to the ear canal.

Pinna reflections occur, of course, for sound in every plane, including the horizontal, but since the horizontal plane uses two-eared listening time and amplitude differences effectively, pinna effects are more important for localizing sound in the vertical dimension than the horizontal. Because the pinna are fairly small acoustically, the effects occur mostly at high frequencies, where the wavelengths are short, greater than 6 kHz. The perceptual outcome is that vertical resolution is quite a bit worse than horizontal, so film sound systems are designed to produce localization effects largely in the horizontal plane, since that is the most effective plane.

The third dimension of localization is the depth dimension. In this dimension, perception is the most rough, since there is less information to distinguish sound distance than the other dimensions. Still there are several mechanisms for hearing to obtain depth estimates. These include:

- Amplitude and brightness of the source, compared with experience: a closer source is louder and brighter than a distant one, as occurs acoustically (see Chapter 1).

- Audibility of the ground reflection and how it changes with time out of doors.

- Doppler shift for moving objects.

- In rooms, the pattern of early reflections tells us information about the size of a space, and helps locate the surfaces (something that the blind do remarkably well; sighted persons rely much more heavily on vision for this).

- In rooms, reverberation. Longer reverberation times usually mean larger spaces.

Even though the depth dimension is the "worst" perceptually, it is nevertheless very useful and is manipulated continuously by filmmakers. Differences in the depth dimension can be used even in the simplest, monaural (one track or channel) productions to "place" sound in space, at least in one dimension, and thus have been used since shortly after the introduction of film sound.

Examples of the use of the depth dimension are many. A few follow:

- Making a voice-over narration much less reverberant than on-screen action, thus separating the narrator to a "voice inside the head," is used widely in documentaries, and also in narrative films, such as the voice-overs in *Apocalypse Now*. There, closeness to the narrative voice was accomplished by recording Martin Sheen in a small, dead room which added no acoustics of its own to the recording, close miked on a very bright microphone, with all of the technique aimed at achieving intimacy. The result is a very "in your face" style of recording that sounds quite different from his on-screen appearances, which have the reverberation of the set and a less intimate ("looser") microphone technique.

- Making a voice-over narration much more reverberant than the on-screen action is a method for indicating that we are hearing the inside thoughts of a character. Dating back to radio plays, this method seems rather quaint today but, nevertheless, when we see a cut to a contemplative character, and hear his voice reverberated without his lips moving, we know what to think—these are the character's inner thoughts.

- There is a process used deliberately to add the roomlike character of a venue to a recording. Let us say that we want to be present at a high-school dance, circa 1960. We obtain records from that era and dub them into the film, but the sound is too direct; it lacks any sort of room sound except that of the original recording. What is done in such a case is to *worldize* the sound by re-recording it over a deliberately less than great sound system in a reverberant gym, which thus has all the "flaws" of typical reproduction in the new recording. An addition to this effect is to move the loudspeaker and microphone continuously while recording, making the sound "swirl" by the constantly changing acoustical path. This was done for the music in the gym scenes in *American Graffiti* by sound designer Walter Murch and filmmaker George Lucas, who picked up the loudspeaker and microphone and moved them while making the new recording.

- In a complex scene representing several layers, the different layers are likely to employ different methods of recording and re-recording to make them more or less reverberant. Starting from "in front" of the screen, dryly recorded narration stands out. The next layer back is often the foreground production sound, complete with the reverberation present on the set. Within that context would be source music, for example, music playing on a radio in a scene. Further back may be off-screen effects, and the deepest part of the depth dimension is often scored music, especially if the score is orchestral.

So even relatively simple monaural production includes a strong potential for the use of "spatial" hearing because the depth dimension can be used. In more elaborate production, stereophony is used. *Stereophony* is the use of two, or preferably more, sound channels from production through distribution to the end user environment, delivered by more than one loudspeaker, spaced apart. Stereo offers two vital perceptual features that make it important to film and television sound: the ability to localize sound in various directions, and the ability to create enveloping, spacious sound having no particular direction but reproducing recorded reverberation more correctly spatially than any monaural system can do.

> These two factors, localization, on the one hand, and envelopment, on the other, are the two limits of a continuum. Sounds may be pinpoint localized, or a little vague or spacious, depending on your point of view, or they may be completely directionless, like the diffuse sound field we expect from high-quality reverberation. A stereo sound system will reproduce these two effects within limits imposed by the number of channels.

> Stereo film sound systems routinely employ five or more channels, whereas home stereo systems before the introduction of home theater used only two channels; the increase in the number of channels is so that fewer compromises are made in the dimensions of localization and envelopment.

The cocktail party effect (binaural discrimination)

Standing at a party in a reverberant space, with background music and many conversations going on, we are able to understand the one conversation in which we are participating with a friend. If we replace ourselves with a microphone, make a recording, and listen to it, we find that the recording is usually completely unintelligible. The fact that we can understand the conversation only when present is apparently caused by a number of factors:

- Spatial hearing allows us to concentrate on sound coming from one direction.

- Visual cues—we lip read to some extent.

- Both participants in the conversation are likely to share a huge amount of background, restricting the range of possible topics, messages, etc.

- When all else fails, we fake it, smiling knowingly and filling in gaps in the conversation from our shared background and experience.

Sound recording is at an enormous disadvantage to actually being there when the cocktail party effect is considered, because it is much less likely that the factors that make the effect work in person can be made to function in a recorded medium. The technical name for this effect is *binaural discrimination*, in other words, the ability to discriminate sounds better through the use of two ears rather than through recording, but every psychoacoustician knows this by its slang name.

The cocktail party effect has a strong impact on the method of recording on sets. In a bar scene, with a master shot, several close-ups, cut-aways to the crowd, etc., the most rigorous way to proceed is as follows:

- Record the master shot by having only the principal performers speak their lines. Everyone else mimics conversations.

- For close-ups, record the actors normally, in silence. If some other people show up in the background, they can mimic conversation, as in the master.

- For cut aways, record the extra (non-principal performer) saying his or her lines so that there is sync sound to cover obvious lip movement (or we would be left with *lip flap*, a defect in which we see but do not hear a person speaking), but watch out, for once a performer has a "speaking role" his or her pay goes up.

- Record "room tone" to serve as a continuous background presence under the scene, easing the way across cuts as described earlier.

- Record a "babble" or "walla" track, either in production or post production, with the right number of people, gender, and level of activity.

- Direct the speaking actors to keep their energy level correct for the finished scene, not what they are encountering in shooting. That is, if the scene is a noisy bar, they need to speak up over the background. Keeping the energy level correct from take to take, and not slipping, marks good direction and acting.

Using all of these methods, a sound editor can prepare a scene, cutting multiple sound tracks to represent principal dialog, background dialog, walla, and presence, and build a complete structure in which the sensation of being there is invoked.

Auditory pattern and object perception

Up to this point we have discussed traditional psychoacoustics. While the principles in this field are useful to film sound, with concepts such as loudness compensation, some decades ago it was realized that further work along this path, although interesting, was not coming any closer to answering some fundamental questions. The main such question was, How do listeners separate auditory objects from one another, and from the background? An *auditory object* is a sound that can be distinguished from other sounds: It can be thought of as a sound "molecule," composed out of component parts, like atoms, but perceptually indivisible and dis-

tinct. For example, we can distinguish two different actors speaking; each is an auditory object to us. In re-recording, we often combine many sounds, such as dialog, music, and sound effects, into one channel. The waveforms of all of the sources are added together and essentially cannot be taken apart by technical means once combined. It is the human perceptual capability that resolves the various elements into separate auditory objects, at the very end of the chain.

This is a little more difficult to think about than the same problem in vision, since anyone looking at a scene can tell the difference between a table and a chair. People do not have the same facility with the variety of sound objects presented in films without training, and this is a core idea. It explains why sound is so valuable to filmmakers. Its relative subtlety compared with picture elements allows filmmakers to manipulate an audience's emotions in a way that is not obvious. The flip side of this effect is that it produces a frustration in those who specialize in sound, because if their work is good, it will never be "understood" by a wider public than specialists. (About the only comment one ever hears from the general public is when the dialog is hard to understand!)

So here we examine those aspects of perceptual sound that have received less treatment by classical psychoacoustics and that may help illuminate the processes by which listeners are able to separate the various sounds presented to them into a sensible internal representation of the world.

Information used to separate auditory objects
Timbre
We have described frequency and its primary correlate, pitch, as well as amplitude and its correlate, loudness, extensively. What is left after differences in loudness, pitch, and duration are made equal is called *timbre*. Timbre is multidimensional; unlike loudness and pitch, which can be placed as a point along a line, timbre is more complex. It depends on:

- Spectrum, that is, the relative amplitudes of the fundamental and its harmonics.

For example, turning up the treble control on a stereo makes the sound brighter by increasing the level of higher frequencies in the sound. This is a change in timbre. Track 15 of the CD illustrates different timbres from different instruments.

- Onset transients: A piano played backwards in time does not sound like a piano anymore, but more like a kind of reedy organ, because the attack transient of hitting the strings comes at the end of a note instead of the beginning. Track 16 of the CD illustrates the importance of onset transients.

The way that the spectrum changes over the duration of the event is important to timbre. A starting transient may have a wide frequency range, but this range may narrow and become more tonal as time goes by. The spectrum changes during the course of the sound event, and we come to associate these changes in time with particular sounds, particularly musical instruments.

Reproducing timbre well is a primary goal of high-fidelity reproduction systems, although reproducing timbre may in practical situations yield to even more important goals, such as dialog intelligibility. There are many films in which the dialog sounds honky or nasal because the mid-frequency range has been overemphasized[5] to promote intelligibility, given the competition from music and sound effects. Listening to these films sometimes sounds as though we are hearing two different movies simultaneously, since the dialog seems to have a narrow frequency range and an emphasis within the narrow range of midrange frequencies, and yet the music and sound effects sound wide range and well balanced. The compromise that has been reached in these cases comes from the observation that understanding speech is little interfered with by such tactics, and in fact this emphasis may promote intel-

---

5. Either through the choice of microphone and technique of its use, or by post production manipulation, called *equalization*.

ligibility when the film is heard under suboptimal conditions.

Reaching the goal of accurate timbral reproduction generally requires that all the equipment in the chain from the source to the listener cover the full audible frequency range, without emphasizing one frequency band over another. All notes of a piano should be reproduced with the same strength as they were played during the original performance, so that the reproduced sound accurately represents the instrument.

Fundamental frequency
The fundamental frequency of various sounds is used to separate them. While we generally do not listen individually to a fundamental and each of its harmonics (although we can be trained to do so), a better representation of what we typically hear is the fundamental plus the timbre (in music, the pitch of the note being played and the instrument playing it).

If we wish to increase the richness of a sound effect, one way would be to layer two sounds together. In order to get them to merge into one auditory object, one trick can be to match the fundamental frequency of one of the tracks to the other. This can be accomplished by simply playing a source at varying speed, until the pitches match.

Correlated changes in amplitude or frequency
If the component parts of the above mentioned example change together, such as all the harmonics fading out at the same rate, this will also promote the formation of a single auditory object composed of all the parts that are changing together.

Location
The localization mechanism helps greatly to separate auditory objects. Spatial separation for sound is akin to spatial separation for vision: If we hear a set of sounds from a single location, we are likely to combine them into an auditory object. For instance, all the various sounds constituting a given dinosaur in *Jurassic Park* are placed together through a process of "panning" the sound effect elements all to the same place. An auditory ob-

ject can be formed using location, even in a monaural sound track, by matching the apparent depth of the various elements. This is accomplished by adding more or less reverberation to each of the components so that they match one another in depth.

Contrast with previous sound

A negative example of this principle is what occurs when background sound is mismatched on picture cuts within a scene: We perceive a change in the "space" that we do not wish to perceive. The mismatched cut adds contrast where there should be none, and a separate auditory object (new background sound) is formed, drawing the audience's attention away from the content.

A second negative example comes from documentary production. In such shooting, the filmmaker usually cannot exercise as much control as in narrative production, and some sounds are recorded that are inevitably annoying. Adding filters for these background sounds also affects the foreground, desired sound. It would be possible to "switch in" such filters, by editing or in mixing, only during the occurrence of the noise, but the effect this has on the foreground sound has to be considered. It is better to leave the filter process in for the entire scene than to switch it in just as needed. This is because of the contrast that would be caused from moment to moment in the foreground sound, something to be avoided since we wish to obtain good continuity, implying a lack of contrast.

A unique example of the use of contrast by film and television program makers is using *pre-lap* edits. If the sound changes ambience to that of a new scene before the picture changes, we draw the attention of the viewer/listener in an interesting way to the edit. While this technique is subject to overuse, it may also be an extremely good one for certain cases. It is well used extensively in *The English Patient* for instance. Picture and sound editor Walter Murch gives credit to director Anthony Minghella for suggesting this method, which involves complex storytelling with interwoven flashbacks associated with particular sounds.

Time-varying pattern

The rate at which the elements of a sound track change gives us a perception of the size of the sound object: A large object probably moves more slowly than a small one. The distant thumps of the footsteps of the dinosaur in *Jurassic Park* are well separated from one another, illustrating this principle. The footsteps are also, of course, bassy, following the principle of bass representing threats aesthetically.

In sound effects as well as music, rhythm causes the formation of an auditory object, since a rhythm forms an expectation in time that something is going to happen in the future at just a certain moment—beats, as in musical beats, will occur. Another rhythmic factor is that musical rhythms have a preferred higher order pattern of beats, the notion of the downbeat. In a waltz rhythm ,for instance, we come to expect not only the beat, but the downbeat as well, emphasizing every third beat.

Gestalt principles

A group of psychologists working in Germany starting in the 1920s, examining classical psychoacoustics, came to the conclusion that there were other, more holistic methods to apply to how humans perceive sound, including the following. One of their ideas was the necessity of separating auditory objects into *figure* and *ground*, terms borrowed from painting.

Similarity

Sounds are grouped together into one perceptual "stream" in a process called *auditory streaming* if they are similar in pitch, loudness, timbre, and location. An application of this principle in filmmaking is in combining together various sounds to make one composite that we think of as the "sound" of a particular auditory object. The dinosaurs in *Jurassic Park* were formed from multiple recordings, mostly of existing animals, modified and summed together. The summing process had to consider the similarity of the elements being summed, so as to produce one sound from the whole.

Good continuation

Smooth changes, with all the constituent parts correlated with each other, probably arise from one sound object, whereas abrupt changes usually indicate that the source must have changed. The example of background noise from shot to shot is valuable here as well: If two shots within a scene have mismatched background noises, it is more acceptable to crossfade the sound between the shots around the picture cut than it is to abruptly cut, in order to promote good continuation.

Common fate

If two components of sound undergo the same changes in time, they will be grouped together and heard as one. This is essentially the same factor as *correlated changes in amplitude or frequency* mentioned earlier but was given the interesting name, *common fate*, by the Gestalt psychologists.

Belongingness

A single element can only form a part of one stream at a time. Hearing will try to impose such an order upon hearing multiple sounds.

Closure

A sound that is intermittently masked is perceived as continuous, provided there is no direct evidence to the contrary. An example of the use of this principle is a scene with music underneath that is the wrong length and needs to be edited to fit. Music imposes a lot of restrictions on where edits can be made, since in order to make sense, melody, rhythm, tempo, orchestration, etc. must match. This may make it impossible to perform a cut, but if there is a loud sound effect in the scene, an edit can be made in the music "underneath" the loud effect, which is concealed by masking. If the discontinuity in the music is not too great, and the sound effect is loud enough and long enough to cover the edit, closure will work and the edit will appear seamless.

Attention to streams

Usually listeners pay attention to one auditory stream at a time, with that stream or object standing out from the others for that listener. This does not mean, however, that

there needs to be only one sound at a time. Interestingly, different listeners will latch onto different streams, at least some of the time, and in listening multiple times listeners may find themselves attending to different streams upon various hearings of the program. Walter Murch, sound designer for *Apocalypse Now,* explains this idea in different terms. For him, hearing can only attend to one of three sounds presented at a time, so he would argue for up to a maximum of three foreground audio streams occurring simultaneously. He says "there's a reason why circuses use three rings; more is confusing." If there are more principal sounds at one time, the listener is unlikely to be able to separate them out into individual streams.

Forming streams places constraints on attention. Probably the most relevant example from film and television sound is the necessity that the audience feels to hear the dialog. Dialog may well suffer from speech intelligibility problems due to the competition from sound effects and music, and the filmmaker may even want it that way, but, nonetheless, the audience demands to hear the words, and they spend all of their concentration on forming the dialog stream. When this process is frustrated by masking from sound effects and music, they become highly annoyed, and poor-performing sound systems and room acoustics exacerbate the problem.

Auditory stream formation is strongly impacted by visual information. Probably the simplest definition of sound in a Hollywood movie is "See a car, hear a car." That is, everything that we see on the screen that we expect to make a sound does make a sound. What we don't know upon first hearing the film is that it is a conscious decision on the part of the sound editors to record, edit, and mix sound effects to cover all of the objects on the screen.

A related topic is that auditory streams sometimes need visual explanation. For instance, in a documentary film, if there is an aquarium out of the picture during an interview, but bubbling, the audience will spend its time wondering what the heck that sound is rather than paying attention to the interview. A cutaway to the aquarium, or its inclusion in a master shot, provides an explanation to the audience, who can concentrate on the content.

Multisense effects

Sound for film and television is by definition presented along with a picture, and sound and picture have interactions. As we have seen earlier, picture has an impact on sound localization, and sound has impacts on picture as well. Most people who see a complex scene with the sound tracks broken down are surprised by how much faster it seems to run when all of the sound is present than when it is heard a layer at a time. Items like the title crawl in *Star Wars* seem to take a long, languid time rolling up the screen when shown silently, but seem to march along when heard with the theme music.

The size of presentation of the picture also has an impact on the apparent speed of action. Larger picture displays, probably due to their greater stimulation of more faculties of the brain, seem to cause action to move more quickly than smaller editorial displays. For this reason, it is a bad idea to edit film silently on a small editing system because when sound is added and the display size is large, the pace will seem faster, almost frenetic, compared with the action in an editing room.

Speech perception

Speech seems to be a special case for perception. There are several pieces of evidence for this, and the idea has a strong impact on the way that film sound is practiced. In 1967 Liebermann showed that the basic blocks of speech, *phonemes*, could be understood even when sped up to a rate of 30 per second, whereas the time boundary for other sounds to cross into confusing order was around 10 per second. This finding was made use of in devices that sped up playback of recordings which, when combined with a corresponding correcting pitch shift, allows listeners to perceive the spoken word at greatly sped up rates. At 10 notes per second, musicians could not tell the order of the notes, but subjects could tell what the content of speech is at the three times higher rate. Brain scans

while subjects listen to speech versus music show different brain activity centers stimulated by speech than by other sounds.

The overall pattern of sound in speech is what is important: frequency, amplitude, timbre, and how they change in time—a multidimensional effect. This is known by adding deliberate distortions to any of these factors, and finding that speech is still intelligible despite very dramatic distortions. For example, for World War II bomber crews, the earphone sound was restricted to a very narrow high-frequency range because the aircraft noise was so loud, with lows predominating. Despite this reduction in bandwidth (frequency range), speech was still intelligible. The multidimensional nature of speech is equivalent to high redundancy, making it difficult to corrupt to the point of complete unintelligibility (although high quality is a different question).

Speech for film and television

A special issue facing speech in the movies is the interaction between two perceptual factors. If localization error of 4° is noticeable to professionals and 15° is annoying to laymen, what about placing speech sounds to be coincident with the picture of the actor speaking?

When stereo sound was introduced into films in the 1950s, dialog was routinely "panned" from left to right on the screen to match the action. This process has dropped out of use, except in certain circumstances. One possible explanation for the demise of stereo dialog could be the fact that producers won't pay for the time necessary to get it right in post production nowadays, and there might be some truth to that, but it isn't the right answer. In fact, there is a problem of perceptual mechanisms competing to determine what is going to cause the greater disturbance, localization error, or something else of importance. Let us say that a scene, like the interior of General Allenby's office in *Lawrence of Arabia*, is shot with a wide master shot encompassing a large office, and that close ups are shot of each of the characters. When the scene begins, picture editors almost always start with the master shot, since the very width of the shot sets the stage for the action. It is an expositional shot really, showing us the scenery, in effect, although of course it may also contain content. Then, as the scene progresses, more and more use is made of close ups, helping to build the tension and intimacy of the scene. This is a standard progression we know from seeing it many times, and we are never confused about where we are and what we are looking at. Now consider the sound. In the master, sound positioned to match the performers is all right, coming from the left or right as the characters face off across the desk. At the cut to the first close up, with the actor centered in the frame, there is a jump in the sound: It must cut from the side where the character was to the center. This cut seems unlike the picture edit, it is not smooth but rather jarring. The principle of good continuation has been violated by the jump[6] cut. The reason for this jarring quality may well lie in the fact that so much training has gone into the way we look at pictures and their cuts that we "know" the film grammar of cutting so well that it seems completely natural, having grown up seeing so much film and television. This kind of sound edit, on the other hand, is something with which we have practically no experience. The question might be resolved by showing edited films to primitive tribespeople who have had no exposure to film or television, and seeing what they make of it, but we have to leave that to some visual anthropologist who is not afraid of disturbing their own object of research.

Certainly, a factor in how jarring this kind of edit seems is how well matched the sound of the two loudspeaker systems is. If the side and center loudspeakers don't match perfectly for timbre, then we are distracted by the timbral change from position to position that we would not notice if the character stayed in one place. This problem was ad-

dressed industry wide in the 1970s, and while not quite a thing of the past, has been greatly reduced, leaving the first reason as the most prominent.

So stereo dialog positioned line by line into the correct position has dropped out of use due to these competing perceptual factors. The standard is now to place most dialog in the center channel, despite its not matching the picture in each shot.

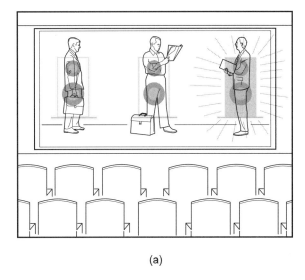

(a)

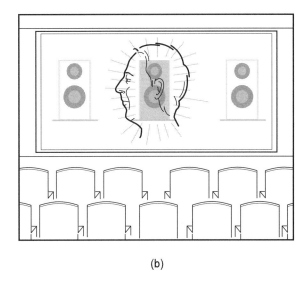

(b)

Fig. 2.5 The master shot (a) calls for dialog to be panned right, while close up (b) calls for it to be panned center. The cut between the two shots thus causes the sound to jump, an aural discontinuity, which leads to most dialog being panned to the center in most films.

---

6. This is a new use for the term that is applied to picture edits that violate continuity rules, such as "crossing the line," or are otherwise abrupt.

Panned dialog does have its uses however:

- Off-screen lines are routinely panned to far left or right as makes the most sense in order to distinguish it from on-screen dialog.

- Dialog lines which are well separated in time from others and for which the character speaking is well off center may be panned.

- Slight panning off center for two characters speaking to one another is occasionally used, since it is less jarring in cuts to jump by a smaller amount than the large amount from the extremes.

Conclusion

We have observed in this chapter issues in hearing and perception which affect filmmakers daily. In sound production, many of these factors are given consideration, either explicitly, or more often, through the training and experience of practitioners. Sound editors may not call it temporal masking, but they have come to know where the best places to make edits are, such as just before a "plosive"[7] in speech, or the downbeat in music.

Re-recording mixers may not have the equal-loudness contours in front of them, but they know that music, faded under, becomes thin sounding, worthy of correction. The lesson of perception is that film and television editors and mixers tailor sound tracks to fit the human psyche, just as much as they fit it into any technical requirement.

---

7. Speech phonemes having a hard edge, such as "p's" and "t's."

Chapter 3: Audio Fundamentals

Audio defined

Audio is the representation of sound, electrically or by various methods on media, not sound itself. We usually say *audio tape*, not *sound tape*, for instance.[1] The advertising tag line that was tried some time ago, "It's audio that surrounds you" is also wrong, because you would be wrapped up in electrical signals or in tape, not in sound, by this image. *Sound* is the term used for acoustical energy, whereas *audio* applies to electrical signals, and magnetic and optical recordings.

Sound is the input for audio processes by way of microphones, which are *transducers,* turning sound energy into electrical energy, at that point called generically a *signal. Re-cording* is the process of converting the electrical signal into a form that is stored on a medium, from which it may be played back and converted to an electrical signal. *Mixing* involves a variety of processes to manipulate audio, and in this way winds up indirectly manipulating sound. Finally, for conversion from electrical signals back to sound, loudspeaker transducers are used.

We have already seen one primary consequence of the overall process of sound track preparation—mixing together sounds from various audio sources. For all intents and purposes, this means that they cannot be separated again by technical means, but rather the parts are separated by the final listener into a variety of auditory objects or streams, using perceptual processes. This causes us a lot of trouble and makes for a specific method of working in post production mixing, which we discuss later.

Tracks and channels

Technically, the word *track* refers to the space on the medium for the audio represen-

---

1. Although of course we do say, "sound track." Are we talking about the physical track on the film representing sound or what we hear? This is usually ambiguous because a mixer will say, "That's a great sound track," and an engineer will say, "The density of the sound track shows that it is underdeveloped." They are both right, thus it is the term itself that is ambiguous.

tation of sound. Thus, we say that we use *24-track* tape recorders because there are 24 parallel stripes of area on a 2 in. wide piece of tape on which we can record separate signals. The sound track on a piece of film is the area devoted to sound and the recording made on that area. In nontechnical usage, the term applies more broadly to everything recorded and its overall effect, as in "That was a dramatic track."

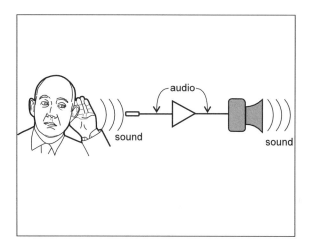

Fig. 3.1 Audio is distinguished from sound by its being the electrical representation of sound, a physical phenomenon.

The word *channel*, on the other hand, does not apply to the representation on the medium but is a more abstract term describing a signal path. It may describe a pathway for signals inside a piece of equipment, as in, "Assign the first input channel of the console to the output," or in a broader sense, as in "The transfer channel is not working at this time" (meaning that transfers from one medium to another cannot be made now).

Signals: analog and digital

There are two primary ways to represent sound as audio, by analog and by digital means. Each is important today, and each has its own strengths and weaknesses. As a trend, it has to be said that digital techniques are growing much more rapidly than analog ones at this time, but nevertheless there is a huge market for both methods. Furthermore, certain parts of the chain from microphone to loudspeaker will probably remain dominated by analog techniques for some

years to come because digital techniques that will do the same thing are much more expensive, at the least.

Both analog and digital methods may also be practiced well or poorly, and may result in good or bad sound at the end of the day, although there are large differences in what the potential problems are. Probably the popular notion is that digital audio is good and analog is passé, due to the large success of the compact disc as a music medium and its obvious improvements over the phonograph record. Still, this view is naive when it comes to wider uses in professional audio, where each type of technology is seen as having particular areas where it excels.

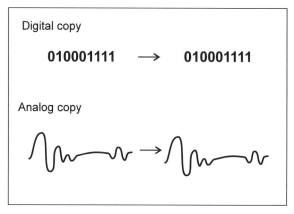

Fig. 3.2 The difference between digital copying and analog copying is the difference between copying numbers and accurately representing a waveform in a medium. This gives the advantage to digital copying, for if the copy can be read at all, it can be restored to its original values.

For instance, the strongest suit of digital technology is replication. The nature of digital recording and distribution is such that it is *potentially* far more impervious to outside influences than are analog recording and distribution chains. The word "potentially" is emphasized because an underlying medium impervious to outside influences is also needed to realize the most important benefit of digital—its permanence. This is what makes digital superior at distribution technologies, such as digital sound tracks for films and the compact disc, than competing analog technologies.

The fundamental difference between analog and digital ways of representing sound occurs in the amplitude domain. In analog, the amplitude of the audio waveform is represented as an *analogy* to the original waveform, whether that is electrically in wires or recorded on a medium. That is, there is strict proportionality between the original sound waveform, its electrical representation, and its amplitude[2] in the medium of choice. These analogies can take many forms, such as the displacement of the diaphragm of a microphone, the consequent strength of a magnetic field on audiotape, the electrical voltage in a console, or the motion of a loudspeaker cone turning audio back into sound, all looked at moment by moment.

Note that for both analog and digital methods there are two dimensions that describe a signal. The instantaneous amplitude is one dimension, and time is the other. Amplitude varying over time describes a waveform.

The fundamental difference between analog and digital signals is that the amplitude domain in digital is *quantized*. Imagine a set of bins stacked on top of one another. Quantization is the process of measuring the practically instantaneous amplitude of a waveform and "binning" it, assigning a particular numerical value by using the number of the bin closest to it in height. The number is what is stored instead of a signal strictly proportional to the waveform itself. The number is no longer strictly analogous to the waveform, since analog-to-digital conversion has been performed.[3]

The beauty of storing the amplitude as numbers is the "ruggedness" with which numbers can be stored; that is, despite many corrupting influences, the numbers can still be read. By adding powerful *error codes* to the quantized numbers, especially the Reed-Solomon code,[4] the numbers are made highly robust, since most errors in their transmission can be corrected, and when uncorrectable that fact is known to the equipment so that a variety of tactics can be brought into play, such as guessing what the original waveform was, ultimately giving way, in the worst case, to no sound. Here is the Achilles' heel of digital audio: It can easily lull one into thinking that all is well, when what is actually happening is that we are operating closer and closer to the edge of not working at all, and there is no way to tell that from the sound quality.

Analog systems, on the other hand, tend to have a more gentle curve of failure, that is, they often sound increasingly bad before outright failure, giving some time to take corrective action before no sound is heard.

One primary difference between professional and consumer digital audio equipment is that professional equipment usually gives some indication of how much error correction is occurring to indicate to the user how solid things really are.

> The first strategy that digital equipment uses on finding an error is *error correction*. In error correction, the error decoder completely restores the original numbers, and there is no change in the sound whatsoever. On the other hand, if there are many occurrences of error correction it means that the medium is potentially damaged, which is likely to lead to more serious problems later.

> The next strategy used, after the error correction mechanism is overwhelmed, is *error concealment*. Here the playback decoding circuitry makes an educated guess about what the numbers were, based on what came before and what comes after the missing data. The sound cannot be said to be identical to that produced by the

---

2. In the strictest sense, the amplitude of the audio waveform may be represented by analog means other than by amplitude in a medium. Schemes such as FM (frequency modulation) convert amplitude variations to frequency variations for transmission, then back to amplitude variations for the output, and are still considered analog methods.
3. Although we could say that the numbers are still proportional to the waveform, the proportionality is no longer strict, since in the act of binning the amplitude, there is a range of possible waveform amplitudes that still fit within one bin before the quantizing device "snaps" to the next bin.

---

4. This was a key technology to make the compact disc, among other digital audio media, possible and was developed by Professor Irving Reed of USC.

original, but may be good enough for all but mastering purposes. If error concealment occurs on a digital audio master, the master is usually remade. Finally, when both error correction and error concealment can no longer be used because the data are so corrupt, most equipment "mutes," that is, switches to silence.

The analog method of representing sound as analogies to the amplitude of the original waveform has the problem that the analogy is only a representation of the original, not the waveform itself. The difficulty that this causes is that with multiple-generation copying, something is inevitably lost during each generation, ultimately resulting in audible quality problems. Distortion and noise, to be discussed later in this chapter, increase from generation to generation, sometimes by tolerable amounts, but they nonetheless do inevitably increase. The popular term for this is *generation loss.*

> I spent a great deal of time on *Return of the Jedi* (1983) trying to sort out why the 70mm prints sounded more distorted than the master in brief passages. Naturally the first place we worked was on the printing process itself, since that seemed to be indicated. In the end, it was found that this stage was not at fault because it was essentially equal in quality to all of the other generations, but rather it was simply that we had accumulated distortion from generation to generation to the point of audibility. (This affected only a few moments of the movie.) On the other hand, by improving the foregoing generations before the printing process, more difficult scenes had inaudible distortion by the next year in *Indiana Jones and the Temple of Doom* (1984).

Digital copying and transmission do not rely on making an analogy each generation, but rather the correct copying of numbers, a far easier task because even if the numbers are "blurry," they can still be read. So all other things being equal, and with certain assumptions, a 10th generation digital copy is indistinguishable from the first generation, whereas a 10th generation analog copy will certainly show audible defects.

Paradigms: linear vs. nonlinear

In film and television production the term *linear* and *nonlinear* are used to describe the means of access to the portions of a program to be edited or mixed. Linear in this usage means that the material is recorded along the length of a medium, which could be an analog or a digital tape. Examples include 24-track analog and digital tape machines. In order to get from one part of a program to another, winding the tape or other medium is required over the intervening portions of the tape, and this can take a considerable amount of time. nonlinear means that access to the material is available by jumping over all of the intervening material. An example is a phonograph record, where you can lift the tone arm and jump from cut one to cut ten with reasonable ease. More importantly, computers store their files in a way that permits nonlinear access. Digital audio workstations generally operate in nonlinear way, able to jump from one part of the program to another, saving time.

> Some picture and sound editors, notably Walter Murch and Randy Thom, have pointed out that there are drawbacks to the enormous speed advantage of nonlinear editing, because viewing the material at high speed, such as on a flat bed editing table, can yield ideas for editors, but nonetheless the sheer speed gains of nonlinear systems make them increasingly the method of choice.

In editing systems, linear storage devices are rapidly giving way to nonlinear ones, because if a decision over the length of a shot is changed on a linear editing system, all the subsequent work in that particular reel will have to be re-done. This problem for linear systems, and the rapid access to material of the nonlinear ones, means that nonlinear systems are growing rapidly, while linear ones are shrinking in importance. The terms linear and nonlinear mean something different when describing the audio quality of a product or system, which we will take up later.

Level

The amplitude dimension of a waveform may be represented in a variety of ways, such as:

- An electrical voltage, for example, at the output of a microphone.

- The strength of a stored magnetic field on an audiotape.

- Numerically, as in digital audio.

Since program[5] waveforms constantly change amplitude with time, the value of each of these representations is also constantly changing. This constant motion makes thinking about the relative level in the various parts of the system difficult, so the idea of level is usually simplified to that which corresponds to a simple sine wave. For sound in air, we have already seen that 0 dB SPL was set as a reference at about the threshold of hearing, and practically all acoustical measurements are referenced to this "level," giving the scale to acoustical measurements shown in Chapter 1.

Microphone level

To characterize the output of a microphone, though, a reference at 0 dB SPL is inconvenient because it is difficult to obtain spaces quiet enough to make a sound of 0 dB SPL without masking by room noise, and it is nowhere near the SPL typically seen by the microphone. Thus, for most microphone measurements it is commonplace to choose as a reference sound pressure level 94 dB SPL. The microphone is rated for *sensitivity*, delivering a specific voltage at 94 dB SPL. Conventional microphones may deliver anywhere between 2 and 60 mV[6] under these conditions, depending on their type. This is a 30 dB possible range from one microphone type to another, a very large difference.

Although 94 dB SPL is a relatively high sound pressure level, the electrical voltage is still quite small, so microphones are routinely connected to *microphone preamplifiers* which amplify the output of the microphone to an electrical level that is more useful, with the amount of amplification depending on system requirements. The wide range of output levels from various microphones means that preamplifiers must be matched to the microphone type. We say that the low output level of microphones is *mike level*, and that the output of the microphone preamplifier is at *line level*. A typical microphone level taken as a snapshot on speech is 2 mV, and a microphone preamplifier may boost this to a 1.2 V line level.

Line level

Line level signals are those that are routinely interchanged within a studio environment, used for connecting different pieces of equipment together for signal processing, for instance. The method of routing such line-level signals may be by cables connected to the input and output connectors on pieces of equipment, or by way of patch bays (which look like the old-fashioned telephone operator switchboards on which they were based) or electronic switches. The electrical voltage of line level varies depending on the studio and whether the equipment is professional or consumer grade (Table 3.1). The most common professional reference line level is +4 dBu, which is 1.23 V, called here Pro 1. Pro 2 is an older reference level still found in a few broadcast applications. The most common consumer equipment line level is −10 dBV, which is 0.316 V.

Many problems in professional audio relate to interfacing equipment intended for different line levels. Patching consumer equipment into a professional studio, for instance, is difficult due to the large level difference in the reference levels of the different equipment. Typical consequences of patching in equipment without compensation for the reference level include excessive distortion, or noise. A proper method to employ such equipment uses a "pad" at the input to the consumer equipment to attenuate the higher studio level down to the consumer equipment level, and an amplifier on its output to restore the level. Boxes are available to make both these changes for the input and output of the consumer equipment. They are called *match boxes*.

A common problem in audio is connecting a microphone to an input jack on a portable recorder, such as a Betacam SP unit, and setting the level, forgetting that there is a switch

---

5. *Program* is derived from broadcasting practice, where *program* means the desired material to be heard by the listener, as opposed to test tones or leaders that may also be on the same medium.
6. mV is one-one thousandth of a Volt.

that sets the input sensitivity of that jack to mic or line level. Connecting a microphone to a line level input will usually result in excessive noise. Connecting a line level source to a microphone level input will usually result in gross distortion.

Speaker level

The third level used in a recording chain is speaker level. It is higher than line level and is provided by power amplifiers capable of delivering up to hundreds of watts to loudspeakers. A typical speaker voltage level is 4 V to produce 85 dB SPL in a theater, a typical reference sound pressure level in post production.

Level comparison

There are thus three principal levels used in a system—mic, line, and speaker—which correspond to a few milliVolts, around 1 Volt, and a few volts (and with high-power capability), respectively. While speaker connections would rarely be confused with line and mic connections, being of different connector types, that still leaves mic level and line level connections to be confused with each other. Perhaps no problem is so prevalent in audio as mixing up these two levels, with

gross consequent distortion or noise. Often, the two levels may be presented even on the exact same connector, such as at the output of a mixer, and on the input to a professional video camera, by means of switches. If the output of a mixer is set to mic level, and the camera input is set to line level, the result will be excessive noise. Conversely, if the output of a mixer is set to line level, and the camera input is set to mic level, gross distortion at least on signal peaks will almost certainly be the result.

Interconnections

Signals are usually routed from microphones to preamplifiers, from consoles to tape machines, and from power amplifiers to loudspeakers over conductive wiring, usually copper. There are two principal ways to do this, by balanced lines, used in mostly professional applications, and by unbalanced lines, used mostly in consumer applications. Due to the differences in balanced versus unbalanced conditions, different connectors are used, generally distinguishing the types. An alternative to conductive wiring sometimes used is optical fiber interconnections among pieces of digital equipment.

Table 3.1: Line Levels

Application	Level (dB re stated reference)[1]	Voltage, (rms Volts)
Consumer and semi-pro equipment	−10 dBV	316 mV
Pro 1	+4 dBu	1.228 V
Pro 2	+8 dBu	1.946 V

1 dBV reference is deciBels relative to 1 Volt. dBu reference is deciBels relative to 0.775 Volts.

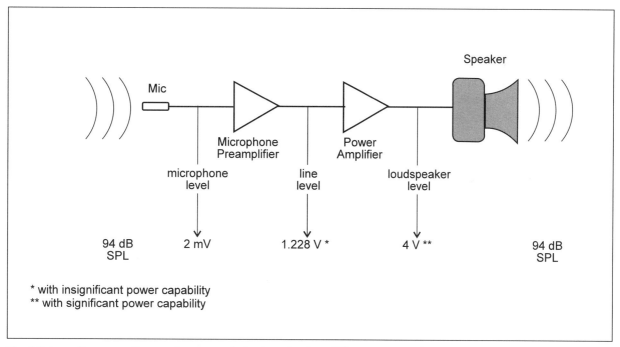

Fig. 3.3 An audio system diagram showing typical voltage levels at different points in the system. Note that although line level and loudspeaker level are similar in voltage, the loudspeaker level comes with far higher power capacity than is available at line level.

Balanced vs. unbalanced lines

Conventional home high fidelity system wiring is unbalanced. That is, there is one signal conductor contained inside a shield, and then the whole cable is wrapped in an outer insulator. The outer shield serves as an electrical ground, as well as providing shielding to prevent electrostatically induced hum.

The difference between unbalanced and balanced wiring schemes occurs when there is interference from external *magnetic* sources, such as the magnetic field set up around lighting cables on a set by virtue of their carrying large amounts of current. In an unbalanced connection, the magnetic field induces a voltage in the principal conductor, which the receiving equipment sees as the same as the desired signal; thus, hum may be heard at the end of the chain.

Balanced wiring provides a means to reject hum caused by stray magnetic fields. It uses two signal conductors contained within a common conductive shield. Thus, there are three conductors altogether. At the instant when one of the two conductors has a posi-

tive-going signal voltage on it, the other one will have an equal and opposite negative-going signal voltage on it. External magnetic fields induce a voltage in the conductors, but it will be equal in magnitude and polarity in both conductors. The receiving equipment is deliberately made sensitive only to the *difference* between the two conductors, and because the voltage induced by the magnetic field is the same in both conductors, it will be rejected by the receiving equipment.

> These two modes of signals in balanced wiring are called the *differential mode* for the desired signal that is in opposite polarity in the two wires, and the *common mode* for the induced hum that is in phase in the two wires. The measure used to quantify this effect is called the *common mode rejection ratio*, a metric that compares a deliberate differential mode signal to a common mode signal and expresses the difference in deciBels. A good common mode rejection ratio is 80 dB, providing a reduction in hum of a factor of 10,000:1.

Balanced wiring is considered essential for microphone wiring, since the signal voltages are low at mike level and the cables are often in hostile environments, leading to high induced noise. Balanced wiring is also used in professional studios in between pieces of equipment, although the added expense is sometimes unneeded when the signals stay relatively local, such as within one rack of equipment, and unbalanced wiring is sometimes used in these instances.

There is one problem possible with balanced wiring compared with unbalanced: If the two signal leads inadvertently become interchanged, through wrong cable wiring, for example, then the signal will be inverted and yet still work. This condition is called *polarity reversal* or more commonly, *phase reversal*.

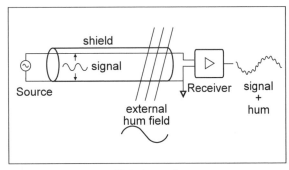

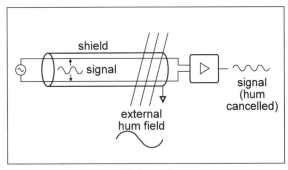

Fig 3.4 An unbalanced system is susceptible to hum pickup by magnetic fields being converted into voltages. The balanced system is much less susceptible because a balanced input is sensitive to the differences between the two conductors, both of which see more or less identical magnetic fields.

If the same inversion occurs in unbalanced wiring, the signal is shorted out, since the outer shield is grounded at its ends. The inadvertent "polarity reversal" of a miswired

balanced line may be inaudible for some purposes, but if two microphones cover a scene and the performer is equidistant from the two, then the subsequent addition of the signals in mixing will cause the two signals to at least partially cancel. Thus the polarity of all cables must be observed in balanced wiring to prevent such cancellation.

Impedance: bridging vs. matching

Today, most audio wiring proceeds in a manner familiar to anyone who has ever plugged in multiple lamps on one electrical circuit: no matter how many are plugged in, the same voltage is delivered to the lamps (they don't get dimmer as more are plugged in), up to the capacity of the circuit breaker. So audio signals can be routed freely, and a single source can feed multiple devices, up to a reasonable limit. Such a system is called *bridging* because each of the devices connected to a source is said to *bridge* across the output of the source.

> The technical description of this condition involves a concept not yet presented—the idea of impedance. In the case of bridging systems, we say the source impedance is low and the load impedances are high, which is the same condition as exists with electrical generators supplying house wiring. This means that the source will, practically speaking, maintain the same voltage despite the number of loads bridged across it.

The alternative system of matching impedance is a system where each source is *terminated* in a specific design load impedance. It is principally useful today in very long lines, such as transmitting audio over telephone lines, but has little utility in studio environments. Still, there are some hold-over applications in broadcasting where matching is employed, because it was commonplace in earlier eras.

Connectors

Unfortunately, there are a great many connectors used for audio (Table 3.2). It is useful to know the names and area of application of audio connectors because they so frequently must be interconnected that even for the simplest jobs one must often specify an adapter for connecting two types, and this must be done by naming the types correctly. In professional use, connectors coming from a source, such as the output of a microphone, are usually equipped with male plugs, while connectors accepting signals are usually female thus giving an immediate indication of the direction of the signal, although there are exceptions to this rule. Male connectors are those equipped with pins for the conductors and are called *plugs*, while female connectors are equipped with receptacles to accept the pins and are called *jacks*, so the "sex" of a connector is determined by the conductors, not the outer shell.

In consumer use, it is common to use hi-fi-style interconnects, where both ends of cables use male connectors and chassis connectors are female. Thus the "direction" of the signal is not indicated by the sex of the connectors. A common problem that arises as a result is finding jacks labeled "Tape Out" on the back of a receiver. What is meant in this instance is actually "Out to Tape," that is, a signal destined for the *input* of an external tape recorder. One could easily think the converse, that Tape Out should be connected to the output of the tape recorder, but that would be wrong.

Table 3.2: Some Connectors typically used for Audio[1]

Name(s)	Conductors	Photo	Usage
XLR Canon	3 – 5		Most widely used connector in professional audio, for microphone and line level analog signals and digital AES 3 (two channels on one cable). Pin 2 positive signal, pin 3 negative signal, and pin 1 shield ground.
$1/4$" Mono Phone	2		Mono headphones, other monaural uses such as microphones and line level signals. Tip positive signal, sleeve shield ground.
$1/4$" Stereo Phone $1/4$" Balanced Phone	3		Stereo headphones with the tip conductor the left channel, the ring the right channel, and the sleeve ground; balanced inputs on some equipment with the tip positive signal, ring negative signal, sleeve ground.
$1/4$" TRS Patch Bay	3		TRS=tip, right, sleeve. For patching balanced lines in patch bays (note the tip diameter is smaller than on a conventional $1/4$" plug: the two are interchngeable only in some jacks). Tip positive signal, ring negative signal, sleeve ground.
TT Tiny-T	3		A smaller version of a balanced patch bay connector

Table 3.2: Some Connectors typically used for Audio[1] (Continued)

Name(s)	Conductors	Photo	Usage (Continued)
3.5 mm Mini Mono Plug	2		Mono consumer headphones, microphones (may be called ¹/₈ ").[2]
3.5 mm Mini Stereo Plug	3		Stereo consumer headphones, microphones (may be called ¹/₈ ").[2]
2.5 mm Micro Mono Plug	2		Miniature recorder input plug.[2]
2.5 mm Micro Stereo Plug	3		Miniature recorder input plug.[2]
Phono Pin Plug RCA Cinch	2		Common unbalanced hi-fi system interconnects at consumer levels including for both analog and digital signals.
BNC	2		Professional audio test equipment, video, some professional digital audio use especially in video facilities.
Banana	1 per lead		Nagra tape recorder outputs, test equipment
Tuchel	2–8		Nagra portable recorders

1 many other types are used for specific circumstances, such as multi-pin connectors for multi-channel use, special connectors for radio microphones, etc.

2 The variation in body style among these four is typical of varaitions found among connectors in the field, and some large diameter connector bodies prevent full insertion into corresponding jacks due to obstructions. Also, variations in the precise dimensions, particularly the diameter of mating surfaces, vary from jack to jack. Thus if a large diameter plug has been plugged into a jack, that jack may subsequently not make good contact with a smaller diameter plug, within the tolerances of parts found in the field.

Quality issues

Audio equipment is assessed by means of measurements and listening tests. Measurements can quickly tell if certain factors are optimum in a given piece of equipment, and whether problems found are likely to be above or below audibility. Nevertheless, it is also necessary in the final analysis to conduct proper listening tests to check for factors that may escape conventional measurements. Generally, when something is heard in such listening tests, a measurement can be devised to quantify the effect.

Dynamic range: headroom and noise

One difficulty facing film and television production equipment is the very wide volume range, from the softest sound to the loudest, present on a typical set. The background noise may be at 20 dB SPL, and an actor shouting can easily reach over 120 dB SPL. The consequent more than 100 deciBel volume range is a challenge to record. There are two limitations to the ability of any item in the audio chain to reproduce the volume range from soft to loud. At the bottom end of the range, noise is the limiting factor, and at the top end distortion is the limit.

Noise is inevitable in microphones, amplifiers, tape, analog-to-digital and digital-to-analog conversion, and ancillary electronic equipment. It arises from the underlying randomness associated with the electrons comprising the signal-carrying mechanism. Even the simplest dynamic microphone (defined in the next chapter), containing no electronics and sitting in a vacuum, produces noise. This noise is caused by the Brownian motion of the electrons in the conductor comprising the voice coil and wiring of the microphone at room temperature. The only way to eliminate this noise is to cool the microphone to absolute zero temperature, where all motion ceases. Thus, at practical temperatures a noise floor is established right at the microphone, below which desired signals are masked. Ultimately, then, the way to achieve minimum noise is to capture lots of signal by using high-sensitivity microphones close to the source.

Unfortunately, using high-output microphones close to the source leads to a potential problem at the other end of the dynamic range: So much signal will be picked up when the source is loud that it may easily overload or clip the electronics or saturate the tape and cause severe distortion. The term *clipping* means that the signal peaks are literally truncated by the electronics, grossly changing the waveform and producing distortion that is quite likely to be audible.

Choosing a reference level for the electrical level in a studio, or the recorded level on tape, is like using a gray card in photography: Making an exposure based on a gray card puts midrange brightness tones in an image in the middle of the exposure range of the film. Likewise, reference levels in audio are used to represent an average "exposure" or recorded level of a program. From this reference level, the two limits to the dynamic range are measured. The dynamic range from the reference level to the noise (such as tape hiss) is called the *signal-to-noise (s/n) ratio*, and from the reference level to the maximum undistorted level is called the *headroom*. Adding the headroom in deciBels to the signal-to-noise ratio, also in deciBels, results in a single number for the dynamic range of the device or medium, which is certainly one of the most important aspects of performance.

The signal-to-noise ratio is so named because it is an expression in deciBels relating the reference level (the signal) to the noise. The signal-to-noise ratio may be *unweighted*, that is, the measurement instrument may respond to all frequencies equally, or it may be *weighted*, that is, the meter is made to respond more like a human listener by emphasizing those frequency regions where human hearing is most sensitive, with decreasing sensitivity in regions where the ear is less sensitive.

Headroom is the amount above the reference level that a system can produce without severe distortion. Headroom may be flat with frequency, with frequency components anywhere in the audio spectrum overloading at the same level, or it may not be flat with frequency, often overloading or clipping first at the frequency extremes.

An example is given by the performance of open reel analog tape recorders operating at the studio speed of 15 in./sec compared with cassette decks operating at $1^7/_8$ in./sec. Although a cassette recorder can do a credible job most of the time, one primary difference lies in the ability to record high levels of high frequencies; we say that the open-reel machine has much more *high frequency headroom,* and thus a cymbal crash, consisting mostly of high frequencies, recorded on the open-reel machine is undistorted, while recorded at the same relative level on the cassette machine it is distorted.

Audible distortion is more often a problem in film and television production than is audible noise caused by a source such as tape hiss. That is because the relatively high acoustic noise levels present on most sets thoroughly mask the noise from technical sources. (However, the noise from technical sources may become important in very quiet recording situations.) That leaves distortion as the most obvious manifestation of dynamic range problems in most situations.

There are many points in an audio chain where the signal may get to be so large that clipping or distortion occurs:

- In the microphone, especially in those equipped with their own electronics.

- In the microphone preamplifier.

- On the analog tape, or in the analog-to-

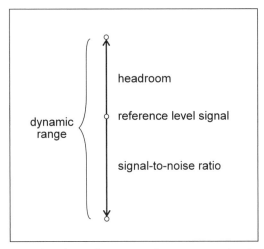

Fig. 3.5 The relationship among dynamic range, headroom, signal-to-noise ratio, and reference level.

digital conversion for digital recording.

- In subsequent signal processing to "improve" the sound quality.

- When multiple sources are summed together in a mixing console: One might not be too great a signal, but many added together may be too great.

- On any intermediate recording stage.

- At the final recording stage to the release medium.

Mixers call optimizing each of these stages for the best compromise between distortion and signal-to-noise ratio *gain staging*. Suffice it to say at this point that the signal in each stage in the chain should be optimized for level so that the widest dynamic range is preserved. This is like optimizing the exposure of film, not only on the negative, but on subsequent interpositive, internegative, and release-print stages so that the "signal," the desired picture, does not become under- nor over-exposed at any point in the chain.

Distortion added at any point in the chain can for all practical purposes not be undone at a later stage of the chain, and thus it is important to keep it low in every stage for the final result to sound undistorted. Likewise, noise accumulates from stage to stage, so under-recording is not the solution to distortion.

Linear and nonlinear distortion
Linear distortion: frequency response, amplitude, and phase

Any change in a waveform constitutes distortion in the broadest sense, but some distortions under this broad definition are benign or even beneficial, while others are quite detrimental. The first class of distortion is called *linear distortion*. These distortions change the waveform, but the effect of the change can be "undone" by equal and opposite signal processing. If, for instance, the treble is boosted a few deciBels by a piece of equipment, an equal and opposite treble cut introduced subsequently in the audio chain will restore the waveform to its original shape precisely, and essentially nothing is lost.

A linear distortion then is a change in what is called the frequency response of the system. A misnamed term, it would probably better be called "amplitude response with respect to frequency," but that being too long, the term has been shortened to the more familiar one, *frequency response*. It means how much one part of the audio frequency range or spectrum is accentuated or attenuated. For instance, a typical frequency response rating is ±1 dB, 20 Hz to 20 kHz, meaning that there is no more than a 2 dB variation from the minimum to the maximum of the response across the range.

> Frequency response actually has two parts, the amplitude response and the phase shift, both with respect to frequency. The two together completely describe the linear distortion that the waveform undergoes.

Many sound qualities are attributed to frequency-response variations, some of them very far away from the expected definition. For instance, midrange sounds around 2 kHz have a larger effect on the perception of distance than do other frequencies. Boosting this frequency range makes sound sources seem to be closer, while cutting it makes them seem further away. Some console manufacturers, knowing this, have gone so far as to label equalization knobs for this frequency range (tone controls affecting a narrow frequency range only) in the boost condition presence and in the cut condition absence. There are many other examples of frequency response variations being ascribed subjective effects perhaps well beyond the expected range of a "tone" control.

In the most general sense, what we most often seek is a flat frequency response (sometimes called a *linear frequency response*) from most items in the audio chain. For instance, a tape recorder that discriminated against bass frequencies and boosted treble frequencies would not be desirable because all sounds going through the recorder would be affected. Although certain sounds might "sound better" with such a nonflat response, the overall average of sounds would not be improved. Thus, flat response is generally desired in most parts of the audio chain, and this is surely one of the most important specifications of any piece of equipment. In fact, in careful experiments, a deviation of as little as $1/2$ dB over several octaves of frequency range is an audible change. For equipment that is not supposed to change the sound quality, specifications on this order of magnitude ought to be considered necessary, especially when considering the multigenerational nature of film and television production in which each sound is recorded and played an average of six times before it reaches the listener, and thus errors accumulate.

Exceptions to the requirement for flat response include the deliberate response changes made by equalizers and filters to improve timbre and reduce noise, which are covered in Chapter 10. Microphones are most often distinguished audibly by two factors: their frequency response and how this varies with the angle to the microphone. There are reasons to make microphones nonflat, which will be taken up in the next chapter.

Nonlinear distortion

Nonlinear distortions are a class in which the waveform cannot be restored to its original shape by equal and opposite compensating equalization. In nonlinear distortions, new tonal components are added to the original ones, and no ordinary process can remove these added components. One of the most egregious examples of nonlinear distortion is *clipping distortion*. In clipping distortion, an amplifier or other device is driven beyond its capacity, with the result being literal clipping off of the peaks of the waveform. Clipping a sine wave, for example, which is by definition only a single frequency tone, results in a great many overtones being generated because the waveform is changed dramatically. Clipping distortion is sometimes heard in production sound recordings because it is difficult to exercise adequate control over all the gain-staging[7] factors in a production sound mixer and recorder. It can usually be completely avoided by correct settings on the various pieces of equipment at hand, including the microphone itself, the mixer, and the recorder. Clipping distortion results in added frequency components at harmonics of the original tone. If the clipping is perfectly symmetrical for positive and negative excursions, the resulting harmonics are the third, fifth, seventh, etc.

Distorting analog tape also creates harmonics, although the brick-wall clipping effect is not so pronounced. Analog tape tends to distort more and more as the level is driven higher and higher above the reference level, with the ultimate limit being complete *saturation* of the magnetic oxide, equivalent to the brick wall of clipping, but with consequences well before the hard limit is reached. For this reason, it is conventional practice to modulate tape so that the peaks of the program reach only a certain distortion, without going all the way to saturation, except on nontonal sounds such as gunshots, where the added distortion is generally inaudible.

The measure usually used for the distortion described is *total harmonic distortion* (THD). THD is the sum of the energy in all of the harmonics compared with that in the fundamental, expressed as a percentage. A typical maximum level for THD in an analog tape recording system is 3% on the maximum peaks of program material. However,

_____

7. A term used to describe all of the various level controls and switches in a recording chain.

THD is not an adequate measure for all types of audible distortion.

To measure various distortion mechanisms beyond simple clipping or tape saturation, *intermodulation* (IM) distortion measures are used. IM distortion comes in a variety of types, but all are distinguished from harmonic distortion by the fact that the test signal contains more than one frequency, and it is the mutual effects of one frequency tone on another that are examined.

> SMPTE intermodulation distortion, for example, two tones at a low and a high frequency are used to drive the system being tested, with the low-frequency tone being 12 dB greater in amplitude than the high-frequency tone. What is looked for is changes in the high-frequency tone as a result of the larger low-frequency tone being present in the system. In a perfect system, the high-frequency tone would be unaltered by the presence of the low-frequency tone, but in a practical system, intermodulation distortion makes the high-frequency tone change level over the cycle of the low-frequency tone. Changes in level of the high-frequency tone at the low-frequency rate are heard as a "roughening" of the high-frequency tone, a kind of gurgle effect.

> High-frequency difference tone distortion tests send two relatively closely spaced high-frequency tones into a system and measure the resulting *difference tone intermodulation* at the difference frequency between the two tones. For example, 19 and 20 kHz tones mixed in a level ratio of 1:1 are sent into a system, and the amount of 1 kHz resulting from distortion coming out of the system is measured.

Generally speaking, the most audible of these distortions is clipping, which must be avoided for all but the briefest instants in order to remain inaudible; the next most audible is harmonic distortion on over-recorded analog tape or film; and the least significant typically is intermodulation distortion. Still, there are special cases in which each one of these distortions can come to prominence in film and television production. For example, early in the history of tape recording, an ornithologist found that bird song recorded on a tape recorder contained lots of audible distortion in the form of low-frequency thumps accompanying the high-frequency bird song.

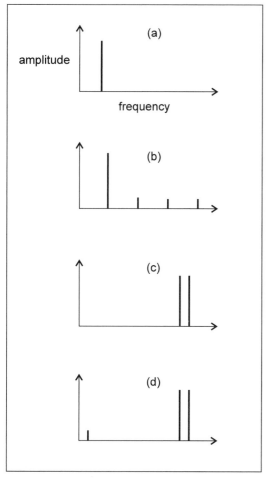

Fig. 3.6 (a) represents the sine wave input to a device under test; (b) the distorted output showing the fundamental plus harmonic distortion; (c) represents the two sine wave inputs for a difference-tone intermodulation distortion test; and (d) the distorted output showing the original sine waves plus distortion at the difference frequency.

What was found was a design problem with difference-tone intermodulation distortion in the recorder model used that had been overlooked by the designers because conventional test signals did not stimulate the effect.

Wow and flutter

Analog mechanical tape and film transports, and phonograph records, are subject to pitch variations as the speed of the mechanism varies slightly around the normal playback speed. After all, off-speed transfers are often made of sound effects in order to make them seem something other than what they are, so one can see that running a tape machine at half-speed produces frequencies that are

one-half the original on playback. It should thus not be surprising that speed variations result in pitch variations. Human hearing is particularly attuned to pitch variations and is able to distinguish a very small fraction of 1% variation under optimum conditions.

Analog tape machines, film transports, and analog optical playback from projectors in theaters and home videotape machines are all subject to wow and flutter, which are pitch variations arising from speed variations. Wow and flutter were originally distinguished as *wow* having to do with once around variations in the speed of phonograph players and *flutter* with higher speed variations. Today, the two phenomena are lumped together and are thought of as one, wow and flutter.

Wow and flutter measurements are standardized differently in different parts of the world, so the numbers derived in Europe, the United States, and Japan are not necessarily comparable. Reliable measures of this statistical phenomenon are also hard to make. Unfortunately, like noise, wow and flutter is something that accumulates over generations, and performance that is fine for one generation may well be audible when accumulated. Wow and flutter is typically most audible on music, including solo instruments such as oboes and piano.

Humans are most sensitive to wow and flutter at a rate of around four variations in frequency per second, and are less sensitive both below and above that frequency. For this reason, most wow and flutter measurements are made with a weighting curve emphasizing this frequency range.

Another form of speed modulation occurs at even higher frequencies than conventional flutter, *scrape flutter*. This is what happens when the stretched tape acts like a violin string and vibrates quite quickly. This causes *modulation noise*, which is a form of noise that is not present in quiet but occurs only when a signal is present. You can hear this easily on a Nagra recorder by recording the reference-level oscillator while listening to the playback in headphones. Stopping the roller closest to the record head with your finger will raise the scrape flutter to audible levels, while letting it move freely will essentially eliminate the audible noise.

Digital audio specific problems

All of the dynamic range and distortion measures outlined earlier apply to digital audio systems. Wow and flutter, however, can be made vanishingly small, due to the nature of digital recording. Any speed variations in tape transports can be eliminated in playback by storing the digits coming from the unevenly played tape in an electronic buffer and withdrawing them at an even rate. Digital systems also provide the potential for no generation loss. These properties constitute some of the best features of digital audio systems, where they are unequivocally better than analog ones.

On the down side, digital systems also come with their own peculiar distortion problems. Unlike analog systems, digital systems quantize the amplitude dimension. This function may cause difficulties, especially when compromises are deliberately introduced to save space on a medium. Particularly in fitting audio to the capacity of computer uses, such as CD-ROM or game boards for PCs, these compromises are likely to be so great that they become audible to the casual listener. Thus, the informed user should know what problems may arise when such measures are invoked.

The digital audio-specific problems discussed here apply to the most common digital audio method of representation, called linear *pulse code modulation* (PCM). In PCM digital audio, quantization occurs by comparing the amplitude of the waveform to the height of a series of stair steps. Each of the stair steps is of equal height. The quantizer (the heart of the analog to digital converter) compares the amplitude of the waveform to the height of the stair steps and assigns a number corresponding to the number of the nearest step.

> There are other problems that occur in practical equipment; the ones outlined here are problems inherent in the basic PCM digital method. For example, an analog-to-digital converter in which all of the steps are not ascending in order (with, e.g., one step missing) is clearly defective.

Resolution

Resolution is the number of bits being used to represent the amplitude dimension, the number of steps in the stairs. For the compact disc, this number is 16 bits of binary (0 or 1) information, or about 65,000 steps. Sixteen-bit representation yields a dynamic range of nearly 96 dB,[8] since each "bit" of resolution buys 6 deciBels of dynamic range ($16 \times 6 = 96$). On the other hand, many low-end computer boards, programs, and CD-ROM recordings are made at only 8 bits, for a dynamic range of 48 dB. This produces audible noise accompanying almost any program material, since there is practically no program material that will mask noise only 48 dB below the maximum signal level. If we were to assign a reference level 8 dB below the maximum, then there is only a signal-to-noise ratio of 40 dB. A 40 dB signal to noise ratio means that the noise will be $^1/_{16}$ as loud as a signal at reference level, and thus clearly audible. Eight deciBels of headroom is also very little to accommodate louder sounds.

In addition, there is an inherent problem with complex productions using digital audio. For the result to be of a certain resolution, for example, 16 bits, if only one track goes into the production, a 16-bit source will do. As the number of source tracks grows, however, the noise from each of the sources will add, and the result will be a decrease in resolution. So a 16-bit multitrack recorder has an inherent design problem: With any degree of mixing it is impossible to deliver an output that has a 16-bit dynamic range. Although a formula can be given for determining the number of additional bits necessary to produce the desired resolution, the formula does not take into account varying levels among the channels, equalization, etc. One emerging trend in digital audio is towards greater resolution in professional equipment, to 20- and 24-bit, which may be a useful improvement in large-scale production.

---

8. *Nearly* is an important word here. Nearly for two reasons, that no practical device reaches the theoretical and due to the need for dither, which is explained later.

Sampling and aliasing distortion

Although quantizing is at the heart of digital audio, another process must occur beforehand, sampling. The procedure is to measure the audio signal so many times per second that all of the nuances of the signal that are in the audio frequency band are captured. The sample rate required is a little more than twice the highest frequency in the desired bandwidth. With 20 kHz usually considered the highest audible frequency, the sample rate for the compact disc became 44.1 kHz, and other professional audio uses 48 kHz. (A lower rate of 32 kHz is used in some broadcasting applications, and some available equipment uses 96 kHz sampling, coming down on the side of extending the bandwidth into what is generally considered to be the ultrasonic domain.)

In order to save space on computer discs and CD-ROMs so that more audio can be stored, it is common to sample at lower rates, usually submultiples of 44.1 kHz, such as 22.05 kHz, 11.025 kHz, etc. The problem encountered with sampling at these lower rates is that frequency components at more than one half of the sampling frequency are likely to be in the signal. The sampling process "confuses" these with lower frequency signals and produces an output tone that is different in frequency from the input one. This is called *aliasing distortion*.

> One half of the sample rate is called the *folding frequency* because aliasing distortion "folds" the signal frequencies around one-half the sample rate. So any input frequency above one half of the sample rate will alias and appear as a new frequency in the output. For instance, if the sample rate is 11 kHz and the signal frequency is 7 kHz (speech recorded for a CD-ROM will contain such a frequency in an "s" sound), one half of the sample rate is 5.5 kHz and the 7 kHz signal will be seen as a 4 kHz signal (7 kHz is 1.5 kHz above the folding frequency, and 4 kHz is 1.5 kHz below the folding frequency).

An example of aliasing distortion in motion pictures is a shot of wagon wheels appearing to run backwards when photographed, or sampled, at 24 fps. Up to a certain speed of the wagon, photography renders an accurate representation of the speed of the wheels.

But at the point where the shutter is open, then closed, then reopened just as the spokes have moved, for example, $1/6$ of a rotation for a six-spoke wheel, the film "sees" a stationary image of a moving object, which is aliasing distortion. At other relative rates between the photography and speed of the wheels, they even appear to run "backwards," which is clearly an artifact.

In audio, the sound of aliasing distortion is distinctive. On speech as a signal, it sounds like a chirp that accompanies "ess" and other high-frequency sounds in speech. It may be fairly benign, or very nasty, depending on the strength of "ess-es" in the speech and the sample rate (lower ones are worse). The way to avoid aliasing distortion is to use a filter that removes the frequencies higher than one-half the sample rate. This filter is called an *anti-aliasing filter*. Unfortunately, most low-sample-rate analog-to-digital converters are not equipped with anti-aliasing filters, and plainly audible aliases are the result on much program material.

Jitter

An issue in sampling and in digital-to-digital interfaces is called *jitter*. This is the variation in time from sample to sample from the calculated time due to imperfections, and can result in pure tones becoming "rougher" sounding, much like with *scrape flutter*, only generally jitter is smaller in effect than scrape flutter. Jitter can even be present in digital-to-digital interfaces. The input of properly designed digital audio equipment "re-clocks" incoming jittered signals and restores them.

Quantizing distortion

The process of quantizing the amplitude dimension of the signal also carries with it the potential for a particular kind of distortion, called *quantizing distortion*. Quantizing distortion arises even in a perfect linear PCM system when the amplitudes of the signals are very small, unless measures are taken to prevent it (see *Dither,* below).

Let us say that a signal is just slightly larger than one step of the staircase and is a pure sine-wave tone. It will be converted as it first crosses above and then below the level of the first tread of the staircase. The digital representation of the sine wave will simply alternate between the higher and the lower bit levels. The result, upon conversion back to analog, will be a square wave, not a sine wave. The reason is that the converter is coarse at these low levels and cannot discriminate the waveform, only the fact that the one tread has been alternately crossed. Thus, what came into the analog-to-digital conversion process as a sine wave is actually converted as a square wave, producing a very significant distortion. Furthermore, a just slightly lower level signal is not converted at all, because it never crosses the tread of the staircase. Thus any lower level signals than the smallest step (called the *least significant bit*) are discarded, another important distortion. There is a way around these distortions and it is called *dither*.

Dither

The effects of quantizing distortion can be fully eliminated by the addition of some deliberately added random noise, which may sound like hiss. Although noise is usually considered to be a detriment in any system, adding dither noise in a digital audio conversion process randomly "agitates" the signal so that even the smallest signals cross the treads of the staircase. The noise pushes the signal up and down randomly, causing it to cross the threshold often. By averaging the signal plus the dither over time, like the hearing mechanism does, signals even far below the threshold of the smallest step can be perceived. The noise effectively smears out the steps in the staircase, turning the stair steps into a linear ramp when averaged over time. The amount of dither is about equal to one step in the staircase, so the added noise to produce these benefits is quite small, although it may become noticeable when many channels are added together.

Another important role for dither is in reducing the number of bits of resolution when a source has more resolution than a copy. If 16 bit recordings are made in the studio, and then transferred to 8 bit for release on CD-ROM, very significant audible distortion results. These effects can be minimized by adding the proper amount and type of dither. With 20 bit storage capability on digital videotape, and 20 bit converters growing in use, conversion to the final consumer format of 16 bits, for example, must add dither in the conversion so that the coarser steps of 16 bits compared with the 20 bit original do not become a source of quantizing distortion.

Dither may be added in a number of forms. The noise needed may "hidden" in the less audible parts of the spectrum, by shaping the frequency response of the noise to be like the equal-loudness contours, with little noise in the 2 to 3 kHz most-sensitive region of hearing, and increasing it above 10 kHz, where sound is less audible. Called *noise shaped dither*, and also by trade names such as Super Bit Mapping™, this process yields an audible improvement in dynamic range over the restrictions of the output resolution. Perceptibly, a 16 bit system can be made to sound as though it has the dynamic range of a 19 bit system in this way.

A digital audio system

There are a number of blocks in making a digital audio system, caused by the needs outlined earlier. In addition, it should be pointed out that we are dealing with only one kind of digital audio in this exposition, and that is linear pulse code modulated digital.

A PCM system has the following parts to its block diagram, in the order that a signal encounters them:

- Anti-aliasing filter

- Dither noise generator

- Summer for the signal and the noise

- Analog-to-digital converter

- Digital circuitry to add error-protecting codes and to condition the signal for recording or transmission

- Medium for storage or transmission of the digital bits

- Digital circuits to decode the error codes and correct for errors

- Digital-to-analog converter

- Reconstruction filter, the equivalent on the output of the anti-aliasing filter on the input, which "smooths" the small steps remaining in the signal from the digitization process into a continuous signal

Specialized application areas, such as digital release prints, employ other techniques. Linear PCM is the most common method of recording and storing audio today, but it consumes a lot of digital audio storage for a given time of track time. For instance, sampling at 16 bits with a 48 kHz clock results in 720,000 bits per second per channel. Due to this high number, lower sample rates and resolution are used for CD-ROM and other such purposes to save space. Another solution is perceptual coding, which works by

"throwing" away signals that would be masked by human hearing mechanisms, achieving more than ten times bit-rate reduction with potentially few audible artifacts.

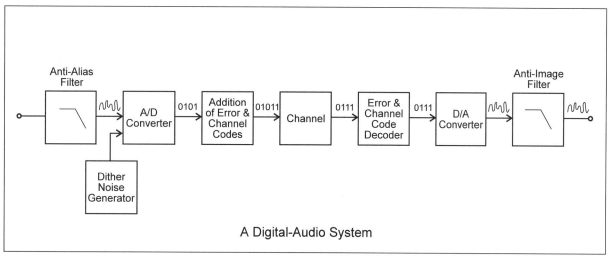

Fig. 3.7 The parts of a linear PCM digital-audio system from analog input to output.

Oversampling

Two dimensions of an audio signal are amplitude and frequency. It is possible to trade one of these off against the other, since the information-carrying capacity of a channel is related to the product of these two factors. Radio microphones, for instance, convert the audio bandwidth and dynamic range from their microphone to a wider bandwidth and a smaller dynamic range for transmission in the radio-frequency channel. The signal is represented by a different means (FM radio), but the information content is still the same. The two dimensions are represented in digital audio by quantizing and sampling respectively. Oversampling can be compared with the process used in radio microphones, trading off bandwidth and dynamic range. By sampling at a higher than normal sample rate, less dynamic range in the A/D and D/A converters is needed to produce results associated with a wider dynamic range in the audio channel.

Oversampling is a process one frequently hears about in terms of the number of times of oversampling that a particular circuit employs, from "4 times oversampling" to "128 times oversampling." The number of times refers to the sam-

ple rate, for example, a 4 times oversampled professional audio system samples at 192 kHz (4 × 48 kHz). The basic idea behind oversampling is that sampling at higher rates spreads the noise of the analog-to-digital conversion process out over a wider than audible frequency range. The portion of the noise that is ultrasonic is inaudible, so the more spreading the better (the higher the sample rate or number of times of oversampling). When converted at the other end of the process back to audio, just the audible frequency range noise counts, so it is possible for an oversampled system to come closer to the ideal than one using conventional sample rates. Oversampling also simplifies the requirements of the anti-aliasing filters, because they need not filter so steeply because the sample frequency is raised so much. On the other hand, there are practical problems involved in oversampling, such as the fact that *jitter*, small variations in the time that the samples are taken from one to the next due to imperfections in the process, becomes relatively more important than in a lower sampled system. So it is by no means clear that the system with the highest oversampling rate is necessarily the best.

Chapter 4: Microphones and Techniques for Their Use

Introduction

Microphones are, of course, fundamental to film and video sound in capturing the sounds present on a set, in a sound-effects gathering expedition, on a scoring stage, or elsewhere, and in converting the sound into an electrical voltage proportional to the amplitude of the acoustic waveform, varying moment by moment. This voltage is generally conducted over wires to a microphone preamplifier. Alternatively, it may be the input to a wireless transmitter which will convey the audio content by radio frequency transmission to a companion receiver.

A microphone is called generally a *transducer*, since it converts energy from one form (acoustical) into another form (electrical); likewise, a loudspeaker is also a transducer, working in the opposite direction from a microphone.

> There are other transducers as well as microphones used very occasionally in filmmaking. These include hydrophones (underwater microphones) and accelerometers (vibration-sensitive pickup devices that are directly attached to the

source, thus obviating air transmission).

Pressure microphones

If asked to make a microphone, one way to proceed would be to copy the way the ear works: Stretch a diaphragm over a sealed chamber (providing a leak, like the Eustachian tube, for pressure equalization with barometric pressure change) and measure the displacement of the diaphragm caused by the sound, converting its vibration into voltage by various means. This is the way the simplest microphones work. Compared with the ear, though, there need to be several "improvements." One is that the ear canal provides a resonant tube in front of the eardrum, increasing the sensitivity in just one frequency range. Since we usually want our microphone to keep timbre constant, we typically want a flat frequency response, so the tube will have to go: The diaphragm should be exposed as much as possible to the sound field. (Some compromise is usually made here, and the diaphragm is slightly recessed to prevent damage.) This microphone construction is called a *pressure micro-*

phone, because the motion of the diaphragm, and the consequent voltage, result from the pressure variations caused by the sound.

Notice that for wavelengths of sound that are large compared with the diaphragm, it does not matter from what direction the sound pressure comes; any compression part of a sound wave pushes the diaphragm into the cavity behind it and produces a positive voltage at the output terminals. This is because the sound waves from behind the mike diffract around the microphone body, and the local increase in air pressure caused by the compression pushes the diaphragm into the body of the mike. Pressure microphones are thus inherently *omnidirectional*, accepting sound from all directions.

At high frequencies, where the wavelength of the sound waves becomes comparable to the dimensions of the microphone, the omnidirectionality breaks down because for sound coming from the direction behind the face of the diaphragm, the body of the microphone casts an acoustic shadow. Nevertheless, sound pressure from the back makes it to the diaphragm through diffraction, but is somewhat attenuated in doing so. Thus, practical-sized pressure microphones "roll off" sound coming from the rear at high frequencies.

Something else happens to high-frequency sounds coming from the front. If the microphone were not present, the sound wave would flow freely. Placing the microphone in the sound field interrupts the field, but this is hardly noticeable at wavelengths at which the microphone appears small, so across most of the audible frequency range there is little effect. At high frequencies, however, pressure "congestion" in front of the diaphragm raises the level; this is the same effect as seen at the walls of rooms, in which sound pressure is raised locally due to the pressure increase at a barrier. So without corrective action, the frequency response of a pressure microphone will "rise" on axis, increasing its output as frequency goes up. This is not a small effect, amounting to 9 dB at 20 kHz for a $1/2$ in.-diameter diaphragm-equipped microphone.

The high-frequency rise on axis in an uncorrected pressure microphone was initially used to add "clarity" to recordings because almost inevitably in older recording equipment there would

be a high-frequency loss somewhere that the microphone was useful in overcoming. Then, as the equipment and methods grew better over the years, a market arose for mikes with a flatter frequency response, and the design was modified to make them flat on axis.

Today, both types are offered as recording microphones, because mikes with rising response are seen as especially useful when placed at long distances, where there are air absorption losses to overcome, and flat on-axis mikes are used for close work or in smaller rooms.

In precision-measurement microphone terminology, an uncorrected mike (with rising response on axis) is called a *pressure microphone*, whereas the models corrected for flat response on axis are called *free-field microphones*. Free-field precision measurement mikes are used where there is a single direction for the sound field, such as in anechoic chambers. Pressure microphones are used in real rooms with mixed-sound fields, with the diaphragm oriented perpendicular to the direct sound, thus eliminating the effect of the congestion on the direct sound. In such an arrangement, the frequency response for the direct sound and for diffuse-field reverberation match reasonably well for $1/2$ in. diameter and smaller microphones.[1] This is why you will see technicians aiming measurement microphones at the ceiling when tuning dubbing stages and theaters; they are using pressure mikes.

The high-frequency effects of shadowing by the microphone body and pressure congestion in front of the microphone are worse for larger diaphragm diameters and are better for smaller ones. On the other hand, a larger diaphragm captures more sound energy and is thus more sensitive, producing a better signal-to-noise ratio. The trade-off between these two results in typical microphone diameters of about $1/2$ in., for microphones designed for the "best trade-off" among these factors. Smaller microphones are usable, as in lavaliere mikes, with some noise compromise, and larger ones are even desirable in some music applications, where the "defects" of larger size may be used to some benefit to make a particular sound quality, such as compensating for distance by the rise on axis.

1.The difference is about 3 dB at 20 kHz for a $1/2$ in. diameter microphone, and 1 dB at 20 kHz for a $1/4$ in. one.

For low frequencies, a pressure microphone may respond all the way down into the infrasonic region. This causes a problem, because just taking the microphone up in an elevator could push the diaphragm to one extreme and cause it to stick there, just like your eardrum in an elevator when you have a cold. For this reason, a small pinhole-size pressure equalizing vent is provided to relieve the pressure changes from the very lowest frequencies. This "leak" is typically the only limit on low frequency response.

In sum, pressure microphones are naturally omnidirectional, generally accepting sound for all directions equally, except at high frequencies (short wavelengths), where the microphone body and diaphragm are acoustically large objects, so there are differences with respect to direction: High-frequency sound from the rear is attenuated, and that from the front is boosted. The latter may be corrected, but to do so "tips" the whole response downward so that sound coming from the rear is even more attenuated once sound coming from the front has been made flat. This is why microphones used on sets most often use small-diameter diaphragms, while recording studio microphones often use larger ones. The difference is that on the set, one can never know for sure the direction of the sound source at all times, but in the studio, under more controlled conditions, the actor or musician can be placed in front of the microphone all the time.

Boundary-layer microphones

A special pressure microphone has been developed for placement on a large barrier, such as the walls or ceiling of a room. These microphones are specially constructed as practically flat plates with the microphone element flush with the plate.

> The advantage of this construction is that the microphone benefits from the pressure buildup at the surface across all frequencies; the "congestion" occurring in front of the diaphragm at high frequencies in conventional mikes is made to work across all wavelengths because the diaphragm is essentially made a part of a large surface. Thus the high-frequency rise seen in conventional types does not occur on axis. The directional response is, by definition, hemi-

spheric.

> Such microphones only work to full advantage when they are placed on very large barriers. Placed on discs of plastic several feet across they suffer from the effects of diffraction around the edge, with poor low frequency response.

Boundary layer microphones have been found useful in settings like car interiors, where their potential visual integration into the roof of the car makes them desirable, as well as their acoustic properties. Practically speaking, any pressure microphone placed up against an acoustic barrier that is not too absorptive will display the boundary layer effect of increased output and hemispheric response.

Wind susceptibility

Pressure microphones are the least susceptible type to wind-induced noise, due to their sealed cavity only exposing one surface to wind, and the relatively high tension to which their diaphragms are stretched, compared to the other types to be discussed.

Pressure-gradient microphones

In a pure *pressure-gradient* microphone, both sides of the diaphragm are exposed to the sound field, unlike the pressure mike. What this arrangement measures is the *difference* in pressure between the two sides of the diaphragm. The diaphragm, in reacting to the difference between its two sides, works in a fundamentally different way from a pressure microphone, leading it to have very different directional properties that make it an essential ingredient in microphones used for a lot of film and television work. There are also consequences of this directionality that can be managed if they are understood.

The first type of pressure-gradient microphone developed was the ribbon microphone. In it a diaphragm, consisting of a thin and lightweight (2 mg.) conductive metal ribbon, is suspended in a strong magnetic field. A compression wave, perpendicular to the ribbon and coming from the front, pushes in on the ribbon, and its movement through the magnetic field induces a positive voltage across the ends of the ribbon, con-

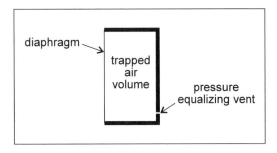

Pressure microphone cutaway drawing

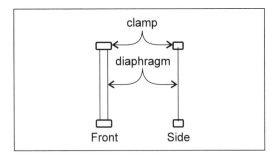

Pressure-gradient microphone

Fig. 4.1 The basics of the pressure and pressure-gradient microphone types. In a pressure microphone, the diaphragm is stretched over a cavity, while in the pressure-gradient microphone, both sides of the diaphragm are exposed to the air.

verting sound into electricity. A compression wave from the rear also pushes the diaphragm, but in the opposite direction of sound from the front, so compression waves from the rear induce a negative voltage, a difference to be discussed later.

We have seen that sound coming from the front and rear are both converted to electrical energy, but what about sound coming from the side of the ribbon? Here the sound field faces the ribbon on its edge, and there is virtually no motion of the diaphragm, and thus no electrical output. Tracing the output characteristic versus angle by moving around the microphone is called the *polar pattern* of the microphone. In this case, the polar pattern is a figure-eight shape, called *bi-directional* or *dipolar*, indicating that the front and back are sensitive, while sound arriving from either side is severely attenuated.

Note that the figure-eight pattern is three dimensional, which is the type of surface we would get by spinning the symbol for the number 8 around its vertical axis.

Pressure-gradient microphones exhibit a behavior that is not found in pressure microphones because they are sensitive to the pressure gradient instead of pressure. As the distance between the source and the microphone is decreased, the low-frequency response is boosted; this is called the *proximity effect*. It is illustrated by Track 17 of the CD.

> This effect occurs because of the curved wavefront close to the source and its measurement at two points in space rather than one. At larger distances, the spreading wavefront, which is actually spherical, when sampled at two points by a small microphone, appears essentially flat.

Old-time radio announcers used the proximity effect to good advantage for their careers. They spoke into ribbon microphones closely, thus boosting the bass and their reputation at the same time.

While the proximity effect is prominent in the frequency range usually considered to be bass, from 50 to 200 Hz, there is another effect that pressure-gradient microphones exhibit that can seem contradictory. At the very lowest frequencies, below 50 Hz for typical microphones, the response is attenuated. This occurs because for the very lowest frequencies, with the longest wavelengths, the difference between two closely spaced points in air is very small as seen by a microphone. So unlike pressure microphones, pressure-gradient ones do not respond to extreme low bass, and in fact tend to virtually no output at infrasonic frequencies. Tracks 18 and 19 of the CD show the difference on very low frequency response of pressure and pressure-gradient microphones. (Note that the sound system you use to play these tracks must have extended low bass response to hear these differences.)

Comparing an omnidirectional pressure microphone with a figure-eight pressure-gradient microphone operating in a room shows some important differences. The room has direct sound, reflections, and reverberation, and the direct sound has a known direction, while the reverberation is practically directionless. If an omni mike and a figure-eight mike are installed side by side and aimed at the direct sound, and have equal sensitivity, the two will pick up the direct sound equally, but the omni will pick up more reverberation than the figure-eight mike. This is because the omni is sensitive all around, whereas the part of the reverberant field that is coming from the side is attenuated in the figure-eight mike.

Keeping reverberation low in recording is generally desirable due to the fact that it is essentially impossible to reduce reverberation in post production, and it is simple and routine to add it. Thus "dead" recording rules, i.e., studios are usually very absorptive, and directional microphones are used, both to reduce recorded reverberation.

> Another difference between pressure and pressure-gradient microphone types occurs due to room acoustics. Heretofore this discussion has generally assumed a free field for direct sound, or a diffuse field for reverberant sound. At low frequencies, where standing waves dominate in rooms we do not observe a free- or a diffuse-field but rather standing waves, and the pressure and pressure-gradient types can be quite different at these frequencies. Just rotating a pressure-gradient microphone about its axis in a room with standing waves can also produce very dramatic changes in the bass because the standing waves have particular directions. The two types respond to different components of the sound field, producing potentially very different output. This can easily be heard using highly directional microphones often used for film sound: their bass frequency response is affected by the standing waves in the recording room, and this effect seems more pronounced for the most directional types.

Wind susceptibility

Pressure microphones are the most susceptible type to wind-induced noise, due to both sides of the diaphragm being exposed to wind, and the relatively low tension to which their diaphragms are typically stretched.

Combinations of pressure and pressure-gradient responding microphones

Thus far we have discussed two polar patterns, omnidirectional and dipolar. These two "primitive"[2] patterns are useful directly in many ways that we discuss later, but most microphones in widespread use for film and television work use a combination of the two types.

Certainly, one of the most popular polar patterns is the *cardioid*, or heart shape. A cardioid (and variations thereon) can be made in one form by placing both a pressure and a pressure-gradient responding microphone element together in close proximity and adding their outputs together. You will recall that we said the difference between the front and back halves of the ribbon microphone was polarity, with one side producing positive voltage for positive energy and the other producing negative voltage for positive energy. The back half is "out of phase" with the front half. It is this characteristic that we can put to use. By adding the negative voltage from the back half of the dipole to the positive voltage received from the omni, cancellation is achieved for sound coming from the rear: $(+1) + (-1) = 0$. Sound coming from the front, on the other hand, sums in phase: $(+1) + (+1) = 2$. The sensitivity compared to one of the mikes alone is doubled. Tracing this characteristic output versus angle around the microphone results in the cardioid shape. Track 20 of the CD illustrates adding the two types together to form a cardioid.

For such cardioid mikes, the suppression of reverberation is about the same as that of the figure-eight mike. Although reducing reverberation is useful, it is the forward preference for sound that makes it favored in film and television applications compared to figure-8 mics.

The method of producing a cardioid polar pattern that relies on summing two mike elements is rather clumsy, but was the first way in which cardioid mikes were made, and

2. In the sense of serving as the basis for derived forms.

some still function this way. After the importance of the pattern was established in the marketplace, other methods of construction were found that achieved a cardioid pattern.

> The methods used include adding chambers, holes, silk, or metal mesh screens and other methods of acoustical phase shifting to sound applied from the outside to the rear of the diaphragm, all of which are aimed at producing a cardioid pattern over a wide frequency region. In an alternative method, two diaphragms are used that are electrically added together to produce various polar patterns. Some types so equipped can even be made with electrically adjustable polar patterns.

The cardioid microphone is without a doubt the most commonly used type among reasonable quality microphones in the world. However, it is used infrequently in film and television production sound, that more likely uses one of the types discussed below. Sound effects recording, music recording, and Foley recording are more likely to make use of cardioids.

Super- and hyper-cardioids

There is a need for microphones that are more directional than cardioids, especially in film and television production sound, where the microphone must often work at a large distance. The cardioid or the figure-eight mike can be used at a distance factor 1.7 times as great as an omni mike for equal reverberant pickup. The cardioid pattern was generated by adding the outputs of two receivers, a pressure and a pressure-gradient one, in equal proportions, causing the null toward the back. If the level of the two receivers is adjusted differently, the pattern can be made with two important differences from a cardioid. The sides are "pulled in" compared with the cardioid, so for sound at 90° the output is distinctly less. In addition, there is a small "lobe" or region of sensitivity pointed to the rear. This polar pattern is called either super-cardioid or hyper-cardioid.[3] These are among the most valuable patterns for filmmaking for several reasons:

3.These two types are so close to each other in performance that, all other things being equal, they are essentially indistinguishable in practice.

- Due to their tighter directivity, the response to reverberation is less than in any mike type discussed up to this point, having a distance factor of 2.0 for pick up of reverberation compared to a pressure mike.

- Instead of a line pointing straight back from the mike being the "null" in the cardioid type, the super- and hyper-cardioid have their null at an angle of between 120° and 135° from the front. This null is rotated in space, and thus forms a cone where the output is minimal. In the overhead position on a boom, the front "hot" side of the mike can be aimed at the actor, while the null "cold" side can be aimed at the camera. Thus the actor can be recorded well and the camera noise rejected at one and the same time, which is important in motion-picture applications (movie cameras are noisy because of their movement of film compared with television cameras which rarely have any moving parts).

Fig. 4.2 Super- and hyper-cardioid mics on overhead booms allow the boom operator to place the actor on the "hot" side of the microphone, and the camera on the "cold" side, thus maximizing the desired performance, and minimizing the camera noise simultaneously.

- Super- and hyper-cardioids are more easily designed for a wide frequency range, with a smooth frequency response on- and off-axis, and thus may preserve timbre more faithfully than the more commonly seen interference-tube microphones (to be discussed later).

Sub-cardioid

If the summation between elements is made different, more in favor of the pressure type, then a sub-cardioid (also called a *limaçon*) pattern can be generated, with no complete null but with a forward preference. Used occasionally in music recording for an appropriate balance between direct sound and reverberation, it is rarely if ever used in production sound.

Variable-directivity microphones

Because these various patterns are generated by summing together the different ingredients of a sound field, it is possible to make either fixed-directivity (fixed polar-pattern) microphones or variable-directivity microphones, with the variation among patterns accomplished either mechanically or electrically. As a general statement, though, variable-pattern microphones are compromises in favor of flexibility over performance on any single pattern and therefore are used in applications where there is an emphasis on flexibility. In film and television production sound, it is rare to find switchable directivity microphones in use, although music recording studios make more use of these types.

> Note that the degree of the proximity effect will vary depending on the pattern to which a variable-directivity microphone is set, so in practical situations, changing the pattern could result in hearing different amounts of bass. This is not a defect but an expected result arising from the various methods of operation.

Interference tube (shotgun or rifle microphone)

The final directivity pattern is one of the most important for film and television uses. It was developed originally to solve the problem of keeping the microphone out of the camera shot while still providing a high ratio of direct-to-reverberant sound. To achieve this, even more directionality was required than the sum of two receivers—pressure and pressure gradient—could provide, as in the supercardioid. The interference tube microphone developed in the United States for the introduction of television in 1939 has undergone several generations of development, with the current one described here.

If a tube is arranged with slots along its length, the slots are covered with acoustical resisting material such as silk, and the end of the tube terminates in a supercardioid microphone transducer, then sound waves progressing along the axis of the tube will be unimpeded. Sound incident on the tube from 90° will suffer interference effects within the tube and will not add together at the transducer. So, in sum, there is an increase in directivity compared with any other microphone type, with an accompanying reduction of reverberation and other off-axis sound.

Fig. 4.3 The Sennheiser MKH416 "short shotgun" is a hypercardioid at low frequencies, and becomes sharper in its polar pattern as the frequency increases due to the interference tube in front of the diaphragm. Photo courtesy Sennheiser Electronics Corporation.

In contemporary production sound, this is probably the most popular type used as a boom mike. It does suffer from the following problems, however:

• Off-axis sound is reduced through interference. This causes peaks and dips in the off-axis frequency response, because the interference becomes constructive or destructive at various frequencies. Although attenuated, the off-axis sound is "colored," that is, the timbre is quite noticeably changed. This can have an effect on, say, footsteps, when the microphone is pointed at the mouth of the actor from 45° overhead. The feet are very far off the axis of the microphone, and they may sound as though they were recorded in a barrel.

- The longer the interference tube, the wider the frequency range over which the narrow directivity is achieved. Thus, the mikes having the most uniform directivity with frequency use long tubes, which may become unwieldy.

- Wind susceptibility is relatively high. This means effective windscreens must be used, which are also necessarily large, to create a region around the mike that is relatively less turbulent.

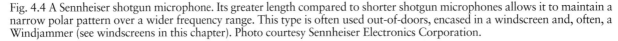

Fig. 4.4 A Sennheiser shotgun microphone. Its greater length compared to shorter shotgun microphones allows it to maintain a narrow polar pattern over a wider frequency range. This type is often used out-of-doors, encased in a windscreen and, often, a Windjammer (see windscreens in this chapter). Photo courtesy Sennheiser Electronics Corporation.

Microphone types by method of transduction

All microphones convert acoustical into electrical energy, but there are a number of ways to accomplish this, with varying areas of application.

Carbon

The first microphones were composed of a diaphragm stretched over a cavity that was loosely filled with granular carbon. Positive sound pressure presses in on the carbon, compacting it slightly. This reduces the electrical resistance of the mass of carbon, so when connected to a dc power source such as a battery, a voltage proportional to sound pressure can be generated. On March 10, 1876, Alexander Graham Bell said into such a microphone the famous first line ever sent by electrical means "Mr. Watson—Come here—I want to see you."

It is extremely difficult to make such microphones both sensitive and have a flat frequency response, and they suffer relatively high distortion due to the nonlinearity of the carbon mass. Still, such microphones formed the heart of the telephone industry for 100 years, so there are many still in daily use. Carbon microphones are rarely if ever used directly in filmmaking, but the output of telephone conversations may need to be recorded.[4] A magnetic-induction pickup coil, or direct wiring, can be used to record telephone conversations over phone lines, for which the source is the carbon microphone in the telephone. Such sound quality may well be more appropriate for a phone conversation than the use of a better microphone. While post production techniques include a "telephone filter," sometimes it is best to simply record a telephone, with all its response variations and distortions.

Ceramic

Certain crystalline, glasslike materials, when struck by vibration, produce voltage directly by way of the piezo-electric effect. The vibration can be conducted from a diaphragm to a transducer element, and thus form a ceramic microphone. Small blocks of such ceramic materials are very resonant, like striking a bell, so it is difficult to get a wide frequency-range receiver. The primary place where such an element is in any use in film and video is in making hydrophones (underwater microphones) for which the very stability of the glasslike structure is highly useful. In this case, the microphone is supplied with it own set of electronics, which produce a line-level signal suitable for recording. On the other hand, underwater recordings can also be made with other microphone types enclosed in water-impermeable housings, but their sound may be muffled by the enclosure.

---

4. Note that there are laws covering permissible recording of telephone conversations.

Electrodynamic (dynamic)

If a conductor of electricity such as copper is moved in a magnetic field, a voltage is induced across the ends of the conductor. The conductor can be insulated wire arranged in a coil and attached to a diaphragm. With the right shape of magnet, the diaphragm motion will cause the *voice coil* to produce a voltage at its ends as the magnetic lines of force cut across the coiled wire.

Dynamic microphones generate their own electricity, without an outside source of power as is needed in most of the other types. They are also typically rugged compared with other types, withstanding both shock and temperature and humidity variations better than other mikes, and thus they are preferred as at least a backup in many kinds of filmmaking. They do contain strong magnets, and some models leak magnetic field, which means they should be stored at least a few inches away from audiotape. The simplest dynamic microphone to make is the omnidirectional pressure type, but other polar patterns are available, with the cardioid probably being the most popular among professional types.

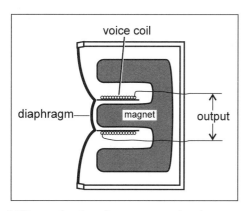

Fig. 4.5 Dynamic microphone cutaway drawing.

Due to the particular combination of strengths in the dynamic microphone, it is typically used in film and video production where requirements for ruggedness and reliability under adverse conditions prevail. The ultimate quality of a dynamic microphone is potentially limited by the requirement that the sound move the mass of the diaphragm and voice coil in order to produce an output, and the mass, although low, is higher than in the electrostatic microphone (to be discussed later). While well-designed dynamic microphones can be very good, as a class they are not considered to be the ultimate transducer.

> Note that the ribbon microphone employs the same principle of transduction as the conventional dynamic microphone, but the smaller amount of conductor in its magnetic field typically leads to much lower output levels, which must be stepped up to a more usable level by a transformer in the microphone. Even with the step up, a ribbon microphone usually has too low sensitivity for most film and television purposes but may find use in music studios, especially in front of louder instruments.

Electrostatic (capacitor, condenser)

The electrostatic microphone has only one moving part, the diaphragm. The motion of the diaphragm is detected by measuring the electrical property capacitance between the diaphragm and a fixed back plate.[5] *Capacitance* is the ability of two conductors, separated by an insulator, to store charge. In the case of a capacitor microphone, there is a fixed amount of capacitance caused by the spacing in silence, which varies up and down by the motion of the diaphragm due to sound. It is the changes in capacitance with sound that are detected, using one of three methods.

> One method is to charge the capacitor formed by the diaphragm and back plate, using a polarizing voltage, generally 45 to 200 Vdc. A set of electronics can be arranged to make the variations in charge resulting from the changes in spacing between the diaphragm and back plate into an output voltage. This method is quite stable and is used in measurement and many recording microphones.

> The second method is to use the changes in capacitance caused by the sound to change the instantaneous frequency of an oscillator, typically operating around 10 MHz. The changes in

5. This property gives this microphone type its common names: capacitor and condenser. (Condenser is an older word, now obsolete in other uses, meaning the same thing as capacitor.) Most texts use one of these words, although the word electrostatic describes the underlying principle better.

frequency are detected by a frequency-modulation detector, which works like the detector stage in an FM radio, and are converted to the audio output signal. This method avoids the use of a polarizing voltage, with a claimed attendant increase in reliability. This technique is labeled "rf microphone," which may be easily confused with radio microphones for which the same term is sometimes applied, although one describes what is going on inside the body of the microphone, while the other describes a wireless microphone.

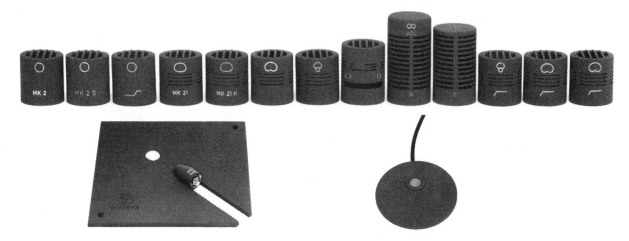

Fig. 4.6 This series of capsules from Schoeps provides a wide variety of polar patterns and built-in frequency response variations to cover a wide range of applications. They include pure pressure (omnidirectional) and pressure-gradient (bi-directional) types, as well as cardioid, hyper-cardioids, sub-cardioids, and boundary layer types. Other variations include capsules that roll off low frequencies, and ones that emphasize high frequencies, along with ones that demonstrate very flat frequency response.

The third method is most commonly used in inexpensive electrostatic microphones, such as those found on answering machines, but there are a number of less expensive recording microphones that also make use of the technique. In this type, the polarizing voltage is applied permanently, by electrochemistry during manufacture, and thus does not require an external voltage source for polarization (although power is still needed for the electronics, which must follow the capsule). These pre-polarized microphones are called *electret capacitor* (or condenser) microphones. While the best of these types can be practically as good as air capacitor microphones, few of the highest quality microphones use this principle.

All three of these methods of converting capacitance variation to output voltage require electronics to do the conversion, and thus require power. Generally the electronics must be placed in close proximity to the pickup capsule of the microphone, although for some types special active cables are available to space the pickup capsule away from the electronics. The power supply may consist of a battery in the microphone proper, in an external box, in the unit into which the microphone is plugged; or as a power supply provided as part of a console.

There is more than one method for supplying the power. In the simplest method, a battery is inserted into the microphone body itself, or into a connector at the other end of a dedicated mike cable. These batteries are easy to forget about because they often last several hundred hours. They are usually specialized types, which are not widely available, and thus it is essential to have spares.

There are some very inexpensive types of electret capacitor microphones available, which, if they have two leads, are powered by supplying the signal lead with DC. If they have three leads, one is the common ground, one is the output, and the third is for battery power. These are suitable for planting on a set or for nature shows, where they might be destroyed or eaten, for example.[6]

---

6. One of these is Panasonic part no. WM-52BM, available from Digi-Key Corp. at www.digikey.com for $1.06.

There are several methods for supplying power to microphones remotely over the required balanced lines. The most popular method is *phantom powering*, in which a positive voltage is applied to both balanced leads from the microphone and the negative voltage to the shield ground. Microphones using this type of powering usually have the letter P in their model number. Such microphones are suitable for connection to microphone preamplifiers that supply phantom power (which may often be switchable on and off).

> Although one intent of phantom powering is to allow interchangeability between powered electrostatic microphones and electrodynamic ones, it is generally not good practice to supply unpowered microphones with power. What may happen is a connection accident where one side of the balanced line becomes connected first, applying the dc voltage to a microphone not designed to handle it. Phantom power is thus often switchable, even on a per channel basis, on consoles so equipped.

A second, less common method of powering is to supply positive voltage to one of the balanced leads and negative voltage to the other balanced lead. Called *A-B* or *T powering*, this method is not as popular as phantom power, due to potential damage to other microphone types that are inadvertently connected. Connecting a ribbon microphone to a microphone input supplied with A-B powering will probably damage the ribbon because it seeks to "transduce" an applied voltage in reverse and act like a loudspeaker; damage may also result to dynamic mikes. Microphones using this method of powering usually contain the letter T in their model number.

Fig. 4.7 Any of the capsules shown in Fig. 4.6 may be combined with one of a variety of electronics "bodies" having various powering options to produce a complete microphone.

Because there is no common designation for which type of powering a certain microphone uses, it is difficult to know which method to use without examining the mike spec sheet. For example, a microphone with a model number ending in P48 is probably intended for phantom powering from a 48 Vdc source.

Electrostatic microphones using air as their insulator with nickel or titanium metal diaphragms and back plates and quartz insulation are extremely stable, and this construction is used for measurement microphones. Recording microphones more often use plastic diaphragms coated with a conductor such as gold. These too may be quite stable. On the other hand, capacitor microphones depend vitally on the quality of insulation. Anything that reduces the insulation can lead to noise or failure. For instance, condensing humidity between the diaphragm and back plate reduces the insulation greatly and causes the microphones to become noisy, increasing hiss, popping, or producing no output at all. Conditions leading to microphone failure are quite possible in the environment of production sound recording, where microphones may be exposed to weather or fog machines on stages. The advanced state of design of such microphones is indicated by the fact that more trouble does not occur. Capacitor microphones can sometimes be restored to their original condition by careful warming if humidity was the cause of their malfunction.

> Electrostatic microphones have been used in arctic and jungle conditions. Here their reliability may be improved by several methods. First, they must be kept dry, and storing them when not in use in air tight containers with desiccant can help. Second, they should not undergo thermal shock, that is, rapid temperature change, since that can lead to condensing humidity. In this way the microphones share a common problem with rotating head tape machines, such as video and DAT machines.

Overall, the principle of the capacitor microphone is applied to what are typically the highest grade microphones, because this principle works with the smallest moving mass and the highest efficiency of conversion from sound to electrical energy, but at a cost that compares with less-rugged electrodynamic mikes, and with a need for power.

Electrostatic mikes may be built as pressure or as pressure-gradient transducers in multiple polar patterns. Some of the pressure-gradient types work by using dual back-to-back diaphragms, while others employ acoustical phase-shift networks behind the diaphragm to accept and delay sound from the rear to produce cardioid, super- and hyper-cardioid, subcardioid, or interference tube designs. Some dual-diaphragm designs claim better signal-to-noise ratios than single-diaphragm designs.

Microphone types by directivity (polar pattern)

Throughout the discussion of the microphone types, pressure and pressure-gradient, and methods of transduction, we have seen that various microphone constructions lead to the following polar patterns:

- Omnidirectional

- Subcardioid (limaçon)

- Cardioid

- Supercardioid

- Hypercardioid

- Club shaped (interference tube or shotgun)

This list is ordered from the most reverberant-field sensitive to the least sensitive when the mikes are compared at equal distances from a sound source at which they are aimed. All other things being equal, the cost of a microphone having wide, flat, and smooth on- and off-axis responses and wide dynamic range generally increases in several steps as one goes down the list, because the conventional pressure microphone is the simplest and the interference tube the most complex of the constructions, with the others being about equal in complexity. Thus, at equal price an omnidirectional pressure mike may well be better than a superficially similar hypercardioid.

Tracks 21 and 22 of the CD feature a "walk around" demonstration of microphones having various polar patterns.

The way that users can typically distinguish

a directional microphone from a non-directional mike is that the directional mike will have more than one primary entrance for sound, whereas a non-directional mike will have only one entrance (neglecting the tiny pressure-equalizing vent).

The axis of a microphone is usually along its length, so the barrel of the microphone is designed to be aimed at the source. These are called *end-address microphones*. There are some microphones, however, that are addressed from the side, especially dual-diaphragm capacitor microphones, often with switchable directivity. They may be distinguished by having a solid end cap or by the shape of the grille, and are called *side-address microphones* or *vertical mikes*. Since some of these mikes are otherwise cylindrical, it is difficult to know which side is the front; thus, they usually have a red dot or a symbol of their directivity on the front side of the mike to indicate the side to be aimed at the source.

Microphone specifications
Sensitivity

Sensitivity is the ratio of conversion of sound pressure level to electrical voltage or power. There are unfortunately a number of ways to rate microphone sensitivity, so it is often difficult to compare one microphone to another numerically without going through various mathematical conversions. Emerging as the most popular way is to rate sensitivity as the electrical voltage produced when the microphone is exposed to a reference sound pressure level of 94 dB at 1 kHz. The rating units are "millivolts per Pascal" because the sound pressure level corresponding to 1 Pascal is 94 dB (re 20 µPa). On this scale, an insensitive ribbon microphone measures 1 mV/Pa and a high-output electrostatic type 60 mV/Pa.

When comparing two microphones by listening, it is important to adjust out sensitivity differences by trimming level controls in the chain, because on a/b tests, the louder device, even if only $1/2$ dB louder, will sound "better." This places a premium on high sensitivity, which may be misapplied, since an adjustment of level can remove the effect of

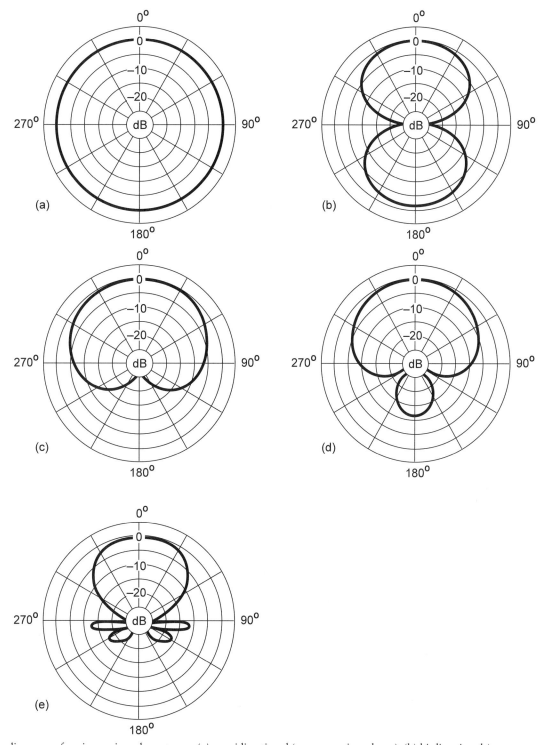

Fig. 4.8 Polar diagrams of various microphone types: (a) omnidirectional (pressure microphone), (b) bi-directional (pressure-gradient microphone), (c) cardioid, (d) hypercardioid, (e) interference tube. All are shown at only one, upper mid-range frequency.

mike-sensitivity differences. What is important is the dynamic-range capability of the microphone and preamplifier combination, as compared with the volume range of the sound source: Can the volume range of the source be "fit" into the dynamic range of the microphone/preamplifier combination? More information on this important topic is presented later in this chapter and the next.

Frequency response

Frequency response is an exceedingly important microphone specification, but it is difficult to tell microphones apart from their data sheet frequency response because the methods used are too variable, and the spec sheets too idealized, to make them comparable across manufacturers. Also, frequency response varies with angle of incidence for direct sound fields, and also differs between direct and diffuse sound fields, making a single curve inadequate to tell the whole story.

> For example, comparing an omnidirectional mike with a cardioid and a hypercardioid from the same microphone series, having practically the same axial response, results in hearing the sound become "harder" when switching from the omni through the cardioid to the hypercardioid. This is caused by the differences in diffuse-field responses, which change the timbre of the reverberation.

> The microphones best characterized for frequency response are measurement microphones, for which a great deal of data is available, including on- and off-axis frequency response, changes due to accessories, etc.

> Because frequency response is dependent on distance from the microphone for all types that include a pressure-gradient component, manufacturers face a choice. They can either make mike response flat at a distance and allow the bass to be exaggerated close up, or they can make the bass rolled off at a distance with flatter frequency response closer. Unfortunately, manufacturers often neglect to supply enough information for users to know what distance would be optimal. It is useful information, even though there are other factors when considering mike placement.

Polar pattern and its uniformity with frequency

The polar pattern is usually portrayed as a set of curves for various frequencies plotted on polar graph paper. An alternative method of display is to make a series of frequency-response curves at various angles. Generally it is desirable to maintain the same polar pattern versus frequency insofar as possible.

On the other hand, the "defect" of narrowing directivity with frequency is sometimes useful in orchestral recording, with mikes spaced at a distance from the players. In this case, the narrowing directivity and rising on-axis response with respect to frequency makes for greater "clarity."

Signal-to-noise ratio

The signal-to-noise ratio measures the difference between the sensitivity of the microphone and the noise floor in deciBels. Alternatively the noise floor of the microphone can be given as the equivalent sound pressure level of the noise. Modern large-diaphragm microphones can have a noise floor ≤ 10 dB SPL, A weighted, while $1/_2$ in. mikes are somewhat noisier.

> Microphone noise measurements are usually weighted for audible effect by using a frequency-response curve that emphasizes the frequencies where human hearing is most sensitive. One frequently used weighting curve is called *A weighting*, and another, producing higher numbers for the same noise, is *CCIR weighting*.

Maximum undistorted sound pressure level

The maximum equivalent sound pressure level that a microphone can produce without gross distortion grows increasingly important as the source becomes closer and louder. It is essential for the microphone to remain undistorted, since any distortion occurring in the microphone or microphone preamplifier will not be able to be reduced in subsequent processing.

> The maximum undistorted output level may vary with frequency, usually with less output capability at the highest frequencies, and sometimes at low frequency. It is usually specified at only one frequency though, in the midrange.

Dynamic range

The dynamic range of a microphone is the "distance" in deciBels from the equivalent noise level to the maximum undistorted SPL. In high-quality microphones this amount may range to over 130 dB, a ratio of more than 3,000,000:1. This causes one of the largest problems in recording because there are few if any microphone preamplifiers that can handle this full range. The job of the recordist is to fit this "gallon" of material (the microphone output), first into a "quart" jar (the preamplifier input), and then into possibly an even smaller "pint" jar (the recording medium).

The factor that ameliorates problems in this area is that the volume range of most practical situations, from the loudest sound to be recorded to the background noise level of the space, rarely approaches 130 dB. There are two methods to bring the large microphone dynamic range to within the capability of the microphone preamplifier:

- The variable gain microphone preamplifier, adjusted by the user for prevailing conditions.

- Using attenuating "pads" inserted between the microphone and its preamplifier.

Probably no area of recording deserves more attention than this one, since recording a wide dynamic range undistortedly and without audible recording noise will boost the reputation of the recordist more than anything else. *Meet Joe Black* had exceptionally good production sound recording, since among other things the shouts of Anthony Hopkins in confronting the devil, played by Brad Pitt, remained remarkably undistorted.

Susceptibility to wind noise

This rarely specified feature of microphones can make or break a production sound recording, because the low-frequency noise made by wind "rattling" the diaphragm directly can pollute the recording so badly that it cannot be repaired in post production. This is not simply wind noise, but rather an added interaction between wind and the microphone. In general, pressure-gradient microphones are more susceptible to wind than are pressure mikes and require a larger volume captured inside a turbulence-free zone, and thus a larger windscreen, for equal performance.

Simple foam windscreen are suitable for omnidirectional pressure mikes used indoors, while basket-type windscreens, having an internal volume free from materials, are better for all directional types.

Susceptibility to pop noise

Associated with wind noise is the noise that many unprotected mikes make when a performer is working near the microphone and his or her plosive "p"-like sounds pop the diaphragm. Again, this is an intolerable noise that is impossible to remove subsequently and must be prevented from being recorded in the first place. Some mike types are specifically designed for this use, with built-in *pop filters*, that is, mesh screens that reduce the air velocity while passing sound. External pop screens are also available as an accessory.

You can easily feel the puff of wind that plosives make by baring your arm and holding it up vertically with your hand in front of your face. Say "p" and "t" and you will feel this effect.

Susceptibility to magnetic hum fields

Electrodynamic mikes, including ribbon mikes, are subject to the direct pickup of magnetic hum fields. Often associated with AC wiring such as for lights, these hum fields can be reduced by moving the microphone away from the source, and by orientation with respect to the source. Of course, the mike cabling may also pick up hum as described in Chapter 3.

Impedance

The impedance system employed today in a microphone-to-microphone-preamplifier interface is called the "bridging" system. The source impedance of the microphone is low, typically 10 to 200 Ω, and the input impedance is relatively high, such as 3 kΩ. This means that virtually all of the voltage available from the microphone is available at the input to the preamplifier. Among other advantages, the bridging system—compared to the older "matching" impedance system—permits mike *splitters* so that one microphone can feed more than one microphone input in cases where this is necessary.

Some years ago, a clear distinction was made between professional microphones, having a low output source impedance and using balanced lines, and consumer microphones, which used higher impedances and unbalanced lines. Today there are few microphones sold that are not low impedance.

Power requirements

Electrodynamic microphones require no power source, because they are electric generators in and of themselves. This is a reason to prefer electrodynamic types in some instances. For example, having an electrodynamic microphone along on a recording expedition far from civilization would be a good idea when the batteries used to supply electrostatic microphones may be in short supply.

Electrostatic microphones are specified according to their type of powering discussed under electrostatic microphones above. Power requirements are given in terms of current necessary to supply the microphone at its rated voltage, and may be used to determine battery life.

Microphone accessories

Pads

An actor screaming, measured at 1 foot, can produce more than 135 dB SPL, a very high level. Therefore, a means must be provided to accommodate such levels if distortion is to be avoided, and that is to use *pads*.

Some electrostatic microphones offer a built-in pre-electronics microphone pad that may be operated by a switch on the microphone body. For other microphones pre-electronics pads are available as accessories, in which case they are inserted between the capsule and the electronics, are usually available in values of 10 and 20 dB, and may be stacked (although the result will be less than 30 dB attenuation). For both of these types, the maximum undistorted sound pressure level is increased by the amount of the pad, but the equivalent noise level is also increased, so the dynamic range is not improved but the capability of handling high sound pressure levels is. These pads are most often used for sound-effects recording, as well as in close miking of musical instruments, and shouting performers.

There are also pads available for insertion "in line," that is, for insertion into the microphone cable. While not protecting against electronic overload in the microphone electronics itself, they may protect from overload in the microphone preamplifier, which is discussed in Chapter 5. Some of these types will affect the power supplied to the microphone, so may not be used for phantom or T-powered mikes.

Shock and vibration mounts

Protecting the microphone diaphragm and its suspension from direct exposure to shock and vibration is the job of special mounts that are either incorporated in the body of the microphone, offered as an external accessory, or both. Noise may be induced in microphones by shock or vibration through a direct mechanical path from the outside to the diaphragm. This noise typically takes the form of large amounts of low-frequency noise, such large amounts that subsequent treatment in post production is likely not able to make the sound usable. An example is using a lectern microphone without an internal or external shock mount and having a boisterous lecturer pound on the podium for emphasis. Not only do we hear the through-the-air sound of hitting the podium, but the sound is far worse because of the direct conduction of shock into the microphone pickup.

External shock mounts work by a mass-and-spring isolation system similar to a spring with a weight hung on it. If we wiggle the top of the spring quickly, the weight stands still; we are above the frequency of the mass-spring resonance, where inputs to the system are filtered out by the time they reach the weight. This is the frequency region in which shock mounts work: they are the spring, and the microphone is the mass.

> Conversely, if we move the spring slowly, the mass follows slowly too, but this condition is not a problem as it induces no noise in the microphone.

It is very important once microphones are suspended within the shock-mount cradle that the effect of the shock mounting not be circumvented by "short circuiting." Stretching the mike cable taut across the mount from the mike body to the attachment point will render the shock mounting ineffective. The cable must be adequately limp and formed into a loop to prevent shock from being conducted across the cable to the mike body.

Mike stands

There are a huge variety of mike stands on the market, with the principal differences being in the flexibility of the positioning of the microphone. Some larger "professional" mike stands may be a detriment to good sound, because the large size (of their "professional" parts) close to the mike body reflects sound from the source back into the microphone. Conversely, small, light-weight parts can rattle in a loud sound field, and being close to the microphone, thus be heard. So small but sturdy microphone stands are to be preferred.

Mike booms

Microphone booms offer a variety of adjustments for an operator, including rotating the boom arm, rotating the mike at the end of the arm, tilting the mike, etc. Using a wide variety of means, and with substantial training, boom operators become very proficient in locating mikes in front of the actor speaking and above the top line of vision of the camera, despite actors moving, cameras moving, and switching from performer to performer. A primary requirement of such booms is the ability to move the microphone swiftly and silently to a new location.

These booms, such as the Fisher boom, are most often used on fixed sets like for sitcoms, and in other studio shooting situations.

Fishpoles

For more portable production than a mike boom allows, mike *fishpoles* are employed. Ranging from fairly simple, with little or no adjustability, to very flexible at much higher cost, fishpoles are commonly used on motion picture and television field production. Again, the primary issue in their design is whether or not they can move swiftly and silently into the position demanded by the shot. Another major issue is weight because, unlike the larger sized mike booms, which offer counterweights and a central hinge point mounted to a dolly, fishpoles are intended to be held up for the length of a take

by the boom operator. Of course, the microphone in use, since it is at the end of the arm, contributes significantly to the total weight.

Fig. 4.9 An unusual articulated fishpole, a K-Tek model. Courtesy m.klemme technology corporation.

Windscreens

Windscreens vary depending on whether they are for use on pressure or pressure-gradient microphones, whether they are to be used indoors as a pop filter, out of doors to tame a gale, etc. Some rules of thumb are as follows:

- Windscreening is needed even in quiet shooting stage settings because just panning the microphone may create enough wind noise across the diaphragm to rattle it. A foam windscreen may suffice for this application because the level of "wind" is limited to mike motion.

- Windscreening is always needed on podium and other microphones placed close to lecturers that would otherwise be subject to "pop" noise, unless such a feature is built into the mike and is effective (and there are not very many of those).

- Pressure-gradient mikes require larger windscreens, so that a volume of air having low turbulence can be created around the microphone. Generally these are woven silk or finely woven cotton stretched over a frame spaced 2 to 3 in. from the mike body. For interference-tube microphones, which are quite often used outdoors, the windscreens are called *zeppelins*, due to their cigar shape.

- When working out-of-doors under severe conditions, multiple layers of windscreening may be necessary, starting from the outside in with fuzzy materials to slow down air but allowing sound through to a woven silk windscreen. For directional mikes, though, it is important to provide a region of low turbulence around the microphone where the wind component is identical at the pickup entrances in the microphone body. For this reason, it is a bad idea to use a foam windscreen inside a stretched windscreen.

It is worth remembering that pressure microphones, although omnidirectional, are less wind susceptible, so if it is possible to get a microphone in close, it may produce better sound quality than a pressure-gradient mike at a distance, where there is wind.

Silk discs

In studio work, a disc of woven silk about 4–5 in. in diameter can be placed between the talker or singer and the microphone to shield the mike from direct breath and prevent pop noises.

Microphone technique—mono

Monaural recording is defined as single-point miking for each of one or more sound sources, with only unintentional overlap among the microphones. The recording may take place on one or more tracks of the subsequent recorder, with dual-track mono not being a contradiction in terms. For a further explanation, see the definition of stereo recording under Microphone technique—stereo.

Distance effect

Decreasing the distance between a microphone and a sound source decreases reverberation and increases direct sound. In production sound recording, and for sound-effects recording both on Foley stages and in the field, the general practice is to minimize reverberation insofar as possible. This is because it is always possible to add reverberation in post production, and practically impossible to reduce it significantly. Thus, all other things being equal, there is a desire to record a source relatively close up. Of course, in narrative filmmaking this must be tempered by the need to get the mike out of the frame.

Decreasing the distance between a microphone and a sound source also may decrease the recording of extraneous acoustical noise, depending on the direction and nature of the noise. It is often useful to aim not only the "hot" side of the microphone at the desired source, but also to aim the "null" of the polar pattern at the source of noise. Although all noise will surely not be eliminated, because the noise as well as the source has its own direct field, discrete reflections, and reverberation, and no mike "pattern" can cope with all of these, nonetheless a significant noise improvement can be gained by this technique.

Decreasing the distance increases the direct sound, and since the noise level of the microphone and microphone preamplifier is generally fixed, decreasing the distance improves the signal-to-noise ratio. Working at a great distance from a weak source will cause the recordist to "turn up the gain" and that will pull up the fixed electronic noise, so close working generally improves the signal-to-noise ratio.

If a directional microphone is being used, moving the microphone in really close will generally need to be tempered by the proximity effect of the particular microphone in use. If it is too close the bass will be significantly boosted, causing an audible timbre problem. In some cases it may even be better to change to an omnidirectional microphone moved in closer to the source instead of using a directional microphone further away, but still within the range where the proximity effect is occurring. This consideration doesn't usually apply to boom miking in production sound because of the distances typically involved, but it certainly is applicable to voice-over or narration recording, and to many kinds of effects recording.

Microphone directivity

Using a more directional microphone generally leads to recording with a higher ratio of direct- to diffuse-field sound, with the intended source emphasized and reverberation de-emphasized. This is why practically all recordings made with boom mikes use directional microphones, usually those with the highest directivity: super- or hyper-cardioid or interference tube club shape.

On the other hand, it may be impractical in a given shot to mike from the overhead boom position, and body mikes may be necessary. In this case, the required small size of the microphone favors an omnidirectional type because the space to make the microphone directional across a wide frequency range just isn't available. In this case, we rely on the fact that the microphone is much closer than would otherwise be possible to increase the ratio of direct sound to reverberation and noise.

Microphone perspective

Perspective is the matching of the sound recording to the characteristics of the picture, in particular, the match of the sound reflection and reverberation properties to what is seen. In early sound recording there was an attempt to match camera perspective, shot-by-shot, to what was seen. A wide master shot was thus more reverberant than the associated close-ups. Then, when the scene was cut together, there was a very noticeable change in the amount of reverberation, as the microphone perspective was "loosened" for the master and "tightened" for the close-up. This tended to draw attention to the sound track due to the unnatural changes at the cuts, which are not duplicated in life. Modern practice thus most often uses relatively small changes in the microphone perspective to correspond to large picture

changes and the reverberation changes are consequently kept fairly subtle—audible if you listen for them, but probably not noticeable to the average viewer who is not "tuned in" to them.

For a microphone perspective that matches the perspective of the camera, you might think that a mike over the camera would do, moving from a wide shot to a close-up just as camera lenses do. This does not work because of the cocktail-party effect; a microphone recording just does not have the same perspective as being there. In fact, the best way to cover a scene that is obviously shot in a reverberant space, such as a large marble covered interior of a museum, is to record all of it with a constant and tight perspective, and then decide in post production whether the judicious use of added reverberation for the wide shots makes sense.

Failure to match microphone perspective between production sound and recordings made on a looping or ADR stage is one of the most telltale differences that may prevent the two from sounding alike.

Another major microphone perspective issue occurs when the microphone has to be placed to one side or the other of the frame, in the case where there is not enough headroom above the frameline to the ceiling to contain the microphone. Whether this is successful or not depends on the blocking of the scene. If an actor should turn towards and then away from the microphone while speaking, they will sound as though they are on-mike when they are facing one direction and off-mike facing the other, even though both angles may be the same to the camera. This then sounds artificial as we come to understand at least subconsciously where the microphone is.

Using a boom microphone below the frame line of the camera is often undesirable. The radiation pattern of the voice, many nearby surfaces, and possibly other factors contribute to this position usually sounding not as good as overhead. It is possible for the best microphone in the world to record unacceptable sound because the microphone position is wrong, but there are times when this placement is the best available alternative, as it can still beat lavaliere microphones.

Using multiple microphones

Many practical situations require the use of more than one microphone. An actress may walk out of range of a boom mike to another part of the set, there may be many actors in the scene who must be covered equally, or there may be many sites of activity such that if a single microphone were used at a distance (e.g. matching the camera) it would result in such a loose perspective that no one area of the scene could be well heard due to the lack of binaural discrimination on the part of the microphone.

In narrative filmmaking, rehearsal makes practical the use of multiple microphones, combined with judicious mixing, for recording to one or more tracks to cover these situations. When the sound from the various microphones is combined, however, whether in the production sound mixer before the original recording or even when separate edited tracks from the various microphones are ultimately combined in post production mixing, several effects may occur that could be unexpected and cause difficulty:

- If one microphone should happen to have been wired *out of phase* (with the two balanced leads reversed) and the pickup of the two microphones overlaps, there will be partial cancellation, particularly in the bass, of the sound.

- Even in cases where the microphones are wired properly, if the source is not precisely centered between two microphones with overlapping pickup, then the sound will arrive at one microphone before the other. In this case, when the electrical output of the microphones is summed there will be constructive and destructive interference effects, leading alternately to peaks and dips in the frequency response of the sum. This may sound as though the source is being recorded in a barrel.

In the case of redundant podium microphones, these effects are reduced by placing the two mikes in use very close to one another, thereby reducing the time of arrival differences between the mikes, even for a performer who moves around. The worst situation possible would be a pair of symmetrically spaced podium mikes wired out of phase with the performer precisely centered between them. The effect will be nearly complete cancellation in the bass, and thin and barrel-like sound above the bass frequencies.

Following are some guidelines to minimize the effects of multiple microphones when the outcome is to be reduced to a single channel, as is usually the case:

- Check that absolutely every microphone and cable in the recording system is wired in phase (just inserting a cable wired backwards, with pins 2 and 3 of an XLR cable interchanged, will change the polarity, commonly called *phase*).

- Choose directional microphones and minimize overlap in their coverage.

When multiple microphones are in use, it is important to do everything possible to match the frequency response of each of the mikes, so that the timbre remains relatively constant throughout a shot and scene. Using mixed microphone types may lead to identifying a different timbre from an actress as she moves from mike to mike, and thus give away the secret that multiple mikes were in use. Even with perfectly matched microphones, as we have seen before, there may be large differences in response in a room due to different angles to the voice, and standing waves and their position relative to the microphones.

Also, using matched microphones may not produce matched sound because the relative position may favor one type over another. For example, if a flat-response pressure mike positioned on a boundary were mixed with a flat-response overhead-boom hypercardioid mike, we could well achieve a better timbre match than if we forced one or the other mike into an "unnatural" role. That is, if we use two matched hypercardioids, one on a boundary and one on a boom, we are less likely to achieve a match than if one location or the other is covered by a microphone type suitable for that specific location.

An example of the use of two microphones occurs in *Field of Dreams*. Near the beginning of the movie, Kevin Costner comes into the house. At first we hear him off mike and reverberant, but as he approaches a doorway and wipes his hands on a towel off screen, we hear him come "on mike." Clearly there was a planted microphone behind the doorway. Then he enters the kitchen, coming closer to camera, but gets more reverberant as he comes onto the kitchen boom microphone, a reversal of the normal order where coming closer should sound less reverberant.

Choice of microphone frequency response

Many microphones are made with a deliberately nonflat frequency response for a variety of reasons, which have some very specific rationalizations:

- All directional mikes suffer from the proximity effect. The microphone designer chooses the distance at which the microphone will be flattest. Generally they are rolled off in the bass when used at a distance, and the proximity effect boosts the bass as the microphone is brought closer to the source. Used at a distance, as on a boom, there is a net low frequency roll off. This rolloff may well be desirable because it reduces low-frequency room and boom noises.

- Also, in most rooms the reverberation time is longer at low frequencies than at middle and high frequencies. It is thought that longer reverberation time at low frequencies may lead to an impression of exaggerated bass in recording when pressure microphones are used, so the use of pressure-gradient types with their low-frequency rolloff at a distance helps to compensate for this impression.

- High-frequency boost is built into shotgun microphones to overcome anticipated high-frequency air absorption when working at a distance from the source, and to deliver a greater sense of

intimacy with a distant source than a flat microphone. A typical amount is +4 dB at 10 kHz.

- Mid-range boost is built into many vocal microphones to increase the "presence" frequency region and to ensure that the outcome is intelligible, despite possible bandwidth and frequency-response limitations later in the chain. Recordings from such microphones tend to cut through other sonic clutter, but at the expense of deviating considerably from the timbre of the source.

Although we generally wish to preserve source timbre and thus desire a flat frequency response, the above-mentioned considerations can cause deviations from such thinking. In general, the microphones that are the most popular for production and sound-effects recording have a wide and smooth frequency response, although they are not necessarily flat. They also have generally uniform polar patterns with frequency such that off-axis sound is only attenuated, not colored, by frequency-response anomalies.

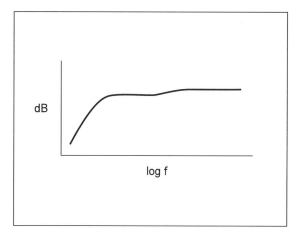

Fig. 4.10 A useful frequency response may not be flat. This shape of response helps control boom noise and increasing noise and reverberation time as frequency goes down, and has a high-frequency boost so that it can be used at a distance and still produce a high amount of presence.

In music recording, microphones are chosen for their frequency response more than any other single factor. This does not mean, however, that one would always choose the flattest mike as the one that necessarily best preserves the source timbre, because representing the source best from a single pickup point is a complex trade-off, as described in Chapter 1. Most practical sources have complex output directivity, and choosing and placing the microphone is an aesthetic choice designed to best represent that source in all its actual complexity.

> Music recording also suffers from a lack of standardization of the monitoring experience. By moving from studio to studio and playing the same source, one finds very great differences in the octave-to-octave balance of the monitoring system. Thus, it is not surprising that competent users make different microphone decisions in different studios.

Typical monaural recording situations
Production sound

There is a preference expressed in Chapter 1 for boom[7] mike recordings over other types, because the radiation pattern of the voice is such that "clearer" sound is achieved for recordings made from overhead, although positioning the microphone straight ahead is also used successfully in narration situations. It is below the plane of the head where problems begin, due to direct radiation by the chest, lack of higher frequencies directed downwards, and more sound reflecting objects being closer, especially the floor.

On the boom the preference is for quite directional mikes, with the super- or hyper-cardioid and shotgun types preferred by most practitioners. Due to the smoother off-axis response, the super- or hyper-cardioid is preferred to the shotgun in situations where the off-axis sound matters, but the shotgun has the longer "reach" (the most rejection of reverberation at the same distance as other types).

"Booming" is such an important job that a boom operator can make or break a recording, even though he or she is subordinate to the production sound mixer in the hierarchy. For narrative filmmaking, the boom operator learns the scene and positions the micro-

7. Equivalently, a fishpole may substitute for a boom.

phone from moment-to-moment to best effect. This may include tracking with the actors, panning the boom arm between actors, rotating the microphone at the end of the boom arm, etc. The operator learns the script extremely well, as well as anyone on the set. Rehearsals are essential. Cinematographer Haskell Wexler says "I can't light a set; let me see the rehearsal," because it is the actors he is lighting, not the set. Likewise the boom operator needs rehearsal to optimize the mic location through the course of a scene. The boom operator is trained to listen in headphones just as much as the production sound mixer, and to affect the position of the microphone from what he or she hears.

Besides the position for optimum recording, the boom operator has two other duties: keeping the mic. out of the shot, and keeping boom shadows from falling on the set where they might be photographed.

For documentary filmmaking, boom operation becomes even more difficult, since rehearsal is often forbidden by circumstance. In this case, a sixth sense is necessary to anticipate what may happen among subjects in a scene. The boom operator must be very alert to what the camera operator is doing too, and anticipate where the next camera move may be. A primary factor in the ability to do these tasks is listening carefully to what the subjects are saying, while still managing to get all the technical details right. This includes, usually above all, keeping the microphone out of the shot, and from casting shadows visible to the camera, just as in narrative filmmaking.

If it is impossible to use a boom due to set conditions, such as an extreme wide shot with the camera at a low angle, then the next resort is to plant microphones. By employing the boundary-layer principle, planting omni-directional pressure microphones on the set may be quite useful. They should generally be flush mounted on large set surfaces to achieve the boundary-layer effect, although, of course, this principle of positioning has to be traded off against getting the microphone in close to the source. Problems include planting the microphone on set pieces that might be handled by the actors and, thus, picking up handling noise directly (the kitchen counter in *Friends* would be a poor choice).

Directional microphones can also be used up against a barrier, where they will exhibit a sort of "folding over" of their polar pattern, with directional preference that could be an advantage over an omnidirectional type.

A large potential problem exists with microphones that must be nearby surfaces but cannot be made nearly integral to those surfaces. The problem lies with the strong potential reflection off the surface, which arrives slightly later at the microphone than the direct sound. This gives rise to constructive and destructive interference, which result in a regular series of peaks and dips in the frequency response that can be quite audible. All in all, microphones prefer either a lot of "air" around them, so that nearby reflections are minimized, or should be made an integral part of the surfaces, as in the boundary-layer method. If a boom microphone needs to be placed near a ceiling due to low ceiling height on a location set, the reflection off the ceiling may be ameliorated by taping an area of absorbing material to the region of the ceiiing above where the microphone has to work. Thicker material covering more area will be more effective than thin material covering a small area.

The final resort is to use body microphones planted on the performers, and either wired to the production sound mixer or used with wireless transmitters. This is a last resort because although the performer should be able to be heard, except in the case of the highest background noise levels, there is nothing natural whatsoever about the perspective reproduced by this arrangement. That is, if the performer turns away from the camera, his or her voice will not change quality in a way that we associate with people turning away from us and the sound will be very disembodied from the picture. Other problems with this approach include:

- The necessity of burying the microphone under layers of clothes to hide it, and thereby muffling the sound quality.

- Clothing noise as clothes in the vicinity of the microphone rub on it or its cable as the performer moves.

- Performer's movements could go so far as to hit the chest, causing tremendous contact noise around the microphone (this happens more often than planned, sometimes during a "take" that was not rehearsed with the breast beating).

- Problems with radio frequency transmission including multi-path dropouts (such as driving around a city with an FM radio on in a car, dropouts occurring when the various direct and reflected paths of the signal cancel at the receiver), which are at least partially overcome in more expensive equipment by redundant reception from spaced antennas (called *diversity reception*).

While this discussion makes the case against the wireless microphone, many real-life television series depend on wireless microphones to limit the size of the crew and to get usable sound from unscripted situations. It must be said here that the niceties of matching perspective between camera and sound to ensure verisimilitude give way to practical conditions of just getting any usable "clear" sound under these conditions, and sometimes the wireless microphone is the best way to do this.

Production shooting and microphone technique

Typically a scene will be shot from several angles to offer the post production editor a range of choices in developing the scene. In conventional film-style production, this is accomplished with multiple *setups*, for example, a master shot, a two-shot, and close-ups, all shot separately by having the actors repeat the scene over and over. The setups may be shot over a period of hours, as the lighting is adjusted for each new camera angle. The temptation in sound is to match the camera perspective for each new shot. While this may even make great-sounding dailies (on which the quality of production sound work is judged), later on in post production it may become clear that all is not well, because intercutting may not be as smooth as desired.

Let us say that you are the production sound recordist for a scene from the latest LA cop show. The duty officers are resting on their motorcycles overlooking a southern California freeway, alert for cars making too-rapid lane changes. The scene will be covered by one master and two close-ups, observing the correct screen direction and not "crossing the line."[8] If the scene is recorded simple-mindedly, the microphone will face the two actors in the master shot, and each of them in turn in their close-ups. In order to be able to cut between them, they need to be looking at each other, rather than having both actors look at the freeway. So conventional wisdom is to have one looking towards the freeway and the other towards the first actor, both in the master and again in the close-ups. Also, the camera must move to different angles with respect to the actors for the three shots, because that is a part of the "grammar" of filmmaking, the way that we expect cuts to be made.

In the master, the microphone and camera "see" the two men on motorcycles with the freeway in the background. It is important that the freeway be seen in the wide shot because that establishes where they are, what they are doing, and, from our point of view, why there is so much background noise. A certain ratio is established between the sound level of the men and of the freeway. In the close-ups, we have to shoot first looking one way, say, away from the freeway, and then looking the other, that is looking towards it. *If the microphone literally follows what the camera sees, there will be lots of freeway noise in the close-up pointing towards the freeway, and much less in the shot pointing away.* Although the production sound recordist might get away with this at

dailies, when the editor puts the scene together the failing will be obvious: Even if the voices of the actors match between the master and close-up, the varying background noise of the freeway from one shot to another will cause huge continuity problems, probably requiring a looping session, and the unhappy producer will wind up paying for the actors and director to come into an ADR stage to replace their dialog, or else live with an obvious problem.

So a primary rule for production sound recording is: Get the big picture. The cleanest dialogue for each of the three shots, combined with more or less constant sound effects of the freeway, will probably make for the most convincing scene.

The problem with recording this scene is that there are two problems being faced simultaneously: microphone perspective and matching the background sound from shot to shot. The microphone perspective is most affected by the distance from the microphone to the actors and is secondarily affected by the angle of the microphone to the performer. The background sound, in this instance, is most affected by the angle of the microphone to the freeway. Since we must aim the microphone at the actors, the best way to mike this scene is to use the overhead boom microphone, keeping the same angle to the freeway in each shot, "panning" the microphone boom arm to cover each actor rather than rotating the mike at the end of the boom, since that would change the angle with respect to the freeway and consequently the background noise.

In another case, let us say that the camera is in an anteroom off a concert hall where an orchestra is rehearsing. Important action is to take place within the hall, and then the action moves to the foreground space. What is called for is an *audio zoom*. We want to hear distinctly what the performers are saying when they are in the background, but we also want to know they are in a hall; conversely, we wish to hear the covert dialog in the foreground as a stage whisper (i.e, a voice tactic that can be heard throughout a

---

8. A line, perpendicular to the camera in the master shot, that crossing with the camera causes editorial problems, such as actors looking in the wrong direction.

theater but that has the timbre of a whisper). There are at least two ways to proceed.

One would be to use either a boom or a planted microphone for the background activity in the hall, and a separate boom for the foreground in the anteroom, judiciously (i.e., sneakily so that it is unnoticeable) crossfading from one microphone setup to the other. The mike in the hall can be placed to record appropriate reverberation, or a second "reverb" mike can be used such that by adjusting the relative level of the "direct" mike and the reverb mike a proper balance can be struck.

> One way to mike the reverberant-field component of the sound field, while picking up practically no direct sound, is to use a directional microphone for the reverb mike, with its null pointed towards the source of the direct sound. Thus the back side of a cardioid, or the side of a figure-eight pattern mike, can be used. One problem with this technique is that the cancellation of the direct sound is often highly variable with respect to frequency, so you may wind up hearing low bass and high treble of the direct sound in the reverberant-field mike. Experimentation with different microphones is definitely needed for this to work, but it is potentially a fine technique.

Another way to approach this same scene is to just use a radio mike on the performer who must move, and leave the changes in perspective and reverberation to post production mixing. One difficulty with this is that the dailies will sound a long way from the final product, yet by proceeding this way it is known that high-quality direct sound is available for the scene. The biggest problem with this approach is the lack of natural change when the actor turns his or her head; for example, when turning around and facing away from the camera the microphone perspective stays the same, but the picture perspective changes.

There are two other sources besides sync sound for dialogue lines: wild lines and ADR. Wild lines are typically recorded on the set, perhaps at the end of the day of shooting, or sometimes along with the scenes being shot. They are recorded in the same acoustic setting, but likely with the mi-

crophone closer and with more noise control. For instance, if wind machines are in use on a shot, the sound is likely to be unusable. Killing the wind machine and having the actor speak the lines the same way as in the camera shot may prevent the need for a subsequent ADR session.

Narration or voice-over

Narration or voice-over recording usually occurs in a purpose-built studio offering low reverberation time and background noise, and relative freedom from room standing-wave effects. Given these acoustic characteristics, the working distance to the microphone can be controlled for the flattest response (when using a pressure-gradient-sensitive mike, i.e., a directional one). Direct-conducted vibration can be eliminated with a shock mount, and by isolating the microphone mounting from anything the performers might touch. Breath noise can be eliminated with a windscreen and/or a silk disc.

One common source of a problem in narration recording is the script holder. If it is extensive and massive, it will reflect sound well and the microphone will receive first the direct sound and then a strong reflection off the surface, causing constructive and destructive interference. It is better to use a fold-up music stand and loose script pages to minimize the reflection off these surfaces.

The choice of the best microphone will often depend on the precise interaction between an individual voice and the range of microphones at hand. I have tried different types with one voice and have found the best mike for that voice, only to find it not good with another voice, for which a different choice is needed. Thus, the absolute quality of the microphones is not in question, but rather the "match" between the timbre of the voice and the response details of the microphone that matters. If this were not the case, one microphone type would have come to dominate all recording, probably the flattest one. In order to be able to make such judgments, though, one first must know with great certainty what the conditions of monitoring are, which are taken up in Chapter 11.

Once a voice and microphone are chosen, then details of the working distance can be managed. Given the environment already specified, there is little trade-off if the microphone is used at 1 or 2 ft., except for the proximity effect varying the response. Another factor is whether the performer is seated or standing, with some attendant changes in voice due to the shape of the chest cavity in these states.

Microphone placement for narration recording is usually best straight in front, or in front and above the horizontal plane, rather than below a horizontal plane that includes the head. This is due to the radiation pattern of the voice, which is generally "chesty" sounding below the horizontal plane.

ADR stage recording

Automated Dialog Replacement (ADR) or *looping* stages have many of the same considerations as narration recording studios, with several added requirements. The first is that the reverberation time, which may be almost arbitrarily short in a narration setting, cannot be so short in an ADR stage. Rooms that are near anechoic are difficult for actors to work in, because they do not hear enough energy coming back from the room and tend, as a result, to force or stress their voices, which shows up as timbre change. In narration and some ADR recording, it is commonplace for the performers to wear headphones so that they can get back all the level desirable by simply turning up the headphones (but watch out: loud headphones can leak sound, which gets to the microphone, changing the source timbre by effectively adding a reflection at the time of the spacing of the headphones and microphone; in the worst possible case, this could potentially even lead to acoustic feedback, for which the British offer the more colorful term, *howl round*).

The upper limit on reverberation time is set by the consideration that we do not wish to impose audible reverberation on the recording at all and would prefer a perfectly "dead" recording, which we could then liven up to taste in post production. A typical compromise reverberation time is 0.4 sec-

onds for reasonable room sizes, flat with frequency, and containing little in the way of discrete reflections, especially those aimed at the microphone. This combined with a low background noise level will make for adequate conditions for ADR stages.

Otherwise, similar conditions exist as for narration recording, except that ADR recording may deliberately use greater microphone distance from the actor to try to match perspective with the production sound recording. Microphones on booms are usually used, and sometimes more than one at varying distances from the actor recorded to different channels of a medium to provide several perspective choices later on in post production.

Another factor that may differ from narration recording is the dynamic range of the actor. An actor may scream or whisper, and the recordist should be prepared with pads and low-noise preamplification to accommodate the full range of a performance.

A performance disadvantage of ADR recording is that the actor faces a dead room with little acoustic response, compared to what is happening on screen. In these circumstances it is commonplace for actors to "underplay" their performance, only to be found later as too low in energy to "read" through the rest of the sound. Hearing Harrison Ford's ADR only in the rolling boulder scene from *Raiders of the Lost Ark* illustrates this. His performance seems "over the top," but he and Steven Spielberg, the director, know that in the final mix there are going to be many more sound elements present that would bury a subtle performance.

There are basically no post production sound techniques that can change the stress in an actor's voice. Post production can enhance intelligibility and smooth out the level variations, and so forth, but no technical process available can change the underlying performance.

Excessive "lip smack" in ADR and narration recordings can sometimes be ameliorated by the actor eating an apple, which seems to clear up speech.

The ADR stage equipment shuttles the picture according to instructions given it, usually by an assistant picture editor, prepares for recording a segment (automatically goes into and out of record), and alerts the actor to the start of the line with three beeps, with the start of the performance expected where the fourth beep would go.

Foley stage recording

Recording on a Foley stage bears a lot of resemblance to ADR stage recording, but with some added considerations. While actors may have a wide dynamic range, Foley recordings usually do have. Foley sound effects, by their nature, may include everything from a quiet clothes rustle to gunshots. Thus, there is a premium placed on all factors that affect the dynamic range, including the background noise of the room, microphone and preamplifier noise, and microphone and preamplifier headroom.

Second, the reverberation time considerations of the conventional ADR stage are relaxed because there is no need to support actors speaking and any added reverberation is generally undesirable, as it is preferable to add reverberation in mixing. Thus, Foley stages are usually very low reverberation time spaces, although at least one studio prefers some reverberation in its recordings so that none needs to be added in mixing. The problem with this is that all the Foley recordings then take on the sense that they are in the same space, when in fact it is better to match the scene.

The lowest noise level microphones may be those with the largest diaphragms, all other things being equal. Although large-diaphragm microphones are not generally associated with the flattest response on axis, and certainly with less uniform control over directionality with frequency than smaller types, Foley stages are a place where the trade-off in favor of low noise will often be made for two reasons:

- Capturing the exact timbre of the source is not as important in sound-effects recording as capturing the much more familiar sound of a voice. Voice and

music timbre are of supreme importance due to our everyday familiarity with them, with sound-effects timbre running well behind these in importance.

- There is just not much off-axis sound for many Foley stage sources. Remember how very dead the stages are, making the off-axis response of the microphone unimportant.

Given these considerations, a microphone such as the Neumann TLM-103 becomes valuable. A large-diaphragm microphone, it has a very large dynamic range, from a noise floor corresponding to 7 dB SPL A weighted to 138 dB SPL headroom.

Typical problems in original recordings

There are some problems that are frequently heard and that can be avoided with some care. These are often audible on television news shows, due to their lack of post production time; somewhat less noticeable on made-for-television productions, as the worst problems are probably eliminated in post production; and hardly audible at all in the best theatrical films, in which if the sound is not good, there has been the time and money available to loop the scene. In any of these productions, though, these situations do cause problems; if not audible problems, then ones associated with spending time and money to fix them. Following are some typical problems:

- Use of lavaliere microphones on an agitated subject who is moving around. The worst example seen was the morning news show that put a lavaliere microphone on a new mother holding her baby, who of course turned to her mother, spotted the shiny microphone, and took it for a toy to play with, causing loud noises.

- News stories reported by on-the-scene reporters in which the "stand-up" part, the on-camera narration, is miked with a lavaliere mike, but the voice-over is miked with a hand-held microphone. As soon as the editor cuts to the voice-over, the sound is clearer due to the microphone quality and location when compared with the lavaliere.

- Teamed news reporters sitting side by side, but with their microphones wired out-of-phase. When the two mikes are live, the bass is attenuated so that the sound is thin and low in level, but as soon as one microphone is faded out, the remaining mike sounds much better. This occurs because at low frequencies the microphones are close together compared with the wavelength of sound, so wiring them out of phase and adding the two together in the mix will cause bass cancellation.

- Low-frequency noise from moving the microphone or wind, which can be limited or eliminated by the choice of microphone, shock mounting, wind screening, and filtering, defined in Chapter 10.

- Simply too much noise and/or reverberation in the environment for good recording. Every location scouting session should include a sound person. It is useful to bring along a sound pressure level meter to show people just how loud the sound is. Remember, they are using binaural discrimination when standing under the freeway listening to you, but the microphone lacks this ability. Sometimes pointing at a sound level meter that shows levels around those of speech can set the question to rest. "But it looks just right" doesn't make it right for shooting. There are far too many examples of shooting where the background looks great, but you have to remind directors and location scouts that sound cannot "pan off" a noise source like the camera can pan off an unsuitable object.

Microphone technique of singers

Watch a good vocalist who has a lot of experience with microphones and you will notice a few techniques that he or she employs with hand-held microphones to improve the natural pickup of sound. Ella Fitzgerald was brilliant at this, although younger performers may be more used to standing in a studio with a microphone on a fixed boom in front of them.

- Sing across the end of the mike, not directly into it, to avoid popping the diaphragm. The effectiveness of this technique depends on the exact microphone and its external and internal windscreens. Some microphones may benefit, while others do not, from this technique.

- Adjust the working distance to account for the proximity effect and loudness.

- Dynamically move the microphone closer to and further away to help crescendos and diminuendos.

Multichannel production sound recording

An infrequently used technique for single-camera film production is to provide multiple microphones connected to a multitrack tape recorder. The microphones may be any combination of boom, planted, and body mikes. The utility of this type of setup is the spontaneity with which the actors can go at a scene, at least in a master. One can have performers walking and talking everywhere in the shot, and selectively "eavesdrop" on any one or more of multiple conversations going on at once. The scene is not usually tightly scripted in such cases—the actors ad lib in character. This was the process used for *Nashville*, which was a remarkable sound track for its time and offered the filmmaker a unique method of unraveling the complexity of many people in a scene at once.

The post production complexity of being confronted with not one track, usually called the "work" track, the "A" track, or the "O" track, but instead perhaps eight tracks limits the applications of this technique. Although interesting, today it would be more common to shoot such a scene over and over, emphasizing each of the participants, in turn, in the sound track.

Multitrack production sound is used extensively, however, on television sitcoms, where the ability to store the output of various microphones—boom mics, planted mics, audience mics, etc.—separately outweighs any potential post production disadvantages.

Demonstration CD

Tracks 23–29 of the CD illustrate various microphone setups on a single talker, recorded simultaneously. These include an omnidirectional measurement type, an omnidirectional recording microphone, and a bi-directional, cardioid, hypercardioid, interference tube, and lavaliere omnidirectional microphones. Each type has been adjusted to a distance that keeps reverberation more or less constant, except for the lavaliere, which is used in its normal position on the talker.

Stereophonic microphone technique

Up to this point, although multiple microphones might be in use, their purpose has been to provide coverage of the action, and the reproduction is expected to be mostly from a single channel centered on the picture. Recording could be on multiple channels of a storage medium, yet we don't say that the channels are stereophonic because the relationship among the channels has not been constructed in that way.

Using stereo produces two effects that cannot be obtained in monaural systems. The first of these is spatial localization at more than one place. We have already seen in Chapter 2 that disbursed localization of auditory objects helps to separate objects psychoacoustically. Thus, all other things being equal, in stereo a more complex sound track can be separable into its component objects by listeners. The second effect is spatiousness, the capability to reproduce diffuse sound fields such as reverberation in a manner that is spatialized, that is, not occupying a single point in space.

A monaural system produces localization, but it is all at the one point where the loudspeaker is, centered on the picture in film applications. It can also produce one dimension associated with spatiousness, the depth dimension, principally by adjusting the direct-to-reverberant sound ratio. In this way, the voice-over in *Apocalypse Now* is distinguished as a separate object from the on-screen voice of the same actor—the amount of reverberation is changed dramatically from one to the other.

Stereo, on the other hand, offers the potential to localize sound on the screen coincident with the picture of the object that is expected to be making the sound, heightening reality. In film sound, the release format standard today is typically 5.1 channels,[9] not the two channels that most people think of when they think of stereo. The 5.1 channels are:

- Three front channels coincident with the left, center, and right of the picture.

- Two surround channels, left and right, arranged around the audience seating area, sometimes supplemented with a separation into left, rear, and right components.

- A low-frequency, and thus low-bandwidth, enhancement channel (the $^1/_{10}$th of a channel).

While the original stereo experiments in the 1930s in the United States used three channels, work in the United Kingdom concentrated on two channels. At its introduction to film sound in the 1950s, stereo had three screen and one auditorium "effects" channel, but when introduced into the home, the number was reduced to two, left and right, because that is all that the geometry of the phonograph record groove could store. Thus we come to know "stereo" as two channels in widespread parlance, but in film sound we always mean a minimum of four, left, center, right, and surround, with 5.1 the current most widely practiced standard.

There are three principal methods of stereophonic recording:

- *Spaced microphones*, usually omnidirectional, spread across the source, with spacing from left to right depending on the size of the source, but never so large that a discrete echo can be formed. This method depends on time-of-arrival and level differences among the microphones.

---

9. Conventional analog optical sound releases are 4 channel, most digital optical releases are 5.1 channel or a quasi 6.1 channel format and one system offers 7.1 channels.

For two channel recordings, three microphones are often used, with the center mike's output split equally to the left and right channels, so that the center of the orchestra, say, is not "further away" in perspective than left and right parts.[10]

- *Coincident or near-coincident directional microphones*, which use the polar patterns of closely spaced microphones to distinguish among the channels. This method depends mostly on level differences between the microphones because the time differences are minimized by their close spacing. There are a number of such methods, so only those most relevant to film sound use will be described further.

- *Dummy head recording*, using microphones placed at the position of the ear canals in an anatomically correct head. This method, when heard over headphones, may be quite spectacular in spatial reproduction of sound from many directions. However, sounds that originated from center front often suffer from "in head" localization. This is the effect you hear from headphones when a voice in a recording seems centered between your two ears. Transforming dummy head recordings into recordings suitable for loudspeakers has proved to be an intractable problem, and no method for doing so has yet made dummy head recordings mainstream.

The spaced-microphone approach was used in production sound recording experimentally at the beginning of the stereo era but has dropped out of use due to editorial problems described with stereo cutting in Chapter 2, as well as the clumsiness of the multi-mike boom. A film that was recorded in this manner is *Oklahoma!*, winner of the sound Oscar® in its time.

---

10. Large-scale users of this technique include Decca and Telarc records, whose orchestral CDs are virtually all recorded primarily with spaced omnidirectional electrostatic microphones.

Spaced microphones have some disadvantages when it comes to the accuracy of timbre and sound imaging because the spacing brings about large amounts of time delay among the microphone channels. There are two problems:

- If the outputs of the channels, spread out in time, are ever combined, such as being mixed together to produce a monaural mix, then the time delay gives rise to constructive and destructive interference, frequency by frequency, which is audible and is called *comb filtering*. Thus the *mono compatibility* of stereophonic spaced microphone recordings is not very good.

- Even without combining the channels electrically, there is a question regarding constructive and destructive interference because the "triangulation" of the source through the channels to the ears creates time-of-arrival differences.

This still remains a popular technique for stereophonic recording, although it is not often applied in mainstream film and video production sound due to its complexity.

For film sound, spaced microphones are used mostly in music recording, with some use for stereophonic sound effects. More often perhaps, coincident microphone techniques are used for sound effect recordings, for their convenience and their special properties. Convenience is obvious; there is only one principal pickup location, although there are several microphones present at that location, so it is easy to pick up and move the whole stereophonic microphone array, which is much harder to do with spaced microphones.

One technique in particular that is useful is called *M-S* for "mid-side." This technique uses two coincident microphones, with a forward-facing cardioid or hypercardioid and a side-facing figure-eight pattern mike. The combined microphone is positioned facing the source, such that it is in the middle of the pickup pattern of the cardioid (or hypercardioid). The source is also centered on the null of the figure-eight pattern mike, such that it picks up practically no direct sound. Remembering that the two halves of a figure-eight pattern mike are different in polarity allows one to understand the following operation: Summing the output of the two elements together results in a left-facing channel (if the figure-eight pattern mike in-phase lobe is left facing), and taking the difference results in a right-facing channel (inverted in polarity, which is easily corrected electrically). This is a method that is compatible with mono mix down, because if you mix the two resulting signals together in a 1:1 proportion, you get back to just the forward-facing microphone's output. Second, it does not suffer from comb filtering in reproduction because there is no time-of-arrival difference between left and right.

> This makes it very useful in systems that employ an amplitude-phase matrix for release (Dolby Stereo, Ultra Stereo), and thus is a preferred method for sound-effects recording.

M-S stereo recording was tried on the principal photography of a picture a few years ago and wound up not being used. The sound recordist reported that the dailies sounded great but the editing problems of stereo sound tracks discussed earlier caused the production sound track not to be usable in stereo—the mono sum served well.

So, although the field of stereo recording is large—offering many techniques—certain methods dominate in specific areas of filmmaking: spaced omnis in music recording and coincident miking for sound effects. It should be pointed out that many monaural sound recordings are combined into complex stereo recordings in post production, with the spatialization created by stereophonic reverberation of the original monaural source. Although this does not satisfy a purist as to how stereo should be done, it is the dominant method used today. The monaural recorded parts of a sound track are usually the dialog, both production and ADR, Foley sound-effects recordings, and some "spot" effects. Other effects, especially ambience, and music are most often original stereo (including more than two channel) recordings.

Worldized or futzed recording

Previously mention has been made of re-recording sound through a deliberately poor "channel," consisting of a loudspeaker and microphone to add specific acoustic effects. Such a re-recording is called *worldized*, and it is not the quality of timbre preservation of the microphone that one seeks in such recordings, but rather, quite often, the opposite. Experimentation is the order of the day for worldizing, and it takes new heights of distortion production in *futzed* recordings. For these, the transmission channel of the loudspeaker and microphone is made deliberately very poor, such that the sound of the transducers intrudes heavily on the recording. A possible use for such recordings is in duplicated telephone conversations. Years ago, simply restricting the original sound to the midrange frequencies by means of an electrical filter was enough to cause the thin nasal quality called the *telephone effect*. With today's better transmission channel, simply filtering the sound is not enough, and futzed sound is commonly used to add nonlinear distortion as well. There is a correct "grammatical" method for portraying a telephone conversation in a film.

- When we see the person speaking, we hear him or her naturally, but if we hear the other end of the conversation at all, we hear it highly modified, by being filtered to a narrow frequency region, and re-recorded through a deliberately poor set of transducers.

- When we cut from one end of a conversation to the other, the roles reverse with regard to sound.

- If we see first one person, then the other, we follow these rules at the picture edits, but, if we then see both of them (by way of a split-screen optical), we hear both of them "direct."

Some films deliberately play with the sensibility of whether the person at the far end of a phone conversation is heard at all, heard through the intermediary telephone, or heard directly.

Chapter 5: Production Sound Mixing

Introduction

Production sound mixing is a potentially confusing term because it is ambiguous. Does it mean the actual process of operating the mixing console or the general processes that go on in production sound, including logging and set relations? Here we will discuss both, starting with the processes that go on in the mixing console. An alternative name for the console is the *mixing panel*. The term *mixer* is also ambiguous, because it can refer to the physical console or to the production sound recordist.

Production sound mixing involves microphone technique, recording, synchronization, and has an impact on editing. Thus all of the factors involved are spread out across the appropriate chapters. Here we take up some of the specific issues facing production sound.

Production sound consoles: processes

Each microphone is connected to an individual microphone preamplifier, either in the recorder or in an external mixer, which then delivers signals to the recorder. Microphone cabling is practically always balanced, using two signal leads and a shield, with three-pin XLR-style connectors, except for some miniature microphones designed to be worn by performers.

Different microphones call for different amounts of preamplifier gain and/or "padding" because of:

- Different microphone sensitivity from mike to mike.

- Different microphone dynamic range capability from mike to mike, with some being more capable than others of reproducing high sound-pressure levels without distortion.

- Different volume ranges encountered by mikes in different locations (a distant mike receives less direct sound than a close-up one).

Also, different microphones use various methods to supply power. None is needed for dynamic and ribbon mikes, 12V T powering is needed for certain electrostatic mikes, and 12V or 48V phantom is needed for other electrostatic mikes. Since mis-setting a microphone power switch can easi-ly damage some microphones, be certain to match the microphone power requirement and the source.

Fig. 5.1 A small, portable, high-quality mixer used for production sound, a Sonosax SX-S with a "break out" box providing extended connectors. Photo courtesy Sonosax.

Accommodating microphone dynamic range

Probably more than any other single factor, this is the factor that leads to poor recordings that are either noisy or distorted. The huge potential dynamic range that can be produced by microphones is quite often greatly reduced due to there being many potential places to adjust the level and some of them being set wrong. The potential consequences of setting one stage improperly, and making up for the error by subsequent gain changes in another stage, are high distortion or high noise.

The methods to maximize dynamic range for microphones and preamplifiers include:

- In the case of electrostatic microphones, a pad between the microphone pickup element and its electronics, supplied either built-in or as an accessory to the microphone.

- A pad inserted into the mike line, although this can interfere with powering.

- The gain of the mike preamplifier.

Note that all three of these devices affecting level are used before the recording level control, also called a *fader*. It is overlooking these potential areas of problems by thinking that "the recording level control will take care of it" that probably causes as many or more distorted recordings as actual mis-setting of the recording level to the medium. The distortion occurs before the level control in these cases.

An example is connecting the Sennheiser 416T short shotgun to a Nagra 4.2 conventional mike preamplifier input.[1] The maximum undistorted output voltage of the microphone is 630 mV, and the maximum undistorted input of this Nagra preamp is 43 mV.[2] With a direct connection, the combination is only capable of capturing up to 101 dB sound pressure level without clipping the input of the Nagra, so a "pad" must be inserted between the microphone and the preamplifier for any sounds that exceed this level if gross distortion is not to result. Peak sound-pressure levels of 100 dB may be hit in even high level dialogue situations, so distortion may frequently result with this unaided combination.

In order for the preamp to pass all of the output capability of the microphone undistorted, we have to make the input overload of the Nagra and the overload of the microphone the same: We say we have to *pad down* the 630 mV to 43 mV, a 23.3 dB attenuation. Then the two will overload at the same sound pressure level, which is 124 dB SPL. Attempting to record any sound above this level will still be distorted, so the only recourse is to move the microphone away from the source.

The microphone also causes another problem. It has 110 dB dynamic range, but the microphone preamplifier only has a 105 dB dynamic range. This illustrates the exact nature of our problem—fitting a gallon into a quart. (By the way, this is not as severe as the dynamic range restriction that will occur subsequently when "fitting" the dynamic-range potential of the microphone and preamplifier into the capacity of the recording medium. While some digital recorders today approach a 120 dB dynamic range, many other digital, and all analog media have much less dynamic range.)

If we pad down the microphone by 23 dB all of the time, we will be limiting our ability to capture the softest sounds possible because the microphone preamplifier noise will exceed the microphone noise. In order for the microphone noise to completely swamp the preamplifier noise, the mike noise should be 10 dB higher than the preamp input noise so that the mike noise completely dominates the noise floor (with a smaller difference the two noises will add). For this case, an 8 dB pad will take the microphone output noise down to 10 dB above the preamplifier noise, as desired for capturing the softest sounds.

So we need a minimum of two pad values available for this combination, 8 and 23 dB. Since these are fairly far apart, a middle "compromise" value of 15 dB is also good to have available. In the end, the case for each combination of microphone and preamp has to be studied individually, and the choices made to also interact with the sound-pressure level range of the program material, making this a very complex area for optimization.

The detailed study above only covers the chain from the output of the microphone to the input of the microphone preamplifier. Many other points in the chain are subject to such "gain staging" problems. For instance, in the case of a Betacam recorder, whether analog or digital, when used with an external microphone mixer, there are many potential items that affect level between the microphone and the mixer's monitor headphones to consider:

- Possible pad between pickup capsule and microphone electronics, built in or an accessory.

- Possible pad between microphone and microphone preamplifier input (but note powering requirements; some are constructed to pass phantom power)

- Mixer input range sensitivity switch: mike or line level on a per channel basis.

- Mixer individual channel level and pan controls.

- Mixer master level control.

- Mixer output range sensitivity switch: mike or line level.

- Camera input range sensitivity switch: mike or line level.

- Camera channel level control.

---

1. This case is common, but note that the manufacturer of the Nagra supplies a different solution to the problem by using a different plug-in microphone preamplifier for this microphone type.
2. The 43-mV input overload point is determined by using a conventional dynamic microphone with a sensitivity of 2 mV at 94 dB SPL, operating at 120 dB SPL.

- Camera headphone monitor output level control.

- Mixer headphone monitor level control.

One not uncommon problem in this chain is for the output level range switch on the mixer to be set to line level, and the camera input range switch set to mike level. In these circumstance, with typical equipment, a "tone" can even be sent and recorded at the right level, but unless the scene is exceptionally quiet, the likelihood is that the line level output of the mixer will overload the microphone level input of the camera on signal peaks, with gross distortion resulting.

The way out of this complexity is to know what the nominal range is for each of the controls, and to be certain that mike level and line level switches are matched between units. For instance, wireless microphone receivers can output either mike or line level; the corresponding mixer input sensitivity switch must be set to the same setting. Also, knowing where the master level controls, the camera level controls, and the monitor level controls usually are set, and setting them there, increases the likelihood that the chain is free from gross problems. One way to do this is to "tape off" many of the controls in line. For instance, it would not be uncommon to find camera input switch and level controls taped off to standard settings, when a Betacam camera is used with an external microphone mixer.

Other processes

After the gain and power issues have been worked out, there are some other potential processing treatments to improve the sound quality. The difficulty with applying these processes in production are many:

- Headphone monitoring conditions don't permit hearing the program under conditions remotely resembling how a standardized sound system will sound at dailies, making judgments of sound quality very difficult on the set or location.

- Any change in the processing from shot-to-shot within a scene may not call attention to itself at dailies, but may well

become a limiting factor on cutting the sound together.

- Any change from scene-to-scene in the processing may also call attention to itself as we come to learn the timbre of one performer's voice. The change from scene to scene may well be noticeable.

With the foregoing in mind, it is clear that minimum signal processing during recording allows post production mixing to produce the best-sounding track in the end. Everyone involved should take special note that good sound on the dailies doesn't always equate with the most editable tracks. Consistency is more important than one shot sounding great and the next shot not so great as background noise, for example, intrudes. Of course, one seeks great-sounding dailies, but the cost of "over mixing" the production sound arises subsequently in post production, when some of the processes carried out in production must be "undone" in order to get to neutral territory, where more effective post production processing can occur.

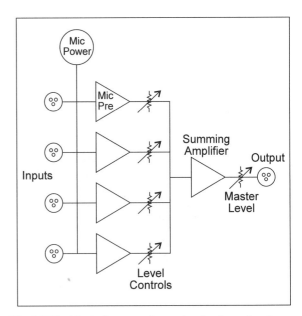

Fig. 5.2 The block diagram of even the simplest mixer involves at least two level controls between the microphone input and the line output.

Quite often in documentary filmmaking, due to the lack of control over the filming conditions, there will be a need for perhaps greater processing than there is in narrative work, but it is these producers who have much smaller budgets and can therefore not afford as complex a production mixing console. Another difficulty in documentary filmmaking is the need for extremely lightweight and portable equipment. Some of the following help to ameliorate these problems:

- It seems to be much more important to maintain consistency of sound quality within a scene than from scene to scene. Changes in timbre within a scene disturb auditory streaming and break up auditory objects, whereas each new scene offers a new opportunity for the formation of streams.

- Unifying factors can be used to smooth the sound quality from scene to scene, such as a consistent voice-over narration or music.

- Recording *presence* (also called *room tone*, and in the UK *atmosphere*) is an essential ingredient in being able to match background sounds. Further, crossfading from one room tone to another at scene transitions may well help ease the listener's job in the formation of new auditory streams without drawing attention to itself. Crossfading presence rather than abruptly cutting it has to be considered among the possible methods to make a scene transition.

Audio processes are described more extensively in Chapter 10. Those available on field production equipment include:

- Low-frequency filtering: Used to eliminate the often large amounts of low-frequency noise present on location, which would otherwise be recorded as rumble. A description of filters appears in Chapter 10.

- Low-frequency attenuation (LFA): This is an equalizer that cuts a broad area of low frequencies, compared with the steeper cutoff filter. It is useful for overcoming the proximity effect and the effects of increasing reverberation time at lower frequencies in large spaces. This system is found on Nagra recorders.

- Equalization: Two- or three-band equalizers are offered on some consoles.

- Limiting: Documentary and even narrative film production sound recording often runs into the unexpected, higher sound-pressure levels than the recording level control was set for. To provide an undistorted recording, a circuit must "limit" the audio signal so that it is capable of being recorded without gross audible distortion. This is often necessary because performers frequently "play bigger" during takes with the camera running than they do during rehearsals. Poor limiters cause audible "ducking" as they reduce gain to prevent overload, but correctly designed and adjusted limiters can be highly useful.

Production sound mixers: signal routing

Production sound mixers, with generally from three to eight inputs, usually have a fairly simple block diagram. Studying the diagram will reveal how a signal makes it from input to output for recording, and possibly separately to monitoring. There may be a "solo" function, permitting listening to one or more microphones individually while the main recording channel remains undisturbed. Also, some mixers provide a "mute" function, cutting off the output of a channel without having to move its fader.

Mixing

In the last chapter we described the various microphone techniques at our disposal, and also the consequences of mixing together various microphones. Here we want to describe just how much "mixing" is desirable at this point in the process of making a program. By *mixing*, we mean dynamically manipulating the level controls of the various microphones during a take for the purpose of emphasizing the desired sound, and the converse. The principles are:

- Producing the best sound within a take consistent with editability from shot to shot. The first consideration may call for a lot of active mixing, but the second limits the amount to variations that can be duplicated from master to close-up.

- Microphones are rarely "potted all the way down,"[3] but instead are simply turned down enough that their contribution to the overall sound is negligible when they are not in use; this means they are already partially up to full value when they are needed, and less of a fade-up is required.

- Performers often react more strongly when the camera is rolling than in rehearsal. After rehearsing to find the correct recorded level, the wise sound recordist will provide a few deciBels of margin for the adrenaline factor.

Level setting

Level setting of recorded level depends greatly on the medium in use, and the type of metering employed. Since this is so, these topics are covered at the end of Chapter 6.

Getting a shot started

In narrative filmmaking, with a director in charge, the following sequence is common:

- The assistant director or director says, "Roll sound."

- The sound recordist turns on the recorder, and if it is a Nagra observes the speed and power indicator is on, meaning that the internal self-check for speed accuracy has been passed. The recordist then says, "Speed."[4]

- The assistant director or director says, "Roll camera."

- The camera operator starts the camera, and after observing it to be on speed says, "Rolling."

---

3. Level controls have a variety of names, including *pot*, short for potentiometer, the actual circuit element that does the adjustment. Alternative names include *fader* and *volume control* (usually reserved only for loudspeaker of headphone monitor controls). Thus, to *pot down* is to turn the fader down in level.

4. The Deva digital recorder has a patent pending feature that records up to 10 s *before* the record button is pushed. This is accomplished by storing incoming sound digitally in RAM all of the time, and transferring it to a hard drive when the record button is pushed.

- The assistant director or director says, "Slate" or "Marker" or "Sticks."

- The clapperboard slate operator says the scene and take number, such as, "Twenty-seven B take one" then hits the clapperboard closed, in view of the camera, and then gets out of the way.

- The director says, "Action" to cue the beginning of the scene.

At the end of the take, the director says, "Cut" and both camera and sound stop. The next decision taken is whether to print that take or not. If the decision is to print the take, the director says "Print it," and the camera log and sound log have that take numbered circled, which is universally recognized as a take that is to be printed, have sound synchronized with it, and shown at dailies.

For synchronization of the sound and picture on a telecine, which is used for both film post production and for television, enough "pre-roll" time is necessary for the picture and sound to sync up. If the sequence described is shortened (usually to save film) by doing everything extremely quickly, there may not be enough recorded time before the slate occurs for equipment to synchronize picture and sound. The detail of how much time is needed depends on the specific equipment in use, so it should be checked before shooting begins with the post production film to video transfer facility. It could be up to 15 seconds.

Dialog overlaps

Overlapping dialog from various actors speaking at the same time causes one of the most serious potential problems editorially. Since for all practical purposes it is impossible for the performers to overlap the dialog identically from take to take, allowing dialog overlaps on the set greatly reduces the possible edit points, sometimes to none! In a very rigorous form of direction, the dialog overlap is created in post production by showing the back of one performer while looking at another and dubbing in the overlapped lines of the actor whose back we see, as appropriate. Today it is probably more common to permit overlaps in master shots and to try to duplicate them roughly in close-ups, due to the naturalness that this brings to the acting, but the editorial problems are formidable and should be thought through by the director and sound crew before shooting.

The reason the sound crew has a strong interest in dialog overlaps is when making the decision about whether actors speaking off camera should be heard directly on mike, "off mike," or not at all. If the actors can reproduce the overlap from shot to shot adequately, then it may be useful to mike both of them (if there are just two) for all of the shots, even close-ups where the off-camera actor is recorded on mike. This permits editorial freedom, as the sound perspective will not change dramatically at the picture cut, but necessitates very careful control of the actors to permit edits.

A second possibility is to record the off-screen actor off mike as well. This means the actor will be heard but will be recorded at a high angle of incidence compared with the axis of the microphone, and thus will be heard mostly as only a small amount of direct sound, and potentially lots of reverberation. The advantage of this approach is that the actor on camera has someone to react to, but the disadvantage is strong: The off-mike recording is very noticeable as being different from on mike, and if a cut is made to bring the off-screen performer onto the screen, the sound perspective will jump and destroy continuity.

The third approach is the most rigorous, and was described earlier. Have the off-screen performer just mouth their words and make no sound so the sound recordist can capture a "clean" track of the on-screen performer, then reverse the roles for the alternate close-up and build the dialog overlap in post production. This has many control advantages but requires more of the performers.

This discussion of methods for dialog overlaps has an impact on documentary interview technique as well because the same issues are often raised. In a one camera interview, it is common to shoot the interview

first, and then to shoot the interviewer asking the questions. If an overlap of speech occurs during the interview, the question is whether that should be on or off mike. Probably the best solution is to record from two mikes, on the interviewer and interviewee, on two separate tracks, because this gives the most control in post production. A problem occurs if only the interviewee is miked and the interviewer asks a question that overlaps. In this case, the interviewer will be heard well enough for dubbing over a direct recording to be impossible, yet his or her voice will be heard grossly "off mike." Of course, these problems are prevented if there are never any overlaps and both parties are shot individually. Then a natural-seeming interview flow can occur editorially, in post production.

Another consideration in such shooting is the need for cutaways. Cutaway shots are those of incidental occurrences surrounding the interview that, above all else, do not show the mouth of the person speaking. This permits editing the audio track to compress time in the interview without the discontinuity of a jump cut. A flaw that must be mentioned occurs sometimes in documentary production in which there is no cutaway to use—*lip flap*. This occurs when the picture shows a speaking person whose voice we do not hear. Although sometimes there is no way around lip flap, it shows very poor technique and gives away the mechanics of the process to the viewer.

Crowd scenes

Another difficulty for production sound is crowd scenes. Generally we wish to focus on the principal performers and what they say in a scene, but what is supposed to be going on in the background may drown them out. Professional extras are good at simulating conversations while remaining silent, and an appropriate matching sound is produced either as "wild sound" during production, or in post production during an ADR session, often with more than one actor, producing what is called a *walla* track, that is, a track containing no discrete audible speech but providing the right sort of level of action to match the scene.

With less professional performers, the degree of the ability to simulate speech, without actually making sound, varies greatly. In some cases it may simply be impossible; this is surely true in documentary scenes played out in a restaurant, for example. There is just no practical method to control a scene in a working restaurant, so shooting should be scheduled outside of normal hours if a scene must take place under such conditions.

The principal actors must speak at an appropriate level and stress in their voices for the eventual situation. Confronted with a quiet stage and well-behaved professional extras, the tendency is to lower the energy level in the performance. However, they have got to "speak up" over the background noise that isn't there! Some actors are very good at this, and develop reputations among sound professionals that they are; whereas other, perhaps more "intuitive" actors may start out with enough energy but drop over the takes. This leads to questions about set politics, covered later in this chapter.

Auxiliary functions of mixers

Production sound mixers also have a number of ancillary functions, such as:

- The *slate microphone*, incorporated or plugged into the mixer, allows the production sound mixer to annotate the recording without having to move the main microphones or shout. *Slating* usually involves scene and take information, although there may be other items annotated for the use of telecine operators and editors.

- *Talkback*, the slate microphone doubles for this purpose on larger fixed consoles in circumstances where there is a separate sound control room. It provides intercom to the main floor from the sound personnel.

- The *director's monitor* is a headphone feed that is generally kept free of intercom and slate content.

- The *script person monitor* is a headphone feed that is selectable for whether it receives audio content only or a mix with intercom and/or slate traffic. It is often useful for the script person to hear the slate information, because he or she marks a script with the picture and sound start and stop per scene and the slate number.

Logging

Logging the sound tapes is the responsibility of the production sound mixer. Usually the log will give:

- Production name/number

- Shooting date

- Reel number

- Producer/studio/director, etc.

- List of scene/take information recorded

- List of any wild lines recorded

- List of any sound effects or other wild sound recorded

- List of any presence recorded

- Takes that are meant to be copied from the production source media to be heard at dailies, with matching picture having their take numbers circled, and the designation "Print circled takes"

Tables 5.3 through 5.5 give production sound reports for various media. The technical information needed to fill out the top of these forms is discussed elsewhere.

At the end of a shooting day, the production sound recordist consults with the script person and a camera crew member concerning the three logs from the set—sound, script, and camera—rationalizing the list of scenes and takes shot that day to correct any errors.

Table 5.3: Conventional Analog Audio Production Sound Log[1]

Prod # _____ Prod. Name _____ Shoot Date _____

Recorder ID _____ Recordist _____ _____ Roll # _____

❏ Full-track, 7 $\frac{1}{2}$ ips, NAB eq., Tails out, 60 Hz Pilot tone sync, sync source recorder XTL

❏ 2-track, 7 $\frac{1}{2}$ ips, NAB eq., Tails out, 60 Hz FM Sync, sync source recorder XTL

❏ Exceptions to above: Camera Frame Rate _____fps

Scene	Take	Track 1	Track 2 (if used)
Head tone		Tone at – ___ dB modulometer level	Tone at – ___ dB modulometer level
Print circled takes. "A.F.S." = after false start. TS = tail slate			

1 Copyright modified for this page: it may be copied by productions for their use when accompanied by this notice. No commercial duplication permitted. Original © 2002 Tomlinson Holman. Used with permission.

Table 5.4: Time Code Analog Audio Production Sound Log[1]

Prod # _____ Prod. Name _____ Shoot Date _____

Recorder ID _____ Recordist _____ _____ Roll # _____

❑ 2-track, 7 1/2 ips, NAB eq., Tails out, sync source recorder XTL, OR _____
SMPTE Time Code: ❑ 30 fps ❑ 29.97 fps ❑ 25 fps ❑ 24 fps ❑ 23.976 fps
　　　　　❑ NDF ❑ DF
❑ Smart slate jam synced from recorder, OR _____

Camera Frame Rate: _____ fps

Scene	Take	TC Start	TC End	Track 1	Track 2 (if used)
Head tone				Tone @ –10.5 dB	Tone @ –10.5 dB

Print circled takes. "A.F.S." = after false start. TS = tail slate
For dailies Indicate ❑ DO NOT SUM TRACKS ❑ SUM TRACKS

IF FOUND, please call _____

Table 5.5: Time Code Digital Audio Production Sound Log[1]

| Prod # _____ Prod. Name _____ Shoot Date _____ |

| Recorder ID _____ Recordist _____ _____ Roll # _____ |

❏ DAT, Tails out, sync source recorder XTL, OR _____

❏ DVD-RAM, 4.7 GB, UDF file system, BWF file format, OR _____

Sample Rate: ❏ 48048 ❏ 48000 ❏ _____

SMPTE Time Code: ❏ 30 fps ❏ 29.97 fps ❏ 25 fps ❏ 24 fps ❏ 23.976 fps

  ❏ NDF ❏ DF

❏ Smart slate jam synced from recorder, OR _____

Camera Frame Rate: _____ fps

Scene	Take	TC Start	TC End	Track 1	Track 2 (if used)
Head tones				Tone @ −20 dBFS	Tone @ −20 dBFS

Print circled takes. "A.F.S." = after false start. TS = tail slate

For dailies Indicate ❏ DO NOT SUM TRACKS ❏ SUM TRACKS

IF FOUND, please call _____

1 Copyright modified for this page: it may be copied by productions for their use when accompanied by this notice. No commercial duplication permitted. Original © 2002 Tomlinson Holman. Used with permission.

Shooting to playback

Quite often it is essential to shoot musical numbers to playback, the logistics of recording music and shooting film or video simultaneously being too demanding for reasonable budgets and time constraints. In order to accomplish this, a playback tape is prepared, often a special mix emphasizing the elements to be "lip synced," and two recorders are needed, one for playback and one for recording. The recording machine records a slate from an open microphone, then re-records the playback directly from the second machine, thus assuring a reference for picture-sound sync. This also permits starting in the middle of a long number for a given shot, and a record of exactly what part of the song the picture is to match is recorded.

For shooting to playback, a number of considerations apply:

- The performers must be reasonably close to the playback loudspeakers, so there is no time delay associated with the air path for their lip syncing.

- For dance numbers, occasionally "thumpers" have been found useful, that is, low-frequency transducers that put vibratory pulses out into a dance floor so the dancers can follow the beat. The advantage of this approach is that ordinary recording can occur, and the low-frequency energy can be filtered out of the recording, leaving a synchronized dance number to music and also well recorded direct sound.

- There must be a traceable path for the synchronization signal from the original music source, through the playback tape, to the recorded tape. Sync will be covered in more detail in Chapter 7. If this "sync lock" chain is broken, then the editor may find it impossible to synchronize.

Time code and audio sample rate

Time code, a method of synchronization, is often an issue in production sound but will be covered in Chapter 7 more comprehensively in order for all parts of the synchronization chain to be understood as a whole.

Sample rates used in production sound are covered in Chapter 8, Transfers. These items are critical for production sound.

Other technical activities in production

The sound crew, usually being the most technically savvy on the set, is also given responsibility for such ancillary electronics as walkie-talkies and intercoms, especially when working on location away from the technical infrastructure available in major production centers. Battery charging, providing music systems for the director and actors, and many other such tasks often fall on the sound crew.

Set politics

Among the factors that make a particular sound crew effective, and hired again, are the skills with which they perform their duties on the set, but also how skillful they are at set politics. Sound may often be considered to be an orphan on the set, since the visual images tend to dominate and sound can always be looped, or replaced, albeit at high expense, later. That is not to say that the performances of the actors during looping will necessarily be as good as they are in front of the camera, with the added tension this brings about. Also, set conditions may prevail, especially on big effects-laden movies, that essentially prevent the recording of high-quality sound. In these cases, the sound crew will revert to recording a *guide track* so that a record exists of exactly what was said, take by take, as guidance in eventual looping sessions. (The ADR or looping session does not occur until after the picture has been cut since there is no point in producing clean sync dialog that will not appear in the film.)

Probably the most contention between the sound crew and others on the set is over the use of the boom microphone. With the potential of dreaded boom shadows being thrown on the set, the boom is controversial from the point of view of the Director of Photography and Gaffer, who may see no way to accommodate the boom and still light the set; it is just one more constraint that "breaks the camel's back." However, as already discussed, this is by far the most effective tool we have for recording production sound that is usable and creates the proper perspective. Cinematographers would rather we resort to body mikes, but that just isn't the same. There are scenes where nothing else will do because the shot is so expansive that no boom can be anywhere near the actors, and planted or body mikes will have to do. In balancing the needs of the various departments, however, it must be said that the accommodation that the camera and lighting departments can give to the sound department in this area is usually well worth the overall impression of a scene.

Chapter 6: Recording

Introduction

Previous chapters have outlined the processes of miking and mixing. Once the signals have been appropriately mixed, they must be recorded on a medium (unless destined for live broadcast). This chapter describes the methods of recording that are in current use in film and television production and post production: direct analog magnetic recording, FM recording, and PCM digital audio recording. More detail about the analog methods may be found in Appendix II.

Direct analog magnetic recording

Direct refers to the fact that the input electrical signal is turned into a proportional magnetic field by the record head of the tape machine, after suitable electronic conditioning for the medium, and the strength of the magnetic field is stored, moment by moment, along the length of the tape to represent the amplitude of the analog waveform. So the amplitude dimension is represented directly as a proportional amplitude of magnetic field strength. The frequency dimension is recorded as well, by the distance between the peaks of stored magnetism along the length of the medium.

> If we record a 1 kHz sine wave along the length of a tape at a speed of 15 inches per second (in./sec), then we would find a positive peak of the magnetic field every 15 mils. (15 in./sec divided by 1000 cycles/sec = 0.015 in./cycle = 15 mils). In this way, the wavelength of the recording on the medium is made proportional to the wavelength of the original sound. It is this proportionality in both amplitude and wavelength dimensions that makes the recording "direct."

Another name for this type of recording that is used on videotape is *longitudinal* or *linear tracks*, meaning recorded along the length, used to distinguish such tracks from others that may be present as well, such as FM tracks. Direct analog magnetic recording is still a popular medium, but it must be said that it has been a mature technology for some time, with few developments left in its life cycle. Also, it must be remembered that despite how well one generation may be adjusted, generation loss with analog recording is inevitable.

AFM recording

Called *AFM* recording in professional applications, and *Hi Fi* recording in consumer ones, the audio signal in this process modulates a carrier in a manner analogous to an FM broadcast transmitter. The instantaneous amplitude of the audio signal is represented as a shift in frequency of the carrier. Instead of being transmitted, however, the FM signal is recorded by special heads installed on the rotating head drum of helical scan videotape machines, such as Betacam SP, S-VHS, and VHS.

This method offers better potential quality than longitudinal recording due to the higher tape-to-head speed achieved by recording with the rotating head drum compared with the low linear speed of videotape. Through clever manipulation of the recorded track geometry, FM recording is made not to interfere with the video recording that is occurring in the same area of tape, but at the cost of not being able to record the audio and video separately; thus, no "dubbing" of sound over existing video is available with this method of recording.

Since FM recording relies on a first step of "tuning in" the FM carrier, it does not work at any speed other than that at which it was recorded. Thus, the utility of FM tracks in editing is very limited, since it cannot be heard at slow speeds to pick edit points, so-called "scrub editing," or at faster than normal ones to scan the tape.

Digital recording

Audio, once digitized, may be recorded to a variety of tape formats, or directly to hard disk or optical recorders. From the standpoint of audio performance only sample rate, word length, and number of channels completely specify a medium. Virtually all film and television audio applications use 48 kHz range sampling[1], and 16-, 20-, or 24-bit word lengths. Virtually all media except digital optical sound on film use linear PCM representation of the audio, although

there is some use of Mini-Disc, which uses low-bit-rate coded audio, in this case ATRAC (see Chapter 11).

In addition to these, there are a great many digital multitrack machines, digital dubbers, hard disk recorders, and digital audio workstations that can be used, both for acquisition and for editing purposes. The formats of these most often offer 8 or 24 tracks. The various types described are different functionally, but not in inherent digital audio quality. We will take functionality up where it is appropriate later.

In videotape production, increasing use is being made of digital videotape machines in a wide variety of formats, with a large range being available to optimize the tradeoffs among optimum picture quality, tape consumption, ease of portable use, cost of operation, and other factors.

Distinguishing features among the formats and media

Open reel tape contains the potential to make an error fatal for sound recording. Once a reel is finished and removed from the machine, nothing prevents one from "turning over" the tape and remounting it on the supply reel and erasing the just made tape with another pass of the recorder. It has happened to a number of professional recordists.

Cassette based formats such as videotape and DAT have a slider or break-out of the plastic case to indicate "recorded" so that re-recording over an already recorded tape is prevented.

Conventional direct analog magnetic recording has a number of limits to its quality that vary greatly among the various manifestations of the method. In general, audio-only media typically offer better audio performance than video media, and higher speeds and wider tracks are typically better than lower speeds and narrower tracks. Also, the raw performance numbers associated with AFM tracks are much better than the longitudinal tracks, especially in VHS and S-VHS, but there are limitations discussed in Appendix II that can make the sound from the con-

---

1. Shot with film the rate is 48048 Hz. See Chapter X on synchronization.

ventional track more acceptable than an AFM track.

The largest distinguishing quality feature among direct analog recording, AFM recording, and digital recording is generally the dynamic range capability of these various types, interacting in the direct analog case with the various media on which they may be recorded. Dynamic range is the region between recorded noise on the one hand, and distortion on the other hand, in which good quality recordings may be made. Recordings that spend too much time at very low level are likely to have the noise floor of the medium audibly intrude, while those recorded at too great a level are likely to produce audible distortion.

Although there are functional and other quality considerations that we will describe later, it is dynamic range that most separates the types and media. That is not to say that all analog media are inferior to all digital ones, for as we shall see, the quality of the various media overlap significantly. Some video tape media have worse audio specifications than even consumer media like the Compact Cassette.

To understand the dynamic range differences among various media, it is first necessary to start with the notion of reference level. Reference level is the level of a sine wave tone on a medium that represents an average level signal on that medium. While program signals vary continuously, and may easily exceed the average, reference level is a continuous tone at more or less the average level of ordinary programs.

There is a parallel used in exposing picture film. A *gray card* serves as a midgray tone reference. By choosing the exposure based on the reflectance of this card, both darker and lighter items within the scene can be captured without excessive under- or overexposure, up to the limit of the film stock. The gray card is meant to represent the kind of average level of items that might appear in the scene.

Reference level—analog

The *reference fluxivity* in an analog recording system follows the gray card idea: It represents something around the average recording level. The units of reference level or reference fluxivity for direct recording are nanoWebers/meter, abbreviated nW/m. The areas of usage of various levels are shown in Table 6.1.

Table 6.1: Analog Reference Levels

Reference level	nW/m
Video Tape	100
Audio Tape, Film: SMPTE	185
Music	200, 250, G320[1], 355, 500

1 G indicates German level, with a slightly different definition for fluxivity

Reference level—digital

Unlike analog media, where both the bottom (noise) and top (distortion) of the dynamic range are somewhat fuzzy, digital audio has an unequivocal level—the maximum undistorted level. This level is chosen because it is the level at which a sine wave will be coded with its highest peak level just touching the maximum coded value, at the positive and negative extremes. The maximum level recordable in the medium is called Full Scale, and other levels in the medium are referred to this level as dB re Full Scale, abbreviated dBFS.

Since no program material could practically be recorded with its average at such a high level without severe distortion, it is common to place the reference level for digital audio some deciBels below Full Scale. Various reference levels are given in Table 6.2. For the majority of professional purposes, −20 dBFS represents a performance such that analog and digital media of high quality match reasonably well, and this is the most commonly used level in film and television production.

Table 6.2: Digital Reference Levels

Reference level authority	dbFS
SMPTE	–20
EBU	–18
Music users/Pro Tools	–16

Headroom

Headroom is the amount in deciBels between the reference level and the level at which a specified amount of distortion is reached, usually 2 or 3% THD. This amount of distortion is typically considered the "ceiling" of the medium, and most recordings are kept below this level, even on peaks.

On the other hand, those dinosaurs in *Jurassic Park* know no such limitations, so they probably reach film saturation, max headroom. The consequences of saturation of analog magnetic recordings range from quite audible distortion on some program material to simply a noticeable limiting effect on other material, where it just doesn't seem to get louder. The audibility of these effects depends on psychoacoustic factors; a piano can be much less distorted than a lion roar in measured fact, but sound more distorted. The difference is that the piano is composed of tonal sound, which is changed spectrally in a noticeable way by the distortion, whereas the lion roar is more noiselike, so the addition of added spectral components is not very noticeable because there is less "organization" to the spectral structure creating the timbre.

Headroom changes from medium to medium, and even with differences in tape stock within a medium. Its character changes from analog to digital. Analog media tend to have a "soft" saturation or overload characteristic, wherein distortion increases with level, and so does level compression, above the reference level. Linear PCM digital systems behave differently. They remain essentially

undistorted so long as the highest peaks of the program stay below Full Scale. Once full scale is exceeded however, distortion is rapid, and nasty.

For analog recording, one of the principal indicators for tape or film quality is how high a level can be reached without exceeding the specified distortion. This is one of the primary differences between videotape and audiotape: Videotape has much less audio headroom because there is much less magnetic material available in the oxide, with its coating being thinner than typical audio-only tapes. Headroom also varies with frequency, and differs from medium to medium. Slower speeds generally mean less headroom at the frequency extremes, due to the record equalization[2] needed to overcome losses. Thirty-five millimeter magnetic film has a fairly flat overload characteristic with respect to frequency. This means that the overload at all audio frequencies is about equal. However, due to the equal-loudness contours, *perceived* overload in the bass occurs earlier. Program material having extremely high levels of low frequencies are probably the most difficult to record, due to flat overload and nonflat hearing. (Hearing requires more stimulus to sound equally loud as the frequency is decreased.)

Slower audio media and videotape fare worse. For instance, $^3/_4$-in. U-Matic videotape has spectacularly less headroom at low frequencies than mag film or audiotape. This leads to problems in post production, where the sound mixer can use quite high levels of low frequencies on the audio medium, which cannot be copied to the videotape audio tracks without severe distortion. On the other hand, the high-frequency headroom of videotape can be the same as open-reel analog audiotape. Thus although it is possible to re-record a cymbal crash from audiotape to such videotapes without distortion, a strong rumble will grossly distort. Fortunately, digital videotape is rapidly supplanting analog methods, and from a sound point of view nothing could be a bigger improvement in

---

2. See Appendix II.

the chain.

Signal-to-noise ratio

Signal-to-noise ratio is the measurement from the reference level to the noise floor of the medium in deciBels.

> What is being done semantically here is to substitute *signal* for *reference*, because what is actually measured is the reference level to noise ratio, with the reference level standing in for the average signal level.

Analog tape noise is perceived as hiss, as is dither used in digital systems to smooth quantization distortion into rather more benign noise. Because human hearing does not have a flat frequency response, especially at low levels, noise is not equally annoying at all frequencies. For this reason, noise measurements are frequently weighted for human sensitivity versus frequency. Such a measurement is called a *weighted signal-to-noise ratio*. In general, tape noise is a greater problem at lower tape speeds. It may be ameliorated by the use of a companding noise reduction system, to be discussed later.

> A special case of signal-to-noise ratio is crosstalk. *Crosstalk* is any leakage of undesired signal into a desired signal. It may arise from physically adjacent tracks with less than perfect isolation. While crosstalk is important in audio-only recorders, because it tends to make the tracks not perfectly distinguished from one another, it is not usually a large problem because the program material in adjacent tracks, in a music application, is all meant to be heard at once in the end. It is more of a problem on videotape machines and on audio machines used for video purposes, in which the signal used for synchronization (SMPTE time code) may crosstalk into audio channels and be quite annoying because it contains audible mid- and high-range audio frequencies.

Dynamic range

Dynamic range is the sum of headroom and signal-to-noise ratio, expressed in deciBels. It is typically the main issue in choosing film or tape stocks for audio.

Table 6.3 gives the headroom at various frequencies and the weighted s/n ratio for various media and recording method. The sum of the two numbers is the dynamic range. The table covers virtually every medium in the channel between the original production recording (or sound effects, music, etc.) and the finished optical sound track in a theater, that will be discussed in Chapter 11. Study of this table may give one pause; if we are to copy a recording made on 35 mm magnetic film to $^3/_4$-in. U-Matic, the headroom difference of 26.5 dB at 31.5 Hz means an enormous amount.

Wow and flutter, scrape flutter

Wow and flutter, and scrape flutter, were discussed in Chapter 3. One difficulty with these distortions is that they accumulate over generations, and distortions not audible at one generation may become quite audible within three generations. Generally, wow and flutter are not a large problem with well-maintained professional equipment, but there are some problem areas—analog videotape and 16mm mag film. In these media, the wow and flutter is worse than on a good cassette deck. In the case of videotape this is apparently due to all the conflicting requirements. In 16mm film it is caused by most transports being built for 35mm film, with the 16mm capability not being considered primary.

Table 6.3: Headroom and S/N Ratio Characteristics of Various Media, in dB re Reference Level

Name of format	Ref. level	Headroom[1] in dB re reference level					s/n ratio, CCIR 2k weighted, dB re ref. level[2]
		31.5 Hz	100 Hz	1 kHz	3.15 kHz	10 kHz	
35 mag film with Dolby SR (3 track)	185 nW/m	+21.5	+17	+17	+17	+19	−81

Table 6.3: Headroom and S/N Ratio Characteristics of Various Media, in dB re Reference Level (Continued)

2 in. 24-track 15 in./sec with Dolby SR	250 nW/m	+16.5	+16.5	+16.5	+17	+20	−77.5
1/4 in. 2-track 15 in./sec with Dolby SR	200 nW/m	+20	+20.5	+19.5	+20.5	+20	−77
1/4 in. 2-track 15 in./sec	200 nW/m	+13	+18	+19	+19.5	+16	−54
1/4 in. full track mono Nagra at 7.5 in./sec	200 nW/m[3]	+4	+10.5	+11.5	+10	+6	−61
Compact Cassette with IEC Type IV tape, Dolby NR[4] and HX Pro	200 nW/m	−3	+5	+6	+4	+3	B: −61 C: −67 S: −67
Compact Cassette with IEC Type II tape, Dolby B and HX Pro	200 nW/m	−7	0	+1	+1	−2	−61
3/4" U-Matic SP with Dolby NR[5]	100 nW/m	−5	+4	+5	+8	+4	−67
Betacam SP linear with Dolby NR[6]	100 nW/m	+2.5	+8	+11	+13	+17	−67
SVHS linear	100 nW/m	−13[7]	+5	+7	+8	−2	−40
SVHS hi-fi	ITA reference[8]	+16	+16	+16	+16	+14	−76[9]
16 bit Linear PCM with dither[10]	−20 dBFS	+20	+20	+20	+20	+20	−72
20 bit Linear PCM with dither	−20 dBFS	+20	+20	+20	+20	+20	−96
35mm analog optical sound track with Dolby SR	50%	+12	+9	+9	+9	+6	−69[11]
35mm digital sound	−20 dBFS	+20	+20	+20	+20	+20	Varies, better than −80

1   The headroom is measured to the 3% THD point for all frequencies except 10 kHz, and is the maximum output level for 10 kHz. Higher levels at all but 10 kHz are certainly found on program material on analog media, but due to difficulty in comparing the level vs. distortion curves of the various media, the 3% THD point is considered a practical limit for comparisons. Headroom and signal-to-noise ratio can be traded off against each other by changing the reference level. The reference levels used for these tests are ones commonly used.

2   The signal-to-noise ratio is measured between the reference level stated and the weighted noise floor. The weighting filter is the CCIR type (now ITU), and the reference gain is 0 dB at 2 kHz.

3   The reference level of 0 dB on a mono Nagra 4.2 modulometer is 320 nW/m DIN.

4   Dolby noise reduction of the type indicated in the signal-to-noise ratio column.

5   On machines marked Dolby NR, C type noise reduction is used.

6   The linear tracks of Betacam machines employ Dolby C type noise reduction.
7   At this frequency the minimum THD is 4%, not 3% as in all the comparative measurements.
8   Reference level for AFM tracks used by the International Tape Association.
9   This high signal-to-noise ratio is accomplished with aggressive companding noise reduction. The noise in the presence of a signal is much larger, and can become plainly audible in the case of leakage of the video signal into the audio, which is apparently often caused by a mismatch in head alignment between record and playback decks.
10   Dither, deliberately added noise, is necessary to eliminate quantization distortion—see Chapter 3. The type of dither used in this example is typical of 16 bit systems: triangular probability density function white noise at ±1 LSB pk-pk. Psychoacoustically noise shaped dither can reduce the measured noise on this type of test by up to approximately 15 dB, while still providing freedom from quantizing distortion.
11   This number is typical of freshly processed, unworn sound tracks, with a 1-mil bias line. Also, SR type signal processing is an improvement over A type on the type of noise encountered with a worn track due to dirt and scratches.

Conditions of these tests were as follows. All the media were chosen to be the best representative of practice available for that particular medium. For example, conventional U-Matic does not employ noise reduction, while U-Matic SP with Dolby C NR was used here, giving the signal-to-noise measurements shown a 20 dB advantage over a conventional U-Matic machine. Here are the machines and tape types used respectively:

1. Mag. film: Magnetech recorder with Inovonics electronics and Zonal full coat film stock.

2. 24-track: Studer A800 Mk III with Ampex 499 tape.

3. 1/4 in. 2-trk: Studer A810 with Dolby SR and 3M996 tape.

4. 1/4 in. 2-trk.: Studer A810 with 3M996 tape.

5. 1/4 in. full track: Nagra 4.2 full track recorder with 3M908 tape.

6. Cassette: Sony K717ES with Dolby NR as shown, HX Pro, and Abex reference Type IV tape.

7. Cassette: Sony K717ES, Dolby B, HX Pro, and Abex reference Type II tape.

8. U-Matic SP: Sony VO-9850 with Sony KSP-30 tape.

9. Betacam: Sony PVW-2800 with Sony BCT-30MA tape.

10, 11. S-VHS: JVC BR-S800U with Fuji ST30 tape.

12. Theoretical performance of 16-bit linear PCM with TPDF white dither; see Chapter 3.

13, 14. Optical track measurements supplied courtesy of Dolby Laboratories.

Setting the level

The bottom line has to be setting the level to be recorded onto a medium. This is because level setting is the one factor that continually faces people using audio media, and many of the other factors that affect performance are fixed by standards or conventions outside the control of the user. So level setting is the main day-to-day activity of a recordist, but technically speaking there is a completely right answer only part of the time. For example, when a copy is made that is to be identical to its source, then there are established procedures for doing this,[3] but this is most commonly not the case with live re-

cording, or even with mixing together several sources. The most common problem with setting a level for live sources is that their range may be so great that distortion is heard on the one hand, or noise on the other, if over-recording or under-recording occurs, respectively.

A parallel situation occurs with exposing photographic film, or in television cameras. The contrast range offered up by natural lighting conditions is usually too great to be captured uniformly on film or video: there is a lack of either highlight or shadow detail in the case of over- or under-exposure, respectively. In order to prevent this problem, lighting is adjusted so that the contrast ratio seen by the camera is limited in dynamic range, so that the film or video camera can capture the scene in a way that appears natural. As anyone who has shot outdoors with direct sunlight and shadows knows, there is a reason to limit contrast by limiting the peak brightness of the light source with diffusion, or filling the shadows with base lighting, called *fill light*, so that there is some definition in both highlights and shadows. Usually the look that a Director of Photography strives for will show details in both highlights and shadows, unless a storytelling element prevails and we aren't supposed to look at the scene naturally, say in day-for-night scenes that are meant to be obscure. In other words, their choice of exposure is the equivalent of our getting the level right. Unfortunately we generally cannot use over- or under-recording to produce such an aesthetic effect in sound as in picture, but judicious gain riding can have a similar effect, bringing up the quietest parts so they "read," and

---

3.   This is covered in Chapter 8.

blunting the excesses of the loudest parts.

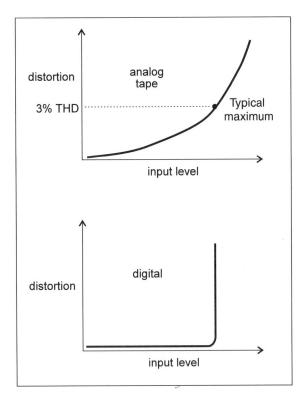

Fig. 6.1 A comparison of distortion versus level for an analog and a digital recorder. Analog tape overloads relatively gradually, while digital converters overload abruptly. The relationship shown is one that is in some use, where a typical analog 3% THD point is some 16 dB above reference level. With the maximum digital converter level, called Full Scale, set to the same value (reference level –16 dBFS), there is level capability on the analog medium that, albeit distorted, exceeds the capacity of the digital medium. The recording region over 3% THD is in fact used by the loudest sounds in film masters, such as explosions, where the distortion is not very noticeable. Thus, the particular alignment of levels implied by the relationship between the two graphs is problematic: it may work well for well-controlled program material, but a digital copy of an analog master of a high-level film made at this level would be quite distorted.

On the other hand, excessive "mixing" of production sound probably should be avoided because it affects intercuttability, as has already been described. When actors are involved, many perform at higher levels when the camera is rolling than when it is not, so this factor may need accounting for by a downward adjustment of level between rehearsal and performance. A good starting point for this factor is 3 dB. Additional information about level setting is found in Chapter 8.

These two contradictory ideas (mixing to fit the program material into the medium and the desired range for listening, and not mixing so as to provide best intercuttability) are resolved principally by learning and by competent feedback from other sound professionals associated with a project.

Historically production sound has been recorded such that the loudest passages of the program material are placed just somewhat below the point at which distortion is audible in order to maximize the signal-to-noise ratio. With expanding dynamic range of digital recording however, this is less of a concern than it was before, because the available range is larger than on analog. Thus when recording digitally it is generally better to be somewhat conservative by leaving some unused headroom for occasional unplanned events. This is not as costly to dynamic range on a 20-bit analog-to-digital converter (24-bit stored) recorder with 116 dB theoretical dynamic range, and an actual measured range of 112 dB, as it was on a mono Nagra, the staple of production sound for many years, which has 72 dB dynamic range[4]. Track 31 of the CD illustrates over- and under-recording of analog and digital media.

Meters
Various meter types are used to indicate level to recordists. The various types are primarily distinguished by the speed with which they register sound levels. The first developed program meter, the Volume Unit or VU meter with its relatively slow 300 msec response time, was adjusted by design to be relatively sluggish, and to read in a long time frame due tothe perception of loudness versus time. A signal must be present for some time to reach full loudness, and that is why the choice was made to have such a relatively long time constant. Unfortunately, VU meters do not read the level of shorter term

---

4. These numbers are not directly comparable, since for the Nagra there is recordable level above 3% THD, and the noise weighting curves of the measurements used to produce the numbers were different. Nonetheless the difference is large.

events, which, while not as loud, can none-theless cause plainly audible distortion. A VU meter reads lower and lower the shorter the event, but even distortion taking only 2 msec can be audible.

Europeans, having taken up these questions later than Americans, looked at the U.S. VU metering practice and thought that it did not adequately cover the potential for indicating the onset of distortion. Thus, they developed country-by-country and user group-by-user group a bewildering array of quasi-peak meters, with internecine rivalries among the groups as to what constituted the best meter. European "quasi-peak" meters basically revolve around the idea that they are faster than the VU meter, most about 30 times faster. The much faster quasi-peak meter thus reads higher on the same program signals than a VU meter, because it is responding to shorter events in the signals than the VU meter. This leads to lots of confusion, because alignment on tone, and how the recordist is to set the level to record on the meter are at variance between the two principal types of meters.

The Nagra modulometer managed to cross borders into U.S. practice. It has a 10 msec time constant, and thus shows even brief distortion. It also reads higher on program material than a VU meter aligned to the same level on a sine-wave tone because the program material contains short-term transients and the sine-wave tone does not.

The introduction of digital recording, with its abrupt overload, has increased the need to know the true peak level, to avoid even moments of the program from exceeding Full Scale. Peak meters with 0.2 ms rise times are often used.

In short, VU meters may indicate more about loudness, but peak meters more properly show the likelihood of the onset of distortion. The professional recordist comes to know the character of the medium and records it to the proper level using either device but may have to make adjustments for particular program material. Both VU and quasi-peak meters were typically designed to

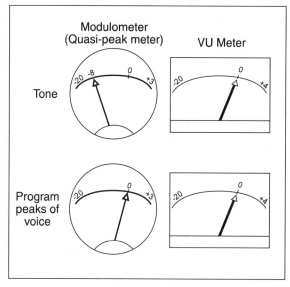

Fig. 6.2 While a modulometer (quasi-peak meter) reads lower on a sine wave tone than a VU meter, its 30 times faster speed makes it read the program peaks of voice as high as does the VU meter. A VU meter only responds sluggishly to peaks and does not reach the true value of the peak. Thus, a VU meter must be used in a system that provides considerable headroom beyond 0 VU, while a modulometer more accurately reflects the actual peak values.

indicate the level of a voice properly, which is not necessarily representative of all possible program material. In particular, short, sharp sounds, such as the mallet hit of a xylophone, are misrepresented badly by a VU meter, so the indicated level may seem proper when what is actually occurring is gross distortion of the starting transient, the hammer attack.

All in all, meters serve as a guide, like a light meter does for a photographer, but professionals come to learn their limitations and work with them.

The bottom line on the combination of level setting and metering is that good quality recording will be made when the recordist sets the level such that typical program peaks on speech just reach 0 VU on machines so equipped, 0 dB on a Nagra modulometer, or −10 to −6 dBFS on a true peak meter of some digital recorders. All of these will leave a little unused headroom for occasional unexpected peaks.

Table 6.4 shows various meter standards. The reason for the differences between film

Table 6.4: Meter Standards

Description	Reference Level	What reference level reads	Time response
VU meter on analog recorder, film/television use	185 nW/m	0 VU	300 ms
VU meter on analog recorder, music use	250–500 nW/m	0 VU	300 ms
VU meter on digital recorder (Deva II)	–20 dBFS	0 VU	300 ms
Nagra 4.2 (mono)	185 nW/m	–8 dB[1]	10 ms
Nagra IV-STC (stereo)	185 nW/m	–10.5 dB*	10 ms
Digital peak meter	–20 dBFS	–20 dBFS	0.2 ms

1   On the Nagra modulometer

and television use of reference level, and higher levels for music use, is explained in Appendix II.

Recording for film and television

Double-system recording

Audio recording for film sound has practically always occurred in a form called *double-system*, in which the sound is recorded on a medium separate from the picture.[5] This allows each medium to be optimized to its task for quality, although using the double-system method also requires a means to keep the two media in sync with each other. Double-system sound applies, practically speaking, whenever film is in use as the originating medium, whether the result is a motion-picture or an immediate transfer to a video medium for editing and release.

Besides improving quality, double-system sound is essential throughout post production in order to accomplish many of the sound processes that rely on the ability to manipulate different components or tracks of sound separately. The reason for this is to keep dialog, music, and sound effects separate until late in the mixing process. The fact

that sound and picture are separate is not a detriment, because various tracks will be added to the original anyway to *sweeten* the sound track, using a television term.

Sound on videotape

Recording sound during video original production usually takes place on the master videotape. However, conventional audio tracks on analog videotape have some fairly severe quality limitations, due to the low linear tape speed and the fact that the tape is optimized for video, not audio, recording. To circumvent these limits, *FM recording is* employed on analog videotape.

Digital videotape formats record audio and video digitally, various of them supporting 12-, 16-, and 20-bit linear PCM. So videotape audio quality covering both analog and digital types spans the range from something worse than ordinary audio cassettes (analog 3/4" U-Matic) to among the best-available media.

Occasionally double-system sound recording is employed with videotape origination, when sound quality is paramount, or especially when multitrack recording is needed. This occurs on, for instance, episodic television shows with multiple microphones in front of studio audiences, where postponing mix decisions until post production is a huge advantage; each microphone may be as-

---

5. There were some historic film formats that recorded sound-on-film in the camera, either optically or magnetically, for newsreels, but these were never applied outside this purpose because the quality was low.

signed its own track of a multitrack recorder during staging for subsequent sweetening and mixdown during post production. In fact, for videotape productions that record production sound on the original videotape (*single-system*), the first process to occur in post production is to *lay down* the audio from the original tape to a separate post production audio medium for manipulation, thus turning a single-system original into a double-system track for post production. The manipulation that occurs is not only mixing of the production sound but also sweetening it, and this must occur in some form of multitrack environment.[6] Once the tracks have been mixed together to form a master mix, the audio is dubbed to the edited master videotape in a process called *lay back*.

Double-system digital sample rates

Digital sample rates for audio accompanying film and television is done at sample frequencies that have a strict mathematical relationship to the frame rate of the picture. The actual rates used varies among different projects due to post production and release format considerations. The sample rate thus also has a fixed relationship to time code, the primary method of synchronization for digital media. These topics are covered in Chapters 7 and 8.

Analog tape recording formats

Analog audio tape recording formats include variations in tape width, number of tracks, speed, recorded frequency response called equalization, and method of synchronization. Among the various widths employed professionally, from $^1/_4$- to 2-in., the $^1/_4$-in. tape is available with the most variations. These variations make it essential to label tapes correctly. With some program material, especially sound effects, it may be impossible to tell what the correct speed is even by listening.

---

6. This does not necessarily mean a multitrack tape machine, because a multichannel digital audio workstation can accomplish the same task.

Quarter-inch-wide tape may be recorded in full-track monaural, with or without a sync signal. Two-channel $^1/_4$-in. recording may also be recorded with or without one of two possible sync signals. Table 6.6 gives labeling instructions for production analog audio tapes. Probably the second most common tape width used in film and video production is the workhorse 2-in. 24-track tape machine, employed extensively in post production. While its "linear" access makes it slower than a nonlinear hard disk based system, the format is still in widespread use.

Compact Cassette tapes see use for gathering background information for documentaries, for instance, in which case the audio from them may wind up in finished programs, as it is the only available source. Since there are variations among tape types, companding systems, etc., among cassette tapes, it is necessary to know what tape works best on what settings of a recorder, and to know the factors that went into making the recording so that it may be played back appropriately.

All of the tape formats, when used in film and television sync sound production applications, must provide a means to record a synchronization track. This is because tape recorders, running "wild" (i.e., without synchronization means) will not maintain lip sync over a long period of time; they drift in speed, lacking an absolute reference such as perforations. Since a one-frame error may be noticeable and a tape may be 1 hour long, 1-frame/hr. should be the maximum error. One frame/hr. is 1 part in 86,400, whereas a professional machine usually has a specification of around 0.1% speed accuracy, or 1 part in 1000. Synchronization thus has to be provided for any professional use of film and video. Methods of doing this are discussed later.

Playback equalization

There are two prominent methods of recording open-eel analog tape used in film and television production that result in different frequency response: NAB used in the U.S., and CCIR used in Europe. Productions that work internationally, or those from countries where the choice is not obvious, must

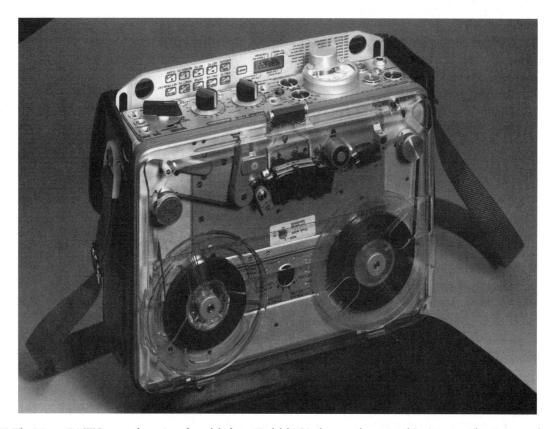

Fig. 6.3 The Nagra IV-STC, one of a series of models from Kudelski SA that are the most ubiquitous production sound recorders for film production. This model is a 2-channel direct analog stereo recorder with SMPTE time code sync. Photo courtesy Kudelski SA

mark the production tapes as to which standard was used. Mono Nagra recorders can play either standard, but are adjusted to record only to one of them.

In cassette recording, there are also two playback equalization response curves in use, called 120 μsec and 70 μsec. The higher number is used with a grade of tape that requires greater compensation for losses. The less expensive IEC Type I cassette tape is used with 120 μs playback equalization, and

the better Types II and IV with 70 μs. Playing a tape recorded at 120 μs, for instance, with a 70-μs response, produces frequency-response errors. Today's cassette machines include "fingers" that fit into "wells" in the back of the cassette shell, telling the machine the general tape type, along with the traditional pre-recorded signal that lets the machine know not to record over an existing recording.

Table 6.5: Open-Reel Analog Tape Formats and Their Uses

Tape width (in.)	Tape speeds (in./sec)[1]	Track format	Primary uses
$^1/_4$	15, $7^1/_2$, $3^3/_4$	Full track plus sync[2]	Film production (principally on Nagra recorders)

Table 6.5: Open-Reel Analog Tape Formats and Their Uses (Continued)

$^1/_4$	**15,** $7^1/_2$	2	Record masters
$^1/_4$	**15,** $7^1/_2$	2-track plus sync[3]	Two-channel film production (on stereo Nagra)
$^1/_4$	$7^1/_2$	4	Semi-pro music studio format
$^1/_2$	**30, 15,** $7^1/_2$	4	Music studio production, 2-ch film masters (typically on trks 1 & 2) with added sync (typically on trk 4)
1	**30, 15,** $7^1/_2$	8	Music studio production, largely superseded by 2 in.
2	**30, 15,** $7^1/_2$	16	First 2 in. machine format, superseded by 24-trk format
2	**30, 15,** $7^1/_2$	24	Music studio and post production workhorse with added sync (typically on trk 24, and possibly 23)[4]

1 The most commonly used speeds are given in bold.
2 The sync system is called Neopilottone, and it utilizes two areas of the audio track recorded out of phase with each other, so that they mutually cancel at the audio playback head, but may be read by a special head.
3 The re are two sync systems: FM sync, and SMPTE time code, discussed in chapter 7.
4 In the case where track 24 is used for a sync signal, such as SMPTE time code or a power line frequency reference tone, it is customary to leave track 23 unrecorded. Crosstalk from track 24 into track 23 potentially degrades the recordings on track 23, and crosstalk from track 23 to track 24, particularly of bass program material, may prevent time code and reference tone readers from working properly.

Table 6.6: Suggested Labeling Items for Analog Tapes[1]

Item	Typical label for Mono	Typical label for 2-channel with FM sync	Typical label for 2-channel with SMPTE Time Code
End that is out	Heads out/Tails out	Heads out/Tails out	Heads out/Tails out
Speed (in./s)	15 ips[2]/$7^1/_2$ ips	15 ips/$7^1/_2$ ips	15 ips/$7^1/_2$ ips
Equalization	NAB/CCIR	NAB/CCIR	NAB/CCIR
Track format	Full track	2 track	2 track
Sync type	Neopilottone[3]	FM Sync[4]	SMPTE Time Code[5]
Sync reference	Internal crystal/external source (specify)	Internal crystal/external source (specify)	Internal crystal/external source (specify)
Sync rate	60 Hz	60 Hz	Time Code Rate & Drop Frame or Non-Drop Frame[6]
Method of sync	Slate	Slate	Smart Slate/Camera Time Code (such as Aaton)

1 These are in addition to the standard production report described in chapter 5, but may be made a part of it.

2　A common abbreviation for in./s.
3　Only on monaural machines.
4　Only on 2-channel machines so equipped.
5　Only on 2-channel machines so equipped.
6　See Chapter 7.

Ultrasonic bias/Record equalization

The fundamental invention that permits good analog audio tape recordings is the addition of an ultrasonic signal called bias. It is discussed in Appendix II. The "bias" is adjusted for each tape type and speed according to manufacturer's directions to optimize a variety of characteristics of the recording. Once bias has been set correctly by a technician, record equalization must also be adjusted for flat overall frequency response of the recorder.

Table 6.7: Running Time at Various Tape Speeds by Reel Diameter[1]

Outer reel diameter (in)	5	7	$10^1/_2$	14
Tape speed (in./sec)	Running Time (min)			
30	$3^1/_4$	$7^1/_2$	15	30
15	$7^1/_2$	15	30	60
7^1_2	15	30	60	120
$3^1/_4$	30	60	120	240

1　This table assumes 0.0015 in. thick tape, which is standard for use in professional audio. Thinner base tape is available for special purposes. The times are given for one pass through the machine (double the times for $1/_2$- and $1/_4$-track recording in both directions—see Appendix II).

Erasure

Erasure of tape or film deliberately may occur at two places: the erase head on a machine, just prior to recording, and on a bulk eraser, also called a *demagnetizer* or *degausser*. Tape machines virtually always use the bias signal, with no audio added, for erasure. This yields a practically random pattern in the domains. It is these random domains passing the play head that forms tape hiss in the absence of any signal, much like the grain that we see in picture film.

A bulk eraser is used to wipe a tape clean without having to pass it through a recorder. These are power line-operated devices with a deliberately strong magnetic field that flips the domains in the tape or film oxide back and forth. By rotating the tape in the strong field in order to cover it all, then *slowly removing the tape from the field*, complete erasure is achieved. On the other hand, if the power is removed while the tape is on the degausser and the magnetic field collapses, or if the tape is removed too quickly from the field, *spoking* will occur. Spoking is a periodic noise that occurs once per revolution of a reel and is caused by the domains on one side of the pack having a preferential direction of magnetization. It is sometimes difficult to subsequently remove this effect with an erase head on a machine, and the result can be a varying hiss level, up and down at the rate of the reel turning. This is most noticeable upon high-speed playback, during which a characteristic "whoop, whoop, whoop" is heard.

In general digital and video tape types are more difficult to degauss than conventional audio tape, and require greater output from the demagnetizing device.

Companding noise reduction

The lifetime of analog recording was greatly extended beginning in the 1970s with the introduction of companding noise reduction, through several generations of developments. Companding noise reduction systems place electronics around tape and film machines that perform an equal and opposite effect on the record and playback sides. In principle, low levels are increased upon recording, and cut back an equal amount on playback. The result is the same sound for desired signals, but the tape hiss that was introduced in the recording process only "sees" the second half of the process, the reduction in level, and so noise is reduced. This is a greatly simplified description of a complex process that is described more fully in Appendix II. The important thing to know is what companding system was in use on a given recording so that the same system can be used on playback. On cassette tapes, for instance, Dolby C noise reduction might be employed, but most machines only have Dolby B, and playing a tape recorded with C-type noise reduction on a machine set to use B-type NR leads to obvious errors.

A prime area for trouble from not setting NR correctly is on Betacam. Since all machines are not equipped with the standard Dolby C noise reduction, many have switches to turn the NR off. Leaving NR off on a tape that is encoded leads to strange artifacts of surging and pumping levels. Tapes must be marked as to their noise reduction status.

Dolby SR is the most sophisticated companding system in use, and it is used on analog magnetic film formats in dubbing, and on analog optical sound tracks for motion-picture prints. It works in multiple frequency bands, some of which are fixed, and some of which are adaptive to the audio signal.

Film recording formats

The distinction between tape and magnetic film is simple: Film is perforated so that teeth in editing and dubbing environments can drive the film by its *sprocket holes* and maintain sync in this brute force but completely effective manner. All recording of sound on film today magnetically is for post production, but release prints more commonly use optical processes, which may be printed at high speed in laboratory manufacture.

Magnetic film is available in two primary widths, corresponding to the gauges that camera film is available in, 35mm and 16mm.[7] Additionally, 35mm film is available in two forms, stripe coat and full coat. *Stripe coated film* has two stripes of oxide on an otherwise clear base, and *full coat* is covered with oxide at a minimum across the area between the perforations, and usually fully across. The two stripes of oxide on stripe coat are (1) a wide stripe meant for recording a single-track monaural signal, and (2) a narrow stripe, the *balance stripe*, coated on the film simply so that the film will wind up smoothly on reels, but occasional use is made of it for recording sync signals.

Stripe-coated film records only one audio track, but full-coat film may be recorded in any of the following formats: three-, four-, or six-track. Because the film is divided into equal track widths for each of these formats, playing a four-track film on a three-track head will result in large problems. Thus labels on masters must contain essential information on the number of tracks (and what they are used for).

Sixteen-millimeter magnetic film is also available in two forms, with perforations down one side, or down both sides called *single-perf* and *double-perf* respectively. Single-perf film may contain two tracks, while double-perf only has room for one. Edge track recording on single-perf film is the most common type in the United States, but center track has the advantage of being able to be reversed head-for-tails, which is occasionally useful for sound-effects editing. EBU stereo is often used for twin-mono tracks for dual-language purposes rather than actual stereo.

Table 6.8 gives information regarding film consumption rates and other information

7. There is in addition a small amount of 17.5-mm film used, 35 mm split in two.

for the three gauges (widths) at 24 fps.

Table 6.8: 35mm, 16mm, and 8mm Film Rates

Film gauge	Frames/ft	Frames/sec[1]	Ft/min	In./sec	Primary production uses
35	16	24	90	18	Theatrical films, movies of the week and episodic television
35	16	30	112.5	22.5	High-end music videos, television commercials, especially those with lots of motion
16	40	24	36	7.2	Some movies of the week and episodic TV shows
16	40	30	45	9	Music videos, TV commercials
Super 8	72	Varies 8–70, typ. 18–32	Varies	Varies	Music videos

1 The 24 fps rate is much more common than the 30 fps rate.

Playback equalization

Luckily, film recording playback equalization was standardized internationally some years ago, so film is more easily interchanged across borders than tape. This is ironic because 2-in. 24-track tape is probably interchanged more often than film, but it, as well as $1/4$ -n. production sound tapes, is subject to these errors.

Companding noise reduction on film

Today where magnetic film is in use it is typical to use Dolby SR noise reduction and signal improvement technology.

Toning reels

Analog tape and film varies somewhat from batch to batch and even reel to reel in such specifications as record sensitivity and response. Thus it is important in professional use to leave a "Rosetta Stone"[8] of information on the tape or film that subsequent us-

8. The Rosetta Stone was the key to understanding Egyptian hieroglyphics. It was found by Napoleon's troops in 1799, and dates back to ca. 200 BC. It contains the same text in hieroglyphics, Greek, and demotic, so provided the first modern understanding of the ancient languages.

ers can employ to play back the tape or film correctly.

On production sound tapes, the head of a new reel is recorded from the tone oscillator in the Nagra recorder at its reference level (– 8 dB on the modulometer of the 4.2 mono machine; –10.5 dB on the IV-S stereo machine).

> As described in the three-head machine discussion, this tone is not a pure sine wave, but contains deliberately added harmonics that can be used to test head alignment and frequency response.

For film pre-mixes and final mixes the usual items recorded before the program on reels are: 1 kHz tone at reference level, pink noise in phase on all the channels, and a "2" pop. The tone provides a reference level setting; the pink noise a reference for physical head adjustments and frequency response; and the "2" pop a sync reference (the "pop," also known as "pip" lines up in editorial sync with the "2" frame of the SMPTE countdown leader.

Digital tape and disk recording formats

The various formats typically used for film

and television sound acquisition are described in Table 6.9. Methods of exporting sound from these formats are discussed in Chapter 8. The primary difference among the methods of export are whether the audio must be "streamed," that is, played out linearly, or whether it may be copied as a file in a format recognizable to a digital audio workstation, a process that can be faster than streaming.

The 24-bit word length machines record the output of a/d converters that have today, at best, about 20 bits of dynamic range. Still, this is more dynamic range than 16-bit machines, which are today "format limited" rather than a/d converter technology limited.

Table 6.9: Digital Audio-Only Formats typically used in Film and Television Sound Acquisition

Format	Medium	No. of tracks	Word Length	Primary uses	Sync method
DAT[1] (aka RDAT)	DAT cassette	2	16-bit	Field and studio recording	Time code on specialized professional machines
Nagra D	$\frac{1}{4}$" open reel tape	4	24-bit	Field and studio recording	Dedicated time code track
DASH[2]	$\frac{1}{4}$" open reel tape	2	16-bit	Studio recording	Dedicated time code track
DASH	$\frac{1}{2}$" open reel tape	24–48	16-bit	Studio recording	Dedicated time code track
Zaxcom Deva II	Removable hard disk > DVD-RAM[3]	4	24-bit	Field recording	Time code
Nagra V	Removable hard disk	2	24-bit	Field recording	Time code
Fostex	DVD-RAM	4	24-bit	Studio recording model now; field model planned	Time code
DTRS[4] ("DA-88")	DTRS Cassette	8	16-, 24-bit [5]	Studio recording	Time code
Mini Disc[6]	optical Mini Disc	2	ATRAC[7]	Incidental recording purposes such as interviews, some sound effects	None internal; use clapperboard slate;[8]

1 (Rotary head) Digital Audio Tape
2 Digital Audio Stationary Head
3 Internal copying to accessory DVD-RAM
4 Usually called DA-88 format for the Tascam recorder that first used the format.
5 Machines are "forward compatible" meaning that a 24-bit machine type can play 16-bit tapes, but not vice versa.
6 Mini Disc is not designed as a professional medium; thus its digital output needs sample rate conversion to work in professional systems, and the accuracy of its quartz crystal may not be good enough for lip sync over long intervals.

7 ATRAC is an audio bit reduction scheme; see Chapter 11.
8 MiniDisc is not conceived of as a professional medium. Although the speed is based on a crystal oscillator (see Chap. 7), the oscillator frequency of a MiniDisc recorder is not guaranteed to maintain lip sync.

Tape/film transports

The purpose of tape and film transports, whether analog or digital, is to move the tape or film past the heads while maintaining intimate contact with them at a uniform speed, and to provide high-speed winding capability to search to other parts of the tape or film quickly.

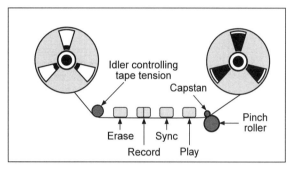

Fig. 6.4 The ingredients of an open reel recorder, including a sync function found only on recorders for film and television sound.

In open-reel tape, a fresh roll is placed on a supply reel, then threaded past a number of mechanical components on its way to the tape heads. Together, these supply "holdback" tension, which provides the pressure needed to keep the tape in good contact with the heads. The tape then passes the head assembly and continues to a capstan and pinch roller. The *capstan* is a cylindrical shaft rotating at a constant speed against which the tape is pressed by the pinch roller so that the tape will take on constant speed. From there, the tape passes by any outgoing motion-stabilizing components to the take up reel.

In total, a tape or film transport provides good head contact and uniform speed across the heads. In direct-analog magnetic recording, speed variations directly result in frequency variations, because if conventional tape is slowed down, all the frequencies are translated to lower ones, and vice versa, by an amount proportional to the speed change. Speed variations in transports take two forms: absolute speed errors, which affect total running time and pitch, and short-

er term variations, called wow and flutter, defined in Chapter 3.

Wow and flutter still mechanically occurs even in digital recording, however, the output from the tape is placed in a digital memory in the machine during playback, and clocked out at a completely even rate. Thus wow and flutter are essentially eliminated. There is one condition under which it may occur, however, and that is if the digital audio machine is being controlled in such a manner as to follow an external source. In this case, wow and flutter may be introduced if the source being followed itself has wow and flutter.

Tape and film electronics and heads

Three-head vs. two-head machines

Professional audiotape and film recorders typically employ a minimum of three heads, one each for erase, record, and playback, in that order. This permits playback off tape while recording so that professionals can be confident that the recording is actually occurring and that it is of high quality. Alternative names used for the monitor modes are given in Table 6.10. Such machines are called *three-head designs* and permit switching between the incoming source and sound off tape for monitor purposes. The idea applies to both analog and digital audio machines. In video, the term for the playback head that can perform this play-immediately-after-record function is the *confidence head*, and the process is *confidence head recording*.

Simple analog and digital audio machines sometimes use just two heads, an erase and a combination record-play head. Commonplace in cassette decks, the difficulty with these machines is, of course, that they lack the ability to monitor what was just recorded, so the professional is less confident that the recording is proper.

Three-head designs are not completely problem-free either. Listening to playback off the tape puts the production sound mixer a moment behind what is actually happening aurally, and thus a required mix action may be timed wrong. Also, it is extremely difficult to speak while listening to delayed sound, thus slating by having the production sound recordist speak is essentially impossible while listening to playback. Many users solve this problem by just listening in playback to the head of takes to be sure of proper recording, then switching to monitor source sound after the clapperboard slate, to be "in sync" with the real world, foregoing play-head monitoring during the bulk of a take.

Analog Nagra recorders have a method to test that bias and equalization have been set correctly by ear, and this depends on their being three-head machines. The tone generator in these recorders used to "tone" a tape, that is, record a reference level signal on the head of the tape to be used later for level setting, contains deliberate harmonics of the fundamental sine wave. By making a listening comparison of the signal sent to the tape, and that returned from the tape, any change in level or timbre indicates a fault in setting up the playback equalization, bias, record equalization, or internal play and record calibrate level controls.

Table 6.10: Alternative Names for Three-Head Tape or Film Machine Monitoring Modes[1]

Send to record head	Return from playback head
Direct	Tape (or film)
Source	Tape (or film)
Direct	PEC[2]
Bus	Film (or tape)

1 The items in the first and second columns are used in pairs.
2 *PEC* is a term left over from the days of optical recording. It stands for Photo-Electric Cell, or playback from the optical path of an optical film camera by way of a photovoltaic (solar) cell, but it is sometimes applied as slang to three-head tape recorder monitoring.

Physical damage to tape or film

Open-reel audiotape and videotape, whether analog or digital, is subject to a number of physical damage sources from handling and in operation. For example, careless winding may cause the layers to be stacked unevenly, and the protruding edges may rub against the reel or storage container. This will bend and crease the tape edges, causing intermittent problems, such as dropouts, loss of high frequencies, etc. Physical damage to open-reel media can be practically eliminated by winding the tape onto the reel at play speed, forming a solid pack, and storing the tape tails out. This is common practice for audio libraries, but is not so common in video libraries, which could benefit from it. Rewinding before playing and then storing the tape tails out is advantageous.

Magnetic film is more robust than tape due to its much thicker backing, so the tails-out, slow-wind method is little used or needed for film, although the quality of the wind in storage can matter, especially with acetate-base films.

Cassette tape, whether audio or video, analog or digital, is generally much less susceptible to physical damage than open-reel tape, but machines with poor mechanical alignment can damage tape, even though it is protected by the shell from most user-caused damage problems.

Tape and film oxides are mysterious chemically, being subject to a great many trade secrets. The archival quality of all magnetic tape, audio or video, analog or digital, is questionable because the oxide can break down into its constituent components over a period of years. Regrettably, no form of tape can be said to have the archival quality of Matthew Brady photographs made in the mid-1800s, consisting of silver on glass. Until such a medium is available, we continue to use tape routinely, but we monitor it in storage for degradation and copy it as necessary to maintain it over a period of years. To prevent physical and magnetic damage in long-term storage of production and post production materials, SMPTE has guidelines for storage conditions that should be followed.

Magnetic damage

Since the purpose of audiotape and videotape, whether analog or digital, is to store magnetic fields for playback, any outside magnetic field strong enough may change the tape and cause damage from the loss of high frequencies through complete erasure. Magnetic tape is called *hard* magnetically, because it is fairly difficult to magnetize it in the first place, and it retains magnetism for later playback. Tape recorder heads, on the other hand, are made of magnetically *soft* materials so that they do not retain magnetism, generally speaking.

However, even though they are not supposed to, magnetic heads and other transport parts can become magnetized, through coming into contact with a magnetized item (like a magnetized screwdriver, which seems to be the most common) and because of the electrical signals applied to the heads. For this reason, heads and metal transport parts touching the tape generally require periodic

demagnetization, typically with a hand demagnetizer that plugs into the wall and generates a deliberate enormous magnetic field. By smoothly moving the demagnetizer over the metal parts of the transport, and *moving the demagnetizer well away from the transport before disengaging its power*, the build-up of stored magnetism is eliminated.

To avoid magnetic damage in storage, production sound tapes should be stored a few inches away from dynamic or ribbon microphones, headphones, and loudspeakers, all of which contain magnets, and should be kept some feet away from any demagnetizer. Another kind of magnetic damage can occur in storage, without any external force. Tape is of course wound on a reel. In this condition, a process called *print through* can occur, where a signal on one layer can be re-recorded to another layer, at a much lower but potentially audible level. This is particularly a problem for production sound, because a lot of it consists of dialog interspersed with silence. Wound on a reel, if a word of dialog happens to be layered with an adjacent segment of silence, either preceding or following it, the word may print through to the silent passage and become audible as a pre-echo or post-echo. High temperatures, such as those in a hot car, exacerbate the process of print through and may easily make it more audible. A great deal of the dialog editor's time in post production has been spent on selectively removing the effects of print through.

Table 6.11: Analog Video Tape Formats[1]

Format Commercial Name	SMPTE[2]	Tape width and form	Manufacturer(s)	Sound capability	Additional sound capability
Quad		2" quad open reel, 15 and 7.5 in./sec	Many, but virtually obsolete	2-ch stereo longitudinal	
B	B	1" helical open reel	BTS	2-ch stereo longitudinal	

Table 6.11: Analog Video Tape Formats[1] (Continued)

C	C	1" helical open reel	Many	2-ch stereo longitudinal, some with Dolby A companding noise reduction	2-ch stereo 16-bit linear PCM, rarely (used in duplication plants, not production)
U-Matic	E	$^3/_4$" cassette	Many	2-ch stereo longitudinal	
U-Matic SP		$^3/_4$" cassette	Many	2-ch stereo longitudinal with Dolby C companding noise reduction	
Betacam	L	$^1/_2$" Betacam cassette	Sony	2-ch stereo longitudinal with Dolby C companding noise reduction	
Betacam SP Broadcast series (BVW model nos.)	L	$^1/_2$" Betacam SP cassette	Sony	2-ch stereo longitudinal with Dolby C companding noise reduction	2-ch stereo AFM with companding noise reduction
Betacam SP P- and U- series	L	$^1/_2$" Betacam SP cassette	Sony	2-ch stereo longitudinal with Dolby C companding noise reduction	
Hi 8		8mm cassette	Many	AFM mono minimum, 2-ch stereo optional	2-ch stereo digital optional
8 mm		8mm cassette	Many	AFM mono minimum, 2-ch stereo optional	2-ch stereo digital optional
S-VHS	H[3]	$^1/_2$" S-VHS cassette	Many	2-ch stereo longitudinal	2-ch stereo AFM with companding noise reduction[4]
VHS	H[3]	$^1/_2$" VHS cassette	Many	Mono or 2-ch stereo longitudinal on all machines, some with Dolby B noise reduction	2-ch stereo FM with companding noise reduction, optional

1 Analog videotape means that the video is analog; audio may be direct analog, FM, or digital.
2 The designation used by the Society of Motion Picture and Television Engineers.
3 Note that both VHS and S-VHS are covered by the same document, so the letter H does not distinguish them.
4 A system was designed to record a third pair of sound tracks on SVHS with 16-bit linear PCM, and was sold in limited numbers in Japan.

Recording

Table 6.12: Digital Videotape Formats

Format Designator	Tape width	Producer	Video format	No. sound channels	Sound channel coding[1]
D-1	19 mm	Sony, BTS	Component	4	20-bit linear PCM
D-2	19 mm	Sony, Ampex	Composite	4	20-bit linear PCM
D-3	$1/2$"	Panasonic	Composite	4	20-bit linear PCM
D-5	$1/2$"	Panasonic	Component	4	20-bit linear PCM
D-9 Digital S	$1/2$"	JVC	Compressed component	2, 4	16-bit linear PCM
DCT	19 mm	Ampex	Compressed component	4	20-bit linear PCM
Digital Betacam	$1/2$"	Sony	Compressed component	4	20-bit linear PCM
Betacam SX	$1/2$"	Sony	Compressed component	4	16-bit LPCM
DVCAM	$1/4$"	Sony	Compressed component	2, 4	16-bit for 2; 12-bit for 4
DV, miniDV	$1/4$"	Many	Compressed component	2, 4	16-bit for 2; 12-bit for 4[2]
MPEG-IMX	$1/2$"	Sony	Compressed component	4, 8	24-bit for 4; 16-bit for 8
D-7 DVCPRO25	$1/4$"	Panasonic	Compressed component	2	16-bit linear PCM
DVCPRO 50	$1/4$"	Panasonic	Compressed component	4	16-bit linear PCM
High definition tape formats					
D-12 DVCPRO HD	$1/4$"	Panasonic	Compressed component	8	16-bit linear PCM
D-5 HD	$1/2$"	Panasonic	Compressed Component	8	20-bit linear PCM
D-6	19 mm	BTS, Toshiba HDTV format recorder	Component	10,[3] 12[4]	20-bit linear PCM
D-11 HDCAM	$1/2$"	Sony	Compressed component	4	20-bit LPCM

1 Although the coding on the tape handles 20 bits in these machines, few if any of them are equipped with 20-bit converters. What is probably most common is 18-bit converters, which are actually monotonic to 16 bits. All the professional formats use 48 kHz sampling.
2 Sample rate for 2 channel is 48 kHz; for 4 channel it is 32 kHz.
3 For interlace scan.
4 For progressive scan.

136

Aesthetic factors in tape recording

Usually when we think about tape recording we do not think about aesthetic aspects of the physical act of recording itself, but rather the sound material that is recorded and its arrangement on multiple tracks. For the most part, if an expert were asked for a definition of a good recording system, the intent would be to record the signal coming in uncontaminated and to deliver it unmodified to the output sometime later. There are several ways though that conventional analog tape recording faults have aesthetic impacts on the material to be recorded.

The first came to light in the late 1960s with the introduction of the first widely used companding noise reduction systems. Upon reducing the noise 10 to 15 dB across the audible frequency range, some users had several complaints:

- The sound lacked "airiness," a sense of space around the sound.

- The sound was duller.

Subsequently it was found that these were both artifacts of tape hiss. Tape hiss is uncorrelated across the channels, because it arises from completely random sources. Uncorrelated noise presented over multiple channels of a sound system does tend to make the sound more spacious, just because the sound caused by such noise at the two ears is distinctly different. Also, adding small amounts of noise to uncontaminated signals made it sound slightly brighter, and that could be interpreted in some cases to be "better." Thus, adding noise to the signal actually improved it, in one way of thinking! The idea that higher noise might be better could not, however, withstand the onslaught of the needs of recording on multiple tracks, with its attendant 3 dB decrease in the signal-to-noise ratio for each doubling of the number of tracks; we would have been drowning in hiss by today's production standards if companding noise reduction were not used.

The second of these kinds of problems occurred with the introduction of digital recorders. Within their bounds, that is, recording so that peaks do not exceed the full-scale value, digital recording is potentially quite undistorted, compared with high levels on analog machines. In music studio use, however, some users complained that the sound of the new digital machines lacked something, and indeed they did—the distortion added by an analog system. Linear PCM digital audio systems overload abruptly, causing what is probably audible distortion as soon as the full scale is exceeded. Analog distortion, however, tends to be gradual in its onset, getting more and more distorted over a range of levels. This very "pillow-like" overload effect is what some people were looking for from their tape recorder. Analog tape at high levels compresses the signal, albeit in a distorted fashion. While this doesn't obey the above-mentioned definition of recording, it is nonetheless a real effect. Sharp transients can be limited in level by tape saturation, possibly permitting louder signals on analog recordings than on digital ones, for the same or less perceived distortion. This factor, plus the greater cost associated with digital recording, has kept analog multitrack recording alive in the music business to this day. The purveyors of digital recorders "know" their machines to be superior in measured performance, but users sometimes prefer analog systems to use the overload "defect" for benign limiting. Therefore, there are aesthetic implications to technical choices.

Chapter 7: Synchronization

Introduction

The need to synchronize audio tape to film or video for lip-sync sound when using double-system recording has already been discussed. Methods for tape media include those that simply maintain synchronization once it has been established, without providing an absolute reference, and newer means, which provide both relative (correct speed) and absolute (correct start point) synchronization. The older methods "invisibly perforate" tape, while the newer ones add a yardstick to the length of the tape so that any position along the tape is labeled with a location or "address." Newer hard disc recording also relies on this addressing method, called SMPTE Time Code. The oldest method, synchronization by perforations in film, has been around since the start of film sound in the 1920s, and is still in widespread, if declining, use.

The methods used to obtain synchronization between double-system audio and film or video are described in this chapter, and the editing methods to "sync up" the two are

described in Chapter 9. This chapter also covers the relevant aspects of film-to-video transfer called telecine, since a basic understanding of the processes used there is needed to establish and maintain synchronization in video-based post production for film originals.

Sprocket hole sync

Starting in the 1920s, the method of synchronization was to mount separate strands of film containing picture or sound onto different machines, to engage their perforations called sprocket holes on toothed wheels, and to drive all the machines at the same rate for synchronization. For production, this was accomplished by driving the film camera and the optical audio recorder with synchronous motors, which locked to the frequency of the power line. In this way, the length of time of one frame of picture film and one frame of sound file matched identically.

By using a clapperboard slate, and finding the correct picture frame when the sticks first come together, and the correct sound frame with the loud "thwack," and cutting the track to fit the picture, sync was established.

Pilot tone sync

The second primary method of synchronization was developed for the introduction of lightweight portable tape recorders for production sound, and is still in use. It has already been pointed out in Chapter 6 that a synchronization method is essential for tape because its speed control is not adequate to maintain lip sync. What was needed was a way to record a signal on the tape proportional to the speed of the camera, and a way in subsequent transfer to use this signal to "resolve" the speed so that a copy to film or a workstation could be made such that each single frame of sound is exactly equal in length of time to a single frame of picture.

Today electronically controlled motion-picture camera motors are used that are referenced to a quartz crystal-controlled oscillator. This device is very similar to those provided in "quartz crystal" watches, giving cameras extremely good speed stability. A separate crystal-based oscillator in the audio recorder produces a sync signal that, although not connected to the camera, provides a reference to maintain lip sync throughout long takes. This method, called *crystal sync,* is the prominent technology in use today.

For historic reasons, the frequency of the sync signal recorded on the tape is the power line frequency in the country of shooting—not the frame rate—60 Hz in the U.S. and Japan, and 50 Hz in Europe, and one of these two standards in other parts of the world (another headache for international productions).

> Some older studio cameras employed synchronous motors, the speed of which was controlled by the power line frequency. In such cases, the crystal oscillator of the sound recorder is not used as the source for sync, but rather a scaled down (1 Volt) and transformer isolated version of the power line itself, in order to match camera speed.

> There are also older battery operated cameras that had a small signal generator attached to

their motor shaft. This generator is also arranged to produce a power line frequency signal when the camera speed is exactly 24 fps, and it must be connected by cable to the sound recorder.

In the case of monaural full-track recording, the problem was where to place the sync signal on the tape, because practically the full width of the tape was recorded. The solution was for the sync signal to be recorded on two narrow tracks down the center of the full track recording, with the two tracks having opposite polarity, commonly called "out of phase," with each other. When the two halves of this recorded signal are played by the full-track audio head, the two opposite polarity recordings cancel each other out, yielding essentially no crosstalk into the audio. On the other hand, when a special fourth head with two narrow tracks reads the signal (the same type that recorded it), the head wiring can be made to *add* the out-of-phase signal and to *cancel* the in-phase signal (the audio) and thus recover the sync signal. This method of synchronization is called *pilottone sync* and is used on all mono sync recorders today.

FM sync

Analog stereo recorders came along later. There is space between the two audio tracks for a synchronization signal track. If this was a direct recording at 50 or 60 Hz though, it could easily crosstalk into the audio channels and be heard as hum. The use of a high-frequency signal to carry the information reduces the likelihood of crosstalk. So 50 or 60 Hz is used to frequency modulate an FM carrier at 13.5 kHz, thus preventing crosstalk. The name for this recording process is *FM sync,* and it is functionally identical to the pilottone system, differing only in the method of recording and track placement.

Resolving

Resolving involves playing the sync signal and using it to control the speed of the playback machine so that transfer of the original production recording onto magnetic film or into a digital audio workstation is at the same rate as the picture. After resolving, each "frame" of sound will be exactly the same length as each frame of picture, and even very long takes will stay in sync. To complete synchronization, all that has to be done is to "sync up" the sound track with the picture, using clapperboard slates.

> The heart of resolving is to compare the frequency of the recorded sync signal to an external reference frequency, such as the power line frequency, and derive a control signal that continuously speeds up or slows down the playback machine in order to match the playback frequency to the external reference. In this way the production tape becomes "locked" to the reference frequency. In addition, the same reference frequency must be used to control the speed of the film recorder or the frame rate of the digital audio workstation. The transfer operator must monitor that sync lock is maintained throughout the duration of the transfer. If these conditions are all met, synchronization is assured.

When sync is lost

Loss of sync renders lip-sync material at the very least extraordinarily difficult to edit, and is a cause for large post production problems. The audio recorder must record a sync signal that relates to the camera speed, usually the output of its internal crystal oscillator. Analog recorders that record a sync track have prominent "tally"[1] features to show that sync is being recorded, and the tally feature should be used.

Sync is widely considered to be an annoyance associated with double-system recording, and thus the responsibility for it always seems to fall to sound personnel. Synchronization can be lost for a variety of reasons. One problem could be that the sound person forgot to record the sync signal, or the right sync signal that matches the camera. On the other hand, it is also possible for a malfunctioning camera to be running off speed.

> Complications can occur if motion-picture cameras are operated at non-normal speeds, such as

---

1. To *tally* is to indicate the presence of something. In the case of television, a red light provided on each camera lights one at a time to show which camera is live; the red light is called the *tally light*. Likewise, in this context *tally* means that an indicator shows that the function is occurring.

to accommodate video or computer monitors in a shot. Without changing the camera speed from 24 fps, a moving black bar or other artifacts may be photographed on the monitors. Shooting sync sound with such monitors portrayed correctly in the scene is a specialty that requires expert advice, and possibly special equipment.

Requirements for synchronization

Note that both the pilottone and FM sync methods only provide the correct speed, thus causing the correct length of a sound transfer so that picture and sound match. The starting point for each take must be determined by the use of a clapperboard slate, called "sticks." Its use in "syncing dailies" is described in Chapter 9 and Appendix II.

The method that provides both correct speed reference and absolute positioning is SMPTE Time Code. Time Code consists of four sets of double digits, representing hours, minutes, seconds, and frames, such as 01:20:17:06. The counter increments 1 minute for every 60 seconds, 1 hour for every 60 minutes, and from 0 hours through 23 hours, before starting over at 0 hours. The number of frames per second and how they are counted depend on the type of time code in use, described below.

Time code is recorded on the audio recorder, and is photographed at the head of shots on the picture by use of a time code slate, or is recorded optically in the camera. Thus audio recordings are delivered in "frames per second" by using SMPTE Time Code for synchronization. The picture and sound time code recordings are then used in post production to establish and maintain synchronization for each shot. Because of its importance in this scheme, telecine transfer is described next, then there is further information about time code.

Telecine Transfer

In a great many cases today, film shot for both theatrical features and for television is transferred to video for editing. Theatrical films are often edited on video, and then a special cut list[2] is produced for a negative cutter to cut the film negative for subsequent laboratory operations. For films shot for television release only, either the original telecine transfer is used for the final output, or a similar edit list is used to make a new telecine transfer at higher quality and in conformance with the "off-line" video picture edit.

There are complications due to the differing nature of film and video that are necessary to understand in order to get and keep picture-sound synchronization throughout the various processes.

Most film in the U.S. is shot at 24 fps, whether for theatrical release or for television shows. But video operates at a higher frame rate, nominally 30 fps. If we were to simply speed up the film from 24 to 30 fps for the purposes of transfer to video, all the action would be much faster than normal, and accompanying sound would have its pitch raised dramatically—hardly a usable result.

So what is done in the film to video conversion is to selectively duplicate some of the film frames into some of the video frames (actually into halves of video frames called fields), so that a ratio of 24 film frames to 30 video frames is produced, a ratio of 4:5. This process is routinely called "3:2 pulldown." Technically a better name is "2:3 insert and pulldown," since the sequence starts with two video fields matching one film frame, then three video fields for the next film frame, and so forth—the 2:3 process constitutes the insertion of extra fields; the added process "pulldown" is explained below. The terms 3:2 and 2:3 are used interchangeably, and mean the same thing. The 2:3 telecine process does the frame conversion from 24 to 30, and viewers typically do not perceive the artifacts produced by repeating the film frames.[3]

If this was all there was to it, there would be

just a few complications resulting from the transfer. However, NTSC[4] color video does not run at exactly 30 fps, but instead at 29.9700261643 fps, routinely called 29.97. All too often this is even further rounded to "30" fps when what is meant is actually this long number. (The reason for the odd number of frames per second had to do with fitting color into a transmission system that had formerly only handled black and white television.) So after the 2:3 film frame to video frame/field conversion there is a remaining difference of practically 0.1%, with the video being slower than the film original, and the film is simply slowed down by this amount in transfer to video. This is the "pulldown" part of the process and is responsible for the potential of sync problems arising, because the original sound recording must be slowed down to match. The process of slowing down the audio to match the picture is also given the name "pulldown." We say, "you must pull down the sound to match the picture," for instance.

The four film frames of the sequence in Fig. 7.1 are labeled A, B, C, and D. The concept of these frame labels is important to be able to generate a correct list to match back to film frames from a video edit decision list. The "A" frame is defined as one which produces two fields in one video frame originating from the same film frame, and is assigned a frame time code of 00, 05, 10, 15, 20, or 25 in 29.97 fps video.

The European alternative
PAL and SECAM users do not face quite so many complications as those in NSTC countries. 25 fps video is matched by shooting 25 fps film for television, and theatrical features shot at 24 fps are simply sped up by about 4% when played on television. This does lead to a pitch shift that should be corrected, but often is not.

SMPTE time code sync
Of all the areas of film and television sound recording, probably none has simultaneously advanced the industry more and caused

---

2. Of several types.: see Matchback and Film Cut Lists, below.

3. Although some specialized film shot for video, such as some music video and television commercials that feature a great deal of action benefit from being shot directly at 30 fps on film.

---

4. U.S. analog standard definition television.

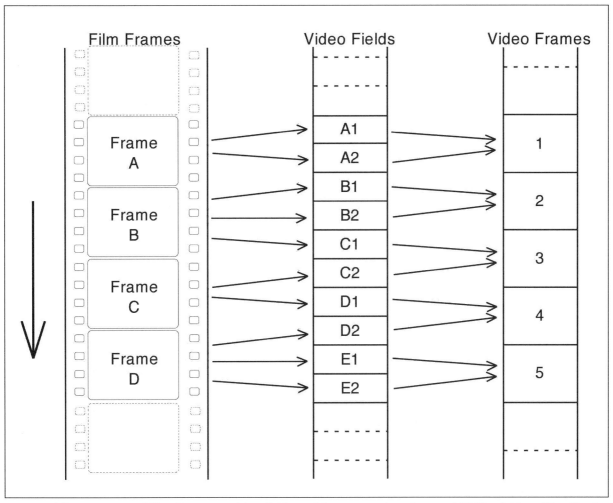

Fig. 7.1 The sequence of film frames to video fields and frames produced on an NTSC telecine. The film is run at 23.976... fps and alternating 2 and 3 video fields are produced from the film frames. The result is video frames running at 29.97... fps having the frames derived as shown. Film frame A and video frame 1 is the only combination that uniquely associates one video frame with one film frame, a fact that can be used to identify the A frame from the associated video. Video fields each consist of one-half of the lines of a video frame, interlaced with each other.

more problems than time code. Originally developed for videotape editing purposes, it was soon extended to keeping multitrack audio machines in sync with video machines for post production,[5] and then to production sound. Planning time code usage in pre-production and having all parties involved carrying out the plan can greatly improve efficiency. The usual way problems are avoided today is to hold a pre-production meeting among the producers, the cinematographer and his or her assistants, the camera rental house, the post-production facility, and the production sound personnel. There all the steps can be discussed, and the most expertise will be available to everyone.

Audio for either film or television originating on film is typically recorded with time code at an actual 30 fps, and played in sync with the telecine at 29.97 fps. Slowing down the audio thus matches the video in length and stays in sync, and the resulting slight pitch shift is acceptable. However, there are several consequences of operating video at a rate slightly slower than clock time: one of them is that the time code numbers no longer

5. The companion use is for studio video recordings when multitrack is in use, such as studio audience shows.

match real time. Since real clock time is desired for some operations, like running a network, this problem leads to variations in types of time code.

Types of time code

There are a number of different Time Codes standardized by SMPTE, and several others that have come into use without being standardized (Table 7.1). Each of them has a spe-

Table 7.1: SMPTE/EBU Time Code and its Uses[1]

Frame rate (fps)	Frame count	Primary uses	Notes
23.976		High definition 24 p video for editing on NTSC 29.97 systems	
24	Non-drop frame	1. Film-only projects to be edited on specialty 24-fps video post-production systems 2. High definition 24 p video	Virtually never used with film
25	Non-drop frame	European video and film shot for television	
29.97	Non-drop frame	post production editorial, original video production, delivery masters for some non-broadcast uses such as DVD-V	One hour of time code runs one hour plus 3.6 sec of clock time
29.97	Drop frame	Delivery masters for broadcast, original video production on episodic television	Skips selected frame numbers to stay on clock time
30	Non-drop frame	Shooting film for music video or commercials for television at 24 fps or 30 fps*	Used where a 0.1% timing error is unimportant
30	Drop frame	Used with 24 fps film origination of episodic or long-form television when the delivery master requirement is 29.97 drop frame	Becomes 29.97 drop frame code when slowed down on the telecine

1 Do not confuse the time-code frame rate with the picture frame rate because the two can be different: Film can be shot at either 24 or 30 fps and will usually use the 30 fps time-code on the slate and production sound recorder, for example.

cific reason for existing, and they are very difficult or impossible to mix in some editing systems, while others may be capable of certain mixtures. It is not uncommon for a project to start out with one time code in production, use another in post production, and a third for delivery on video, for reasons that we discuss later. In many cases today though, the time code type needed for the final delivery master is used all the way from production through post to delivery master. Most problems related to time code have to do with misunderstanding the requirements for each stage of the chain, or loosing trace-

ability somewhere along the way. In order to understand why a project may use three different codes during its production, it is important to understand a little about the function of each of the codes.

• **23.976 fps** code is used for certain high definition video applications, where the HD camera is substituting for film. The rate is chosen so that direct conversion to NTSC by electronic 2:3 insertion like that in a telecine transfer is in a fixed relationship, without necessitating a pull-down.

144

- **24 fps** code exists in the standard, but its use is limited to those cases that use optical time code in the camera and to new *video* applications, called 24 p[6]. This may be surprising, but although film is being shot at 24 fps in the camera for normal motion picture production, the corresponding recorder will almost *never* be set to this rate. The reason for this is due to the nature of video used in post production editing, whether the film is to be released as a motion picture, or as a television program. The actual rate usually used in the U.S. on audio recorders and slates is 30 fps.

- **25 fps** code exists for the production, editing, and distribution of European television programs, whether origination is on film or video. Films for European television are simply shot at 25 fps, and each frame of film transfers exactly to each frame of video, with the European video systems PAL and SECAM being based on the 50-Hz power-line frequency there. If U.S. films are shown on European television, a transfer is made at 25 fps, running 4% shorter in time and generally with the pitch raised 4%. This is a noticeable error, so sometimes a "pitch shifter" (see Chapter 10) will be used during the transfer to return the pitch to the original one. (Theaters seem to be equipped randomly with either 24 or 25 fps projectors. Most theatrical films shot in Europe are made at 24 fps, although films produced by television agencies for both theatrical and television release may be shot at 25 fps.)

- **29.97 non-drop-frame** time code was developed to account for the fact that the frames in color television do not go by at 30 frames per second but rather slightly slower. The frames are numbered from 0 to 29 inclusive, so there are literally 30 frame numbers per "second." For every 30 frames, the time code *counts* 1 second. The problem is that the real frame rate is actually slightly less than 30 fps. Because the rate is *slower* than real time, it takes *more* than one actual clock hour to increment the time code hours counter, an error that accumulates to 108 extra frames per hour of code. In other words, a program that measures one hour long using 29.97 non-drop-frame time code will run one hour plus 3.6 sec of clock time. This 0.1% error is perhaps unimportant in timing short segments, but is important in timing longer programs, and is very important to television networks. Non-drop-frame code is used in many shooting and editing situations, partly at least because it has simpler arithmetic than the next code.

- **29.97 drop-frame** time code was invented so that the time indicated by this code could remain very close to clock time. By not counting certain frame numbers, *drop-frame* code keeps clock time.[7] In fact, real frames of film or the corresponding video are not dropped or lost; it is the frame numbers that are skipped to keep on clock time. Because this results in jumps in the code, it is more difficult for editing systems to deal with these missing codes.

- **30 fps** time code was originally designed to be used with U.S. black-and-white television. Today it is widely used on sound recorders and time code slates as a primary choice for film shoots that are to be posted using video editing systems. When film shot at either 24 or 30 fps is put on a telecine for transfer to video, it is slowed down very slightly (0.1%) to accommodate the needs of color television and it is thus converted to 29.97 fps (with the 24 fps film also undergoing the 2:3 process described above). The sound

---

6. The "p" stands for progressive scan, one method of producing a video picture.

7. The counter frames 00 and 01 are skipped once every minute, except in the minutes 00, 10, 20, 30, 40, and 50 for a total of 108 frames per hour. So the actual displayed time is not exact at many places in an hour but adds up to one displayed hour in one actual hour. There remains a residual error of about 2 frames per day that are skipped in the middle of the night by television networks.

is slowed down the same amount in transfer, so the two stay in sync.

This rate is not used in "pure" video applications shot on video cameras, because even a black-and-white video today generally uses the color television frame rate.

- **30 fps drop frame** time code has come into use for shooting episodic or long-form[8] television programs, where the delivery master is to be at 29.97 drop frame. When the film and tape are run on the telecine equipment for conversion to video they are both slowed down by 0.1%, becoming 29.97 drop frame code in the process.

A typical project for long-form television shot on film may use the following scheme:

- Shoot 30 fps drop frame time code on the slate and on the production sound recorder, using a camera frame rate of 24 fps.

- Transfer the project on the telecine. Both the sound and picture are slowed down by 0.1% to produce a 29.97 fps video picture, with the 2:3 insertion described above.

- Edit the project "off line" with a nonlinear system based on digital video, using 29.97 drop-frame code. Such off-line editing makes use of typically a lower cost and quality video system than the original format. The output of the process is an *edit decision list* (EDL), a list of how to "conform" a high-quality master copy of the original video source to the decisions made by the editor in the lower cost setting. The EDL may be on paper but more likely will be delivered on a floppy disc or electronically from the off-line editing system to the on-line system.

One difficulty with using video editing for 24 fps film projects is the necessity of using matchback techniques that cannot always be frame accurate in providing a negative cut list. In fast-paced commercials and music videos, this is

overcome by shooting 30 fps film as the original, but for television movies this is unlikely due to film consumption, and for theatrical films it is impossible due to universal use of 24 fps projection in theaters and no practical conversion means being available. One way out of this dilemma is to use specialized 24 fps video systems in which every frame of film is represented by a frame of video, exactly, but directly dubbed video tapes from such systems are unusable on standard equipment. Special tape copies must be made that employ an electronic process of 2:3 insertion and pulldown to run at NTSC video rate.

Conform the project from the original telecine transfer tape and possibly other sources to the *Edit Master* tape or disk, usually under computer control in an "on-line" edit suite, with 29.97 fps drop-frame time code. An alternative is to go back to the film original and retransfer it at higher quality, under computer motion control so that scenes can be located quickly.

- Copy (dub) the master videotape to a *delivery master* for broadcast distribution.

- Dub the edit master videotape to another delivery master for video distribution. The delivery contract will specify the type of time code required. In the case of networks, drop frame code is typically required, while for DVD discs, non-drop-frame code is standard.

This represents just one project, shot on film and delivered on tape, illustrating some of the issues regarding time-code usage. There are many more, especially when dealing with mixed film and video projects for release in both media, in which shooting is on film, editing is on video, and release is both on film and on video. Time code is the single part of production and post production in which planning is the most essential.

The term applied to the overall process of shooting on film, posting on video, and releasing on film is called a "film finish," while following the same preliminary steps and making a video master is called a "video finish." *Matchback* is the term applied to using a special type of EDL from a 29.97 fps

---

8. A term covering made for television movies and mini-series.

source to locate and cut film frames to match a video edit. This process inevitably involves some error, but the best systems keep the error to within ±1 frame of film, and maintain sync with sound. A *film cut list* is obtained from a 24 fps video system wherein each video frame matches a film frame, and editing can be exactly to the frame. This process also provides good sound sync.

Time code slates

In film sound production use of time code, a clapperboard slate showing a running time code is closed and at the moment of closure the displayed time code freezes. A time code generator, set to the same time and running parallel to the one in the slate, is included either internal to the sound recorder, or as an external time code generator. The frame on which the sticks have just closed and banged is noted as the sync point for the picture and sound.

Fig. 7.2 A time code slate, courtesy Deneke Inc.

Jam syncing

Note that the camera is equipped with a quartz-crystal speed-referenced motor and that the slate and recorder time codes must

match and are both referenced to their own crystal oscillators. So their relative speed is given by the accuracy of their oscillators, but there must also be a way to "set the time" so that they have the same absolute starting point. This is accomplished by *jam syncing* the two together. Because the recorder and slate may be disconnected for some time, much longer than the length of a reel, the quartz-crystal oscillators in both of them must be much more accurate than for conventional crystal-sync shooting. It is customary to jam sync the recorder and slate at least a few times per day to ensure hard synchronization, although the requirement for this depends on just how good the oscillators are in the two devices.

Syncing sound on the telecine

Usually productions are immediately transferred from film to a video format for post production, even for projects that will ultimately be theatrical features. This is due to the convenience of editing on video, although certain editors still cut on film.[9]

For most projects a telecine transfer operator synchronizes the open-reel analog, DAT, or other digital recorder sound to the picture. The operator does this by reading the time code of the frozen frame on the picture when the slate just closes and typing it into a controller that synchronizes the sound and picture for that take and then makes the transfer to video in sync. The process has to be repeated for each take, but it is quick. There needs to be no other handling of the separate sound source material, unless a sound editor wishes to get out-takes for word substitutions and sound effects.

Tip: An important feature that is required for the telecine operator to do this job is to have enough audio "pre-roll." That is time recorded before the slate, so that the equipment can be backed up, come up to speed, and lock sync before the slate occurs.

9. See for instance the end credits of *Saving Private Ryan* which proclaims that it was edited on the Moviola.

Latent image edge numbers

Film manufacturers supply camera negative exposed with latent image edge numbers, including both human- and machine-readable types. Since these numbers are embedded at the time of manufacturing the film, they are not referenced to the time code used on the set. During telecine, a data base is made of the time code derived from the slate and the latent image edge numbers, for further editorial use.

In camera time code

Several methods have been developed of recording optical time code in motion picture cameras, with separate efforts by Aaton and Panavision on the one hand, and Arri on the other. This capability eliminates the need for slates, and an ancillary data information capability beyond code may be used for date and camera information. This film time code works for both 16 and 35mm film gauges. When used with a double-system sound recorder, the camera and recorder are jam synced together just like the recorder and slate. Then the camera records time code as well as the audio recorder. On a telecine, the two can automatically be synchronized and played out to a video format for post production editing.

Synchronizers

Time-code synchronizers are devices that generally read time code and cause machine transports to come "into lock," thereby assuring synchronization. *Chase synchronizers* are devices that accept code from a master source and cause a locally controlled machine to follow the actions of the master. The master and slave may lock to identical code numbers on the two media for dailies transfer as described, or there may be an offset of time code numbers between the master and slave required.

There are at least two sets of time code used in a production. One is generated at the time of production and is used throughout the editorial processes. But this code would be discontinuous if copied to the *Edit Master* because picture edits would cause "jumps" in code numbers. Discontinuous code would confuse time-code synchronizers, so a second set of time code numbers is introduced. Edit masters are "striped" with continuous time code, that is, time code for which the numbers increase monotonically throughout the tape. So there is one set of time code numbers for production and another for finished edited material. Other sets of time-code numbers may be used for intermediate editing.

Machine control

Synchronizers make use of shuttle commands, such as fast forward, rewind, pause, and play, that are passed from one machine, the master, to another, the slave. The common way to do this is by way of DB-9 connector protocol standard called *Sony P-2 9-pin control* or colloquially just "9-pin" in the industry.

Time code midnight

One problem that occurs with time code is related to "midnight." If the start of the program is at 00:00:00:00, rewinding 30 seconds will yield the time code number 23:59:30:00. If a command is issued to locate 00:00:00:00, some equipment will go into rewind. It is trying to rewind by nearly 24 hours, rather than going ahead 30 seconds! For that reason, it is customary to use 01:00:00:00 as the first frame of the program rather than zero time. The hours digit may be incremented to indicate reel numbers, with the first tape of the program starting at 01:00:00:00 and running for perhaps 20 minutes, followed by the second tape starting at 02:00:00:00, with unused code numbers in between. This avoids the midnight problem and provides simple reel numbering.

Time code recording method

SMPTE time code is recorded by a variety of means depending on the medium. Table 7.2 summarizes the methods and their placement on the medium. Professional formats allocate space on the tape to such a track, such as Betacam SP. Recorded linearly along the length, this type of recording is called LTC for longitudinal time code. Such code can be recorded on the audio tracks of consumer formats that lack a dedicated time code track.

In video formats that record the vertical interval,[10] in addition to conventional longitudinal recording, time code may be recorded as a video signal on an unused line in the vertical interval. The line to use for this vertical interval time code (VITC) is not standardized, but modern time code readers locate VITC, despite its placement. There are some other requirements regarding videotape use of time code, such as the alignment of the code to the color frame sequence of the video frames, that are beyond the scope of this book.

---

10. The lines that are above the picture, usually hidden from view by cropping in the set.

Table 7.2: How Time Code Is Recorded by Medium

Medium	Placement of SMPTE time code[1] (LTC)	Other Code
$\frac{1}{4}$" 2-track Analog Tape	Center track	na
Analog Multitrack	Track 24 of 24 track (typical)	na
Open-reel digital tape	Dedicated address[2] track	na
DAT	Special[3]	na
Motion picture film	Edge, optical (not very widely used)[4][5]	na
Magnetic film	Balance stripe of stripe coat, rarely	na
Analog Video Tape: 1" C format, Betacam, Betacam SP	Dedicated time code address track	VITC
U-Matic	Dedicated time code address track[6]	VITC
Digital video formats	Dedicated time code address track	[7]
Hi-8	No SMPTE time code, but custom RC code plus external converter to SMPTE code is possible	na
8 mm	No	None
SVHS	Use a longitudinal audio track[8]	VITC
VHS	Use a longitudinal audio track[8]	Possible, but not generally reliable

1 All are longitudinal analog direct magnetic recordings unless otherwise stated.
2 An address track is a dedicated area of the tape, usually used for time code recorded longitudinally.
3 Time-code recording is carried in data multiplexed with audio data called *professional running time* or Pro R time. On properly equipped machines, this means that the time code rate and type can be chosen upon playback as a calculation from the running time.
4 A time-code slate photographed by the camera and clapped at the beginning of the take usually serves for film sync.

5 Although SMPTE code is not used very widely in production, a simpler optical code recorded in camera is popular in some applications called *Aaton code*.

6 Early machines lacked standardization in this area, so time code recorded on one brand of machine might not play on a machine of a different manufacturer.

7 The professional digital VTR's also have a special time code placement that is called Audio Sector Time Code (ASTC) that allows time code to be read in stop and at slow speeds.

8 Crosstalk of time code into the other longitudinal audio track should be expected.

na = Not applicable.

For most media, one must choose the type of code from the list of seven available at the time of recording, and a dub to a copy will usually be needed in order to change the code type, with a special synchronizer capable of syncing to one type of code at its input, while putting out a different type of code. DAT avoids this problem by recording hours, minutes, and seconds normally on tape, but instead of choosing one of the multiple frame rates at the time of recording, it records DAT frame numbers in place of film or video frame numbers. Suitable players contain conversion between DAT frames and a choice of one of the types of code, so that the type required can be a decision made at playback, not record, which is a great convenience. Some other types of hard disk recorders employ the same convention.

Conclusion

The bottom line on time code is that it can be very practical and efficient but its use requires continuity throughout a project and a clear understanding from the outset what is to be used at each stage of production. For this reason, interestingly, it is the producer of a television show who has the responsibility to deal with the vagaries of time code throughout the project, because it is the producer who follows the project through all stages of production and post production to delivery.

Slating

Clapperboard slates provide the means to find the start point for most film originated material. There is some use of time code recording directly to film in the camera which has the potential to eliminate the slate, but slating is still more common. When pilot-tone or FM sync are used, slates are required, while with SMPTE time code, a time code slate is still often used.

In some cases, such as documentaries, slates are undesirable because they make subjects of the documentary feel like actors. While methods were worked out to provide less obtrusive sync methods for film, today documentaries are customarily shot directly on video, and the single-system sound of video is employed, so no slates are necessary.

Why are slates important if they're all destined to be the first thing cut off in editing? Slates are the first to hit the screen in dailies, and it is a sign of good management of the activities of the crew if they come off well. Producers judge work on such matters. And even if technical means were developed to eliminate the need and the "wasted" footage that results in doing slates on every take, *The Fugitive* director Andrew Davis says that the slate would still be necessary: it is a part of the mantra that the crew chants together just before the take. It shows that everyone is alert and on board, and it gives the actors a moment to take a deep breath before stepping into the scene.

Slates must:

1. Be legible to a telecine operator and editor. This means being:

- all in frame and right side up for head slates,

- sufficiently large in the field of view, say occupying 1/3 of the frame,

- perpendicular to the line of sight of the camera,

- adequately lit to read,

- in focus, and

- held still until it is closed, then

- swiftly removed.

2. The slate operator and camera operator should collaborate to accomplish the above so that the camera needs minimal or no re-framing and re-focusing between slating and the body of the take, if at all possible. Sometimes this is impossible and the camera operator must say "Frame" so that the cue "Action" is not given prematurely, as shown in the following sequence.

3. The boom operator must "boom" the slate by orienting the mike in its direction. In some scenes, the mike is so far away and sometimes misaimed that the slate cannot be distinguished from other noises of the location. In this case a separate microphone, "opened" only for the slate, such as a radio microphone on the slate operator, may be used.

4. Occasionally it is impossible to head slate due to special camera position or framing. In these cases, it is customary to tail slate, with the slating done up side down to indicate that it is a tail slate.

5. Contain the correct information, especially scene and take. These especially must be legible, because they are the only place to refer to for this information (the can or box has the film title, reel number, etc.)

6. Be closed smartly, without a bounce, and without any fingers in the way.

7. Be correctly timed in the sequence:

- AD: "Roll sound,"

- Production sound mixer: rolls the recorder, observes the Speed and Power annunciator on the Nagra or that the equivalent on other recorders indicates correctly, opens the slate mic, announces scene and take, closes the slate mic and says: "Speed,"

- AD: "Roll camera,"

- Camera operator, when camera is running: "Rolling,"

- Slate: "Marker" or "Sticks" then bangs the slate crisply and exits. In the case of a close up, where the slate may be right in the actor's face, it is a courtesy to say instead "Soft sticks" and then close the clapper softly, so long as it can be heard on the recording clearly.

- Camera operator: "Frame,"

- Director: a breath, then "Action!"

For tail slates:

For tail slated takes, the director must *not* say CUT at the end. Instead the director should say: "Tail slate." The AD repeats what the director says over, only louder if necessary.

The slate person steps into the shot, and waits until the camera person says "Marker" indicating he or she is ready, the slate is in focus, etc. Then the slate person says "Tail slate" and bangs the sticks.

An alternative to the sound recordist stating the scene and take number by way of a slate mike is for the slate operator to do it.

Time code for video

Professional format video cameras with tape transports have built-in time code generators. For NTSC standard cameras, usually 29.97 DF and NDF are available alternatives.

In addition, there is an added concept of *Record Run* or *Free Run* for the time code generator. In Record Run, the time code generator runs when the tape runs, and stops when the tape stops.

> When the tape is restarted in record, it backs up a short amount, reads the time code off the tape, jam syncs the generator, and then begins recording.

The result is that the tapes made in Record Run have continuous code numbers, and this makes life easier for editing systems. Reels are usually numbered by setting the hours counter to correspond to the reel number, although reel numbers must be repeated when the number exceeds 23.

In the Free Run mode, the code generator counts all the time, and it may be set to clock time. For double-system video shooting, free run code is essential because the code must line up with the audio recorder, which has a separate generator that must also be set to free run and to the correct time of day. An alternative is to transmit the time code by wireless microphone technology to the audio recorder from the camera, in which case record run is an acceptable method of operation.

RC code is used on Hi-8 video machines as a substitute for time code. There are conversion boxes on the market to convert between the Hi-8 code delivered by some decks and SMPTE code, so that such machines can be used in editing systems based on SMPTE synchronization.

Locked versus unlocked audio

Professional digital video formats have a fixed relationship between the frame rate and the audio sample rate. 8008 audio samples occur in 5 frames of 29.97 fps video, since this relationship produces the right video frame rate (by definition), and the right audio sample rate, 48000 Hz, at one and the same time.

However, mini-DV has audio that is "unlocked," without such a fixed relationship. While this causes no visible problem in playback of a tape, with about $\pm^1/_3$ of a frame lip sync tolerance, it can cause a problem when sound is separated from picture in an editing system. Since the actual sample rate may be somewhat high, for example, when it is used as a time reference for lip sync long takes may go out of sync, and when resynchronized, clicks or dropouts may occur as described in Chapter 8. These problems may be circumvented by setting options in particular editing software.[11]

2-pop

One of the requirements for synchronization remains the same despite whether one is working on mag film, on the newest digital editor, or on anything in between. That is that the mixes carry a "2 pop," one frame of 1 kHz tone at reference level cut in editorial sync with the "2" frame of SMPTE Universal Leader (which indicates 2 seconds before first frame of program) or the "3" frame of the Academy or SMPTE Projection Leader (which indicates 3 feet before first frame of program), cut into or recorded on the master. This is used for both analog and digital sound tracks to establish a head synchronization point.

Principle of traceability

Sometimes the chain is more complex than just recording a camera-speed reference on the production recorder and resolving it in transfer for dubbing to perforated film. Let us say that we are doing a scene in a movie where the actors are going to lip sync a song, "The Milli Vanilli Blues." During filming, they need to hear a temp mix in which the voices are emphasized so they can be sure to hear them.

There are multiple pieces of tape and several transfers involved here:

1. The original multitrack[12] recording, probably 2-in. 24 track.

2. A temp mix of the original for playback purposes during filming.

3. The production sound recording.

4. A copy of the production sound recording on a Digital Audio Workstation.

5. A mix of the multitrack recording on multitrack tape.

6. A copy of the mix on film for re-recording—the music "track."

How is all of this kept in sync? What must be understood is *the principle of traceable synchronization*. In other words, the sync source for everything in the chain needs to be established and locked to the correct reference signal; if the "traceability" of the signal is lost, it

---

11. For example, in Final Cut Pro this is called the Autosync Compensator.

12. Note that this medium maintains all 23 tracks separately so that they can be mixed down in different proportions for different purposes.

will almost certainly result in the loss of sync. There are specific steps to follow from the beginning to ensure synchronization. Here is how it would be done in this case:

1. If the original 24-track master (a) lacks a sync reference, one will need to be recorded to it. It is customary to use track 24 of a 24-track machine for this purpose, and not to record anything critical on track 23 to avoid potential crosstalk to and from that channel. So, ensuring that the machine is operating on speed (any speed varier is shut off and the machine is in good repair), record a power-line-derived signal on track 24, usually about 10 dB below reference fluxity. This makes a starting point for the traceable synchronization process.

2. Mix down the 24-track tape (a) to a 1- or 2-track $1/4$-in. temp dub (b), emphasizing the vocals as needed. Record a reference on the pilottone or FM-sync track by either copying track 24 from the master or resolving the speed of the source machine to the power line (or other reference) and recording this same reference to the sync track of the $1/4$-in. tape.

3. On the set, play back the temp dub (b) to loudspeakers located close to the actors (remember the speed of sound—if the speaker is 50 feet from the actor, they will be one frame late even if performing in perfect sync). Resolve the playback to whatever sync source the camera uses, probably crystal sync. This is easily done using just a Nagra machine equipped with the correct resolver module.

4. Record production sound (c) by dubbing the temp mix (b) directly (electrically) from playback to the record machine but add in a mike to record the clapperboard slates. Sync the record machine to the same source as the picture, probably crystal sync again.

5. Resolve the production sound tape (c) and transfer it to the workstation (d) for editing purposes only.

6. Mix down the 24-track tape (a) to the fi-

nal mix (e) using the sync method described for the temp mix (b).

7. Dub the mixdown (e) to a workstation (f) using resolving.

8. Edit the temp sound (b) dub and picture to the finished sound track (f) in the workstation. Having two sound tracks, one that syncs with the picture (b) and one that must be the final track (f), provides a check on editing. For instance, if the actor turns up stage, and off camera, then back, and has a line off camera, ensure that the picture cut in from another camera angle is in sync by matching the sound tracks.

9. Deliver the cut picture and the continuous music track (f) to the dubbing stage.

Although this is a long and somewhat obscure discussion, and involves many personnel getting things right (the music studio, the production sound recordist, and the film sound-transfer facility), if it is all done then sync (and "reality") will be well maintained. The principle of traceable synchronization has been illustrated by taking note that a sync lock occurs all the way from the original 24 track to the final sound track, with a detour by way of production filming.

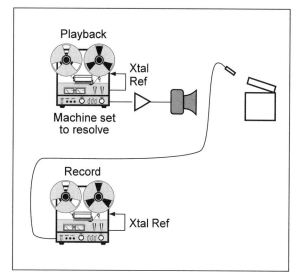

Fig. 7.3 Recording production sound to playback ("lip syncing") is accomplished by two recorders: one plays back the voice or music for reference, while the other picks up live sound to capture at least the slate. The playback recorder must be set to resolve, and the live sound recorder must record a sync reference. In this way, the principle of traceability is fulfilled.

Chapter 8: Transfers

Introduction

Transfers are a necessary if not very creative part of the post production process. In fact, it is important to rule out creativity because the job of making transfers is to produce identical work, week in and week out, during post production so that transfers made weeks apart can intercut with each other transparently. In order to do this it is exceedingly important that tight standards be set and maintained for every kind of transfer.

It is worth pointing out, however, that for this "noncreative" job there are multiple Academy Award winning mixers who started their careers in the transfer room, making transfers from original production tapes, sound-effects tapes, and compact discs, from film to film, and to and from digital media.

In today's world, knowledge of computer systems and how to interface them has become necessary to work in many positions in sound, since digital audio is so important. George Lucas's 1977 invention of a droid familiar with six million forms of communication today seems prescient. There are many file systems and formats with transfers among them an everyday process that need to be understood. Sound transfer operators and sound editors in particular become conversant with words that only a few years ago were only the province of computer sound people.

There are many proprietary digital workstations, recorders, dubbers, etc. on the market, and these may use custom formatting of digital audio within them, with certain import and export facilities to and/or from other formats. With the emergence of interchange standards in the beginning of the 2000s, we can expect easier transfers with less trouble as time goes by, but today a great deal of time is still devoted to solving problems in transfers.

While digital transfer operations are relatively new to the field, there is continuing need to interface to and from analog media. We cover digital transfer operations first, then more traditional analog ones.

Note that most post production sound tracks such as premixes, final mix stems, and print masters (described in Chapter 9) will carry a "2 pop" to permit finding the start point, and that many will also carry a tail pop. Head and tail pops are described on page 150.

Digital audio transfers

Digital recording should make the task of transferring easy: As long as a bit-for-bit copy is assured, then the digital-to-analog converter at the end of the chain sees the same digits as converted by the analog-to-digital converter at the beginning of the chain, then all the intermediate stages should be transparent, no matter how many generations are involved. However, various media are affected by different potential problems, and systems have varying susceptibility to digital errors (some are protected by error correcting codes; others are not). We will describe the sources for potential errors along with the descriptions of the various kinds of transfers, so that they can be recognized and avoided.

Transfers into Digital Audio Workstations

Post production audio workstations get their inputs in a variety of ways:

- by way of files exported from picture editing systems, delivered on removable magnetic or optical disks, fixed magnetic disks, or over a network

- from digital or analog sync sound source machines containing production sound

- from digital or analog source machines for "wild" sound or sound effects

- from sound effects libraries in a variety of forms, most often CD

- from other audio workstations

Types of transfers

Two basic methods of making transfers need to be distinguished: *file transfers*, and *streaming audio transfers*. These are quite different operationally, although the basic function when transferring digital audio is the same, and may even be of identical bits.

File transfers take place in a nonlinear environment and are inherently digital-to-digital transfers, while streaming audio transfers are inherently a linear operation, and may be from either analog or digital sources.

File transfers

The source for file transfers is the audio recorded within a file format on a magnetic or optical disk or computer format[1] magnetic tape. This may be delivered from the output of a picture editing system, or as an original production recording or copy. The medium can be fixed magnetic disks (hard drives) that are transported among systems, or a removable magnetic disk, tape or optical disk made either directly or as a copy of a hard disk drive original.

File transfers may occur at far higher speed than normal audio rates, because bits can be copied at the maximum rate of the computer interface that may be far faster than required for audio, so long as there is no need to monitor the audio at the same time. This makes file transfers potentially better than streaming digital audio transfers due to greater speed. An example of this is that a USB 2.0 transfer (see below) of a 72-minute audio CD may be done in 4 minutes and 20 seconds, a factor of 16 times in speed.

For file transfers there are several basic items that receiving equipment must understand for interchange. The first item that must be known is due to the physical and/or electrical properties of the source:

- For removable media, the basic disk or digital tape type so the receiving computer media player can find the bits on the medium. Table 8.2 gives information about removable media used for digital audio files.

- For fixed hard drives to be "mounted" on a receiving system, the basic drive protocols, such as ATA (IDE), SCSI, Firewire, or USB and the details for each of these for connection to the receiving

---

1. As opposed to DAT or DASH, digital audio tape formats.

computer. Tables 8.3 and 8.4 give information about some of the electrical and mechanical interface standards for contemporary disk drives. While older drive protocols may be usable, and surely new ones are always under development, these are representative today.

- For networked systems, the network protocols to find and read files, along with necessary authorization and contention control (who can read or write particular files and when), for both local and wide-area networks, such as the internet.

Next,

- The operating system and the corresponding file system in use so that files can be located on the medium. Table 8.5 gives examples of file systems.

Then, for all the source types above,

- The audio file format so that the receiving application software can understand what parts of the file are audio, how it is organized, and how to convert it into the representation needed within the receiving software. Table 8.6 gives examples of audio file formats in use.

And/or,

- In the case of systems where the audio has been manipulated before entering the audio post production process such as on a picture editing workstation, a list of instructions for how to duplicate what the former stage did to the audio, called an Edit Decision List or an Audio Decision List. In addition, there may be other information about the files transferred, such as scene, take, camera roll, production notes, clip as named and logged by the picture assistant editor, etc. Table 8.7 gives examples of audio file formats that include EDL/ADLs.

Confusingly, some of picture editing systems may deliver files that have either:

- the digital audio samples *and* the editing/manipulation instructions in one file, or

- the editing instructions in one file with pointers to other files containing the actual audio.

This point has probably resulted in more wasted hours in post production than nearly any other in recent years, because it is commonplace for people to export the second type of these from, say, the picture editor to the sound department, without understanding that they are only sending an edit decision list, and not the actual audio! A clue to this is the size of the file. Editing instruction files are rather small, while audio and video files are usually quite large.

Editing systems take various tacks on how much information they present to the operator about where files are located, and sometimes "automatic" systems place files in areas of the file system that are not understood by users. For instance, an editing system may place a newly generated audio file on the top directory of the drive which is least full, without the editor knowing this. When export to the sound department is necessary, then it may be essential to know where this particular file is located. Overcoming this *media management* problem depends on understanding the types of files in use and their origin and destination locations in a transfer.

Files that contain both edit instructions and media are called "consolidated" on the Avid workstation. Files wherein the audio has been signal processed by the editing system are called "rendered," a term that comes from computer graphics and is now applied to audio. Normally the desire is to export the raw audio plus the instructions for rendering rather than rendered files themselves. However, the export process may not provide enough information so that it can be duplicated in the audio editor for some processes. In this case, it may be useful to produce two versions of a given track, one rendered and one not within a file for export from picture editing to sound editing.

Audio file formats

Today's audio file formats are the result of years of development, with many systems owing quite a lot to older ones. In many lineages, each new "format" is really an extension of older formats, accomplished by placing new "wrappers" around the file recorded in older formats to add new information. In this way some audio file formats today bear a strong resemblance to Russian concatenated dolls—opening each one reveals a new doll within. Some newer formats that wrap around older ones restrict the range of choices of the older ones. For instance, .WAV files may contain low-bit-rate coded audio (see Chapter 11), but when used as an AES 31 file, the coding is restricted to linear PCM.

One of the first of these formats was called IFF, developed for the Amiga computer. It begat WAV, which begat BWF, which begat AES 31, each one adding a layer of additional information to the basic audio.

Basic digital audio files in widespread interchange use are the formats AIFF-C, BWF, WAV, and SDII. There are also numerous file formats used for given proprietary systems. Some of the proprietary system file formats may be interchanged with each other, e.g., Akai machines can read Fairlight files.

The second type of file contains the audio media and editing instructions, and additional *metadata,* or data about the data. These formats include OMF1, OMF2, AAF, and AES 31. Audio file formats that may be embedded within OMF, for instance, include AIFF-C, SDII, and WAV. However, OMF files may also be just edit decision lists with pointers to the actual audio; such OMF files are called "composition only" files.

Digital audio with a sample rate of 48 kHz using 16-bit linear PCM coding requires 5.76 MBytes per track minute (48000 samples/s × 16 bits/sample × 60 s/min ÷ 8 bits/ Byte = 5,760,000 Bytes). So 1 GB[2] of digital

---

2. Normally in computers 1024 Bytes = 1 kB; 1024 kB = 1 MB; 1024 MB = 1 GB, a GB thus consisting of 1,073,741,824 bytes. These values routinely are applied to such items as main memory. However, drive manufacturers use 1 GB to be 1,000 MB, contravening their own convention.

audio storage holds 173 minutes of monaural 48 kHz sampled 16-bit audio. Other sample rates, word lengths, or number of channels can be scaled from this number.

Media are filled to various degrees depending on their use. For instance, while media for exchange can be filled rather fully, media for editorial purposes must leave room for editing changes to the audio, additional editing files, and operational overhead. For editing purposes, 50% full is probably normal operation.

Common problems in digital audio file transfers for film and television

Here are some of the common problems found with digital audio file exchanges, in particular those that come from the picture editing department. Some of the most crucial of the tasks above devolve to picture editing assistants, so sound people can help by knowing what the issues are and communicating clearly what is expected. In addition to the more strictly technical matters above, there are a number of ordinary editing tasks that fall to the picture editing department, but which can have a large effect on the sound department.

1. File operations:

- Different software version of the system that generates the export data than expected between source and destination, or among source, translator software, and destination.

- Changing software version part way through a project.

- File naming conventions unintelligible or illogical. A file named "tempdub" conveys hardly any information as there are a great many of these in a production.

- Leaving file extensions off the end of file names, such as .wav.

- Improper formatting of export media, including fragmentation due to not starting from an empty file structure on export media.

- OMF files transferred between different

editions of an editor before export to the audio system.

2. Editorial operations:

- Illogical track layout, like sounds jumping among tracks such as interchanging boom and lavaliere tracks at random. Consistency in naming and logging of tracks is necessary.

- Audio not in hard sync before export; it is difficult to see sync on low-resolution video. To check sync, it is useful to have a production *A track* that has been carefully checked as a reference. Dialog may then be split across other tracks and their sync checked by listening and sliding the split tracks, playing the edited track and the A track simultaneously and listening for "phasing," a swishy sound resulting from the comb filter that occurs when sound is very nearly in perfect sync. There is software on the market that helps to autoconform sound to sound, such as Vocalign and Titan from Synchro Arts.

- Insertion of wild sounds without a means of tracing sync back to the source. This means the sound department has to do the work all over again if the same source is to be used. For instance, laying in music from a CD in the picture editor provides no means to "traceback" to the source. Instead, copying the CD to a time code DAT machine before insertion into the picture edit, then importing from the DAT with time code, provides a means to get precisely the same sync in sound editing. Note that such sound is exported, but the sound editor may need, for instance, a longer length of it, and this is where it is valuable to be able to repeat the picture editor's work in the sound editing room.

- Over reliance on exporting systems has led to less accurate production of human readable EDLs, but these are the only backup if the export fails.

- Text information on a sound clip.

- Sub clips/group clips in multi-cam shooting.

- Start times for a session do not match sequence time.

- Noisy editing rooms with bad monitoring leads to the picture department saying "it sounded all right on the Avid" in explaining a bad transfer. Picture editing suites are notorious for having bad monitoring conditions, and thus they are no place to judge audio quality usually. The story is told of completely distorted audio being received by a sound department that, when they went to check how it sounded in the editing room, found that the tweeters[3] in the monitor speakers were burned out.

3. Digital audio problems:

- Different sample rates between source and destination. This is particularly a problem when music interests are involved as they would prefer 44.1 kHz sample rate of the CD, yet most film and television operates at 48 kHz. Just importing CDs as sound effects into projects necessitates a sample rate conversion if they are to be imported with the same pitch and duration[4].

- Audio digitized in "draft" mode at 22.050 kHz.

- Sample rate conflicts due to pulldown. Shot with 48 kHz "standard" sample rate at 29.97 fps, then pulled down on the telecine results in a non-standard rate. If audio has been inserted without pulldown, it will drift in sync by 0.1%, with the sound being longer than the picture. This can be checked by measuring the length and calculating the difference. If it is 0.1% which is 1 frame in a thousand with the sound being longer, the likely source is the lack of a required pulldown.

---

3. high-frequency radiator in a loudspeaker
4. but many effects may be all right without correction.

4. Ordinary audio production items caused problems:

- level too low or high,

- channels mixed together or interchanged.

5. Improper set up for export:

- Incorrect consolidation: in the case of Avid, leaving Audio Suite plug ins activated: group information, pitch change, time compression/expansion, fades, levels.

- The sound department needs "handles," that is, sound for each region of audio used in the picture edit before the beginning and after the ending, providing sound editors the ability to make smoother changes than are usually done by the picture department. Handle lengths range from a few frames to the full length of the take depending on the

material, the density of edits on the tracks, and the desires of the sound editors. For long-form work, handles are provided that are the length of the take, so the maximum chance is available to find presence that intercuts.

6. Improper or no labeling of the media. Table 8.1 suggests content for a label for interchange, with examples for hard disks and removable media.

7. One frame or more sync errors in exported files (probably originates in software mathematics) are common. It is useful to have a sync check such as a clapperboard slate once in an export file so that hard sync can be checked after import.

It is highly useful not to rely on a crucial transfer, but rather to test the transfer path ahead of the time when a transfer will be essential.

Table 8.1: Media Label Items and Examples for File Exchange

Item	Example 1: Hard disk	Example 2: DVD-RAM
Medium	SCSI-3 (Ultra 160) 68-pin LD 9 GB hard disk	4.7 GB DVD-RAM
Originating File System	Mac HFS+	FAT32
Export File Type	OMF2	BWF
Export File Names(S)	EXPRTR1.OMF	DAILY*.bwf * shooting day number DAYS 1 – 5
Originating software	Avid 10.0	DEVA II
Sample rate	48k	48048
1st Time Code	01:00:00:00	01:00:00:00
Last Time Code	01:20:00:00	10:27:30:00
Time Code Type	30 NDF	30 NDF
Contact	Name/phone	Name/phone

Table 8.2: Removable Computer Media That May Be Used in Digital Audio

Name	Type	Capacity, GB	Comments
DVD-R	Optical write-once disk	3.95, 4.7	
DVD-RAM	Optical re-writable disk	2.6, 4.7, 5.2, 9.4	Used by the Deva II as an optional interchange medium; used by Fostex on a 4-channel direct digital recorder; used with a DVD-RAM writer for Pro Tools file interchange.
CD-R	Optical write-once disk	0.650	Limited capacity, although very cheap.
CD-RW	Optical re-writable disk	0.650	
MO	Magneto-optical disk	0.1 – 5.2	One form used by Dolby for Dolby Digital mastering.
JAZ	Magnetic	1, 2	Use 2 GB only in its drive.[1]
ZIP		0.1	Too small to be of interest today.
ZIP250		0.25	
DTF	Streaming tape[2]	up to 200	
SD1		up to 100	
4mm DAT data		up to 20	
8mm, Exabyte		up to 20	Used for CD and DVD production.
DLT		up to 40	
SDLT320		160	
AIT		up to 50	
VXA		up to 60	

1 Strong reliability concerns have been voiced about this medium, although it is popular.
2 Streaming tape media are used more for backup than for interchange of files in transfer due to their linear access.

Table 8.3: Hard Disk Drives for Digital Audio[1]

Class	Name(s)	Typical Capacity, GB	Advertised Bus speed[2], MB/s	File transfer rate,[3] MB/s, for representative models
SCSI	Ultra3 SCSI[4] Ultra160 SCSI (68 pin)		160	21.7—36.1, 36.6–52.8, 51–69
	Ultra320 SCSI		320	
ATA (common name IDE)	Ultra ATA/33	9, 10, 15, 18, 20, 30, 37, 40, 73, 80[5]	33	6–12
	Ultra ATA/66		66.6	10.7–19.9
	Ultra ATA/100		100	
IEEE 1394	FireWire, i-Link		12.5/25/50[6]	32
USB	USB 2.0[7]		60	
Fibre Channel	Fibre Channel		200	43

1 These types are given as representative at the time this book was written; however, this is a rapidly changing field, with gains in recorded density of magnetic hard disks from 1991 to 2001 averaging 60%/yr. Obtain the latest information, but understand that the advertised bus speed is much higher than the rate at which digital audio can typically be delivered.
2 Commonly advertised marketing specification.
3 Actual audio performance, which depends on operating system, application software, and disk performance, particularly that measured by seek time.
4 Two types of these are LVD and HVD for low-voltage differential, and high-voltage differential respectively. Older lower speed drives also operated single ended. Note the use of balanced (differential) lines for higher speeds and less interference.
5 Some types are offered up to hundreds or even thousands of GB.
6 These are called 100/200/400 for their rating in Mb/s.
7 USB 1.0 is a desk top accessories interface that is too slow for digital audio purposes.

Table 8.4: Common Hard Disk Connectors

Type	Common Name	Designation	Pins	Rows	Sub-type or explanation
SCSI	DB-25	Standard DB-type connector	25	2	Narrow
	CX-50	Centronics	50	2	Narrow
	HD-50	High Density	50	2	Narrow
	HD-68	High Density	50	2	Wide
	SCA	High Density	80	2	Wide
ATA (IDE)	Standard		40	2	
	Ultra DMA		80	2	

Table 8.4: Common Hard Disk Connectors (Continued)

Type	Common Name	Designation	Pins	Rows	Sub-type or explanation
1394	4 pin		4		Self configuring, hot pluggable
	6 pin		6		Ditto, plus carries power as well as signal
USB	USB				Self configuring, hot pluggable; USB 1.1 and 2.0 connectors and cables are inter-changeable
Fibre Channel					May be copper or fibre optic

Table 8.5: Operating System Disk Formats used in Digital Audio

Name	Operating Systems used for Audio	Where used	Maximum addressable space in one partition[1]
FAT16	Windows 95 original		2 Gbytes
FAT32	Windows 95 OSR[2]2, Windows 98, Apple NFS+	Used by AES31	2 Tbytes
NTFS	Windows NT		
HFS	Apple		2 GBytes
HFS+	Apple		
OpenTL	Tascam	MMR 8/MMR 16 digital dubbers	
Fairlight	Fairlight	DaD digital dubbers	

1 Physical disks may be partitioned into more than one part.
2 OEM Service Release

Table 8.6: Some Digital Audio File Formats without Edit Data [1]

Shorthand	Full Name	Origins	Notes
IFF	Interchange File Format	Amiga operating system	A general file format that may contain sound. Grandfather of RIFF and AIFF, only in occasional use today.

Table 8.6: Some Digital Audio File Formats without Edit Data (Continued)[1]

Shorthand	Full Name	Origins	Notes
RIFF	Resource Interchange File Format	Microsoft developed from IFF	A general file format with two common variations .WAV for audio and .AVI for video.
WAVE, WAV, .WAV	WAVE	Microsoft developed from RIFF	A variation of RIFF specifically for audio; nearly 100 bit rate reduction schemes are registered, but only LPCM is used in film and television production.
AIFF	Audio Interchange File Format	Apple developed from IFF	Standard Mac digital audio.
AIFF-C	Audio Interchange File Format–Compression	AIFF with provision for bit rate reduction	One of the export formats supported by Avid.
SDII	Sound Designer 2	Digidesign	Pro Tools, Avid's Media Composer, Film Composer, Media Express, and others.

1 These are files of historical interest or currently used in film and television digital audio. There are many other formats for computer audio.

Table 8.7: Some Digital Audio File Formats with Edit Data

Shorthand	Full Name	Origins	Notes
.BWF	Broadcast Wave Format	EBU developed for radio workstations from WAVE	WAVE files with added information such as origination time, time of first sample since midnight, description, etc.[1].
AES 31	AES 31	AES developed from BWF with extensions for time code, etc.	BWF with added edit instructions called Audio Decision List (ADL) in human readable form, with among other things sample accurate time code (SMTPE code plus sample number), clip name, source material file, track no., in time, destination time, out time.[2]
OMF1	Open Media Framework 1	Group of companies led by Avid, including Microsoft, Intel, etc.	May contain multiple media including picture.
OMF2	Open Media Framework 2		May contain multiple media including picture. Use with DigiTranslator to export Avid files to Pro Tools.

1 The .wav file extension is still used as then applications that make no use of the additional data in BWF can read the file.
2 This is called a simple interchange format. Exact instructions for recreating an equalizer, for instance, are deliberately left out of the ADL Standards in development allow for more sophisticated project information to be transferred.

Streaming digital audio transfers

More traditional streaming digital audio transfers usually occur over an electrical interface called AES3. This electrical format carries two channels of audio of up to 24-bit word length at 48 kHz sampling rate on one wire, with the audio playing in real time. The corresponding consumer version of this electrical signal format is called S/PDIF (the two versions have incompatible electrical standards, and some bits are used differently between the two), and S/PDIF is what appears on the digital audio output jack of a CD player. The professional version is balanced and uses XLR connectors, but the signal occupies frequencies up to 10 MHz, and the signal should not be plugged into analog equipment inputs. A variant used in professional video systems substitutes unbalanced BNC connectors, and video levels and impedances so that audio pairs can be treated just like video in routing around a facility.

Problems affecting streaming transfers

Inevitably there are digital bit errors with tape or optical media, so there are error codes used that are capable of recovering the original digits for the assumption of transparency to be true. If the error code is capable of recovering the original bits during each generation, then all is well despite the number of generations. But should the error coding break down and start substituting interpolated data into missing portions, then each of these interpolations may accumulate over generations, and what might not be noticeable in one generation could be quite noticeable after several generations.

The difficulty with errors leading to interpolation is that the machine may not indicate to the user that it is interpolating. No consumer digital machine, for example, has indicators of how much correction is occurring, and many professional machines make this an obscure matter, with the user having to hunt for the correction indicator, sometimes hidden inside the machine!

Audio sample rate

The audio sample rate of either file transfer or streaming types of digital audio is affected by the targeted delivery medium. Film and television video is standardized for release at 48 kHz sample rate, and this is widely employed on most machines. However, audio from production recorders shooting double-system for film are destined to be slowed down in transfer. The accompanying slow-down in sample rate would yield a non-standard rate, unless measures were taken in advance to prevent it. Thus double-system production recorders shooting with film normally use a sample rate of 48,048 Hz, exactly fast enough so that when slowed down on the telecine, a 48 kHz sample rate is produced that matches the 29.97 fps video.

Table 8.8: Frame Rates for Film and Video with Time Codes and Sample Rates

Frame Rate	Where used	SMPTE Time Code Frame Counter	Audio sample rate, Hz
23.976	24 p video	0–23, then 0	48000
24	Film 24 p video alternate	0–23, then 0	48000
25	Film or video for PAL television	0–24, then 0	48000

Table 8.8: Frame Rates for Film and Video with Time Codes and Sample Rates (Continued)

Frame Rate	Where used	SMPTE Time Code Frame Counter	Audio sample rate, Hz
29.97 NDF	NTSC Video, some production	0–29, then 0	48000
29.97 DF	NTSC Video, some production and network delivery masters	0–29, then 0, dropping frame numbers at the start of each minute except for minutes 0, 10, 20, 30, 40, 50	48000
30 NDF	On production sound recorders for film to be posted NDF	0–29, then 0	48048
30 DF	On production sound recorders for long form television and film projects	0–29, then 0, dropping frame numbers at the start of each minute except for minutes 0, 10, 20, 30, 40, 50	48048

Locking sample rates in streaming transfers

Another problem, especially in mixed audio-video environments, is synchronization. The word *synchronization* used by a sound editor means elements cut typically with accuracy to within a fraction of a frame, close enough for all picture-sound sync issues, but not sample accurate. What is meant here is not frame-based lip sync as provided by time code, but rather synchronization of audio samples between the source machine and the recorder, with a much finer resolution than editing sync. The variance here is as small as 1/48,000 of a second.

Each recorder must synchronize either to the incoming data stream or to a separate sync signal that the incoming stream also is following, or else clicks or dropouts may occur. Normally this is simple if both machines are digital audio ones and are locked to a common external sync source.

The input for this sync signal may be called *word clock, word sync, sample clock, reference clock, color black,* or *line reference.* These are different signals, but all have integer relationships to the audio sample rate. For instance, word clock, which is a signal at 48 kHz, has a precisely fixed relationship to 29.97 fps video of 8008 audio samples per 5 frames of video. Interconnection details must be worked out with specific equipment to make use of one of the references.

Without both sender and receiver locking to the same source for sync, or the receiver following the sender, the two may drift, if even slightly, with respect to each other in speed, and eventually cause a click or dropout as the digital audio words cross the boundary of available buffering in the receiving recorder. Normally in a production facility, the recorder will be connected to *Word Clock* or its equivalent, so that it runs in complete synchronization with the facility. The source machine must also be "locked up." However, not all sources of digital audio are capable of locking to an external sync signal. For instance, CD players very rarely have this facility, and consumer DAT machines also do not. Thus for an error-free digital transfer from a CD or consumer DAT, the recorder has to be taken off the facility's Word Clock, and made to run with synchronization derived from its input signal. Then, when playing back such a recorder into the rest of the facility, Word Clock must be re-established.

In mixed audio and video environments, the audio machines must be synchronized to the video studio master generator, just as all the video machines are so that audio can be exchanged between the machine types. When all the studio's audio and video machines are not locked to the same source, the result will be errors.[5]

Wrong sample rates

The CD runs at a sample rate of 44.1 kHz, non-standard for film and video use. In order to import a CD file into a session for picture by either the file transfer or the streaming audio methods, it is necessary to undergo sample rate conversion, for which hardware and software programs exist. These vary greatly in quality, mostly based on the available resources to do the mathematics involved. Sample rate conversion can also provide clickless transfers in the case of near, but not quite equal, sample rates. This would apply for instance to a consumer DAT machine with recordings at 48 kHz. The inability to "lock up" the machine to external word clock means that transfers could contain errors, that can be overcome by an appropriate sample rate converter.

> For file transfers, sample rate conversion software must be used, or the file must be played out usually after copying through an AES3 port on the equipment into a hardware sample rate converter, and thence re-recorded.

> Sample rate conversion may occur in one of two modes, synchronous and asynchronous. Synchronous sample rate conversion is done when both the source and the destination machines are locked to the same reference, but are at different rates, such as 44.1 and 48 kHz. Asynchronous sample rate conversion is done when one machine is "unlocked," such as a consumer DAT machine feeding a professional recorder locked to house sync, where the source is at 44.1 and the destination at 48 kHz, but the two are not "locked" to each other. In this case the sample rate converter continuously changes its multiplication and division ratios so that clicks or dropouts do not occur.

Revert to analog

In some cases, digital transfer is impossible because the conditions required for locking sample rates cannot be accomplished, for in-

stance, if sample rate conversion is not available. In such cases, it may be necessary to go through digital-to-analog conversion on the playback machine to analog-to-digital conversion on the recorder. In such cases, the biggest issue is perhaps level setting. Head tones on source reels recorded at a known digital level, such as –20 dBFS can help to make a 1:1 transfer despite having "gone back" to analog. This is rather similar to making an X copy in analog, as described below.

Digital audio levels

Level change across a digital-to-digital interface is rarely used, with most copies being bit clones of the source.

> If a level change downward is needed between the source and copy, then the level change should be accompanied by the proper amount and type of dither (deliberately added noise to eliminate quantization distortion) to maintain low distortion at low levels, as described in Chapter 3. Level changes upwards across a digital interface will probably result in the dither present in the source properly dithering the output, so no special measures need to be taken.

> In the case of some computer digital audio boards, there may be multiple level controls such as one provided by the application software, and another provided by the operating system software. If levels recorded digitally across an interface to or from these systems seem especially low or high, it may be due to there being multiple "hidden" level controls that must be set.

Analog transfers

In general, the job of making a transfer is to produce as identical a copy of the source original as it is possible to make in the target medium. The idea of extensive signal processing to "improve" on sound quality at this point is generally misdirected for several reasons:

- Monitoring facilities in transfer facilities are generally nowhere near as good as in purpose-built facilities such as dubbing stages and mixing rooms, so aural judgments are hard to make.[6]

- Repeating an exact treatment weeks apart to make perfectly intercuttable

5. The clicks or dropouts may occur as infrequently as once in a program or as often as many times per minute, depending on the difference in sample rate clock between the source and the receiver.

transfers may be difficult or impossible.

- Processing is usually better done after editing, because it is important to maintain consistency within a scene, and at the time of transfer the order and edit points of the scenes are not yet known.

Thus, unless there is a compelling reason to do so, it is better to make unprocessed transfers. The only reasons to process are:

- If the source recording is recorded at such a high level that to copy it at that level would result in added audible distortion on the copy.

- If the source recording is recorded at such a low level that to copy it at that level would result in added audible noise on the copy.

In general, professional recording is done near optimum levels, so these considerations do not typically apply.

In order that transfers be intercuttable, there have to be tolerances on how much variation is allowed. A good starting point for this is $\pm^1/_2$ dB for level and within ± 1 dB for frequency response across the frequency range that encompasses the program material for analog copies. If these standards can be maintained week in and week out, there will not often be a problem.

Methods for standardizing transfer levels

Analog systems

Direct analog magnetic recording

In direct analog magnetic recording, the reference levels used are fluxivity and the units are nanoWebers/m (nW/m). As pointed out in Chapter 6, this is a level set medium by medium as a midrange "operating level," analogous to the gray card used to determine average photographic exposure. Nei-

---

6. The reasons for this include the non-uniform bass response in small rooms caused by strong room modes, monitor systems not aligned to electroacoustic response standards (see Chapter 11), and the fact that double-system transfer rooms typically operate without picture, yielding a different impression of sound and its problems.

ther black nor white, this midlevel when it was standardized was supposed to represent something like the average level of the program peaks measured on a VU meter. This means that the maximum peaks of program material usually deflect the meter to about 0 dB, with only occasional deflection above that level. The reference fluxivity is then the setting at 0 dB on a VU meter for a sine wave tone.

However, film and television on the one hand, and the music industry on the other, have generally used advances in magnetic tape and film performance differently over the years. With each improvement, the music industry raised the reference level fluxivity to account for the improvement, keeping headroom more or less constant and improving the signal-to-noise ratio. Reference fluxivity for 0 VU moved from 185, to 250 +2.6 dB re 185), then 355 (+5.6 dB), and even 500 (+8.6 dB) nW/m. The film industry in contrast stayed with 185 nW/m reference level, but recorded the magnetic film to higher peak levels as time went by. Film personnel placed a greater emphasis on uniformity of day-to-day reference level standards to achieve greater interchangeability, partly to keep transfer room operations consistent, especially when considering level alignment of companding noise reduction systems, described below.

This means that today if you observe VU meters on a film mix, they will often be "pegged," up against their maximum reading of +3–4 dB. This does not necessarily mean anything is wrong, because today's magnetic film has a much higher level capability than when the 185 nW/m reference level was standardized.

X-copy

The simplest transfer is also one of the most common and is called an X-copy. This is a transfer made from a source medium to a precise copy of itself. The idea is that the copy is intercuttable with the source, although it is a generation "down" from the source and inevitably, with an analog copy, not perfect. In order to make an equal-level transfer, it is necessary to make an equal fluxivity transfer, as follows:

1. Start by adjusting the playback level on both the playback and the record machines using a test tape or film with a known reference fluxivity, typically 185 nW/m for film. Set the output level of the machines to the standard studio electrical bus level, such as +4 dBu.

2. Adjust the input level control of the recorder so that an oscillator tone at studio bus level produces the same reference fluxivity.

3. Assuming all other parts of the alignment for playback and record frequency response are correct, then connect the playback machine's output(s) to the recorder's input(s), play the source tape, and record the X-copy.

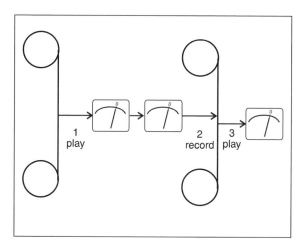

Fig. 8.1 Making an X-copy involves matching the levels of a new recording to playback. With well set up analog machines it should be possible to then intercut the X-copy with the original to, for example, extend the length of an ambience.

There are three other cases besides X-copy to consider. In the first, although the medium is not the same between source and copy, the headroom and signal-to-noise ratio are similar. In this case, the same procedure can be followed as for an X-copy, with the reference fluxivity of the recorder set to the standards for that medium, and the references fluxivity of the playback source set to the standards for it. Conventional production sound transfers from 7$\frac{1}{2}$ in./sec. Nagra

tapes to 35mm mag film fall roughly into this category, and all transfers can be made at the same level.

If the source medium has both larger headroom and a greater signal-to-noise ratio than the medium of the copy, then the correct procedure depends on the nature of the program material. If the program material uses the available dynamic range of the medium, and that won't fit into the copy, it is the same situation as encountered by trying to record wide volume range real-world sources to limited dynamic range media. In this case, limiting, compression, or judicious mixing may be necessary to keep the program material within the capacity of the copy. Limiting and compression are mixing processes that are covered in Chapter 10. Mixing, on the other hand, can produce better results, because human intervention can anticipate problems and alleviate them before they occur, without the side effects that may be caused by mechanical processes. See Table 11.3 for details of headroom and signal-to-noise ratio of various media.

An example is a recording of Mahler's *Symphony of a Thousand* prepared for cassette-tape release. The volume range of the recording certainly exceeded the dynamic range of the Dolby B compact cassette. Faced with the choice of distorting in loud passages and sounding noisy in quiet ones, the way out is to "mix" the sound for the medium, containing the volume range to what can be tolerated in the target medium. It is natural to think that the level should be turned down in high-level passages and turned up in low-level ones, to "contain" the volume range of the program to that of the medium. While this is true on the surface and is what a compressor would do, it is actually not the best representation of the program material. This is because the dynamics of the program have been altered by this process so that it seems to lack contrast between sections. We thus use the cinema mixer's trick: To make something sound loud, put something soft in front of it. Movie mixers learned this in the 1930s when they had a very narrow dynamic range channel to deal with. In the case of the Mahler tape transfer, the trick was to keep a quiet passage before a loud one relatively low in level, and then to turn it up as the program got louder, which is opposite of intuition, but is effective nonetheless. In other words, the program really does get louder when one expects it to, but the total amount by which the level is increased is not so great as to cause distortion—the real trick is to bring down a soft passage preceding a loud passage, and then restore the level to something higher, but less than an equal fluxivity transfer, when the program gets loud.

The third case is simple. In the case where the dynamic range of the source is smaller than the copy, then just proceed as for an X-copy. This would apply, for example, to compact-cassette recordings dubbed to mag film.

Using companding noise reduction

Most companders in use today require strict maintenance of reference levels so that the playback expander "sees" exactly the same level signal that is produced by the record-side compressor. Thus, for most transfers it is necessary to first decode the source playback correctly, and then to encode the record side. There is one case in which strict observance of decoding, then encoding, is not necessary—an X-copy, for which the copy is made at an identical reference level as its source. Because no level change deliberately takes place, it is possible to enclose within one compressor-expander pair the two generations consisting of the source and the X-copy.

FM recording

For recording levels on AFM and hi-fi tracks of videotape, consumer machines offer no level controls, instead using the limited range expected of incoming sources and the wide dynamic range available on this type of track to ensure decent recording levels. On professional machines, even those in consumer formats, level controls are provided.

Generally VU meters are used, and 0 VU is set at adequately below 100% modulation[7] so that all likely signals are accommodated

by the manufacturer.

Analog-to-digital and digital-to-analog systems

Any conversion operation between analog and digital brings with it the potential for level shifts, but these are simply removed through calibration. If all machines in a facility are aligned in the same way, then there will be no unexpected level changes throughout the generations required by post production processes.

In an effort to make digital machines more like analog ones, some manufacturers have placed a 0 dB reference level at anywhere between –12 and –20 dB re full scale,[8] with –12, –14, –18, and –20 dB being the most popular. It should be noted that these are purely arbitrary references. They have little or no meaning for any real program material because the program is dynamic, moving continuously both below and above the reference. These references should not be treated like some maximum for program material, because to do this would be to lose 12 to 20 dB of dynamic range. For this reason, most professional digital audio metering has 0 dB at the top of the scale, corresponding to exercising all of the bits in the system. This is sensible because it ends arguments about how much headroom to leave above 0 dB: The simple answer is none! Still, there is reason to leave some of the top of the dynamic range unused, typically just for the occasional "over the top" source.

Using equipment designed for one purpose in a system with a different purpose may lead to unintended level changes. For instance, a consumer digital tape recorder with a reference level of –10 dBV is brought into a professional studio, where the reference level between devices is +4 dBu. The 12 dB difference (not 14 dB because the references are different) must be made up in transfer by

---

7. The full scale of an FM signal is called 100% modulation.
8. Written –20 dBFS, meaning –20 deciBels referred to full scale. *Full scale* refers to the maximum possible undistorted level.

an amplifier called a *match box*. When using analog sources to be copied to digital media, the analog source should be decoded for any

companding noise reduction before recording digitally.

Table 8.9: Reference Electrical Studio Bus Levels Used for Reference Digital Coding Level[1] or Reference Fluxivity[2]

Reference Level	Voltage (Vrms)	Users
–10 dBV	0.316	Home, semi-pro equipment (where it is often abbreviated "–10")
+4 dBu	1.228	Most music and post production studios, some broadcasters
+8 dBu	1.950	Other broadcasters

1 such as –20 dBFS
2 such as 185 nW/m

Modifications during transfer

While standardized and thus repeatable transfers are emphasized at the outset, there are a number of processes that generally go on in transfer if mag film or multitrack tape is the post production medium. If digital audio workstations are the editorial mechanism, these processes may go on during editing.

One of the most common is *off-speed transfers* for sound-effects recordings. It is quite common to record at one speed and playback at another to produce a pitch shift in an effect, which will be accompanied by a corresponding change in duration. Most commonly the pitch is shifted downwards to make the sound source seem bigger. Because we don't have a pitch reference for effects in the same way that we do for voices or music, quite strong changes may be permitted in some kinds of effects.

This is an area where plain old analog tape recorders can outperform digital methods. The method of pitch shifting digitally involves interpolating samples that are not actually present in the original, and this limits the range over which a digital pitch shifter can work, and the quality in that range. An ordinary analog tape machine equipped with a wide range speed varier works well as a pitch (and duration) shifter.

Videographers say that you only have to get the colors of the skin, grass, and sky right to have people "believe" the colors, whereas any other color can be completely distorted and still work (this really bothers sponsors of commercials, who insist on getting their product colors right). Pitch shift is the audio equivalent: We can't afford pitch shift on recognizable items, but lots of pitch shift can be used on the less recognizable ones.

Another modification is *reverse transfers*. Less often used than off-speed transfers, reverse transfers also help to make sound effects less recognizable. A limitation on this is recording the reverberation in the source recording, which, because it appears backwards, usually sounds quite strange. Digitally, some systems can reverse head and tail of a sound segment editorially, so this is performed by sound editors and not transfer operators.

A third process involving special transfers occurs in making certain kinds of loops, in which an audio segment may be joined head to tail so that it can play continuously. Sound editors make loops of sound, particularly of background ambience, for use within a scene. Usually the trick in making loops is to find a place within the loop where an audibly transparent edit can be performed. The other trick with loops is to be certain that they do not have a kind of signature sound that draws attention to itself through repetition.

Another special case involving reverse transfers also occurs in making loops. Some sounds that are otherwise useful for loops are polluted with, say, a rising tonal sound over the course of the loop. What is heard at the splice point of the loop is a jump in pitch of the tonal part of the sound—a sawtooth effect over the course of the loop. On the other hand, if one makes two transfers, one forwards and one reverse, and then splices them together into a loop, first forward then reverse, the discontinuity at the splice is eliminated—the pitch rises and falls smoothly.

Chapter 9: Editing

Introduction

In this chapter, after a general introduction to the overall scheme of sound editing and mixing, the specifics of editing for feature films are discussed. This is described first because feature films generally have the most elaborate sound tracks, and other forms use many of the same techniques at various levels of intensity. Next, a television sitcom and a documentary production are described. Note that the methods used for each of these is meant to be indicative of certain working styles, which in fact are used across multiple genres. Also, although people tend to specialize in particular sound jobs, dialog editing for instance, they may do this job one week on a feature film, and the next on a sitcom. What is transferable is the particular skill set of dialog editing, whether the editing mechanical system consists of a workstation, multi-track recorder, or film.

A wide range of equipment and methods are now used in editing, from traditional sync blocks and flat bed editing tables through multi-track audio recorders with sound laid to them in sync, to Digital Audio Workstations. While it must be said that the use of DAWs for sound editing has become very widespread, there is still magnetic film editing going on due to the very low cost of the editing equipment for film.

In some instances, digital is just being used as a substitute for analog equipment, and operationally there is little difference. For example, recording on a time code DAT machine instead of a Nagra IV-STC time code analog recorder changes little in the overall production. On the other hand, some digital developments are more revolutionary. For example, one person at a digital audio workstation can both edit sound and process it, including mixing, tasks that had been traditionally performed by different people in different spaces. This potentially changes the whole process of post production, with implications for personnel, equipment, and buildings.

In order to understand sound editing in context, it is necessary first to understand the various stages used in making a sound track. This is because the sound editing process is sandwiched in between so-called picture editing,[1] and sound mixing, with free flow of material back and forth across picture editing, sound editing, and mixing as revisions are made.

Overall scheme

In overall form, the process of making a sound track follows an hourglass shape. At the top are source sounds and their media. These are edited into cut *units* or *elements,* so called if they are separate pieces of film, or called *tracks* if they are on a multitrack tape recorder or a digital audio workstation. Sound editing principally works at the top layer of the hourglass model choosing sounds and placing them into logical order within tracks.

The following issues affect where a given sound will be placed:

- Like sounds are first grouped by discipline, for example, whether they belong to dialog, music, or sound effects. While for most sounds this is a simple decision, there are subtleties that arise even within such an apparently straightforward set of choices, as described below.

- Within each category sounds are further broken down to a finer level of detail. For example, sound effects are broken into cut (foreground) sound effects, Foley effects, background or ambience effects, etc.

- Sounds are next assigned to individual tracks to be edited. In this process, due consideration is given to the layout of tracks for the mix. For example, all of the sound units to make a given car effect, such as car steady, car braking, car screech to a halt, and car door open and close, will be cut into adjacent rather than widely separated tracks. (This is not to say that the sounds from one source would never be cut into one track; they may be if they match well enough.)

- Within each cut sound track, there is a certain complexity that is optimum. Cutting too many sounds into one track makes it too difficult for the mixer, who must be constantly adjusting for the changes from cut to cut. On the other hand, spreading out the sounds across a great many tracks, with only a few effects per track, will strain the facilities, for example, taking up too many dubber tracks. The sound editors cut the tracks with a view to making the mixing easiest on the mixer and on the facilities, prepare cue sheets, and deliver the tracks on the medium of choice and cue sheets for the first stage of mixing. The units are then mixed together into *premixes*. In the premix process, typically one premix is made at a time. Thus, for example, all of the various Foley elements of a reel would be mixed together in this process. These might include footsteps, clothing rustle, creaking doors, and the like, but all would be consolidated on the one Foley premix.

The various premixes are then mixed together to produce the *final mix*. The final mix represents the waist of the hourglass, because this stage has the minimum number of tracks needed to represent fully the overall sound track. The final mix is divided into *mix stems*, parts such as dialog, music, and sound effects, and each of these is likely to be multichannel, representing directional information like left, center, right, left surround, and right surround. The final mix process has combined as many tracks as possible in order to get down to the minimum number needed to:

- contain all the required sound,

- minimize the number of tracks for simplicity, consistent with the following,

- keep separate those parts that may be needed separately later, such as keeping separate English-language dialog so that foreign-language dubbing is simplified.

The advantage of keeping the various mix-stem component parts on tracks separate from one another is the convenience with

---

1. So called because cutting picture virtually always involves cutting sound as well, and the two interact.

174

which a variety of different types of output mixes, called *print masters*, can be prepared for different purposes. For example, it is relatively straightforward to substitute a foreign-language dialog track for the primary-language dialog if the dialog stem has been kept separate. It is also simple to produce an *M&E mix*, which contains only the music and sound effects, for dubbing to foreign languages in countries where such dubbing is done locally. Another purpose is to fit the dynamic range of the mix stems into various media, emphasizing dialog for an airline mix, for instance.

Remember that once sounds have been mixed together, they are only "taken apart" by human perception, so there is an advantage to keeping tracks separate in the mixing process to provide the maximum flexibility at the final mix. In theatrical film mixing, the director may or may not sit in on the premixes, and if not, then the sound professionals working on the show must make decisions about what kinds of sounds are appropriate. If the director subsequently disagrees with some choices, then it is best if little combining has gone on so that new sounds can be substituted, and new premixes made, on short notice. On the other hand, if no combining of sounds ever goes on, the final mix becomes a nightmare, because all decisions have been postponed until that time. So an orderly progression of mixing together like sounds is the best method.

One principle that grows out of this approach is *checkerboarding*, which means that one premix might occupy the red squares of a checkerboard while another occupies the black squares. Each is active only a part of the time and is otherwise silent when the alternate premix is playing. However, note that the lines on the checkerboard are not hard and fast: Premixes may also overlap one another, playing simultaneously. The advantage of checkerboarding is the momentary silence between the alternating sounds, permitting the editing of premixes. This is an advantage for last-minute alterations because if the director doesn't like one particular effect at the time of the final mix,

it is possible to remove just one portion of one premix and substitute a different sound.

From the mix stems a series of *print masters* are made, representing the sound to be copied in 1:1 correspondence to each medium of release. A moderately big show might have many print masters:

- 5.1-channel English-language digital stereo master
- 2-channel English-language Lt Rt matrixed stereo master
- 5.1-channel M&E
- 2-channel M&E
- 5.1-channel French
- 2-channel French
- 5.1-channel German
- 2-channel German
- 5.1-channel Spanish
- 2-channel Spanish

This list is long but by no means exhaustive.[2] These types are more fully described in Chapter 11. Suffice it to say that the various print masters fill out the base of the hourglass due to their number and variety.

So there are seven generations involved in typical film work:

- Original source recording or library effect
- *Cut units*, also called *elements* or *tracks*
- Premixes
- *Final mix*, composed of mix stems
- Print masters
- Optical sound track negative

2. Italian is missing from the list because Italian dubbing must go on in Italy by law, so the M&E masters, along with a mono English track for reference, are sent there. Asian, Dutch, and Scandinavian languages use English-language sound tracks with subtitles traditionally, although some films might be dubbed, probably locally.

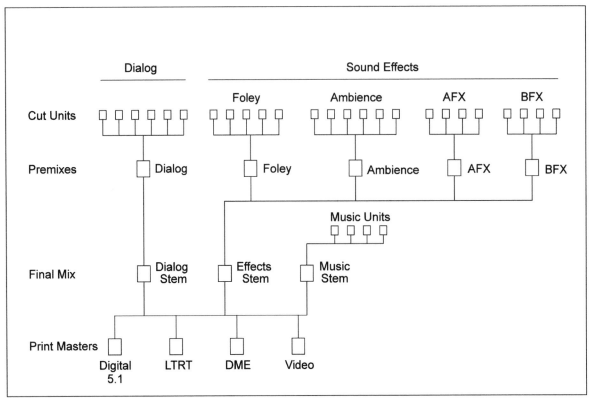

Fig. 9.1 A block diagram of the overall mixing process for a feature film. Each row represents a generation, so units are mixed together into premixes, premixes together to form a final mix, then the final mix stems are mixed together to produce the print masters that are the output of the sound post production process. Note that each of the premixes, final mex, and print masters are likely to be multichannel.

- Prints

Television production, having tighter schedules than film production, and also virtually always working with a "locked"[3] picture, may proceed somewhat more simply:

- Original source recording or library effect

- Multitrack or workstation edit

- Mixed stems

- Master mix

- Layback to video master

---

3. Although sound work starts in earnest after picture lock on a feature film, the picture is still subject to change, even after picture lock. There is no such luxury of time in television post production, where the time frame is measured in working hours, not weeks.

Feature film production
Syncing dailies
Production double-system sound may be acquired on a variety of analog or digital recorders, either of which may be with or without time code. After resolving of non-time-coded tapes and copying to the editorial medium, the picture and sound need to be synchronized. Often this will be done as a part of telecine operations, as described in Chapter 7. If it is done by on film, the procedure is described for film cutting in Appendix III.

Whatever the source, either time code slates or, more rarely, in-camera time code, is used either manually or with an autoconform program to sync the production sound on the telecine, as described in Chapter 7. Video is most often used for editing today whether the source is film or video, although film dailies still occur on large productions shot on film since the cinematographer needs to look at projected work print to know precisely what was captured. To show synchronized sound at film dailies, methods have been worked out of running digital audio sources in sync with film.

Table 9.1: Methods of Syncing Dailies

Source Material	Basic Method
Analog double-system production sound with neopilottone or FM sync resolved and transferred to film	Assistant picture editor matches slate clapper close on pix and snd
Analog double-system production sound with neopilottone or FM sync resolved and transferred to digital audio workstation	Assistant picture editor matches slate clapper close on pix and snd
Analog or digital double-system production sound with time code, with time code slate[1]	Telecine operator reads time code at clapper close and slaves playback audio machine to make in-sync transfer, shot by shot
Analog or digital double-system production sound with time code, with in-camera optical time code	Autoconform by chase synchronizer on telecine
Analog or digital single-system sound	Already synchronized, but use time code to *laydown* to sound editing medium in sync

1 This method is probably the most common today for theatrical films, television movies, and the like.

A single-track linear representation of the production sound in sync with the picture is called an *A Track,* and it may be left intact throughout picture and sound post production to form a *guide track.* A guide track is always left in sync with the picture to have a reference sound track known to be in sync with the picture. On a workstation, the *regions* or *clips* corresponding to the shots may be copied and pulled into separate tracks so that overlap and cross-fade editing from shot to shot can be performed for smoothing dialog edits. The guide track pro-

vides a continuously available check that this process of moving copied regions to different tracks has occurred in sync.

Traditionally film picture editors would cut just the A Track in sync with the picture while editing. However, more elaborate editing in the picture suite soon occurred, as the importance of sound to pacing the action, driving the story, and so forth, was noticed, and "B" and even "C" tracks came into being. Today, with picture cutting workstations like Avid Film Composer, more elaborate sound editing is done in picture editing than ever before.

However, the primary focus of picture editors has to be getting the story into coherent shape, and sound inevitably takes a back seat, especially sound quality. For this reason, among others, re-transfers of the original production materials may be needed once the picture is delivered to the sound editors, although when working with digital workstations and with files correctly transferred into the picture editor and exported to sound editing as described in Chapter 8, this step should be able to be avoided for most production sound.

Dialog editing specialization
Sources for dialog
Dialog editors depend on several sources for their tracks:

- *Production sound tracks* (probably retransferred if the production A track has been modified).

- *Out-takes* of the production sound from alternate takes, even out-takes that were never printed, to cover miffed words.

- *Wild lines.* These are dialog lines that the actor records under the director's guidance, often at the end of a production day. Recording wild lines on the set after hours gives a quieter place having the same acoustics as the rest of the production sound, and may avoid the added expense of an ADR session. For instance, noisy lighting equipment, generators, wind machines, and the like, can all be shut off. The situation is optimized for sound recording because no cameras are operating, so a boom mike can be employed in all cases. The job of the actor and director is to repeat the performance that has occurred during shooting, not to "improve" on it, at least insofar as sync goes, so that there is a chance that the dialog editor can get it into sync by manipulation of the track, cutting in between words and even syllables to synchronize the wild lines with the original production sound for the takes that are used in the picture.

- *ADR (Automated Dialog Replacement) recordings.* The ADR editing supervisor or an assistant does the preparation for the ADR session by producing a log of all the required lines by footage or time code for a given actor. This allows quick work on the ADR stage, where the equipment will fast forward to a line, then play the line over and over, and record it when the actor is ready, as many takes as are needed, then fast forward to the next line by that actor. Actors are typically brought in one at a time to loop their lines, although there are certainly exceptions to this rule. In particular, where overlapping dialogue may occur, it is difficult for the actor to perform alone.

There are three major considerations in getting good ADR: sync and performance, mostly in the hands of the actors, and recording, mostly in the hands of the ADR mixer. Sync can be accomplished by good acting, skillful editing, and with help from software that slides ADR performances into sync with production sound (Vocalign). Performance is another matter; some actors can perform ADR well, but others are not so good at it. It must be said that if you've ever tried it, you would find it to be a highly artificial thing to do, and require a special skill. When a particular actor is known from the outset not to be a good "looper," the production sound recordist can be told to concentrate on them. Recording attempts to mimic the per-

spective of the original, with in particular the correct amount and type of reverberation, if there is to be any attempt to use any of the production sound from a given scene.

Track breakdown

The dialog editor constructs a number of tracks from the production sound. The objective is to make the most mixable sound track, so if all sound can be cut perfectly so that the foreground says the right thing, and the background matches perfectly at the edits, there would be no reason to split the sound segments into separate tracks at edits. Dialog editors say that they listen "through" the dialog to the backgrounds in order to choose edit points. Of course they are not ignoring the dialog, since saying the right thing comes first, but they choose their edit points more on how well the backgrounds match at the edit point than perhaps any other single factor.

Whether to split the sources into separate tracks or to keep them together on one track depends on whether the match is perfect at the edit. Most times it will not be, and the tracks will be split by shot. Dialog editors make use of the principal on-screen dialog, wild lines, and outtakes in pursuit of the best combination of performance and technical quality. Whether these three sources can be intercut depends on the noise on the set present during shooting, the microphone perspective, and the actor's performance.

On large Hollywood features, another set of sound editors works on ADR. ADR must always be cut on tracks separate from production dialog, since it will virtually never match. This is so the tracks may be separately available for different kinds of signal processing, such as equalization and reverberation, during mixing. By separating them by source, one maximizes the possibility that the post production mixer can produce a smooth-sounding track, because, for example, it will probably be necessary to add reverberation to ADR recordings to get them to sound like production sound recordings, so the processing on the two has to be different.

With source of the sound being the first level of splitting off dialog tracks, things get more complicated on the next level. If there is a two shot, and both characters are recorded well on mike, then there may be no need to split the track. If, on the other hand, one character is "off mike" in one shot, then there is the possibility to improve the sound by using sound from an alternate take, placed on an alternate track. By the way, this "off mike" sound example shows up another difficulty with dialog overlaps: if an off-mike line overlaps an on-mike one, to replace the off-mike one with ADR would result in "doubling" of the part of the line during the overlap, and this is usually painfully audible. That is why it is important to exercise discipline on the set, particularly over off-camera lines, since they can be so easily constructed by dialog editors, and so difficult to take apart should the need arise.

In the end, the objective of making the most mixable sound track is the ruling principle. Choosing how to split tracks is mostly achieved by careful listening, and through experience.

Presence or fill

In order to smooth dialog, it is essential to have a recording to fill in between the gaps when things must be cut out. The difference between having this *presence* or *fill* and not having it is like the difference between seeing an unpopulated set and going to black. Black equals silence in this example, and cutting to it would be just as obvious as missing the picture—so with sound. Material for fill is often gotten by copying the background sound between the actor's lines, and looping it to lengthen it as required. The advantage that this has is that it is sure to match, at least at the portion from which it was lifted, to the production sound.

Another source for presence is the space between the various things going on at the beginning and end of a take, as described in Chapter 5. For example, if the director waits a moment between the exit of the slate person and calling "Action," there will be some sound recorded that will exactly match the start of the take and thus can be used as

presence. Even as little as less than 2 seconds is very useful because that sound can be looped and extended as needed.

Another recording made for this purpose by the production sound mixer is *room tone*, or in England, *atmos* (short for *atmosphere*).

Obviously, the ability to intercut presence into a scene depends on the exact nature of the background noise present on the set or location. Intermittent background noise will make it hard to intercut presence. For a relatively noisy New York street scene there may be difficulty in cutting between presence and production sound, because there can be quite audible components of the two that do not match. We could not cut, for example, in the middle of a taxi passing by the microphone to presence recorded without the taxi without drawing attention to the lack of continuity of this stream.

Dialog editors thus usually "clean" individual sound tracks of such intermittent background noise as they can by cutting, and sometimes provide another track of matched, continuous fill called a fill track or a fill loop that the mixers can use so that the "bumps" that remain at the edits in the dialog track can be masked. They may also cut hard effects from the dialog track, such as a door close, into a PFX track, for "Production Effects," that may be used as one choice along with others such as Foley at the mix.

A difficult dialog editing situation occurred on *Mosquito Coast*. Harrison Ford has lines while lying down in a boat surrounded by lapping water. The sound editors had to manually clean out the "laps" between each word of dialog, hoping that laps under dialog would be masked by it, and simultaneously match a second track with laps matching those seen so that the re-recording mixers could have the capability of adjusting the relative levels of dialog and water sounds, all in sync of course.

For illustration of how dialog editors cut when there is significant background noise, play cuts 32–35 of the CD.

Presence is cut into dialog tracks where it

matches well. To produce a separate continuous presence track may seem to make sense at first glance, but then you realize that the presence would be doubled up underneath the dialog lines, and be singular in between the lines, and this could easily be audible as bumps. The rule is, if presence intercuts well, then cut it into the dialog track; if it doesn't match too well, split it out into a separate track.

The importance of "handles," sound recorded before and after the actual dialog lines, was discussed in Chapter 8. For dialog editors, handles are very important as they provide a means for the mixer to make smooth transitions, and provide an important source for fill. Picture editors do not typically deal in handles, but they should export them so that dialog editors have adequate material with which to work.

Sound-effects editing specialization

Due to their complexity, sound-effects editing is often broken down into subspecialties, along the lines of the premixes: cut effects, ambience (backgrounds), and Foley. Often on a large film production, these will be the sub-departments of sound editing.

Hard or "cut" effects

The simplest definition of hard effects is "see a car: hear a car," a trademark of the craftsmanship that goes into filmmaking. It is the expectation of the audience that everything we see on the screen that makes a noise should be heard, and thus covered by a hard sound effect. *Hard* in this context means that the sound was obtained from a source other than production sound, Foley, or ambience, and the sound was *cut* in by a sound-effects editor to match the picture.

The relationship between the picture and a hard effect can be in one-to-one correspondence, such as the car example, or it may be more tenuous, such as the high-pitched processed insect sound effect in the jungle scene in *Apocalypse Now* that acts as a builder of tension.

The sources for hard effects, in order of their likelihood of use, are as follows:

- Commercial or private sound-effects libraries. Virtually no filmmaking activity has enough backing to record all new sound effects for each film, so libraries are relied on to provide many of the basic effects. Commercial libraries are made easily accessible on series of compact discs. Still, to make use of CD recordings, they must first be copied to an editorial medium, such as film, or a digital audio workstation, which is likely to involve a sample rate conversion. However, note that sound effects are usually less damaged by pitch shift associated with off-speed transfers than are the more recognizable voice or music, so some effects may work without conversion.

- Custom recordings. When working on *Top Gun* the sound-effects editors probably ran out of jet recordings from libraries rather quickly, using up the whole recorded repertoire from sound-effects libraries in a few minutes of screen time. While it is possible to reuse recordings, if done too much the pattern of usage becomes audibly obvious. This seemed clear in the 1983 helicopter cop movie *Blue Thunder*. Many new recordings are needed for such a specialized sound track.

There are at least two ways to find a source for given sound effects: literally, and those that bear a more tangential relationship to what is being portrayed. Table 9.2 gives some of each of these types.

Table 9.2: Some Sources of Sound for Movie and Television Sound Effects

Sound Effects	Source
Emperor's blue lightning, *Return of the Jedi*	1930's tesla-coil-based "Jacob's ladder" machine used in James Whale's *Frankenstein*
Pile of rats in cave under the church, *Indiana Jones and the Last Crusade*	Petaluma, CA free-range chicken ranch, standing among the chickens, pitch shifted up to multiple frequencies, plus horses moving gently in corral, pitch shifted up
Biplanes, *Indiana Jones and the Last Crusade*	Kenosha, Wisconsin annual air show of antique planes
Distant thunderstorms on Dagobah, *The Empire Strikes Back*	Blind midwestern farmer who records all passing storms, layering together multiple storms
Fly bys of alien craft, *Independence Day*	Screaming baboons
Footsteps on grass	Foley stage walking on unspooled audio tape
Footsteps on ice and snow	Foley stage walking on rock salt
Device for killing aliens, The *X-Files*	Producer close miked saying "pfffft"

Built-up elements. Many sound effects are built up from multiple recordings layered together to achieve the needed level of complexity. Today this layering can be accomplished quickly in a digital audio workstation, at reasonable cost and investment in time. The sound of a face punch in an Indiana Jones movie, for example, has the sort of "Kabamm Pow!" character that cartoons have. This is accomplished by layering together different recordings, including throwing a leather jacket onto the hood of an old fire engine and dropping overly ripe fruit on concrete—together they sound like neither, but like something new altogether.

Hard effects are organized according to their type into a variety of premixes. Like sounds are usually grouped into the same premix. They could be grouped by event, such as one car door close, start, and drive away may be assigned to one premix, if that makes sense as a unit. On the other hand, a single event might not be so grouped, but rather the grouping could be organized by the kind of sound, such as Wind, Metal FX, Water-A

FX, and Water-B FX for a given film, say a sea-faring one, whereas the breakdown for another type of film could be quite different. In this case, Water-A might be more or less continuous water sounds, but not necessarily having a 1:1 relationship with picture, while Water-B could be specific water events that "sell" the veracity of the track by having what sound editors call *sync hits*, those effects in hard sync that convince you everything you hear is real.

An example is that of the Imperial Snow Walkers in *The Empire Strikes Back*. Seen in a long shot, three of them menace the rebel forces. With four feet each, that's twelve big footfalls to cover—a lot of cutting. This can be simplified by cutting two tracks, one an effects *bed*, with the sound of multiple feet falling, in this case a slowed down punch press from a machine shop, at about the correct rate. The second track, run in parallel, "sells" the shot by cutting single foot falls in hard sync with the most prominent visible feet falling. The two together work, and all the individual feet don't have to be cut.

Another method used to sell the verisimilitude of a shot is to change the perspective by changing the effect. In the case of a closer shot of the Imperial Snow Walkers, the sound of a bicycle chain dropping on concrete was added in sync with the punch press sound, since as we know from Chapter 1, closer sound is louder, and brighter, than more distant sound.

The editing is performed so that not only do the source tracks checkerboard in time, but the premixes are organized to also checkerboard the sounds in time, making some of the combined effects at the premix stage first appear in one premix, and then in another.

One consideration in assigning sounds to predubs is their place in the frequency and dynamic ranges. This idea is based on frequency masking. It would be typical to have the ambience predub contain low-frequency sounds, while Foley provides higher-frequency ones, thus helping to discriminate the two despite their similar levels. Quiet effects would not typically be intercut with loud ones, as that would make mixing too difficult.

Combining sounds together to create denser sound effects is a principle often used. Special manipulations may be done on either individual elements of a complete effect, or on the whole, mixed effect. These include speed change, used to produce a corresponding pitch change, making a sound "bigger" by slowing it down; lengthening by mechanical or electronic looping; and pitch shifting to make a sound seem to move past a point of observation by faking Doppler shift.

Foley sound-effects editing

Foley sound effects are those made in a recording studio called a *Foley stage* while watching the picture and performing the action more or less synchronously with the picture. More than any other single part of a sound mix, it is the Foley sound effects that often make the sound seem real, because Foley recording exaggerates real-life sounds to make them audible.

Foley recording was invented early in the history of film sound by a man named Jack Foley, working at Universal Studios. The coming of sound had brought international distribution headaches to an industry that had enjoyed simple means for foreign distribution. All that had to be done to prepare a foreign-language version of a silent film was to cut in new title cards translated into the target language. The coming of dialog spoiled that universality. At first, to solve this problem some films were shot on a 24-hour-day schedule, with three casts working in three shifts recording three languages. The casting for the foreign-language versions had two concerns, that the actors could speak the language and that they could fit into the costume made for the English-language star! It wasn't long before foreign-language dubbing was invented, lip syncing a foreign language to the English original.

The difficulty with these foreign-language dubs was that they lacked all the low-level sounds of the actors moving around the set, sitting down, pouring a glass of water, etc. While these sound effects could be provided by a sound editor cutting in effects from a library, this was an exceedingly tedious process. Thus, the stage was set for the invention of Foley recording. The idea was that many sounds could be recorded "to fit" the time that they appear on the screen by simply performing the action in sync with the picture, and recording it.

Today, Foley recording is likely to involve a multitrack recorder or workstation so that different record passes can be used to add layers of different effects, building up to a complete whole. There are a number of people involved in producing a Foley track:

- The Foley artist's job is typically done by one or two persons, who spot the picture with the Supervising Foley Editor (that is, assign what sounds are needed from Foley as opposed to hard sound effects), gather props, gather Foley props, and perform for the recording.

- The Foley editor prepares the cue sheets, attends the recording session, works with the Foley recordist in track layout and aesthetic recording issues, and prepares the Foley units for re-recording.

- The Foley recordist chooses the microphone technique and operates the equipment, layering sound to separate tracks and monitoring the ongoing work as needed to be certain everything needed is covered.

After the recording has been made and monitored for completeness, it is possible to send a multitrack recording to the dubbing stage to form the Foley premix. Often, however, the sync between Foley sound and screen action is not perfect, and on a larger scale production each of the tracks of the Foley is adjusted on a digital audio workstation for sync. This *fine cutting* consists of moving the recorded sound with respect to the picture by usually just a frame or two to put it into *hard sync*, which is certainly one of the most important things to do to achieve verisimilitude.

Ambience sound-effects editing

Ambience, also known as "backgrounds" ("BGs"), is sound that produces a space for the film to exist in. Although superficially similar to production fill, there are some distinguishing factors. Fill is sound that can be intercut transparently with production sound. It is a record of the background sound present on the location or set. Ambience is a separately built sound track, selected by sound-effects editors. Ambience is artificial presence in the sense that it provides a "space" that wasn't there during shooting.

> The dictionary gives the primary spelling to be "ambiance," but the secondary spelling "ambience" is most often seen for this type of sound track.

Ambience most typically consists of more or less continuous sound, often with a low-frequency emphasis we associate with background noise of spaces. Thus, in reel 1 of *Raiders of the Lost Ark,* the scene in the cave has low-frequency rumble acting as a more or less distant threat once Indy triggers the ancient mechanism by appropriating the idol.

Ambience plays a significant role in scene continuity. If ambience stays constant across a picture cut, it says subliminally to the audience that while we may have changed our point of view, we are still in the same space. Conversely, if there is an ambience change at a picture change, it says the opposite—we are in a new scene. Ambience may even be overlapped across certain scene transitions, either to create an effect of the former scene lingering into a new one or to anticipate a cut to a new scene.

In the cave scene in *Raiders* there is an ambience change accompanying a picture cut that is significant in explaining the story at that point. Indy leaps the chasm to get away, and as he scrambles up the other side of the hole, the picture cuts to a view from the other side of a portal that is starting to close. Although realistically speaking the level of the ambience rumble would be just about the same through an open door as in the first space, in fact the level changes abruptly downwards with the picture cut. The subliminal indication to the audience is that by making it through this opening before the stone comes down into place, Indy will have reached a place of safety, away from the threatening ambience rumble.

Ambience is one of the most interesting sound tracks from a spatial point of view, using stereophony to achieve its goals. One crucial spatial question about ambience is whether it should include sound in the surround channels. The difference between an ambience on the screen and ambience that includes surround sound is related to the degree of involvement of the audience. A good example is from *Apocalypse Now.* In the jungle scene, we first see the boat on the water with the jungle in front of us. As two characters get off the boat to gather mangoes, we follow them into the jungle. The sound of the jungle remains present on the screen channels, but also creeps up in the surround channels, enveloping the listener. This use of surround sound creates greater involvement on the part of the listener by breaking the bounds of the rigid screen edges, and brings the audience into the action. Then when the tiger jumps out, the action is much more frightening because we accompanied the characters on their search, rather than observing them from afar.

Another way that ambience may be used is to smooth over small changes in presence that may otherwise draw attention to the artificiality of building the scene from different shots. Suppose the presence changes because the microphone is forced to shoot a different direction from shot to shot and a directional noise source is involved. As long as the level of the presence can be kept quite low and the discontinuities in it masked by a continuous ambience track, all is well. So the use of ambience varies, from providing a sonic space for the scene to exist in to the practical covering up of presence discontinuities, auditory "perfume."

Music editing specialization

Music scored for film is composed to fit the time given it by the film. While this might seem to be a limit to creativity for the musician, perhaps the following story is illustrative.

In producing a ballet from a work by Stravinsky, the stage director had a problem. There was a certain amount of stagecraft that had to go on in order to change the scene, but there was no music to accompany the change. This was the premiere of the work, and Stravinsky was the conductor. With fear of what might happen when he did so, the stage director approached the famous composer with the problem.

Stravinsky replied, "How much?"

"Eight seconds. That's no problem is it? You can have as much time as you want."

"Of course not. I'm delighted to have a requirement!"

The first step in the process of composing the music is that the composer, the director, and the supervising sound editor or sound designer *spot* the picture. *Spotting* refers to going through the picture and noting where music should be present and what kind it should be. (The term is also applied to any process of matching required sound to picture.) This process has to take place after the picture is locked and before the composer can begin to work in earnest on the film or television show (although he or she might be able to write some musical themes before picture lock, in order to write the actual music cues the exact length of cuts, available only after picture lock, is needed).

It is at the stage of spotting that the composer finds out the general outline of the sound effects for a given sequence, so that attention can be paid to producing music that not only matches the mood of the picture but that is kept relatively free from frequency-masking effects. Thus, if the sound designer says that a scene will have a loud rumble to indicate a threat to the audience and there isn't any dialog to be heard, the composer may concentrate on higher instruments, say, violins and brass, rather than double-bass and timpani, to accompany the scene, maintaining the most separation possible.

In theory, the practice of music editing should be straightforward: Just cut the music in where it was written. In practice, things are much more difficult. The single largest problem is that it takes weeks to write the music and record it, and this must be started early enough to ensure that it will be finished well in time for mixing. The start date on composing the music is as early as possible, usually right after picture lock. The problem is that picture lock is often not all that firm, and the picture continues to be edited while the music is written. By the time the music is recorded, the version of the picture has often changed, and sync is no longer ensured. This is where the art of music editing comes into play. The music editor cuts the music tracks with great sensitivity to both the integrity of the music and the needs of the picture. There is potentially a required trade-off between these two issues because the music must, for example, pay off at the end of a scene and yet be cut to make musical sense within the scene.

One trick to accomplish music editing is to make cuts that will be masked by other sounds on the sound track in case "perfect" cuts cannot be obtained that are inaudible. While the general outline of the music, its orchestration, key, tempo, etc. probably need to be the same before and after an edit, a difficult edit is hidden by masking by putting it "behind" a loud sound effect.

Music editors for film are generally trained musicians who read music, help the composer prepare for the scoring session, sit through the mixdown from the multitrack original recording to the music tracks, and then cut the music tracks so that they may be played during the final mix. Table 9.3 gives the track formats for music delivered to dubbing stages.

Table 9.3: Track Formats for Scored Music

Name	Tracks
1-track	used for source music within a scene and for recording to playback
2-track	L,R for television use only
2-track	LT, RT[1] usually for television use
3-track	L, C, R (the most common)
5-track	L, C, R, LS, RS
7-track	L, LC, C, RC, R, LS, RS (rare)

1 See Chapter 11.

One technique that should not be overlooked is the possibility of cutting the picture to the music instead of the other way around, which is frequently used in montage scenes. In this case it would be typical to be using either existing pop music (such as in the babysitter scene in *Risky Business*) or "source" music,[4] which is music present in the scene, heard by the characters, rather than "scored" music. In the documentary, *The Wonderful Horrible Life of Leni Riefenstahl*, the subject explains with utter delight how she cut a scene in *Triumph of the Will* to the music and how that tactic helped to move the audience (in all the wrong ways, as

4. Also called *diegetic* by our critical studies colleagues.

it turned out!).

In filmmaking that cannot afford custom-written music, or for which there is a need to adhere to existing music as a storytelling method, there is a danger in using existing music sources that should not be overlooked. Each audience member brings a lot of potential baggage to bear, such as associations from circumstances of hearing the song formerly. This makes it difficult for the filmmaker to stay in control of the storytelling process, since there is an outside influence that is out of control. On the other hand, known music can bring with it known emotions, that being old and familiar may just fit like an old pair of shoes.

Music also imposes its own order on a scene, whether the picture is cut to the music or not. It is surprising how many times music will be laid underneath a scene of someone walking, for example, and the walk appears to be "on the beat." Somehow our brain searches for order out of chaos and imposes it, finding order where none was intended.

There are two basic music issues regarding rhythm—beats, and downbeats—that impose their own temporal order on a scene. The beat is the "atomic clock" of music, propelling the music through time. The downbeat is one beat of a repeating sequence that has an accent —4/4 time emphasizes the first beat of each measure of four beats over the others. Each of these can affect the match to picture. The tempo of the beat is quite important to motion. For instance, "andante" is said to be a walking tempo, and compositions at andante tempo could best be expected to match walking on screen. Key signature has an impact too. Major keys are said to be bright and happy, minor ones sad or contemplative. But this idea is a vast oversimplification of a very sophisticated field.

Types of cuts

Sound editors use a mixture of types of splices or cuts. Butt splices are instantaneous ones. On film and tape, these are straight across the mag or tape, and on workstations they are simple vertical cuts. While they may work in several situations, the use of butt splices is actually a fairly low percentage of audio edits. The problem is that the audio waveform is being chopped off instantaneously, usually at a non-zero amplitude. Cutting instantly to zero, or to any other non-matching level, will probably result in an audible click.

Diagonal splices are therefore favored for audio editing, with a typical crossfade time of one perforation of film, about 10 ms. Longer ones are easy to perform on digital audio workstations, and are routinely used when a smooth transition is needed. Where butt splices may be used are: 1. in silence where it doesn't matter, therefore Foley editors, cutting between effects for instance, make use of butt splices, and 2. when backwards masking is needed, like cutting in the middle of a word on a "hard" phoneme, to prevent hearing the edit.

Premix operations for sound editors

The output of the three subspecialties—dialog, music, and sound-effects editing—are the *cut units* or *tracks* delivered to post production mixing, along with the *cue sheets* prepared by the editors, organized to explain the placement of sounds in the units to the re-recording mixers.

One likely breakdown of the premixes is:

- Dialog
- Foley
- Ambience
- A FX
- B FX
- C FX
- Music

Foley, ambience, and the cut-effects premixes A through C constitute the sound-effects premixes. Consolidating them in the final mix results in the sound-effects stem. The most commonly found breakdown of the tracks at the final mix stage is:

- Dialog

- Music
- Sound effects

Called *DM&E*, these are known as the mix stems.

Another possible breakdown, used on sitcoms is:

- Dialog
- Music
- Effects
- Audience reaction (Laughs)

Finally, special films call for special breakdowns. For instance, *Return of the Jedi* used:

- Dialog
- Music
- Effects
- Creatures

  The reason to keep creatures separate from dialog is that the creature utterances are to be used in foreign-language versions. They cannot be mixed into sound-effects units because if a different balance between dialog and the rest of the mix is needed in a language other than the primary language (which is quite often the case), then the creatures need the same adjustment as the dialog, so they need to be separate. Let us say that the Italian mix has dialog some 6 dB louder relative to music and effects than it was in the English-language mix, which is often the case (the Italian mixers trying to be certain that the dialog is intelligible in poor venues, and given that lip reading on the part of the audience, a part of the cocktail-party effect of improved intelligibility, is unavailable to the audience in a dubbed version), then creatures will have to be raised 6 dB as well.

This brings up one large problem facing sound editors, the "purity" to apply to the breakdown along dialog, music, and sound-effects lines. Let us say we are shooting a pirate movie and there is to be a battle scene where a set of pirates boards a ship. Is all the shouting that is heard dialog or sound effects? Is it intelligible or not? The advantage of all of the utterances being dialog is that all the sounds having a given principal language are grouped together, foreground "dialog" as well as background shouting. Then the effects tracks remain "clean" of dialog.

The problem with this approach comes when it is time to dub the picture into a foreign language. The process has been enormously complicated by the requirement that all of the background shouting must be looped. In point of fact, this is often not done due to the time and expense involved. Therefore, the foreign dubs seem surreal to the producers, because so much winds up missing in this case.

The alternative is to put the shouting-crowd noises into sound-effects units. Then the sound will appear in the M&E for the foreign-language dub, with the problem that background language may be recognizable. The audience has the problem that the principal acting is in the dubbed language but the fight in the background is in the original language! A factor that can ameliorate this problem is to divide the background shouting into the lines that may be recognizable, put them in the dialog stem, and those that are mutters or indistinguishable shouts, put them in the sound-effects stem. There is no easy solution and the problem is routinely faced by productions that have foreign distribution.

Television sitcom

Let us say we are shooting a four-camera television show. While shot on film in the camera, a *video tap* also provides a simultaneous video output from the camera that is sent by radio to receivers in the studio, and thence to video tape machines. There will probably be five video recorders in use, one for each camera and one to record a live, switched composite. A live audio mix is sent to each video recorder. Additionally, a multitrack audio machine records a separate track for each mike on the set. For instance:

- Boom mic 1
- Boom mic 2
- Radio mic 1
- Planted mic 1
- Planted mic 2

- Audience mixed mics L
- Audience mixed mics R
- Live mix

To maintain sync, the same time code is sent to all five video recorders, as well as to the multitrack audio recorder. Because of the nature of the production, this will be drop-frame 29.97 fps SMPTE time code, starting at 1 hour for the first reel, 2 hours for the second, etc. In this case the motion-picture cameras operate directly at 23.976 fps and no pulldown is needed. 2:3 insertion is carried out electronically to make a 29.97 video directly.

The production delivers six reels of tape to post production, five video and one multitrack audio, as well as production logs. Each of the camera tapes is dubbed to an editing format and sent to the off-line editor. The edit produces a cut videotape and an EDL. Once the EDL is done, the production multitrack is dubbed into a digital audio workstation. The EDL is used by the sound editor to conform the dubbed audio to the picture, maintaining sync (in some systems, this mechanical synchronization process may be automatic, called *auto-conform*).

The production sound tracks are first cleaned by having extraneous noise removed, and then sweetened by adding additional tracks of sound effects and music. Once the sound editor is satisfied with the cut, the multichannel output of the digital audio workstation is dubbed to an analog or digital multitrack tape format for use in mixing. The mix occurs from tracks of the multitrack, to other tracks of the same or a synchronized multitrack. Once mixed into stems, the stems are simply summed together to make a master mix, and this is then dubbed back to the video tape master in a process called layback.

This description has been of a hybrid system, involving original sound capture on a multitrack, editing digitally, and then dubbing to a new multitrack linear format machine, analog or digital, for mixing. This is not an unusual situation, because each technology is used in its strong suit: Multitrack for massive capture and storage, and random-access digital for its editorial capability. Historical trends favor increasing use of nonlinear digital technique over time, but the current cost/performance trade-off favors hybrid systems.

Documentary production

Documentary production most often today originates on videotape, with sound recorded "single system" on the longitudinal and/or the AFM tracks of an analog format, or to the digital audio tracks of a digital video format tape.

> The AFM tracks have a performance advantage but an editorial disadvantage over linear tracks of an analog medium: They cannot be recorded over existing video—no "dubbing" is possible. Original recording may thus be done on the AFM tracks, leaving the longitudinal tracks for a voice-over, added onto the camera original after shooting. Extremely simple productions may get away with just using these four tracks, but such a procedure is usually reserved for time-pressured production such as news.

Time code is recorded on a dedicated track on professional cameras to be used as a means of maintaining picture identity in post production, that is, to keep track of the exact position within the program as editing proceeds and as a sync signal for double-system audio post production.

An off-line "picture" edit is performed on a nonlinear editor in an *edit bay* also called an *edit suite*, or *off-line room*. In doing this, the typical edit is in a form called *audio-follows-video*, that is, each picture cut is accompanied by a simultaneous audio cut, without intervention from the editor.

There is a critical feature of such nonlinear editing systems that makes them especially useful in this case: they record *non-destructive* edits. This means that what an editor is doing in cutting is really just making a list of pointers to the media files, with discontinuous jumps in the media for edits. These appear continuous (if they are intended to be!) because the machine is so fast that the jumps around the media are not seen.

The way that sound editing works in this environment is the following. First sound is exported from the nonlinear off-line system to the sound editing system using a high-level file transmission scheme that sends the required media files along with the editing instructions that have been produced by the picture editor.[5] Intermediary software may be needed to get the translations to occur correctly. For instance, transmitting from Avid's video-based editor to Pro Tools requires DigiTranslator software.

The sound editor treats the sound delivered by the picture editor just like feature film does their A track, and proceeds to split that track out whenever there is a discontinuity by copying the A Track across to other tracks. What is actually going on is that no new recording is being made by the "copying," but rather, new pointers are being written to the media file. The advantage of non-destructive editing now comes into play. If the export has been done correctly, the sound editor has sound from before the beginning of a picture edit to after the ending of the shot, and it is these "handles" that provide a means to smooth transitions across the edits.

Then dialog *cleaning* is done by editing the dialog tracks to improve them, and substituting "room tone" in those places that need to be filled. In documentary production, usually there is no available "retake" from which to grab a word, should one not be clear, but we live with a style in documentary work that includes people talking as they do, with "flubs," more readily than in narrative filmmaking.

One of the biggest problems of documentary production comes from the huge amounts of material that are often available. To make the editorial task easier, transcripts of interviews are typed. It is tempting to build the story by editing the pieces of the transcript into a logical whole. The problem with this is that it ignores sound quality and the huge shifts that may take place for different loca-

---

5. The media files may be embedded in the edit file, or separate, as described in Chapter 8.

tions. By recording under a variety of conditions, completely different patterns of reverberation and background sound are present in each of the venues used for interviews. It may be tempting to cut the interviews together as a voice-over for other footage so that the picture does not appear to pop back and forth from one scene to another, but to do the same thing with the sound track should be seen as equally troubling as changing the picture.

The program is then *sweetened* by adding additional tracks of sound effects and music. Mixing proceeds along the same lines as for feature films, with some simplification. Since no foreign language dubbing is done, there is no reason to keep things separate, and since there are fewer tracks to begin with, and console automation to help out today, it is common to mix from all the available tracks directly to the final mix. Still, premixing is not unknown in documentary sound.

The off-line edit is usually done with video copies of the original material, not the original tapes, and after the edit is approved an *on-line session* is scheduled and done with the original tapes. The output of the off-line edit is an *edit decision list* (EDL), which is often delivered from the off-line system to the on-line one on a floppy disk. The on-line room is equipped with a more expensive automated editing system, with higher quality machines and capabilities, and higher per hour charges than off-line systems. So the bulk of time that the editor spends is on the off-line system, determining the edit. Once the edit has been made, and documented by an EDL, the on-line system essentially duplicates the actions of the editor, shuttling machines back and forth, making insert recordings at each cut, and assembling an *Edit Master* videotape, all under computer control. Thus on-line edit bay time and consequent costs are minimized. In a final stage called *layback*, the audio master tracks are x-copied onto the master videotape in sync.

Conclusion

The role of sound editing in the overall process has been put into perspective. While a variety of different recording and editing methods are used at different places within the industry, the basic idea of being able to manipulate sounds separately and then combine them is fundamental to all of the solutions. What changes among the methods is the relative cost versus the capability for fine manipulation of the material. Cost is a complicated equation because there are large differences among the types of cost: capital equipment for digital editing vs. mag film for transfers, labor for hand work on cheap editing equipment vs. faster speed on more expensive equipment, and so forth. The economics are also rapidly changing as the price of digital storage continues to drop precipitously, making workstations more attractive. Free but limited capability software is also available on computers, making the tradeoffs even more complicated. Table 9.4 describes some of the tradeoffs.

Table 9.4: Tradeoffs Among Competing Sound Editing System Approaches

Parameter	Traditional film editing	Multitrack based editing	Digital audio workstation
Editing equipment cost	Cheap to fairly expensive (sync block to flat bed)	Expensive (analog or digital multitrack plus source machines and mix console)	Free to very expensive
No. of editors available with skills	Many, and skills are easily transferable	Fewer, and skills are reasonably transferable	Rapidly growing, but each system requires specific learning curve time before high productivity is achieved

Table 9.4: Tradeoffs Among Competing Sound Editing System Approaches (Continued)

Storage capacity limited by	No. of units which a post facility can play simultaneously, transfer costs for mag film	Storage capacity in coarse increments of 24 tracks at a time, no. of multitracks available	Disk drive recorded density grew 60%/year over last 10 years, so strong trend in this direction
Sound quality of recording	Fair to Excellent	Fair to Excellent	Good to Excellent
Technological age	Mature technology more than 45 years old, essentially no innovation expected	Mature technology more than 20 years old, little innovation expected[1]	New technology less than 10 years old, innovation follows computer developments (an advantage since that market is so huge)
Ability to handle picture changes	Possible, but costly as so much labor is involved	Terrible, requires dubbing off to an intermediate medium, then re-dubbing in new position on multitrack	Potentially very good, although practicality depends on system details
Largest limitation	High labor costs	High equipment costs, difficult to get uniform year-round utilization, editor must also act as transfer operator, slowing down editing	Storage capacity limitations, time to load and un-load disks is large, big systems are still expensive

1   The use of digital or analog multitracks fulfills the same operational needs, having the same advantages and drawbacks, although there may be sound quality differences.

Computer-based digital audio editing

The fundamental difference between mag film and multitrack systems, on the one hand, and digital audio systems, on the other, is random-access-based editing, also called *nonlinear editing*. In film and tape editing systems, by cutting a segment of mag film in, or by recording a sound to a multitrack recorder, a sound editor commits to a particular time sequence of effects. If the picture subsequently changes, the sound tracks must be changed. This is clumsy with either film or multitrack.

The random-access nature of digital audio workstations makes these problems potentially much simpler to handle. You can think of the difference between digital audio workstations and either mag film or tape-editing systems like the difference between a phonograph record and a tape. To get to a new cut of a phonograph record, all we do is pick up the tone arm and move it to the cut we want by counting the "lands" in between the program segments. We can do this at

random, going from track 1 to 10, to 2, to 5, if we like, with no difficulty. A compact disc works more or less the same way on many of the more elaborate players. A tape, on the other hand, must be shuttled to the new cut through all the intervening program material. This is one fundamental difference between nonlinear editing, and linear editing—lifting the phonograph tone arm to skip all the intermediate cuts is nonlinear, while having to spool through tape is linear.

The other major difference between these two systems is illustrated by a scene extension. In the linear case, the editor must find the corresponding head or tail trim in order to cut in the correct sound. In nonlinear editing, by contrast, all of the sound of a given effect may reside on the medium all of the time; it is an EDL that determines which sound to play for how long and when from a larger "database" of sound resident on the medium. Random-access editing works very much like a phonograph record on which we can move the tone arm to the desired groove (not just the desired cut) when we wish and play it at the appropriate time.

Digital audio editing duplicates many of the same features as linear analog-based systems, including butt and diagonal splices. In addition, due to the capability for local signal processing within the editing system, more effects, such as reversing the head and tail of a sound, or changing its speed editorially rather than in transfer, may be used. Other modifications are available to be made during sound editing but are actually rather risky. These include filtering and equalization, which belong more properly to the province of mixing. The difficulty in making such decisions this early in the process is the same as that in making such judgments in transfer: The monitor system is probably unsuitable to make such judgments, and any mistakes made may be irre-

vocable. Digital audio workstations have brought with them somewhat more features than can actually be exploited, but some of them have opened up more sound-manipulation capability for sound editors.

Ultimately the job of sound editors is to pick and place sound, and any of the systems described can do this. What sounds are chosen and where they appear is certainly more important than the technology used to achieve the goal. All three systems—film, multi-track, and digital workstation—coexist at this time, with rapid expansion on the part of digital nonlinear techniques and the others declining in use, but still available.

Digital editing mechanics

Fig. 9.2 shows an editing screen from a Digital Audio Workstation. Traditionally, tracks

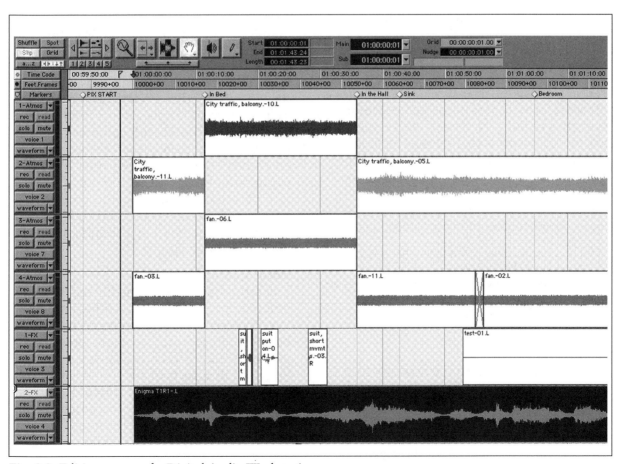

Fig. 9.2 Editing screen of a Digital Audio Workstation.

are represented horizontally, flowing from left to right. They allow "cut and paste" sound editing to be done rapidly, following a visual track metaphor.

> Interestingly, this is in contrast to cue sheets, where the work flow is from top to bottom. The reason for this difference appears rooted in the history of digital audio workstations: music came first with its horizontal representation.

Edit screens show progress of playback along a time line, the individual tracks with their associated sound regions displayed, and potentially many other items such as input and output assignments of signals sent to and from the tracks, "mode" of the tracks such as play or record, "solo" functions described in Chapter 10, and where sounds are located on the media so they can be quickly accessed and dragged into a track in the desired sync along the time line. Other screens are more mixing oriented, described in the next chapter, and they may include "overlays" for transport control, time/footage readout, etc. Individual details vary and are a point of competition among workstation manufacturers.

Perhaps one of the most remarkable things is the waveform display of the audio within the active regions. Not every workstation has these, but those that do may include as much as a sample-by-sample display of the amplitude through time, the actual digitized waveform. This is remarkable because it turns a task that for cutting mag film was done completely audibly into a visual task.

> The amazing thing about this is that it is a reversion to pre-1952 film sound cutting, when work was done on optical sound tracks that were visible. Sound editors at the time thought mag would never catch on because it wasn't visible, therefore you couldn't edit it!

Fade files
We've already described the necessity for making "diagonal" vs. butt splices in audio. A diagonal splice is a fade in, a fade out, or a cross-fade. Fading involves level change, which in digital audio means doing multiplications, in fact, thousands of them per second. In order to have the equivalent of a diagonal splicing capability on each edit, the workstation signal processing requirements are formidable. While some high-end workstations do such cross-fades in real time, on all the channels, others use a different method, the idea of *fade files* to accomplish the same thing. Fade files are derived from those regions of audio files where the sound is being changed in level. The computation of the fade can be done slower than real time, and the corresponding snippet of sound stored away as a fade file. Then, in real time, all the workstation has to do is play the fade file at the correct time, splicing it instantaneously to the main file once outside the audio region affected. The instantaneous splice is not audible because the waveforms are perfectly matched at the edit point. Some systems divide their media recordings into *audio files* and *fade files*, with the fade files having the potential to be lost and re-generated from the audio files through the editing instructions.

Cue-sheet conventions
Sound editors prepare two things: sound elements and cue sheets, so that mixers know where sound is located. The cue sheets are essential for premixing, and subsequently they may be used as a reference for where an individual sound is placed in a premix. Cue sheets are organized with columns representing what is going on in each element. Within an element, they indicate whether a sound is to cut abruptly or fade in and out. They also give the critical footage or time code numbers corresponding to the start or, if needed, an intermediate point in a sound effect. See Fig. 9.3 for an example.

Sound design
The term sound design encompasses the traditional processes of both editing and mixing. The origin of the term seems to have been the film *Apocalypse Now* where one person, Walter Murch, was given responsibility for all aspects of the sound track. Today, a person in charge of sound design could have responsibility over a range from the overall conception of the sound track and its role in the film, to making specialized complex sound effects.

Ben Burtt[6] likes to say that each of us carries

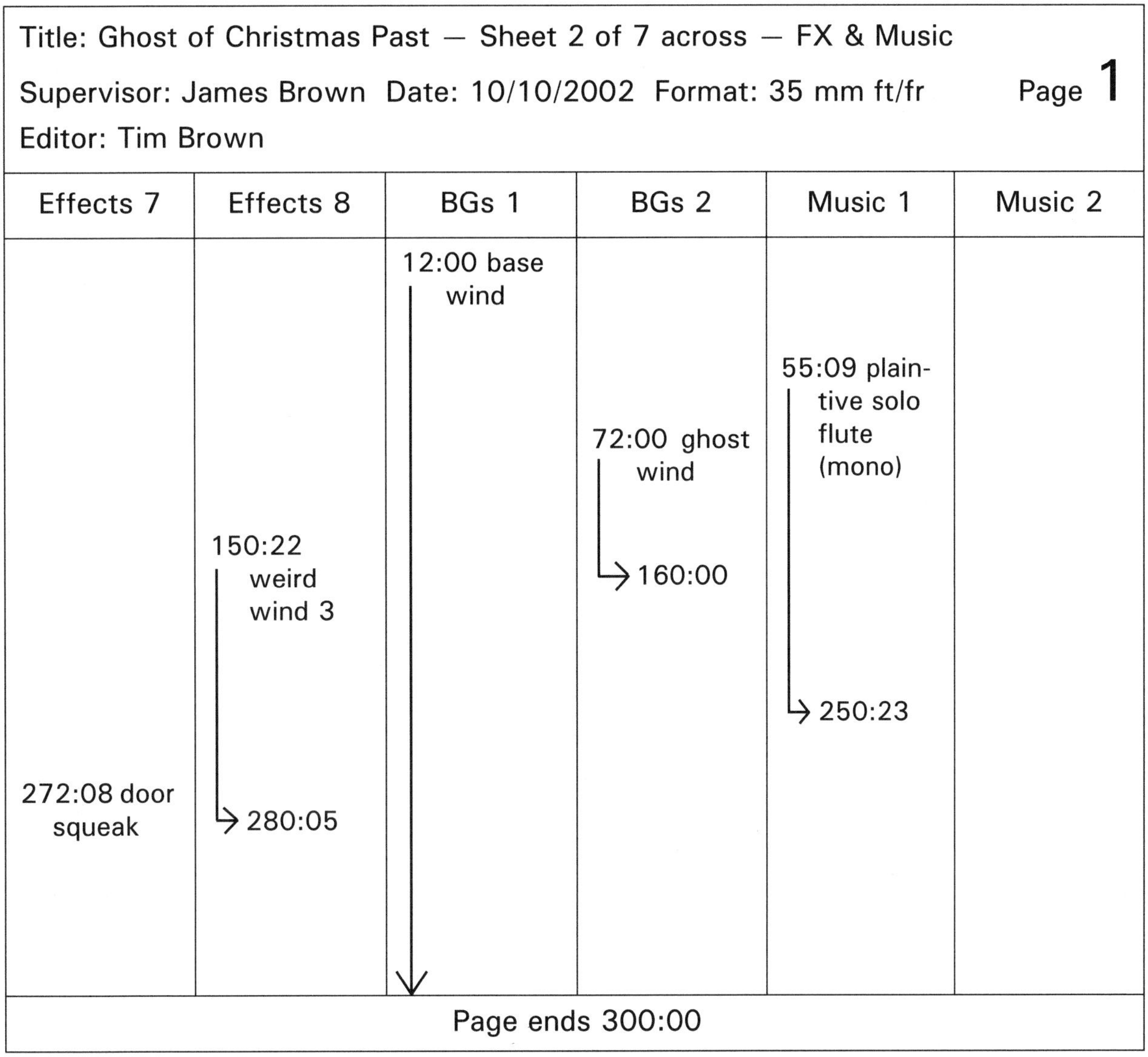

Title: Ghost of Christmas Past — Sheet 2 of 7 across — FX & Music					
Supervisor: James Brown Date: 10/10/2002 Format: 35 mm ft/fr Page **1**					
Editor: Tim Brown					
Effects 7	Effects 8	BGs 1	BGs 2	Music 1	Music 2
272:08 door squeak	150:22 weird wind 3 ⤷ 280:05	12:00 base wind ⬇	72:00 ghost wind ⤷ 160:00	55:09 plaintive solo flute (mono) ⤷ 250:23	
Page ends 300:00					

Fig. 9.3 A cue sheet showing conventions such as length of effects and continuation across pages. Courtesy WildSync L.L.C.

around in our heads an emotional dictionary, associating certain sounds with certain emotions. The low-frequency rumble means threat equation is one of the simpler manifestations of this. Doubtlessly, this is true because it is known that a smell can evoke a memory, and certainly a sound can. Walter

Murch, editing *The English Patient,* used aural memory for transitions to the flashbacks that the title character is having. But even below the threshold of producing a specific memory, there is subliminal feeling, for example, the feeling that something just isn't right when a low-frequency rumble is present. A sound designer uses the sound to tap into this emotional dictionary.

Another duty of the sound designer creative-

6. Academy Award winner for special sound effects editing of *Star Wars* and *E.T. the Extra-Terrestrial.*

ly may be to produce new sound effects. For example, a believable sound for a dinosaur is needed so recording all kinds of animal noises, then combining them in new ways, potentially using the transfer tactics discussed in Chapter 8, will work. In *Jurassic Park* some of the dinosaur sounds designed by Gary Rydstrom originated with penguins and another from a baby elephant trumpeting. For *Star Wars* Ben Burtt had to make a creative decision as to what the laser guns and spaceships would sound like, and this decision substantially influenced the film. (Imagine the space battles in *Star Wars* with the sounds of *Star Trek* instead.)

Sometimes the source for finding effects is aural memory. When Indy enters the cave with his guide, he knows to spring an arrow trap by taking a burned-out torch and pressing on a "loose" rock in the floor. The arrow springs out of the trap in the wall, and naturally just hits the torch squarely. The sound that the arrow makes on striking the torch is a sort of twang. Ben Burtt remembered the kid sitting next to him in grade school, who would twang his ruler on the edge of the desk to make a "neat noise," and that's what Indy's arrow sounded like because that's what it is!

One way in which sound effects are made to seem like something other than what they are is by recording technique. While many practitioners concentrate on the very best quality recording methods to capture the actual sound of a source, others are more interested in what variations can be achieved with invented techniques. For example, the sound of Luke's land speeder in *Star Wars* came from another transportation sound— the Harbor Freeway in Los Angeles[7]—by recording that sound through a vacuum-cleaner tube. The tube acts as an organ pipe, emphasizing one frequency range to the exclusion of others, and makes a vaguely "transportation-like" sound, without revealing the source identity. Other methods include contact microphones used, for example, on bridge structures, hydrophones

used underwater, and many more experimental ones. Some of these are aided by disposable microphones referenced in Chapter 4.

Sound design is the art of getting the right sound in the right place at the right time. The right sound means that the correct aesthetic choice has been made for that moment in time. The right place relates to the high degree of organization that is necessary over the process, combining sound where possible within a premix for simplification of the final mix, but also keeping the various sound elements separate enough so that necessary changes can be made late in the process. It is the balancing act between these two issues that is at the core of the sound designer's work. The right time refers to the correct position in editorial sync. So sound design can be seen to embrace both aesthetic issues and "manufacturing" details, from the inception of temp sound for temp mixes through the preparation of print masters for release on a wide variety of media.

Because of its northern California origins, the term *sound designer* is not well liked in parts of Hollywood, where the traditional terms breaking down editing and mixing into the jobs supervising sound editor and re-recording mixer still prevail. The term *sound designer* was also taken up by some people to describe themselves to clients, saying they could perform all of the tasks themselves well, and this raises the ire of some in the post production community. One would be wise to enquire about which terms are in use on a given production before plunging into a description of one's expertise either as a "sound designer" or "supervising sound editor."

Coincident with the use of the term sound designer came a difference in working style that has served well. In the old style Hollywood assembly line method of editing, sound editors were assigned reels. With this approach, there were coordination problems, since if, for instance, that door opening of the bridge of the *Star Trek Enterprise* was cut from one source for reel 1, then it had to be the same sound effect throughout the rest

---

7. One block from the USC campus.

of the reels. This meant the supervising sound editor had to keep logs of all of this information, and transmit it to all the editors. Walter Murch realized that if the organization were to be done "horizontally" rather than "vertically," productivity improvements could result. Thus the specialization that one person would go through all the reels and cut the "bridge effects" came into being. Today, these two methods of working, assignment by reel, and assignment by type of effect, coexist.

Film sound styles

Films and videos have sound styles, which can elevate the story line. By style is meant the aggregate of sound perspectives, methods, correlation or lack of it with the picture, and other factors such as the degree of reality vs. constructed space that is used.

Sound style may vary within a given program, and usually does over longer programs to keep things interesting. While listening to all programs we encounter sound style continuously, and it is a more or less conscious choice on the part of the film- or video-maker throughout the piece. While the field encompasses all decisions about what sound is heard when, and thus is difficult to quantify, a few organizing principles can be given.

- Musical score heard alone usually distances us from the picture content, because there is no synchronous sound (dialog, cut effects, or Foley) to make things seem real. This is why many, perhaps most, films start with music and then add more real effects as the action gets started: it is a way to start with an abstraction and then to draw the viewer/listener into the story.

- Likewise, a break in the middle of action to hearing just music tells us that we are in montage. The old vaudeville plea from the stage for the orchestra to produce "a little traveling music please" still works in film. For instance, *Days of Heaven* opens on score underneath black and white photos with titles, and moves on to the interior of a steel mill, with such

loud sound effects that we can't hear the language building up to a fight that loses Bill (Richard Gere) his job. We have gone from filmic montage to reality. Next there is a scene change to a very dark interior and we hear some distant train effects and voice-over narration as the characters travel west. Then we hear music, and see the train in a long shot—the little traveling music—in pure montage again. One definition for montage is: "A process in which a number of short shots are woven together in order to communicate a great deal of information in a short period of time."[8] and the end of this sequence certainly qualifies. Another definition might be: A period in a film where the picture and sound are less associated than usually, such as when the sound track is music and the picture combines shots spaced over time.

The debate on the dubbing stage for *Out of Africa* must have been interesting: just how much of the airplane should we hear while it flies through the flamingoes underneath the great big string score? The answer chosen was just a little bit. It could have been none—pure montage—but that would have been a distance from reality that was too great at that point in the film—it wasn't the beginning or ending, but rather a pause in the middle.

- Foley sound effects seem to make things more real. Their "hyper-reality," achieved through close miking of small-scale events ,helps make this so. A movie that combined ADR sound unmodified in mixing so that it seemed disembodied and passages with no Foley sounds is *A Room with a View*. The overall effect is one of an undesirable abstraction—it just doesn't seem real.

- Ambience is the connective tissue of film sound tracks. As described before, its constancy across picture cuts provides an

8. James Monaco, *How to Read a Film*, Oxford: Oxford University Press, 1981. pp. 183-4.

anchor for the visuals that means we are in the same space, with a different perspective on the action. Conversely, its abrupt change at a picture cut means we have changed scenes. This idea is played upon by pre-lap edits wherein we hear the sound change before the picture change, in effect "warning" us of the scene change. This effect can even be heightened by changing the source for sound sent to the surround channels before that sent to the screen channels.

- Besides its connective nature, ambience has a particular story-telling effect. In the language of semiotics, the study of signs and how they work (that includes aural experiences), certain effects, many of them ambient ones, are "signifiers." That is, such sounds have near instantaneous accepted meaning, shorthand for describing the "signified." For instance, after the lid falls back onto the ark in *Raiders of the Lost Ark,* and the ruckus it has made subsides, we are left with one sound, that of a cricket. The signified is peace and quiet, that the storm is over, the climax has occurred, and dénouement begins. All from one sound effect.

- Dialog has its own set of conceits. Quite often we are able to hear sound through walls or windows, or at a very great distance, just as if the actor speaking was in a close-up. While this is neither good nor bad necessarily, it certainly does not match reality. In some cases it can be disturbing to an audience when they don't know who is supposed to be speaking, and so it may be useful to provide this information before such a sequence.

- It has been standard practice since the beginnings of film sound to have dialog heard over a telephone restricted in bandwidth, usually by a telephone filter. This convention has started to unravel recently. For instance, in *The Deep End,* conversations between a blackmailer and his victim occur. In cutting back and forth, re-recording mixer Mark Berger explained that there were picture cuts in the middle of speech phonemes. Cutting

the tracks to match the picture meant abrupt changes in the middle of a word. This difficulty started the process that led to a decision to hear the opposing end of the conversation to the one being portrayed on camera in full bandwidth, with background sound, thus "putting" the blackmailer right in the room with his victim aurally.

After all, we have an ability to "fill in" the gaps when sound is reproduced poorly. For instance, a small transistor radio can become fascinating with the right story told over it—despite its technical limitations, the characters become real for us. Essentially that is what removing the bandwidth limiting filter is doing: producing a more subjective experience more like our own than the actual experience.

Progress in film sound on this topic is interesting. The very earliest sound films portrayed the telephone conversation by cutting back and forth between the participants. If we were left on one visually while the other one spoke, which was unusual, we heard nothing of the far end of the conversation, but instead must deduce what was being said by the reaction. Within a few years, filters were introduced and the standard fiction came into use: that we hear the far end of conversations filtered. *The Deep End* sets up a new "reality" by starting out using unfiltered voice for the other end of conversations in a relatively benign phone call early in the film, so that when it is used later on the audience can understand it, and the blackmailer is projected into the victim's room, along with the casino background from which he is operating.

A related effect is used in *Vertical Limit.* In this mountain climbing movie, a character knows he is going to die on the mountain, but has a satellite phone conversation with his loved one. The extremely narrow audible frequency range of the phone is set up earlier, but over the progress of the crucial scene, the bandwidth constriction is removed, projecting his love into the tent where he will expire.

- There are several juxtapositions at work in selecting sounds. First is the juxtaposition with picture. Critical studies thinkers have been at work on this since the introduction of sound, although much less critical work has been done in sound than in picture. Some writers have said sound operates in counterpoint with the picture, using the musical term for parts having independent motion of pitch and rhythm played simultaneously. But this would be true of any juxtaposition of picture and sound. Michel Chion argues for the term "harmony" instead, with picture and sound different, but related. In the end, it is the production of meaning in the mind of the viewer/listener that is sought in selecting sounds, whether simply illustrating the picture, or providing a extension to it into other aesthetic domains. If anything, sound professionals complain that directors tend to be overly cautious and conservative in this area, using sound to match the picture rather than provide extensions to it.

- Picture and sound have mutual subjective effects. Picture without sound runs slower subjectively than with it. The presence of a picture makes sound slightly less loud and bright. Color pictures sound slightly clearer and softer than black and white ones of the same material.

- There are also juxtapositions within the sound track. In *Band of Outsiders* Godard has a character bang her bicycle up against a railing, ending her ride and the scored music abruptly at the same time. Sound designers pay attention to the effects of frequency and temporal masking, leaving, for instance, "little holes"[9] for dialog. In *Platoon*, the crucial battle near the end of the picture has lots of shooting and artillery, but none of it is over critical lines of dialog necessary to the story. Lines such as "Get out of the hole!" stand out against the background due to the space carved in the sound effects for it, not some mix manipulation. At the beginning of *Apocalypse Now*, the sound of a helicopter and that of a ceiling fan are juxtaposed, by blending them in a crossfade that takes us from one reality to another.

- The sound can be very clean and bright, or it can be more obscure. Comparable to the filters that cinematographers use on lenses to soften the image, it may be undesirable to have everything completely clear on the sound track all of the time.[10] However, convention demands that all dialog be intelligible, even when the director says the line is of no importance, and need not be heard. If it is not, it will provoke wonder in the audience: "What did he say?" must be one of the most said things in movie theaters.

- Each film or television show has the freedom to establish its own conventions, but generally it must pay attention to them. *Ally McBeal* has meditative sequences where we are taken inside a character's thoughts to what is occurring, and we are jerked back out to reality by a sound that is like that of a phonograph tone arm skated across a record. It becomes a convention through use that this sound has this meaning, for that show. Used in another context, the same sound could be a reality one: say in a disco club it could indicate frustration on the part of the record spinner.

- Not all films use the conventional DM&E breakdown because some use virtually no dialog or effects. An example is a film of the ballet *The Nutcracker*.[11] It would be possible to have only a music track for a film of a ballet, although in this particular instance, the

---

9. Ioan Allen's term for this effect.

10. An idea expressed by Randy Thom.
11. The 1993 edition, sound design by Randy Thom.

filmmakers chose to add a Foley sound track of the dancer's movements in order to heighten the "reality" of the film, rather than to use the more abstract music with no other sound, "distancing" the audience from the work.

- Beginnings and endings are important. As we've already said, music often begins a program, which then crossfades to realistic sound. The ending is often signi-

fied pictorially by a crane shot, starting on the level of the characters, and then moving up to an extreme wide shot. The equivalent for sound is also usually music, moving us "away" from the reality of the picture.

Table 9.5 gives some common film sound conventions, along with their short-hand meaning.

Table 9.5: Sound Conventions in Films and Television

Sound	Meaning	Example
One cricket heard alone	Peace and quiet, rural. The fact that it can be heard proves the point.	*Close Encounters of the Third Kind* *Cocoon* *Raiders of the Lost Ark*—after the lid has reclosed on the ark
Low-frequency sound effects such as distant thunder	Portent of bad things to come	Numerous
Gentle rain	Heard from an inside perspective it forms a protective, enclosed space, isolated from others.	*Hedwig and the Angry Inch*
Foley sound effects	Heightened reality	Most films, strange by its absence, such as in *A Room with a View*
Acoustic feedback	Public address system in use: practically all films use the cliche that the sound system portrayed feeds back at first, then settles down—since ongoing feedback would be so annoying.	Numerous—note its avoidance is unusual in *Jurassic Park III* in the opening scene
Red Tail Hawk	Lonely western scene	
Three crow cries	Death	
Dial tone right after a phone call	The other end has hung up. This is movie reality—it doesn't happen this way in real life.	
You can always hear speech, despite seeing though a window, or at a long distance out of doors.	Not much. It is a convention that we can hear dialog so that the question is not asked "what did he say?" fatal to staying connected to the story.	
Multiple galloping hooves in the distance.	Threat over the horizon, using the low frequency equation again.	Super Posse in *Butch Cassidy and the Sundance Kid* and stampede in *Dances with Wolves*

Chapter 10: Mixing

Introduction

The process of mixing sound tracks together has slightly different terminology applied to it depending on the field of use. In film work, mixing is called *re-recording* or *dubbing*. In television production, the words *mixing* or *sweetening* are more commonly employed to name the process.

The term *re-recording* is perhaps the most self-defining of these terms. The term *mixing*, on the other hand, can be applied to a wide variety of tasks, from live sound mixing at concerts, to combining the tracks of a multitrack recording into fewer tracks for release of a music compact disc, to making adjustments in level in transferring one two-track master to another. *Re-recording* is a more limited term, meaning taking something already recorded and distilling it down by mixing processes to a more convenient representation from many units, elements, or tracks to pre-mixes, or from pre-mixes to final mixes. *Dubbing* is synonymous with *re-recording* when applied to the mixing process, but it is also applied to any copying process that may occur in audio or video recording.

Laydown, layover, and *layback* are terms that essentially mean x-copying at the various stages of a television production. Laydown means capturing from the production sound medium into an editing environment, usually a workstation. Layover is synonymous with dub (used as the second definition above), and with x-copy, but these two terms are more associated with film than video. Layback is the copy from the sound master to the composite video master, usually the last step in the process.

Re-recording is typically done on a dubbing stage by from one to three mixers working simultaneously on the program material. Arranged to be like a theater, with the mixers occupying the best audience seats, the basic idea is to combine the tracks of the relevant stage of processing, while simultaneously manipulating them for the best sound quality and the desired effect, while hearing the movie under the same conditions as an audience would in a theater.

In post production, it is necessary to have a system that can "rock and roll," that is, respond to commands and go forward or backward, at high or normal speed, while maintaining sync. In fact, one of the distinguishing factors of film dubbing compared to other methods is the ability to "play in reverse," which is revered by mixers who work on the sound processes during reverse play and so maximize their productivity.

Film has traditionally been projected for film dubbing, but its slow speed access to different parts of the reel has given way in recent years to dubbing while showing a projected video image, which may be available from a nonlinear editing system and thus able to "reset" to another time instantly. Entering the mixing room has also been the Digital Audio Workstation, usually of the same type used by the sound editors. In this way, a sound editor can be on standby to make rapid editorial changes if called for. Also, digital film dubbers offer offset capabilities, so sound can be slipped in sync relative to other sounds during dubbing without tying up editorial facilities.

Sweetening for television programs is typically done in a relatively small studio by one or two mixers working simultaneously, which is arranged to be closer to a living room than to a theater in size; however, more expensive TV dubbing is done in larger rooms.

Sound source devices used in re-recording

Traditional dubbers played magnetic film across virtually any number of machines interlocked by a signal called *biphase*. Magnetic film could carry from one to six tracks per strand of film, and interlocking multiple machines meant a very large number of audio tracks could be played simultaneously. Large studio sound departments had machine rooms with up to about 100 machines, each of which could theoretically carry up to six tracks, but this centralized room served multiple dubbing stages simultaneously, and none of them could handle 600 tracks, al-

though 200 was not unknown. Devices were built to provide a slip sync function for one machine at a time, so sound effects could be quickly resynced if relatively simple changes were needed. Edit/change rooms were usually made available so that sound editors could quickly revise units more thoroughly as needed. Television post production has relied on 2-in. 24-track recording for many years as standard, until recently.

Modern post production has mostly done away with the magnetic film dubber in the last few years, although a few low budget films still use them, and they will be in use for a very long time to come to play back legacy recordings. The number of 2-in. machines in use has also begun declining. At first the replacement was a generation of multichannel digital audio tape recorders called MDM as a class, for *modular digital multitrack*. The colloquial name for these machines is "DA-88," named for the first machine of the class, but the tape format is more formally named DTRS. These 8-track machines cost about one-tenth the price of an analog dubber, so were quickly adopted. They could be ganged by control functions, so that a large number of tracks could be supported. The sound quality was decent, although the machines were 16-bit linear PCM, that did not have as much dynamic range as the magnetic film or tape with Dolby SR that they replaced (see Table 6.3). Combining many 16-bit tracks results in a dynamic range of less than 16 bits, so this is seen as a limitation. Also, the first machines lacked confidence head recording, although this was added to later models.

Modular digital multitracks were a way to store a lot of digital content cheaply, but access to that content was limited to the linear domain. To go from the end to the beginning of a reel, the tape had to be rewound, and then on pressing play, would have to "sync up." Although the machines were relatively cheap, faster operation could be achieved if a random-access based system were to be used. Also, MDMs could not play in reserve as dubbers could, so mixers considered them to be a step backwards.

Thus digital dubbers were developed, characterized by random access, quick lock up, play in reverse, and control integration features for dubbing, and control over record insertions called punch ins, described later in this chapter. The format of storage is hard disk or magneto-optical drives. With this development, software was made available to read some standard DAW file formats directly, so putting sound up on a digital dubber usually means simply plugging in a SCSI drive mounted in a carrier.

Digital dubbers are on the order of double or triple the cost of MDM machines, but being purpose built with the features desired for the film and video post production market, have been successful. Meanwhile, digital audio multitrack machines based on hard disk drives have come on the market too. Usually in a 24-track format on hard disks, they are used more widely than dubbers for all kinds of recording. Their large-scale of manufacture makes them cost about what an MDM machine costs, with the added benefit of random access. However, they have limitations in dubbing applications, such as no play in reverse function, etc. Their low cost makes them attractive, though, for those willing to give up on features.

DAWs are also increasingly making their way onto dubbing and mixing stages. An advantage is instantaneous ability to re-edit. This is also a disadvantage if the process is not disciplined. Using an expensive dubbing/ mixing stage as an editing room is not a productive use of the producer's cash. DAWs may deliver their output over digital audio interfaces such as AES3, in which case the workstation is tied up supplying sound to the console, or their media can be demounted and placed in a digital dubber or multitrack, assuming there is file format interchangeability between the DAWs and console. Some dubbing stages have been built recognizing this trend, with booths open to the stage on one side, but surrounded on the others.

Mixing consoles

Mixing consoles used for dubbing are often large and intimidating, with hundreds to thousands of controls. Luckily, there is a great deal of duplication among the controls, so by learning just one area of a console one learns nearly all of the areas. Fundamentally, what goes on inside consoles can be broken down into two ingredients, processing and configuration. Sound processes are the devices used to affect the sound, including all the way from simple internal level controls to sophisticated outboard reverberation units. Configuration issues are about signal routing from the input to the output of the console through the various processes. Of the two, it is processes that are easier to study, because they are represented by the knobs, switches, and other controls on the console. Configuration, on the other hand, is more obscure, since modern consoles are so dense with controls there is no room to draw diagrams on them showing the electrical order of the controls. Given this outlook, we will look into processes in some depth and give the general principles of organizing them by configuration.

It is worth pointing out that each new console faced by a professional is just as much a sea of knobs to them, as it is to the pre-professional until the array can be broken down into logical units and addressed singly. While a professional will recognize a great many of the knobs for the processes they represent, everyone inevitably needs training on the configuration of the processes.

Before describing processes, one organizing feature is worth noting. In many consoles, the construction is such that a series of processes that are associated with one input are arranged vertically in a console *slice*. This means that a primary issue in configuration is accounted for by this fact: An entire column of knobs is likely to be associated with processing the signal from one source. With that in mind, various processes that may appear in an individual slice are first described, and then variations from this standard.

Obscuring the classical distinction between editing and mixing is the fact that DAWs today have many mixing features, and may even have more potential different processes available as software "plug-ins" than major consoles. Console control surfaces that operate the functions of DAWs are becoming popular. The distinction between DAWs equipped with a control surface and large consoles is usually that, if the console is digital, it will have dedicated digital signal processors for each channel, and thus may be designed not to "overload" under the burden of signal processing, and possibly crash or lose signals. DAWs are more likely to dynamically assign resources like digital audio signal processing power, so could run out if a great many signal processes were in simultaneous use. This can often be solved by plugging in more hardware to the DAW, but then its cost may approach that of a console.

Processes

Level

Setting the level of each of the elements of a mix is surely the single most important item to be done in mixing. Even the simplest of equipment has a means to adjust the relative level (also called *gain*) or volume of the individual elements by way of *faders*, also called *potentiometers* or *pots*. The reason is simple. If each recording has been made to make best use of the medium, then a Foley recording of footsteps, for example, will be recorded about as loud as a dialog recording. When re-recording, though, it is necessary to get these various elements into balance with one another, so inevitably the Foley element will be turned down relative to the dialog element in order to assume its proper relationship in the mix.

The main level control for each input is given more weight than any other console process by the placement and type of control. On re-recording consoles, the main channel fader is always the control that is largest and closest to the operator, and is usually a vertical slider type of control with markings for resetability.

Another related primary control is called a *mute*, which is simply a switch that kills the signal altogether, allowing for a speedier

turn-off than turning the fader all the way down rapidly. Mutes are probably more commonly used during multitrack music recording than during film mixing because in music all tracks are on practically all of the time, whereas workstations produce silence when there is no desired signal, thus accomplishing muting right at the source. Music mixes may mute individual channels for whole sections of the mix, say, the string channels during a brass solo, to prevent audible crosstalk into the unused channels from the open, but unused, mikes. The mute function also provides a means of identification of where a sound might be. By activating the mutes in turn during a trial run, the mixer can learn where the various sounds are, in case the cue sheets are faulty or unclear.

In cases where there has been too much sound cut for a sequence, and not enough time to change it editorially, a mute function may become valuable. Here, a computer follows the action of switches throughout a reel, keeps track of what is muted and what is unmuted, and performs the mutes on subsequent passes. Like fader automation, mute automation can be built up into a complex pattern over many passes.

These two functions, level and mute, are so important that they are the first functions to be automated in more elaborate consoles. A means to mute all other channels and to monitor only what one channel is contributing to the mix is very useful. This function is called *solo*. Pressing the solo button on a channel will make the monitor mute all other channels. Pressing more than one solo button will produce a mix of only those channels.

> There are variations on the solo idea. Most solo systems offer only a "cue" or "audition" function, so the signal processing, such as the position in a stereo mix, is lost when solo is activated. Some offer "solo in place," representing the sound being soloed correct spatially. Many solo systems are "destructive," that is, the output mix of the console is affected by the solo function so it cannot be used during principal mixing, but others are "nondestructive," affecting only what is monitored, not what is

recorded. So individual consoles vary greatly in their possible solo functions.

Multiple level controls in signal path

On its way through a modern console, a single signal may well pass through a large number of level controls—individual channel fader, subgroup master fader, master fader, and monitor volume control. This multiplicity of controls, while offering high utility and flexibility, also creates problems. The problems are similar to those of recording on a medium: If a tape is under-recorded, when the level is subsequently restored by "turning it up," noise will become evident. Conversely, if over-recorded, the resulting distortion is permanent and will not be removed by "turning it down" at a later stage. While consoles generally have a wider dynamic range than recorders, hitting the dynamic range of each of the intermediate stages correctly is an important issue to avoid excessive noise or distortion.

On the best professional consoles, with their multiplicity of controls, attacking this problem of the correct setting of the variety of controls is accomplished relatively easily. The scale on them is the clue, with 0 dB the nominal setting of the controls. Many of the controls have "gain in hand," which goes above 0 dB, that is, one can "turn it up" from the nominal in order to reach for something under recorded as needed, but the nominal setting is clear. On consoles that lack this feature, it is necessary to determine which settings of all of the controls are the nominal ones. It is usually the channel fader for each slice on which most of the actual mixing is performed. The other controls, such as submasters or master level controls, are used for slight trims to the overall section-by-section balance, or for the main fade-ins and fade-outs of the overall mix. On the other hand, since the individual channel slice gain controls can be used to set the "balance" among the parts of an effect, a submaster can be used to set the overall level of an effect.

One problem with using DAWs as mixing consoles is that they don't typically provide very much "gain in hand." Their design assumes properly recorded levels coming in. Older film consoles had as much as 25 dB gain available over the nominal to accommodate under recorded material, whereas today, with wider dynamic range available on source media so that under recording can be better tolerated, some DAWs only have 6 dB. The designers probably do this to avoid clipping distortion that would otherwise be a strong potential for some material—to keep the operator out of trouble. Other digital console designs have as much as 45 dB gain in hand, so are designed to better tolerate under-recorded sources.

Dynamic range control
Compression

Each track used for re-recording has a volume range. When tracks are combined in mixing, the problem of unintentional masking of one signal by another arises. Let us say that we have a dialog recording, with a volume range, and a music recording, with its own volume range. Starting at the beginning of a show, we have music as the foreground, but it is not theme music in this case that fades out before the dialog begins, but rather source music, fading under the dialog. The problem is that while most of the time the music will lie underneath the dialog, there may be a point in time at which the peaks of the music correspond to the minimum level of the dialog and the dialog is obscured. On the other hand, there will also be times when the music is faded under so that it seems to go away altogether. The alternating presence and absence of the music is distracting.

In order to solve this problem, we could "ride the gain," turning the level of the music down during its higher level passages and up during its softer ones, to maintain a more even level behind the dialog, but this would be tedious and time consuming. The process can be automated by a device called a *compressor*, which does just what we have described. A compressor is equipped with a number of controls to vary the volume range over which the action of the compression occurs, the amount of the compression, and how fast or slow the compressor acts. Each of these devices is fairly idiosyncratic as to control functions, so the number of knobs associated with them varies.

A typical compressor may have the following control knobs:

1. A "threshold" control, below and above which the compressor exhibits a different "transfer function." Usually below the threshold, the compressor acts as a linear amplifier, such that each deciBel in yields a deciBel out, and above the threshold each deciBel in results in less than one deciBel out.

2. A compression ratio control with markings such as 2:1, 4:1, 20:1, or more. This is the ratio between input and output in deciBels above threshold. A 4:1 compression ratio would mean that a 4 dB change in the input produces a 1 dB change at the output, above threshold.

3. An output level control. Because compression often has the effect of lowering the overall level, this control is used to make up the gain and to raise the overall level after the compression process.

4. An attack time control. This control modifies how quickly the controller circuitry responds to an increased level. If it changes too quickly, short sounds that do not reach full perceived loudness may control the gain excessively and "pumping," (audible gain riding) may result. If it changes too slowly, then loud attacks may be heard followed by a level change downward, also leading to pumping. A typical starting value for this control is 80 msec.

5. A release time control. This control modifies how the controller acts when the signal decreases. If the control function is made too fast, the gain will change within one cycle of the signal, which leads to harmonic distortion. If the gain change is set too slow, then soft sounds following loud ones could be lost completely. A typical starting value is 0.5 seconds.

Of course, technically speaking it would be equally possible to compress the dialog into a narrow volume range in order to keep it above the music continuously, but even with the music in correct overall balance then, it may seem to come and go, which can draw attention to it. The principle of "least treatment" for this scene would say that the mixer should process the background sound first rather than the foreground sound, to leave the fewest artifacts present. On the other hand, I have found is useful to use small amounts of compression on dialog to make it sound more natural. The reason for this may be that we are recording dialog typically at one point in space, but we hear at two points. The spatial averaging of level that occurs by averaging two points tends to reduce the stronger level differences observed at one point. Thus slightly compressed sound may actually be a better representation of what we hear than "pure" uncompressed sound. But note that I am speaking of small amounts of compression, on the order of 6 to 8 dB of maximum gain reduction from the linear condition.

If the dialog and music tracks have already been combined, then compression is not an option. The louder track dominates the "thinking" of the compressor, moment by moment. A likely outcome of this condition is that the level of the music would audibly go up and down with the level of the dialog. Assuming the dialog is practically always above the level of the music, when the dialog is soft the compressor will "turn it up," bringing up the music as well; and when the dialog is loud, the dialog and music would be "turned down." This is an effect known as *pumping*, when the level of one element of a mix audibly affects another element in level and is generally undesirable. It is thus best to compress each individual source alone and then to combine sources, rather than to try to compress the entire program.

An aesthetic use for a compressor has been described for keeping music "under control" while faded under a dialog source. This use would be made despite any other consideration in the overall system because it is an aesthetic one, but there is another reason to use compression. Generally, post production works with media that have a wider dynamic range capability than that of the ultimate release format.

Another use for compression is to reduce the large dynamic range of a theatrical presentation to the smaller range felt necessary for home video. Such compression is not routinely used in video transfers, but may be used in special cases where the supervisor of the transfer is certain of the conditions of use. If all users are expected to listen to a program over a television set internal loudspeaker, then that may be given weight in a compression decision. For instance, children's VHS video and airline and hotel video copies are compressed compared with the theatrical version of the same movie. So, there are different uses for compression—in re-recording to control certain tracks to make them more manageable, and subsequently to "fit" the program material's volume range to the range needed by individual media or users.

Expansion

The opposite of a compressor is an expander. An expander increases the volume range of a source, and may do so across a wide dynamic range, or may be restricted to a narrower region by control functions. Restricting expansion to just low-level sounds is often used in re-recording. Called *downward expansion*, *noise gating*, or *keying*, this function turns the level down below a threshold set by a control. For example, all sound below say −40 dB could be rapidly turned down to essentially off. The advantage of this is that there is often low-level noise on each of a number of tracks, that is undesired, and that would be a problem if all of the noise sources were mixed together continuously. With use of a noise gate (which would be more properly called a program gate because it essentially "turns on" for signals above a certain level, and off for ones below that level), such additive noise can be reduced because only tracks above a certain level will "get through" the gate.

Noise gates have a number of audible problems. Let us say that we have a dialog recording with some air-conditioner noise in it. The threshold of the noise gate can be set to distinguish between the dialog and the air-conditioner noise because the air-conditioner noise is lower in level than the dialog. The problem is that we hear air-conditioner noise "behind" the dialog when speaking is going on, and we hear its "absence" in between lines. The dialog is pumping the level of the air-conditioning noise. The exaggerated difference between the noise being on and it being off may well draw more attention to it than just leaving it alone, unprocessed.

For this reason, traditional "all-or-nothing" noise gates are not used too often in critical re-recording tasks. They are used, however, in multitrack music studio work. For example, suppose we have recorded an orchestra and have placed the instrument groups on different tracks. Upon playback, we find that the string track is polluted with acoustical crosstalk from the brass section. In order to eliminate the brass from the string track during passages where the strings are not playing, we can use a noise gate, set so that when the strings are playing the gate is on, and when they are not it shuts the signal off. This operation depends on the string level being higher thatnthe crosstalk of the brass, and on setting the noise gate so that it can discriminate between them. In this application, the noise gate is used on playback, where the control function can be changed and repeated if necessary, rather than on the record side, where any mistake could not be corrected subsequently.

An advancement on the all-or-nothing approach is frequently used in dubbing. Some noise reduction devices work like gates but don't turn the signal fully off, so changes are less abrupt. A more sophisticated approach breaks the audio spectrum up into four or more frequency bands, and applies a downward expansion below a certain threshold separately in different frequency bands. Also, the expansion is not made as dramatic as turning the signal all the way off. These two strategies have the effect of producing much less objectionable side effects. Audible pumping is greatly reduced or eliminated by these approaches. The generic name for such a device is a *multi-band low-level expander*, although because that is such a mouthful, the actual units go by their trade names. These operate in both the analog and digital domains, with potentially many parallel frequency channels. All of them attempt to distinguish desired program material from background noise content, and decrease the level of the background noise without affecting the program material.

Single-ended noise reduction devices based on Dolby A or Dolby SR, known as the Cat. 43 and Cat. 430, respectively for their Dolby catalog numbers, are widely used. These devices use the multiple frequency bands of the associated type of Dolby noise reduction, but not in a manner complementary to what is usually associated with companding noise reduction. Here "single-ended" means that the signal to be processed has not been previously encoded. The Dolby units combine both level and frequency domains because they do their work in multiple frequency bands, basically turning down the level below a certain adjustable threshold. If a desired voice can be set above threshold and an undesired noise below threshold, the equipment can distinguish the two and turn the noise, but not the voice, down. Their use is usually dialog cleanup of production sound recordings.

Limiting

A variation on the idea of a compressor is a limiter. A limiter acts on signals above a certain threshold as a compressor does. Then above that threshold, the level is controlled so that for each deciBel of increase on the input of the limiter, the gain is reduced by the same amount. Thus, above the threshold, the level simply stays practically the same despite any increase in level.

Limiters are useful in production sound to "catch" occasional events that might not otherwise be controlled as to level, to bring them into a range where the recording medium can handle the signal linearly. They are routinely included in production recorders, such as the Nagra, and in camcorders for the utility they offer in keeping unexpected signals under control.

> Limiters are very useful for keeping unexpected high levels from distorting, such as an actor "going over the top" and shouting more loudly on a take than in rehearsal. With mixed program material, though, there may be a problem. Let us say that there is a gunshot in the middle of a scene. With a limiter in use, the gunshot will certainly "trigger" the limiter and the gain

will be dramatically reduced. The difficulty is that it will be reduced for sounds coming after it as well, and the "duck" in level may well be noticeable for speech coming immediately after the shot. In such a case, it may be better to proceed without using a limiter, letting the tape distort on the gunshot briefly. In that way, a post production editor can "clean out" the gunshot from the production sound track by cutting it out, leaving no artifact other than a hole, and cut a clean gunshot into the sound effects track. The limiter must reduce the gain quickly and keep it that way for a while, because if it did not, the result would be distortion of low-frequency sound, so the "duck" after a very loud sound is a natural artifact of limiting.

Limiters are also useful in post production in several ways. They can:

- Put an upper limit on one track, so that it cannot rise in level so much as to interfere with another track. An example is Foley recordings of footsteps in which one or a few footsteps sound like they stick out of the mix, but lowering the overall level of the Foley track is not satisfactory, because then the overall impression is too weak. So applying a limiter set so that it catches the highest level footsteps and keeps them under control is a useful function.

- Probably the most common use of limiters is to control the highest level signals on a sound track so that they can be recorded on a particular medium without distortion. Examples include limiting for analog optical sound tracks, which have much less headroom than the magnetic tracks used as their source.

- Another use for a limiter is to raise the overall loudness without affecting the maximum level. By limiting the highest peaks of the program to a lower level, the average level can be raised without exceeding a particular maximum. With the proper sort of limiter, 5 to 6 dB of limiting can be practically inaudible, and this amount is a large advantage in fitting into the requirements of, say, an optical sound track or any other limited headroom medium.

De-essing

One particular specialized form of limiting is de-essing. This refers to the fact that many media are sensitive to reproduction of the "esses" in speech. By limiting strongly only on such high-frequency sounds in dialog tracks, the resulting sound track can be easier to record to certain media, such as optical sound tracks. Sibilance distortion is the result of imperfect waveform reproduction, when the high-frequency sounds in speech, especially "esses," are affected.

A de-esser is a limiter with one difference—the control function for limiting is made sensitive only for high-frequency sound, so most signals are unaffected. Should an "es" sound cross the threshold of limiting, then the level will be "ducked" for the duration of the "es." You might think that this would make the sound dull because high frequencies are being reduced in level, but de-essing can be surprisingly benign, having little audible effect except to reduce the sensitivity to such distortion at subsequent stages.

Conclusion

All of the items so far discussed affect the level of audio signals. By far the most commonly used of these processes is level controls, which is used even on the simplest of mixers. Muting and solo are also found on most re-recording consoles. Dynamics processing, including compression, expansion, limiting, and de-essing, are also frequently used in re-recording, but more rarely than level controls. Some re-recording consoles include all of these processes in every input path of the console, while others do not have dynamics controls in each input, but rather route signals from the inputs to separate dynamics processors, either built into the console or external to it.

Processes primarily affecting frequency response

Processes that affect principally the frequency response of the signal are probably second in importance only to level control. These processes can "clean up" the audio signal, make it more interchangeable with other signals (for instance, adjusting the tim-bre of production sound and ADR recordings to be more equal), adjust for the loudness effect (by adding bass for sound portrayed at lower than its original level), and generally make the sound more intelligible or pleasant, or, for effect, deliberately worse.

Most of the ear training necessary to become a re-recording mixer is involved with level and frequency response processing, with other factors such as dynamics playing a subsidiary role. The reason that this is so is that the maintenance of good continuity depends much of the time on the sound track not drawing attention to itself through unexpected changes to level or frequency response. The changes must be "smoothed out" so that the audience is not distracted by them.

The two principal frequency response determining processes are *equalization* and *filtering*. Although either of these processes may affect any frequency band from low bass through high treble, there is a fundamental difference between them. Filtering is done essentially to eliminate certain frequency ranges from the output, and thus the action of a filter changes abruptly across frequency. In fact, filters are rated for their frequency and their slope in deciBels per octave. The slope of a practical filter, how much its output changes across frequency, is generally greater than equalizers.

Equalization

Almost everyone has some experience with bass and treble controls on a stereo system. Equalization is the professional name for the process of altering the frequency response in a manner similar to what tone controls do on a stereo system. However, only the simplest professional equipment devotes only two controls to this important task. For professional *equalizers*, often found in each input channel slice in re-recording consoles, and possibly in other parts of the chain, the audio spectrum is more frequently broken up into three or four parts, which might be called low-bass, mid-bass, mid-treble, and high-frequency controls. Alternatively, the two middle controls could be labeled midrange 1 and 2.

Each of the main equalizer controls, called EQ, are rated for how much variation they produce in deciBels when set to their extremes, such as ±12 dB. These main controls may be supplemented by other continuously variable knobs or switches to provide more flexibility in use. If provided, these extra controls affect the parameters of frequency and curve shape, resulting in the name *parametric equalizer* for the device.

The first of these subsidiary controls usually available is one that changes the *frequency* range in which the EQ control is most active. Note that the frequency range of the various controls may be set to overlap, producing the possibility of up to twice as much boost or cut as for one control on analog consoles, or up to potentially four times as much on a four-band digital equalizer with a range of 20 Hz to 20 kHz in each section.

The second most likely control is one that changes the general shape of the curves produced by the equalization control. The two shapes offered are bell shaped and shelving. Bell-shaped curves are centered around a specific frequency, and at maximum boost or cut look like the outline shape of a bell, right side up or upside down respectively. Shelving curves are like conventional tone controls: Once boosted or cut, the whole frequency range from the center frequency of the control to the audio band extreme is equally affected. Thus, this type of control is usually found only on the lowest and highest frequency bands of a multiband equalizer.

The use of the two depends on why the equalization is being done. For example, a shelving characteristic is used to overcome a muffled sound associated with too much cloth over the mike, while a bell-shaped curve may be used for precise equalization of musical overtones of particular instruments. The shelving equalizer is a broad stroke, and the bell-shaped equalizer is more specific.

The third most likely control is called Q. This relates to the "sharpness" of the control function with respect to frequency. Two controls can have the same center frequency and boost, say +8 dB at 2 kHz, but they may get to that boost in a manner that is either very narrow, having little effect on neighboring frequency ranges, or wide, having effects well away from the center frequency of the equalizer. A "narrow" equal-

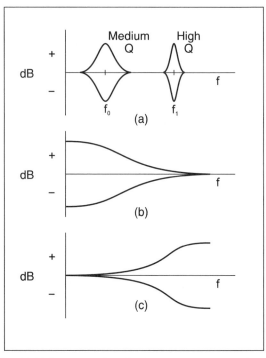

Fig. 10.1 The curves given by (a) represent commonly found "bell shaped" equalization curves, with the "Q" as well as center frequency varied between the two sections. Curves (b) and (c) represent low- and high-frequency shelving curves respectively, most commonly found as the bass and treble controls on a stereo system, but also useful in re-recording.

izer has high Q, and a wide one has low Q. Because low Q affects the response in more critical bands, it is generally more audible. Low Q is usually used for program equalization unless a particular problem in a narrow frequency band is the trouble, and then the high-Q version is valuable for having little effect away from its center frequency.

Professional equalizers could then have as many as 3 knobs or switches per frequency section of an equalizer, and 4 sections is not uncommon, so 12 controls affect frequency response in this scenario, and these program equalizers are usually found in every channel. On a large post production console with many inputs, controls just for equalization run into the hundreds, demonstrating the importance that equalization has for the post production process.

Another type of equalizer is also found on dubbing consoles, but usually not in each slice. *Graphic equalizers* consist of a row of multiple knobs that can be used to "draw" a desired frequency-response curve, offering a very easily grasped human interface. The number of knobs across frequency varies with the model, with six to eight being common. The curves are usually bell shaped, and most graphic equalizers offer no means to become parametric—the frequency of the controls and the curve shapes are fixed. This type is patched into the channels as needed, either into individual channels, or more likely, into groupings of channels. Due to the lack of space on the console operating surface, the use of graphic equalizers has declined in recent years.

Filtering

Filters are distinguished from equalizers by being more brute force in their action. They are intended to essentially eliminate certain frequencies from the output. The utility of filters is in corrective action generally, compensating for noise in the recording, especially low-frequency noise.

Filters may strip off any part of the audio spectrum. Probably the most commonly used filter attenuates low bass, and passes the rest of the spectrum essentially unchanged. Such a filter is called a *high-pass filter* in professional circles because it passes highs while attenuating lows. On consumer equipment, on the other hand, exactly the same device is called a *low filter* or *low-cut filter*. Equipment whose pedigree isn't certain, the category *prosumer*, uses uncertain designations, either high-pass or low-cut, to mean the same thing.

The various filter types and a typical use for them are as follows:

- *High-pass (low-cut) filter*: Used to remove excessive room noise, which is often concentrated at low frequencies.

- *Low-pass (high-cut) filter*: Used in music recording to help isolate a low-frequency instrument playing in a recording studio along with others. Isolation from crosstalk is improved by stripping off the highs from other instruments in the studio that are leaking into the open mike in front of the bass instrument.

- *Bandpass filter*: A combination of high- and low-pass filters. One use is as a

"telephone filter," so-called because restricting the audible frequency range in this way sounds like one of the primary things that a telephone does to sound.

- *Notch filter*: A filter that greatly attenuates only a narrow frequency range. It is useful for removing tonal noises such as certain whines or whistles. Notch filters usually can be adjusted for center frequency and the width of the notch.

- *Hum eliminator*: A filter that has a notch at the line frequency and its harmonics, for use in reducing recorded hum.

Most of these filter types are rated by the frequency where they attenuate the signal by 3 dB, and by their slope versus frequency in deciBels per octave. Typical filter slopes are 12, 18, and, more rarely, 24 dB/octave. The notch filter is not usually rated in deciBels per octave, because its slopes are extremely steep.

Developing an ear for timbre

Perhaps the most important issue in training for mixing is developing an ear for timbre. This is quite complex on program material because it is constantly changing, and so takes a lot of accumulated impression to hear. One way to short circuit the time needed to learn to hear timbre differences is to listen to equalized pink noise, and to match the equalization with a program equalizer at hand. An unknown can be arranged by sending pink noise through a console and using one channel's equalizer to make a particular sound, and then through switching arrange for a second equalizer to be available for matching the first by ear. Of course, the first equalizer should be covered up, and shown only after a "solution" is found. Pink noise has two advantages over program material: it is constant in time, and it has all frequencies present. These two combine to simplify the experience as a starting point.

Processes primarily affecting the time domain

The former processes work practically instantaneously, in real time. Some processes, however, work deliberately to change the time characteristics of the signal, in particular, adding reverberation or deliberate echoes and echo-like effects.

Reverberators

Reverberators are very useful, like equalization, in matching the difference between production sound and ADR recordings. They are also used to "sweeten" music that may have been recorded in too "dry" a space. Another use is to help distinguish among auditory objects; thus, all sound having one reverberant character will be categorized together by hearing. This is an important feature in "layering" sound in depth from in "front" of the screen to behind it.

In the early days of filmmaking, shooting stages were made very dead acoustically, in part because theaters were reverberant, and any added reverberation in recordings detracted from speech intelligibility when heard in these theaters. In the same film, however, it was more pleasant to hear music with added reverberation, so scoring stages were built with moderate reverberation times. This dichotomy started a feature that is still present today: Dialog is generally less reverberant than the orchestral score underlying the scene, partly for speech intelligibility and partly for the aesthetics of music listening. If the music was recorded in too dead a space, then reverberation was added to the recording by playing the recording over loudspeakers located in a reverberant room, and the reverberation was picked up with a microphone, amplified, and added back to the direct recorded sound in a re-recording console. Thus, the reverb chamber became a part of film sound technique as early as the mid-1930s. While these lasted well into the 1970s, the real estate they took up became very valuable and they were not very flexible (one could change the reverberation time only by changing the absorption in the space). Starting then in the 1970s, mechanical and then fully electronic reverberators came to dominate the scene. There are many types of reverberators available today, most of which are based on digital electronics. Most reverberators are designed for mu-

sic enhancement, and have "good sounding" reverberation, but these often do not have an adequate range of reverberation types for film sound because many spaces, needed to be synthesized to make the scenes portrayed, range from acoustically good to downright bad and from short to long reverberation times. For synthesizing smaller and less reverberant spaces, a *room simulator*, which is a variant on a reverberator using many of the same techniques, may be applied.

Echo effects

A digital delay line (DDL) is a device that simply delays sound by converting audio into samples and storing the samples in a digital computer memory, and then withdrawing the samples at some later time and converting them back into audio. *DDLing*, as this has come to be known, adds a variety of effects depending on the delay time and the relative strengths of the direct sound and the artificial reflection. At relatively short times, between 1 and 20 msec, strong timbral effects, like speaking into a barrel, are heard. This "thickening" of the sound is what makes the distinctively metallic voice of C-3PO in *Star Wars*, for example. Longer time delays and stronger artificial reflections sound progressively more like separate echoes.

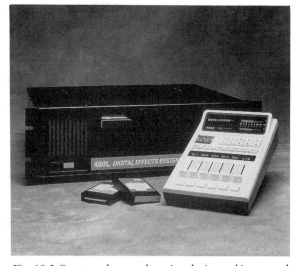

Fig. 10.2 One popular reverberation device and its control panel, which often finds its way onto the tops of re-recording console controls. This is the Lexicon 480 and its LARC controller. Photography courtesy Lexicon, Inc.

Pitch shifters and subharmonic synthesizers

Pitch shifters are digitally based units which take in sound of one frequency range, and translate it up or down to a different frequency range. Pitch shifters are sometimes known by the trade name Harmonizers. They are useful in affecting voices that are meant to be in a different range than the actor's natural voice, and to change the quality of sound effects.

Subharmonic synthesizers are devices that find the fundamental in program material, and synthesize subharmonics, as described in Chapter 1. They are useful for adding desired "weight" to effects.

Combination devices

There are devices on the market that combine two or more of the above-mentioned processes for use doing one task, such as equalizing and compressing for a vocal track to be heard in a mix with other music tracks. These are given names by their manufacturers that emphasize the purpose for which they are built, such as Vocal Stressor.

Configuration

Each of the above-mentioned processes may be needed to manipulate a channel during the mixing process, but no practical console has all of the processes present on each and every input channel. Thus, the configuration of the console becomes important in order to organize the various processes and to reduce the number of control functions to a (barely) manageable number.

Early re-recording consoles

Early film sound consoles had relatively simple signal paths. Each console input channel was equipped with a fader and patch points to insert processing equipment (which at that time included all equalizers, filters, and the like). Processing equipment was patched into input channels as needed. The input channels were summed to produce the output and were sent to a recorder. A loudspeaker monitor system was switchable between the signal sent to the recorder and the return from it, in the manner of three-head tape machine monitoring described in Chapter 6.

If reverberation was needed, the summed output of the channels was additionally sent to a reverberation chamber, and the amplified output of the chamber's microphone was summed together with the dry sound in an added summing stage before the recorder.

Adding mix in context

One difficulty with this arrangement is that it is hard to make predubs[1] having all of the necessary fades because the mixers can only hear the elements belonging to one predub at a time. Thus, if a sound-xeffects premix needs a fade under to accommodate narration, and only the effects can be heard while making the predub, it is difficult to judge the timing and the amount of the fade that is needed. This is the origin of a technique called *mix in context,* which uses two consoles in effect, although they are typically in one housing.

The actual mixing for recording is done on the first console, with its output sent to the recorder. This output is also sent to the second console, along with the other existing predubs. The second console is for monitoring purposes only, and little actual mixing is performed on it, because its output is not recorded but rather is sent to the monitor loudspeakers. The second console is usually set for "unity gain" on all of its active inputs, so the predubs are represented in 1:1 level correspondence to each other. By such a setting, the mixing that is occurring on the first console is "in context" with the rest of the existing material. If the dialog predub is played through the mix-in-context inputs, then the premix that is occurring on the first console can be done with respect to all of the dialog.

Busing

In order to account for the separation of D M & E (as they are traditionally abbreviated), the absolute minimum console must contain three signal buses, one for each part.

---

1. Synonym for premix.

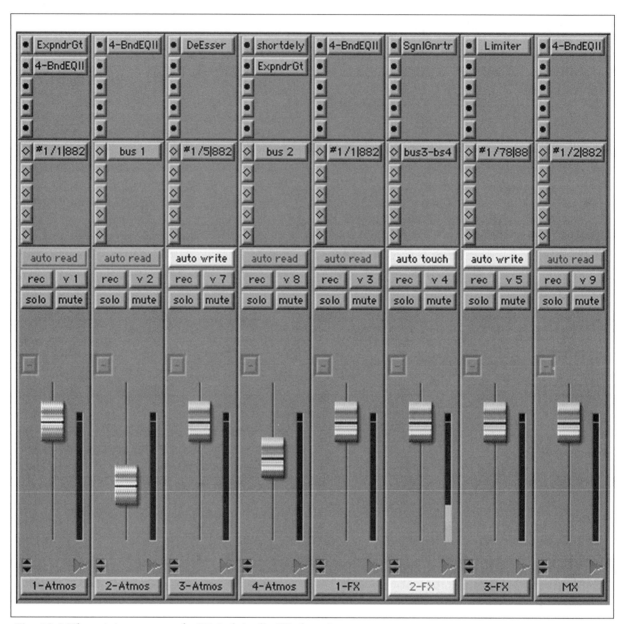

Fig. 10.3 The mixing screen of a Digital Audio Workstation.

A *bus* is an electrical connection that brings together and sums multiple inputs, much like a milk tanker driving among farms, picking up milk and delivering it to the processing plant. Note that once mixed together, we can no longer separate out the individual contributions—summed is summed, and reversing the process is practically impossible. This puts summing at the heart of the sound mixing process, because it is necessary to combine sources in order to simplify mixing, but going back on a mix is very difficult, usually requiring work to be redone.

To account for stereo production, each of the three *stems* (DM&E) needs multiple channels to represent at least left (L), center (C), right (R), and surround, with two surround channels (LS, RS) the norm today, as well as a possible extra low-frequency—only enhancement channel for effects. Each of the stems is thus recorded, either on a separate 6-track film recorder, or alternative methods provide the same functionality (e.g., 18 tracks on a 24-track machine).

Each of the three sections of major re-recording consoles usually have a minimum of six output buses in order to produce multichannel outputs capable of being panned anywhere in the sound field: left, center, and right screen channels, left and right surround channels, and the auxiliary low-frequency effects channel (that would not be panned to but rather "hard assigned").

The term *tracks* applies in several ways and may be ambiguous. Technically, a track is a space on a medium assigned to carry one signal. So a tape recorder capable of recording more than two signals[2] is called a *multitrack recorder*. The term also applies to the cut units or elements, or to the overall *sound track* of a film.

The term *channel* refers to a conceptual model of a signal path. We would think of a microphone channel as originating with the microphone and winding up on a track of a multitrack machine. An *input channel* of a console includes all the signal processes from the input to the buses, which may also be called *output channels*. The assignment of an input channel to buses is set by either hard switches or by panning among the output channels. (*Channel* is the more global term, allowing for signal processing after the summing accomplished by a bus.)

Patching

Because all facilities are not generally available to all input channels directly, there needs to be a means to *patch* specialized processes into the signal flow within a channel. All large consoles provide a way to do this, usually by way of *patch bays*, with many jacks, permitting insertion points within an input channel, or an output channel, so that

processing may be applied to an individual track, or to a sum, such as to all the dialog. Alternatively, on digital consoles specialized software programs called *plug ins* may be "patched" into the signal flow. Alternate terminology is *insertion point,* into which processes may be patched.

Each physical console has its own specific rules governing patching. Some general rules that usually apply are as follows:

- Inserting a piece of equipment into a single console input channel involves patching the equipment from a source signal (called *insert send*) to the input of the process, and from the output of the process back to the signal path (called *insert return* or *receive*), usually to the point in the chain immediately after that point from which it was originally detoured.

- Patching that connects two outputs together is impermissible: They short circuit each other.

- Patching that forms loops around equipment is not permissible: The signal must always progress, not backtrack. The consequence of forming loops is the potential instability oscillation, which audibly or inaudibly (ultrasonically) is feedback, much like the acoustic feedback we hear when a public address system has too much gain and it feeds back.

- Some processes, such as older passive filters, must be patched into points with known source and load impedances so that the filter characteristics (in that case) are maintained correctly. This comes from the notion of matching versus bridging impedance discussed in Chapter 3. Although such devices are disappearing, there are still some in use, so source and load impedance conditions must be observed on those units to produce the correct results.

Panning

A fundamental part of configuration in a multichannel re-recording console is panning. *Pan pots* are devices that place sound among the channels described earlier: L, C,

---

2. 1-track are mono recorders; 2-track are stereo.

R, LS, and RS. There may be several knobs, such as three panning among L, C, R; front/back; and LS/RS. A joystick somewhat like that used with video games may also be used. Each input channel of the console is typically equipped with a panning section or, at the very least, with switches that hard assign an input channel to an output bus. In some cases specialized panners such as joysticks are provided on a console separate from the input channel slices and without a particular channel assignment; in these cases they are designed to be patched in as needed. In digital consoles fitted with joysticks, the stick is a controller that can be switched to take over the pan function for a slice to make the adjustment of the panning control more visceral. When the setting has been made and the moves, if any, recorded, the joystick can be switched to another channel. Some digital consoles use trackballs or graphics tablets instead of a joystick.

Many source sounds are monaural, single-channel recordings. When re-recording these sounds in a multichannel production, there are rules governing placement. These arise from aesthetic considerations based on psychoacoustics and practical considerations based on the nature of film production and viewing. One of the psychoacoustic issues was described in Chapter 2 in reference to dialog panning in the section *Speech for film and television*.

Some of these rules areas follow:

- Dialog in ongoing conversations is usually either centered or kept close to center because otherwise sound edits that match picture edits cause the sound to noticeably "jump" around the screen.

- Off-screen lines are usually panned hard left or right, as makes sense; panning them to the surrounds in the auditorium breaks the "box" of the frameline too much.

- Lines that are isolated from others in time may be panned.

- Foley is routinely recorded in mono and panned into place to match.

- Ambience is most often from original stereo recordings that are placed from two or more source channels into two or more output channels. The principal aesthetic concern of ambience panning is whether or not to include the surrounds, depending on whether or not the audience is supposed to be sharing the space portrayed on the screen.

- Cut effects could be either mono or stereo source recordings. Mono cut effects are panned into position to match their on-screen image. Stereo effects are usually two-channel recordings that are also panned in place, such as into left and center for a stereo effect located left of center. A danger arises when stereo effects are panned left and right, skipping center, discussed in Chapter 11.

Auxiliary and cue buses

So far the kind of bus discussed is called an *output bus*. Destined ultimately to reach a loudspeaker monitoring channel such as Left, such buses may be further separated by discipline, such as a left sound effects bus or channel, as we have seen. The idea of these output buses does not, however, cover all possible purposes for which we may need to combine channels. For example, we may wish to send signals from multiple input channels of the console to the same reverberator, especially for sounds that share the same space, and because reverberators are generally more expensive than other processing equipment, it is useful to share resources. For this reason, auxiliary buses have been developed. Auxiliary buses have two primary purposes, effects send and cue send. Effects send auxiliary buses are used for the purpose already described, to gather signals from multiple inputs and to deliver them to a processor. Effects return modules, similar to input modules,[3] then direct the return signal, such as reverberation, to the main buses. See Fig. 10.5.

---

3. But hopefully lacking, above all else, effects sends themselves, because if an effects return module could send to an effects unit, an unstable feedback loop is likely to be formed.

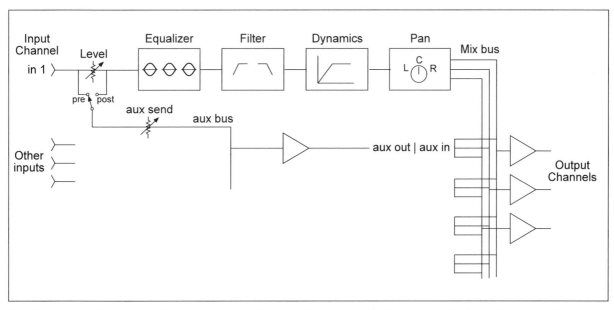

Fig. 10.4 A single-line drawing for a simple re-recording console. A main signal path routes the input channels to the output channels by way of various signal processors, while the auxiliary system provides a means to send a proportion of the signal to an output processor, such as a reverberator, and return it to the main mix bus.

The second purpose is cue send. *Cueing*, in general, in film and television production means any activity meant to alert an actor, newsperson, or musician to a timed event, so that he or she can start on time and perhaps even maintain time. In a multitrack music studio, it has a more specific meaning. There, the first track recorded is often a *click track*, the output of an electronic metronome, used for keeping musicians on time. Then, during recording the cue send feature of the console is used on the click track to send the clicks to headphones on the musicians. Because the musicians cannot play well without hearing themselves, some cue send level is added from their own instrument tracks so that they can hear themselves. Because different parts of the orchestra may wish to hear different balances among instruments (usually with themselves louder of course), there may well be multiple cue send buses so that separate mixes can be made for different groups of musicians.

Punch-in/punch-out (insert) recording

Punch-in recording is a very important concept in post production, because it allows updating mixes without remixing whole reels. Punch-in recording relies on the ability of a mixer to achieve console settings that are identical to those used during a prior mixdown. This is assured by switching back and forth between the source (the mixdown from units produced by the console) and play back off the recording. This switching is given the possible names Direct–Film, Bus–Film or PEC–Direct as described in Chapter 5.

Once throwing the direct-film switch back and forth reveals no sonic difference, the mixer can punch in, that is, activate timed erase and record circuitry so that a new recording is begun seamlessly. Then the mixer can proceed to remix a portion of a reel and, coming once again to a place where he or she can match the console settings with the original, can *punch out*, yielding a newly mixed section without abrupt changes at the transition between the new and existing mixes. This process saves a great deal of time and money in post production and relies on the use of three-head machines to know what the prior recording was, and what the new recording will be, by activating the source/film switch.

Punch-in recording is also used in music studios

working on multitrack recorders. Let us say that all tracks are all right, except one, which contains a wrong note. What is done is to punch in and out just before and after the note, having the musician play the right note at the right time. The musician is "cued" by listening to sound from the other tracks, and he or she performs continuously (because it is hard to play just one note at the right time). The engineer punches in and out at the right moments to substitute a new performance of the one note.

One difficulty occurs in both of these cases due to use of three-head machines. With separate record and playback heads, if one listens to playback and plays in sync with the music, the musician will be in sync with the sound at the playback head, but not at the record head where sync is needed. This problem was solved early in the history of multitrack recording when guitarist Les Paul devised a method to listen to tracks *played back* from the other channels of the *record* head for cueing purposes. Called *sel-sync*, *sel-rep*, or by other trade names, this method of recording ensures sync is maintained despite the three-head configuration. In TV sweetening it is commonplace to use machines in this mode, so that all the signals are always coming from or going to the record head, to prevent any sync errors.

Automation

Increasingly, mixes have gotten so complex and are under such time pressure that it is impossible to "perform" the mix by operating the controls in real time, even with more than one mixer doing the job. While some complex mixing can be done during premixing because of the multistage nature of film and video sound re-recording, nevertheless it is important to have sophisticated control over all of the premixes at the final mix because this is the stage at which the producer, director, and others become most involved.

There are several levels of automation possible. The most fundamental automation is over level control, because this is by far the most active part of the console typically. Several types of fader automation are available, basically breaking down between moving-fader automation and voltage-controlled amplifier automation. In moving-fader systems, the re-recording mixer performs moves on the faders during one pass of the film, and a computer memorizes the moves and reperforms them during subsequent passes. On these later passes, more faders can be brought into play and the computer continues to move already established faders. In this way, one person can do an extremely complicated mix, by adding more and more sophistication over time. Voltage-controlled amplifier automation systems also accomplish the same thing, but without the physically moving faders and thus are somewhat harder to update, because the physical position of the faders must be matched to an old setting in order to take over the adjustment task. The position of the faders is indicated by some kind of metering function of the console.

Usually fader automation is accompanied by automation of mutes, as described previously. A few consoles exist wherein the control surface is not directly connected to the circuits they are controlling, but rather operate as a user interface, sending all control functions as messages to a rack of equipment located in a machine room. These consoles may use "rotary shaft encoders" for their control functions, which means that the setting is no longer tied to the physical setting of the controls but rather to changes in the controls. In this system it is possible to take a snapshot of all of the controls and to restore the console to a precisely known former condition as long as a snapshot was taken. Full automation is possible, with all the control functions affected.

On fully automated digital consoles, it is possible to work on a program without committing it to being recorded, because the console will continue to reproduce all the fader moves, equalization changes, et cetera, in all subsequent passes through the material. Once the program is finalized, then it can be recorded to the medium.

Chapter 11: From Print Masters to Exhibition

Introduction

Print masters are the final output of the re-recording process and are the delivered movie sound track in the eyes of the producer and studio, because subsequent processes are not aesthetic, but manufacturing ones. Following various manufacturing steps to be described, motion-picture release prints, television masters, and video disks and tapes are made. Then, the prints or videos are shown on theatrical, commercial, home theater, or computer systems for the enjoyment of the audience.

Print master types

Print masters are made for each medium of release and possibly in multiple languages, so there are many different print masters of a theatrical feature. We examine print masters in the order in which they are typically made for a large theatrical release. Print masters may be recorded on mag film, on digital multitrack, on disk drives, or on read-write optical computer discs. Permanence is important as print masters represent the value of the product to the producer and studio,

but the problem of what constitutes a permanent digital medium has not been solved. Until it is, formats for storage of the print masters proliferate.

Each release medium has two primary factors that together determine the parameters of the associated print master, the number of available audio channels and the dynamic range capacity of those channels. Each print master must be tailored to the capability of the specific target medium. There is simply no point in sending to the optical recording camera a print master that exceeds the dynamic range capability of the target medium, yet this is an everyday occurrence. The best way to proceed is to have the original mixers of a show prepare separate print masters that respect the limits of the individual release formats because they are in the best position to make such compromises.

Another factor in making print masters for both film and television shows involves foreign-language distribution. For dubbing purposes, it is commonplace to supply M&E

masters, containing mixed music and effects, without dialog. The dialog is usually supplied as a separate track for translation and synchronization purposes at the foreign-language dubbing site. In some instances, the foreign-language premixed dialog stem is returned to the original mixers to make new print masters in the various foreign languages; in other cases, the dubbing site prepares the print master.

Print master work on television entertainment programming parallels that of film, with some simplification due to the faster post production schedules. Usually a television show will have one primary master, the English language composite, and one secondary master, an M&E, if foreign-language dubbing is contemplated.

All print masters must carry a "2 pop." This is one frame of 1 kHz tone at reference level recorded on all the tracks of the original print master, and in edit sync with the 2 frame of the SMPTE Universal Leader (time countdown) or the 3 frame of the Academy or SMPTE Projection Leader (footage countdown). It is used to synchronize the sound track negative with the picture negative, described below.

Print masters for various digital formats

These are the first to be made, because they involve little compromise to headroom or to the number of discrete audio channels. The preparation of such a print master is therefore relatively simple because little or no tailoring to the specific requirements of the medium are needed.

There are three prominent digital sound formats in practice today. They are the Digital Theater Systems (DTS) system, the Dolby Digital system, and the Sony Dynamic Digital Sound (SDDS) system (as titles of movies say, "appearing in alphabetical order"). These are fairly similar in their print-master requirements, except in the number of channels. The minimum number of channels for digital sound on film was determined by an SMPTE standards committee in 1987 to be 5.1. *Five point one* channel sound, as it is called, includes left, center, right, left sur-

round, right surround, and low-frequency enhancement channels. The DTS and Dolby Digital systems provide 5.1 channels. The SDDS system adds the potential for two more screen channels, for a total of 7.1: left, left center, center, right center, right, left surround, right surround, and low-frequency enhancement, although many installations are simplified to 5.1 channels. In all cases, the "0.1" channel designation means that a separate low-frequency channel has only a small bandwidth requirement compared with full-frequency range channels.

The amount of headroom available in each channel of the release print is 20 dB, which is the same headroom that is available on digital stems. However, note that adding the multiple final mix stems together—dialog, music, and effects—could add up to more than the headroom available. This occurs when the peaks in one stem coincide with the peaks in either one or both of the other stems. The result is potential overload of the digital print master, with attendant hard clipping. Some peak limiting may thus need to be done, usually in audibly benign amounts, to "fit" the dynamic range of the mix stems together into one print master channel.

The preparation of print masters for these three formats thus involves what is more or less a transfer operation, mixing together the final mix stems to a 5.1- or 7.1-channel master, as needed. In the post production schedule, this usually represents a small fraction of the mix time, at the very end.

Low bit rate audio

5.1 channels of digital audio coded by linear PCM coding with 16-bit word length and at a 48 kHz sample rate requires 3.8 Mbits/s of data rate. The space available on the film can only accommodate between 584 kb/s (in the space between the perforations on one side of the film in the case of Dolby Digital) and roughly four times as much (outside the perforations on both sides of the film in the case of SDDS). Furthermore, besides the digital audio, strong error coding to protect the audio bits is needed since there will surely be dirt and scratches on a motion-picture print

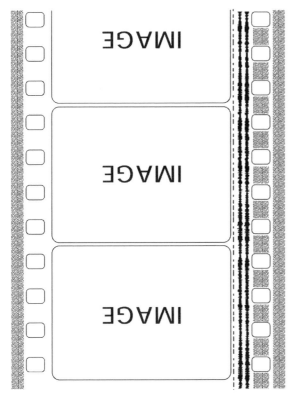

Fig. 11.1 A representation of a release print picture and sound negatives showing the relative position for four types of sound tracks: (a) conventional stereo variable area in the standard analog sound track area next to the picture, (b) DTS time code located between the picture and conventional sound track areas for synchronization of an external disc, (c) Dolby Digital between the perforations on the sound track side of the film, and (d) Sony Digital Dynamic Sound located outside the perforations on both sides of the film. Frame lines of a Cinemascope picture are shown for reference. A positive release print is the inverse of the negatives.

run in exhibition, and the audio payload comes down to 320 kb/s. Thus a means to reduce the number of bits per second by a factor of about 12:1 is needed. While normally we might think that throwing away $^{11}/_{12}$ths of something might cause it severe damage, a clever solution was worked out. By using psychoacoustic knowledge, particularly of frequency and temporal masking, systems were devised to transmit just the audio signal that is relevant to normal human listeners, and to discard information that would be masked, achieving great "coding

gain," equivalent to bit rate reduction. While such systems are not necessarily perfectly transparent all the time, they are on a great deal of program material, and the audible "cost" in terms of audio quality is relatively low. The three main systems, only two of which store the digital sound on the film, compete based on different trade-offs among bit rate, quality of the bit rate reduction coding, unrecoverable error rate, and flexibility.

Print masters for analog sound tracks

While there are more than 60,000 installations of digital playback equipment in theaters around the world, conventional analog optical sound tracks are always also recorded on all theatrical release prints, because *all* of the world's 35mm film projectors can play them. Also, the analog track serves as a backup in case the digital track should become unreadable. There are some severe constraints to consider in making conventional optical sound tracks that must be factored into the print-mastering process, however. The two primary factors are limitations in the number of recorded channels and in dynamic range.

Due to size limitations of the sound-track area on film (it occupies only about one-tenth the area of the picture), practically speaking there is room for only two physical audio tracks to be recorded within the area assigned to the sound track on the 35mm medium. In order to carry the multichannel presentation prepared in post production through this limited capacity medium, a method of encoding four audio channels worth of information into two tracks was developed. Called generically *4:2:4 matrix technology*, this process has several trade names, including Dolby Stereo. Four channels of content can be stored within two audio tracks with some compromise by use of *matrix* technology, and this is one process that occurs in preparing stereo analog sound track masters. The name given to print masters in this format is *Lt Rt*. The "t" refers to "total," meaning a left and a right track carrying information, which may be decoded into left, center, right, and surround.

The other primary limiting factor is that the headroom of an analog optical sound track is quite limited compared with the post production generations that have come before it. Today's analog optical sound tracks employ *Dolby SR*. This involves the application of the SR companding system around the sound track channel, with the SR encoder being part of the preparation of the sound track at the laboratory, while the decoder is located in the theater's equipment. This system is adjusted for 9 dB of headroom in the midrange, with somewhat more at low frequencies. The 23 dB of noise reduction available from Dolby SR[1] in this configuration lowers the noise of the reproduced sound track to levels below that of the background noise level of most theater auditoriums, but the 9 dB of headroom is a large limitation for some program material compared to the 20 dB of digital formats. On the other hand, there are programs that fit completely within the 9 dB capability, and these are less affected by the limitations of the analog system. Although the term *Dolby SR* applies to the companding system, the 4:2:4 matrix technology is also used on these prints.

The job of the post production mixer in preparing print masters for each of these release media is to do the best job possible of "fitting" the typically wider volume range of the final mix stems into the capacity of the media. This can range from being simple to nearly impossible, depending, to a large extent, on the original sound track. *Driving Miss Daisy* is easier to fit into a medium

1. Not the standard 26 dB because the reference level on SR is lowered 3 dB to give more headroom than former formats.

with less dynamic range than is *T2 Judgment Day.*

Specialized multiband limiters and clippers are often used to get the best representation of the wide dynamic range master into the print master.

> Multiband clippers are called *containers*. The idea behind a multiband clipper is that while clipping of audio signals is certainly a bad distortion, constraining the distortion components to the narrow frequency region causing the clipping produces a greater likelihood of the distortion being masked. These devices consist of a series of bandpass filters abutting one another in frequency, followed by individual clipping stages for each band, a second series of bandpass filters, and an output summer. The whole arrangement keeps frequency response flat, while containing clipping at one frequency to the band nearby it, thus not producing the higher order harmonics, which would be more audible.

For the digital formats it is typical to record the print master onto a digital recorder in custom formats supplied by the companies involved. Some of the formats, such as Dolby's use of MO recordings for print masters, contain both multichannel and 2-channel LtRt masters on the same medium.

Other types of delivered masters for film uses

In order to produce foreign-language dubs, it is customary to make intermediate masters that are very much like the English-language print masters, minus the dialog. By mixing these together with dialog premixes in the various languages, final print masters can be made in a variety of languages for various types of prints.

Table 11.1: Print Master Types and their Characteristics

Name	Print technology	No. of audio tracks on print master and print	No. of audio channels delivered	Midfrequency headroom [1] of target medium
Dolby Digital	Digital sound on film	5.1	5.1	20 dB

Table 11.1: Print Master Types and their Characteristics (Continued)

Dolby Digital Surround EX	Digital sound on film	5.1	6.1	20 dB
DTS	Digital sound on synchronized disk	5.1	5.1	20 dB
DTS ES	Digital sound on synchronized disk	6.1	6.1	20 dB
SDDS	Digital sound on film	5.1–7.1	5.1–7.1	20 dB
SR Lt Rt	Analog optical with 4:2:4 matrix stereo[2]	2	4	9 dB
16 mm	Analog optical	1	1	6 dB
DTS 16 mm	Digital sound on synchronized disk[3]	5.1–6.1	5.1–6.1	20 dB

1 See Table 6.3 for more information on headroom vs. frequency and signal-to-noise ratios of the various media.
2 The LtRt print master tracks are recorded on the same MO media as the Dolby Digital tracks.
3 The analog sound track area is used by the digital time code, thus 16 mm prints in this format are not compatible with conventional analog playback on unmodified projectors.

With multiple languages, each with its own print master requirements, the number of "masters" can grow to be very large. Usually, the post production house prepares one or more of the types shown in Table 11.2 for these purposes.

Table 11.2: Other Types of Delivered Masters

Name	Purpose	Number of tracks
Multi-channel M&E	Preparation of digital foreign language dubs	5.1–7.1
Lt Rt M&E	Preparation of stereo foreign language dubs	2[1]
DM&E	Preparation of mono foreign language dubs	3
M&E	Preparation of mono foreign language dubs	1
Dialog	Translation and synchronization purposes in the preparation of foreign language dubs	1

1 If supplied on mag film, typically recorded on tracks 1 and 2 of the 3-track format.

Masters for video release

Once theatrical print master types have been made, sound masters are typically prepared for the video market in one of several formats:

- 5.1 channel for multichannel DVD, usually identical to the theatrical 5.1 channel master, recorded as six-tracks

- Lt Rt for two-channel PCM and analog tracks of hi-fi and longitudinal tracks of consumer tape formats

- Mono, used most often for historical or documentary works, which may be supplied as a DM&E, recorded as a three-track

For the 5.1-channel market, an x-copy of the theatrical print master will do. For the Lt Rt matrix market, on low-budget projects an x-copy of the theatrical print master will serve, but the limitation on dynamic range used for the theatrical master may be misplaced. For example, DVD digital tracks have 20 dB of headroom, and if the Lt Rt has been limited for optical sound tracks having 9 dB headroom, a good deal of the dynamic range of DVD's two-channel capacity would be unavailable to be used. It is common to make a separate Lt Rt for video release, using a full 20 dB headroom.

Not all video-release media can handle this 20 dB headroom though, so on transfer to a digital master videotape with four digital audio channels, two pairs of Lt Rt sound tracks are often recorded. One pair uses the full 20 dB headroom and the other just 10 dB headroom, accomplished with a combination of limiting and reducing the level, each typically by 5 dB. In this way, the producer winds up with a "one size fits all" video master with two stereo sound tracks, one with a large and one with a restricted dynamic range. Thus far this discussion has considered the primary release media, such as theatrical release, pay-per-view, cable, satellite broadcast, conventional broadcast, etc., and the master described with two pairs of recordings can be used for all of these purposes (one or the other pair will service any of these markets). Subsequent exploitation of the work in ancillary releases, such as hotel and airline viewing, requires even less dynamic range than any of the types already discussed, so compression and limiting are liberally applied to specialized copies made

for these purposes, and possibly a new print master made from the final mix stems emphasizing the dialog.

A glance at Table 6.3 shows one of the largest problems in film and tape dubbing—the coexistence of media separated by large differences in headroom capability means that it is simply not possible to capture the full dynamic range of one medium in another for many instances. For example, to copy a digital video master to a U-Matic cassette could mean that as much as 20 dB of level reduction and limiting would be needed, an amount so severe that the average level would be so low as to make the copy unusable.

Television masters

Typically Lt Rt or mono masters are x-copied onto the master videotape in the process called layback, which already has the video program recorded on it. An M&E Lt Rt may also be prepared for foreign-language dubs and supplied in one of a variety of formats.

Sound negatives

For 35mm and 16mm film, a sound-track negative is photographed on a special sound camera, processed, and then used to print the release prints. Unlike picture prints, no intermediate stages can be used, so if many prints are to be made, multiple sound track negatives will be prepared.

The sound-track negative may contain one or more different types of tracks, distinguished by their position on the negative and subsequent print. It is possible for one 35mm negative to contain a conventional analog optical sound track and all three of the competing digital film sound formats. This is called a *quad format negative*.

Conventional analog sound tracks today are of the variable area type, in which what is varied to carry the sound waveform is the width of clear area within an otherwise black sound track on the print. In the sound camera, a light source and a condensing lens system concentrates light onto a device that varies the width of a beam of light in accordance with an applied signal. These light variations are in turn imaged by a second lens assembly onto the negative. The area of each recording is symmetrical about its centerline. This is called *bilateral recording*, and its use reduces distortion caused by uneven illumination across the width of the sound track. In 35mm use, the two tracks needed for recording the Lt Rt signals are placed side-by-side within the area devoted to the original mono sound track, an arrangement called *stereo variable area*, or (SVA). In addition to the conventional analog sound track, one, or even two, of the three possible digital recording formats may also be recorded by the sound camera at one time.

Quality control of sound tracks starts with correct exposure and processing of both the sound-track negative and the release print. If any of these four stages is incorrect, then sibilant distortion (distorted "es" sounds) is usually the first problem heard with analog tracks, while dropouts or no sound at all could result with the digital tracks.

Theater and dubbing stage sound systems

Motion-picture theater sound systems consist of two basic parts called the A and B chains. The *A chain* consists of the sound-track recording on the print itself and all of the equipment needed to recover audio from the print and process it to the point where it may be interchanged with signals from other formats. The sum total of the recording plus processing together constitute a film sound format. In this way a format is like the combination of a compact disc and a player, which produces a standardized output but no sound by itself. The end of the A chain is just after a switch that selects the format of the sound track to be played, such as stereo variable area or digital.

The *B chain* consists of the rest of the sound-reproduction channel, from the volume control through to the room acoustics of the auditorium, including equalizers, power amplifiers, and loudspeakers. Note that although a theater may switch sources by changing the A chain that is in use at any given time, the B chain is the part of the theater sound system that remains constant. In this way it is like the rest of a home stereo used with the compact disc and player given in the above-mentioned example.

A-chain and B-chain components

The precise elements contained in the A chain depend on the format, and are shown in Table 11.3. The table is arranged from top to bottom in the order the signal is processed, and the bottom of the table represents the output to the B chain.

The B chain consists of the following elements:

1. Multichannel volume control
2. Room equalization and level setting to set the sound system to frequency response and level standards
3. Power amplifiers
4. Loudspeakers
5. Screen
6. Room acoustics of the theater

The combination of a selected A-chain format and the B chain together produce the final overall impression of the sound track to listeners. Each of these chains is standardized to promote interchangeability from theater to theater and from print to print. The idea is that once the production has left the filmmaker who approves it on the dubbing stage, all the following downstream processes are technical ones, meant to reproduce the approved sound as it was made.

Theater sound systems

Sound systems in theaters range from the simplest mono system, with one loudspeaker centered on the picture, through commonplace stereo 4-channel systems (left, center, right, surround), to more than 60,000 installed 5.1-channel systems (left, center, right, left surround, right surround, and low-frequency enhancement). More than 5,000 theaters are also equipped to split the surround channels into three, left surround, right surround, and back surround. Some specialized theaters also add two intermediate front channels, left center and right center.

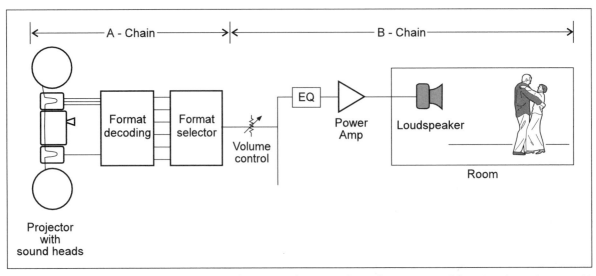

Fig. 11.2 The A- and B-chain of a motion-picture theater sound system. The A-chain consists of the print, the projector and its sound head(s), electronic decoding of the format, and selection of the format. The B-chain constitutes that part of a theater sound system that is common for all of the various formats, from the volume control, progressing through room and speaker equalization, power amplifiers, loudspeakers, and the effects of the motion-picture screen and room acoustics of the theater.

Table 11.3: A-Chain Format Devices

Trade or common name:	Dolby SR	Dolby Digital	DTS®	SDDS®
On release print	Stereo variable area optical sound track with SR-type signal processing	Digital AC-3-coded 5.1-channel sound recorded between the perforations on the sound track side; variant is Dolby Digital Surround EX which adds a matrix process to the surround channels to derive three surround channels from two.	Custom time code recorded between sound track and picture areas. The DTS ES variant provides 6.1 channels.	Digital ATRAC-coded 5- or 7.1-channel sound recorded outside the perforations on both sides of the print
On projector	Optical sound head with stereo pickup	Proprietary digital sound head	Proprietary time code pickup head	Proprietary digital sound head
A-chain preamplifier	Stereo optical preamplifier	Release print	CD-ROM follower	Release print
+	Dolby SR decoder	Proprietary processor	Proprietary processor	Proprietary processor
+	4:2:4 matrix decoder			

Note that no motion-picture theater sound system uses two-channel stereo. Two-channel stereo was a simplification of foregoing stereo systems for the home market, introduced in the late 1950s.

Dubbing stage and theater sound systems are calibrated to a reference level of 85 dB SPL.[2] The maximum undistorted sound pressure level of each of the five main channels is 105 dB SPL. The low-frequency enhancement channel, however, is calibrated to a higher reference level, yielding a maximum undistorted sound pressure level of 115 dB SPL in this channel.

> The reason that the low-frequency headroom is made greater is to provide more equal *perceived* headroom across frequency, because more low-frequency level is required to sound equally as loud as a more midrange sound. This is in accordance with the equal loudness contours discussed in Chapter 2.
>
> Also, note that the headroom here is given one channel at a time. With all channels operating, the instantaneous peak sound pressure level could approach 120 dB SPL.
>
> A picture such as *Forrest Gump* contains both high- and low-level passages, well exercising the dynamic range of the medium. Played at the reference sound pressure level (the standard theater fader setting), the average SPL over the whole length of the film measures 80 dB SPL, with an A-weighted, fast-reading sound-level meter.[3]

Theater acoustics

Motion-picture theaters are unlike other large venues as they are meant as spaces for *re*production of a sound track rather than for *pro*duction of sound. A concert hall plays an important role in the sound of an orchestra, but if a cinema added its own sound to that of the film, then all scenes would have the same added sound, and that would not make sense. In other words, cinemas should be acoustically neutral so that the filmmaker can place the listener in the correct setting. This basically boils down to control over reverberation, discrete reflections, background noise, and intrusive noise. If these factors are brought under control, then the capability of the sound system to deliver the sound track as it was prepared is greatly improved.

One system that seeks to standardize sound quality in theaters is the THX® Sound System. It starts with the premise that the room acoustics are equally as important as the sound system. Prerequisites for installation of THX are meeting room acoustical requirements for background and intrusive noise, and reverberation. Specific, patented installation methods are used for the sound-system components. When properly applied, the result is greater uniformity of performance from auditorium to auditorium in sound quality.

The factors subject to standardization that can improve uniformity from venue to venue are as follows:

1. Calibrated reference sound-pressure level, which helps to standardize loudness which is 85 dB, C weighted, slow reading, for each channel playing alone at reference level for the medium.
2. Calibrated frequency response to match a standardized response curve, the X-Curve, typically accomplished by means of loudspeaker design and one-third-octave room equalization, which helps to standardize timbre perception.
3. A high ratio of direct-to-reflected and to direct-to-reverberant sound for the screen channels, which helps dialog intelligibility in the midst of interfering sound (music and effects) and helps to correctly localize sound in multichannel.
4. An array of multiple loudspeakers for the surrounds, split into left and right sides for 5.1-channel systems, promoting a diffuse sound field that remains differentiable into left and right sides. About 12% of digitally equipped theaters have the added

---

2. With a C-weighted, slow-reading sound-level meter, for an audio level of –20 dB full scale.

3. Although this is a different measure than used for calibration, it is common practice to measure program levels with A weighting to better account for the equal loudness contours. A weighting roughly reflects a mid-level frequency response of hearing. The fast reading is usually used with program material, and the slow reading is for setting the calibrated level on pink noise.

equipment to play three separate surround channels.

5. Low-frequency system to accommodate the 0.1-channel formats.

To these, THX adds a specific method for installing the screen channel loudspeakers that involves the local acoustical environment around the loudspeaker, and the screen. In addition, there are quality requirements on sound systems, which include many issues. Primary among them are the frequency and dynamic range capability of the sound system.

> Interestingly, film sound has some distinct differences compared with the design of other large-venue sound systems. This occurs primarily because the standards are so explicit as to maximum level versus frequency and so forth. Whereas large-scale music systems may have to play at any level demanded of them by the occasion, film sound systems just have to reproduce correctly standardized film, so the range of variations presented to the designer of the system is less.

Most equalizers meant for program equalization are one of the types already discussed, but there is another important use for equalization, for setting up a sound system in a room to a specific standard, so that sound in that room is more interchangeable with other rooms adjusted to the same standard. For such equalization, a device having a control for each critical band of hearing is useful, so that fine equalization can be carried out. One-third octave bands approximate the critical bands of hearing (which are broader in the low bass and narrower in the treble), so one-third octave band equalizers are routinely used to equalize dubbing stages, screening rooms, and theaters to achieve the same balance across the audible spectrum (Table 11.4). Although details vary, the typical range is from a center frequency of 25 Hz to 20 kHz, at one-third-octave spacing, for a total of 30 bands.

> This large number of bands makes such equalization unwieldy for program equalization. There are simply too many parameters to deal with. Technicians equipped with measurement equipment can make good use of such equalization by producing a signal containing all frequencies at equal strength for equal-frequency divisions on a log scale, called *pink noise*, and by measuring the pink noise electro-acoustically with one or preferably more measurement microphones and positions, and thus *equalizing the room*.

Table 11.4: One-Third-Octave Band Center Frequency, Hz, by Band Number

Band No.	Center Frequency, (Hz)
1	25
2	31.5
3	40
4	50
5	63
6	80
7	100
8	125
9	160
10	200
11	250
12	315
13	400
14	500
15	630
16	800
17	1,000
18	1,250
19	1,600
20	2,000
21	2,500
22	3,150
23	4,000
24	5,000

Table 11.4: One-Third-Octave Band Center Frequency, Hz, by Band Number (Continued)

25	6,300
26	8,000
27	10,000
28	12,500
29	16,000
30	20,000

Sound systems for video

Home theater

Today a very large fraction, much more than one half, of Hollywood studio revenue is derived from video releases. Home theater has become a widespread trend, with over tens of millions of installations of multichannel equipment worldwide. This trend had its beginnings in the widespread acceptance of video media, VHS videotape and laser discs, as a consumer product (Table 11.5). While tape started with only mono sound, and both tape and disk started with limited dynamic range, ongoing technical development, such as the introduction of hi-fi tracks on tape and especially 5.1-channel digital sound on DVD, has brought them to a high level of performance.

With thousands of movies released on video this way, there was a "hidden" capability when these media were first introduced to the market. That is, most people played them over two-channel stereo systems, recognizing them as stereo, but without knowing that there was an embedded surround-sound capability. When 2:4 matrix decoders such as Dolby Pro Logic were subsequently introduced to the market, the home theater movement got its start. Virtually all of the tapes and discs of "stereo" movies were in fact surround-sound capable. Combined with a large-screen television, good surround sound systems can create a highly engaging experience in the home, which is attractive to millions of people.

The home environment is very different from the theatrical environment, however, often requiring some changes to ensure good translation of sound from one venue to the other. While the goals of theater systems are well known and at least sometimes met through the application of widely respected standards, home systems are not well defined by standards. Also, equipment for the large and fractious consumer market shows a greater range of quality than does the equipment designed for theatrical use.

Home THX is a system designed to provide better translation of program material into the home environment and to set minimum standards of performance for the hardware of the system. Among the developments for home THX is re-equalization. This uses a high-frequency equalizer to rebalance the spectrum for the home, where fairly flat loudspeakers are heard at fairly close distances compared with the more distant and rolled-off loudspeakers in theaters.

Desktop systems

Computer-based workstations are already important as professional tools for manipulating sound. Also, computer users are increasingly involved in video games and other forms of entertainment offering a combined audio and video experience. Computer sound, however, has grown out of a background that started when the computer could only make beeps, which then progressed to an environment with a small, internal loudspeaker just able to distinguish sounds from one another. Today, CD-ROM games with 8-bit sound are commonplace, as are inexpensive stereo computer loudspeakers of dubious quality to play them back.

As the home computer grows more sophisticated, computer audio will take a quantum leap in quality. This is because the trend is to step up to 16-bit resolution, having suddenly the full expressive capability of films, compared with the telephone quality of 8-bit audio. This trend means that higher quality sound systems for the desktop systems will be necessary to reproduce the capability of new media. Two loudspeakers placed in front of the listener, to either side of the

Table 11.5: Video Release Media Characteristics[1]

Format name	No. of audio channels	Method of recording	Headroom (dB)	Approximate signal-to-noise ratio (dB)
VHS linear	1 or 2	Longitudinal edge track, mono or stereo, possibly with Dolby B noise reduction (rare)	6	40
VHS hi-fi	2	AFM buried layer recording with "hi-fi" companding noise reduction	16	76[2]
DVD PCM	2	16-bit linear PCM Digital	20	72
DVD AC-3 or DTS	5.1	Low bit-rate coded multichannel digital	20	>75

1 See table 11.3 for more information.
2 This raw number is subject to reduction during modulation due to compandor mistracking.

screen, can be supplied with signals that can audibly place sounds in three-dimensional space, called *3D sound*. This involves computing the sound that should be present at the two ears for a source to one side, for instance, and compensating for the acoustical crosstalk from the left loudspeaker to the right ear, and vice versa. With signals that represent the inputs to each ear independently, a sound can theoretically be generated at any angle. Practical implementations of this have limitations in timbre reproduction but can make a convincing display of sound that breaks the bounds of the screen. A very high-quality sound system for the desktop

has been built. Called MicroTheater®, it reproduces the full frequency, dynamic, and spatial ranges of theatrical film program material. Used with a digital audio workstation, it is a powerful tool for making films and video on the desktop. The design uses audio technology to solve the problems posed by small room acoustics and psychoacoustic principles to scale theater sound to the desktop. Using this system and a digital audio workstation, sound personnel can design, edit, and mix sound in an inexpensive environment. We have now come full circle, because this system represents a fusion of the principles found throughout this book.

Appendix I: The Eleven Commandments of Film Sound

1. Separate physical sound cause and effect from psychoacoustic cause and effect. The advantage of doing so is that problem solving is best handled in the domain of the cause. Human perception of sound fields wraps together physical and psychoacoustic sound. Test equipment virtually always works in the physical domain, and thus may not show best what is perceived to be a problem.

2. Allow the sound crew on the set an overhead boom microphone. The overhead position is usually decently far from the room boundaries so that directional microphones can work properly, and it is usually the best location to capture actors' voices.

3. Always wait a moment before calling "action" or "cut" so that the sound editor has some footage that matches the scene for a presence track. This is often overlooked in production, but a few seconds on each shot saves a great deal of time in post production. The few seconds can be made into a loop and an x-copy made of any length necessary to fill out the scene.

4. Make sensible perspective choices in recordings. Extreme perspective changes are jarring as the direct-to-reverberant ratio changes from shot to shot; only subtle changes are typically useful. Remember that it is always possible to add reverberation, but exceedingly difficult if not impossible to remove it in post production.

5. In narrative filmmaking, exercise discipline and control on the set by minimizing all undesired noise sources and reverberation, and maximizing the desired source. When you are making a fictional film, you have the ability to "pan off" an undesired object; use the same control for the sound.

6. Make sure the sound is in sync with the picture. Nothing is more amateurish than out-of-sync production sound: there is a need for traceability of sound sync and camera sync to a common or to matched sources.

7. Organize tracks during editing with a strong eye to mix requirements. Fit tracks to the available number of dubbers or tracks of a multitrack, leaving as much space between different sounds as possible. Keep similar sounds in the same units, and different ones in different units.

8. Normally, provide a complete audio world, including adequate fill and Foley or equivalent effects. Many poor films simply do not have enough effects: silence is rarely found in nature, and should not be found in films either. The lowest level sounds, such as background noise of rooms, must be brought up to such a level that they will "read" through the medium in use. This means the noise will have to be louder than natural to be heard on a 16-mm optical sound track, for instance.

9. In mixing, one job is to get the program material to best "fit" the dynamic and frequency ranges of the target medium. It is silly to mix an 80 dB-wide dynamic range for a 16-mm optical sound track, and it may be equally silly to mix a 40 dB-wide dynamic range for a Dolby SR 35-mm release.

10. Storytelling always comes first: if it works, break the rules. Other than doing damage to people or equipment, all the "rules" given are breakable for artistic purposes, if breaking the rules results in art being produced.

11. Separate strongly the requirements of production from those of reproduction. The filmmaker is highly involved with the first, but the second should be practically a mechanical process.

Appendix II: Recording Details

Ingredients of tape recording
Tape or film
Tape and film have already been distinguished: Film has perforations, which tape lacks. Both are composed of at least two parts, a base and an oxide coating. In addition, some tape and film use a secondary back coating as well.

A little history
The principle of direct analog magnetic recording originated in the late 1800s as a part of work on the telegraph, but this was even before the invention of the vacuum tube as an amplifying device, so magnetic recording had to wait for other technologies to catch up for further development. Recording on steel wire occurred in the 1930s, but the reels needed for any reasonable length of time were huge because the speed needed was very high. Splicing was next to impossible, and the speed was so high that if a reel should get loose, it could do major damage before coming to rest.

During World War II, when the U.S. Army Signal Corps monitored German broadcasts they found that Hitler was portrayed as being first in one town and then instantly in another. It became clear that what the Germans had was an editable recording medium of higher quality than theretofore known. An enterprising Army captain, John Mullin, upon liberating a German broadcast station, found the secret: tape recorders. These used a paper-backed tape with a layer of magnetic oxide coated on it, and a new discovery the Germans had made, ultrasonic bias. While tape was easy enough to conceive, it was this method of *biasing* that contained the leap needed to yield high-quality recording. Mullin took two machines apart and shipped them, along with 50 rolls of the paper-backed, oxide-coated "tape," back to himself in the United States, in many separate packages, and when he got home put the machines back together.

Mullin and his partner, San Francisco filmmaker William Palmer, took a machine to Hollywood and demonstrated it for MGM. The founder of Ampex Corporation, then a small electric-motor manufacturer looking for a postwar market, heard a demonstration and set out to build a machine of their own. Meanwhile, Mullin showed his recorder to Bing Crosby. Crosby's show at the time was delivered to the network on phonograph records because he had a legendary fear of live radio. Crosby hired Mullin to tape record his 1947–48 season, and Mullin did so on the captured German machines and tape, but the network insisted on dubbing the finished tapes to phonograph records for broadcast because they were uncertain as to the reliability of the new medium. Subsequently, Ampex delivered 20 machines to ABC for time shifting in network operations, these saved the then-faltering company, and wide-scale use of tape recording started. While this rather prosaic first use seemed to pigeonhole the idea into the back room of networks, it was not long before its use as an editable medium came into prominence.

Note that film already had an editable medium in optical sound tracks. Used since the late 1920s, they had provided Hollywood with a way to edit, but once film was exposed it needed to be developed, and to reduce certain distortion, to be printed and the print developed, which was certainly far more time consuming than tape recording. When magnetic recording finally did make it into filmmaking a few years later, the reason the studios bought it into the technology was not the higher quality it offered compared with optical recording, but rather the fact that it could be erased and re-used, and was immediately available for use after recording.

Continuous development of direct analog recording has occurred for more than 50 years, and quality has been brought to a high state, limited by issues regarding cost/benefit trade-offs more than any underlying problem. On the other hand, analog methods inevitably encounter generation loss, and film and television production uses a number of generations to accommodate the complexities of modern film productions. They are typically:

1. Original production recording

2. Cut *unit* or *element*

3. Premix

4. Final mix

5. Print master

6. Print

    Television production may skip several of these stages, principally because of time limitations.

The reasons for needing six generations will become clear later, but suffice it to say that this is a large number for an analog-based system to sound transparent from one end of the chain to the other, although it is possible.

Milestones in the development of direct analog magnetic recording include the introduction of stereo, then multitrack in the late 1950s and early 1960s, and the addition of companding noise reduction starting in the late 1960s, which must be seen as combined with many continuous improvements in tape and film stock, heads, and electronics.

Tape recording formats

The first tape developed in the United States was $1/4$ in. wide, and the first machines recorded in one pass practically across the full width of the tape, in monaural, at 15 or at $7^1/_2$ in./sec. While the higher speed consumed a lot of tape, running a $10^1/_2$ in.

diameter reel in 30 minutes, it also offered the best quality recording for the time. Broadcasters needed a reel to run for an hour in order to cover a program, so used the lower tape speed of $7^1/_2$ in./sec. The lower quality was not noticeable over the air, so this was adequate for time-shifting purposes. Still, they sought a means to make the process less expensive, so the track width was narrowed from nearly 0.250 in. to a 0.075 to 0.082 in. wide track along one edge. This allowed one to reach the end of one pass through the machine (heads to tails) and then to exchange the supply and take-up reels, rethreading the tape to continue recording in the opposite direction. The names for the heads-to-tails pass and the tails-to-heads pass were called *side 1* and *side 2*. (Although called *sides*, what is actually meant is opposite positions from one another across the tape on the same oxide layer of the tape.) This is called *half-track recording*, and it became a broadcast standard. It has a four times advantage over the initial full-track high-speed format in tape consumption, and the convenience of having the reel wound heads-out after one is done playing (no rewind required if both sides have been played).

When two-track stereo tape recording was needed in the late 1950s (because the stereo phonograph record had been invented as a consumer medium, and a mastering tape format was required to feed the new medium), it was simple enough to adopt the half-track format and make it two-track by equipping the recorder with heads that could record simultaneously on the two tracks spaced across the tape from each other. Note that two 0.075 to 0.082 in. tracks, placed at nearly the edges of a 0.25 in. piece of tape, leaves a large area in the middle unrecorded; this was subsequently to be of great importance in filmmaking applications, as we shall see.[1] Note too that a given piece of tape is not prepared in any particular way to record one of these formats. It is not *prestriped* in any way. This means that without proper labeling, if one were to play a half-track recording on a two-track machine, one would hear both "halves" of the program at once, one forwards and the other backwards, on the two channels of the two-track. This is why it is essential to label tape as to its format, which we expand on later.

Mastering of two-channel stereo records and radio shows was thus done at 15 in./sec and $7^1/_2$ in./sec with two-track machines, and this remained the

---

1. To achieve a better signal-to-noise ratio, some stereo machines, especially in Europe, record two-channel stereo on $1/4$ in. tape with special wide tracks, 0.104 in. wide, which are incompatible with placing other recorded tracks in between the two stereo tracks.

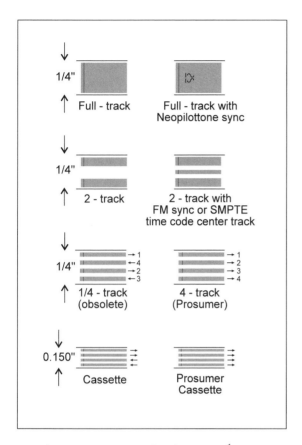

Appendix II Fig.1 Tape recording formats on $^1/_4$ in. tape and in the compact cassette.

most widely used professional standard until digital recording. In order to make a consumer medium out of tape recording though, a method was needed to record two-channel stereo and not consume much tape, so the first thing done was to lower tape speed to $7^1/_2$ in./sec or even further to $3^3/_4$ in./sec. Next, the use of the "two-sided" method of half-track recording was doubled to *quarter track* also called *four-track* (not four at once, but two "coming" and two "going"). Another trick played was to interleave the track positions on the "sides," which gave more space for the tape heads to handle the two channels. This meant that consumer quarter-track recordings, played on professional two-track machines, would play both forwards and backwards programs at the same time, and even for those tapes recorded in only one direction, there was an error because the track positions do not line up, so the level of the right channel of a four-track tape played on a two-track machine is quite low. All in all what this means is that the consumer and professional formats were very incompatible (Fig. 1).

When two-channel stereo became available to consumers via first the LP record, then open-reel tape and FM broadcasting, the need arose for having more tracks in production so that all mixing did not have to occur live, in real time, to just two recorded tracks. Starting in the middle 1960s, music studio production rapidly advanced from 4-track $^1/_2$ in. on which the Beatles breakthrough album, *Sgt. Pepper's Lonely Hearts Club Band*, was made, to 8, then 16, then 24 tracks, which has become the format of choice for multitrack work and dominates the pop music scene today. The more popular open-reel analog tape formats are listed in Table 6.3, along with their areas of application. This table is not meant to be a comprehensive listing of all formats ever in use, but to illustrate those that achieved some measure of commercial viability, and the primary speeds at which they are generally used, with the most common in bold type. Note that only two of the $^1/_4$ in. tape formats use tape in both directions. All the primary professional uses of $^1/_4$ in. tape in film and television production use it in only one direction.

One way generally to achieve better quality is to run the tape or film faster. Studio recorders sometimes run at 30 in./sec, and 70-mm striped magnetic release prints run at 22.5 in/sec. But there are limits to the process of obtaining higher quality with higher speeds. While high audio frequencies are generally better reproduced at higher tape speeds, low audio frequencies may suffer frequency response problems as the tape speed is made higher. This is due to the size of the heads and how they work at long wavelengths, with physically larger heads doing a better job at low frequencies.

The compact cassette, otherwise known simply as a cassette, is a miniature reel-to-reel system enclosed in a standardized hard shell. It is the most popular music medium today and was originally thought of as a kind of business machine for recording meetings and the like, functions served today by the microcassette (an even smaller format). The cassette format has two tracks in each direction, and interleaving is not employed as on the open-reel format.

Technical developments, including better tape formulations and the use of companding noise reduction of the Dolby B type, as well as better transports, brought the compact cassette to a reasonable level of quality that it became acceptable by most people for incidental music purposes.

The base of tape stock today is a polyester plastic material.[2] The polyester base is quite tough, but it will stretch once its rather high elastic limit is exceeded. The base is available in several thicknesses

2. Polyethylene terephthalate.

depending on the required playing time for the tape, although professionals use the thickest available base typically, 1.5-mils[3], as it tends to be the most reliable. This idea applies equally to audiotape and videotape, and to analog or digital tape stock as well.

There may be some reasoning behind using thinner base materials for some applications. Thinner bases are more supple, permitting potentially better head contact, so that high-frequency performance may improve.

For example, among compact cassettes, tape lengths from C-20 through C-90 use one base thickness, but the length of tape wound into the cassette is increased to increase the playing time. At the C-120 length, however, in order to fit the tape into the cassette shell, the tape base had to be made thinner, and this leads to many more potentially damaged tapes, so professionals using cassettes employ lengths up through the C-90 type generally and avoid the C-120 length.

Magnetic film stock is available in both tricellulose acetate and polyester bases. Acetate is an older base stock that is easier to cut for editing purposes, but it is also hygroscopic, that is, it is sensitive to moisture in the atmosphere, absorbing it or giving it up depending on the temperature and humidity of storage. Acetate is also not as stable as desired for archiving purposes, although it is much more so than the nitrate base that it replaced many years ago. It is subject to "vinegar syndrome" wherein opening an old can of it smells like vinegar due to the acetic acid released by the film when it breaks down. Due to these properties, acetate-base film stocks are generally employed where editors must cut them, in the individual cut tracks, called *units*. By being hygroscopic, acetate base film cannot be relied upon to form good continuous tape/head contact, thus high-frequency stability can suffer in particular. It also seems to be a fairly difficult product to manufacture consistently, because tricellulose acetate is basically wood pulp. Acetate base film is available in a thickness that matches picture film, which in post production is acetate based, so that the diameters of equal-length pieces of picture

and sound film are the same. This makes it easy to wind up a double-system work print and a matching sound track on parallel reels.

There is still some variation from type to type in the thickness of the stock, which causes a potential problem. Variations in thickness of 10% from type to type may not produce acceptable performance on a given film recorder or dubber. Once one thickness has been run for some time, the heads wear to a pattern that accommodates that particular thickness. Changing to a new-thickness film then results in poor level stability, but in this case it is not the film stock that is at fault but the "match" between the recorder and the stock.

Polyester-base film stock, on the other hand, is a more stable material. Unfortunately, it is very hard to cut, requiring very sharp cutting tools and a lot of work, so editors do not like it. Therefore, its use is typically reserved to those parts of a film mix that are not usually edited: premixes, final mixes, print masters, and the like; that is, everything except the original cut tracks. Polyester-base stock is available in two thicknesses, one that is close to picture stock so that it winds up being of the same diameter, and the other thinner to accommodate longer playing time for a given diameter. The two thicknesses are around 0.005 in. and 0.003 in.

The oxide layer is composed of a number of materials, the actual magnetic particles, binders, stabilizers, dyes, plasticizers, lubricants, and dispersants. The actual compositions are highly proprietary. The history of magnetic tape recording, including audiotape and videotape, and analog and digital forms of the tapes, shows ever-increasing potential for a higher and higher density of recorded information. That is what makes it possible for a Hi-8 consumer videotape, for example, to be so small, not much different from an audio cassette, because the tape stocks are fundamentally different. (The bandwidth requirement for video is many times that of audio, so this is a remarkable feat.) This is accomplished by magnetic oxides having been developed to have ever higher capacity (Table 1). One measure of this capacity is *coercivity*, the magnetic field required to demagnetize a completely magnetized sample.

_____

3. 1.5 thousandths of an inch.

Appendix II Table 1. Magnetic Materials Used in Tape and Film Coatings

Type	Coercivity (Oersteds)	Uses	Designation when used as compact cassette tape/ videotape
Iron oxide	300–360	Ordinary low-cost analog cassette tape	IEC type I

Appendix II Table 1. Magnetic Materials Used in Tape and Film Coatings (Continued)

Cobalt-doped iron oxide	500 –1200	"High bias" analog audiotape and video-tape, cassette, open-reel audiotape, videotape	IEC type II
Chromium dioxide	450 – 650	CrO_2 cassette tape, videotape	IEC type II
Iron particle	1000 –1500	Cassette tape, analog and digital audio and video-tape for acquisition and editing	IEC type IV in audio cassettes, MP in video cassettes
Plated or evaporated metal	1300 –1500	Videotape for acquisition*	ME

* Not as suitable for editing as MP types due to wear concerns created by the very thin oxide layer.

The thickness of the oxide coating is important, and thickness, like the oxide composition, varies according to a juggling act among the desired properties. Analog video and all digital tape formats rely on short-wavelength recording, that is, a good ability to record high frequencies. To optimize for this requirement, a thin oxide layer is needed. On the other hand, audio-only tape and film generally use a thicker coating because that means there is more magnetic material available to magnetize, and low-frequency capability is maximized.

For direct analog recording of audio on videotape, the thickness is not great enough for high quality and headroom suffers. The former studio workhorse analog videotape recorder, 1 in. C-format open reel, has 8 dB less low-frequency headroom than mag film, a very significant amount. Furthermore, such videotape is also significantly noisier than mag film. Increasingly, there is a shift from analog to digital videotape, aligned for 20 dB of headroom, so there is much less concern among sound practitioners over committing their mixes to digital videotape than there was with analog.

One further factor besides oxide composition and thickness can have an impact: the *velour effect*. This is a characteristic caused by the manner in which the magnetic oxide particles were aligned in manufacture. After the oxide has been coated on the base but while it is still wet, the tape or film passes over a very strong magnet. This magnet aligns the generally needle-shaped oxide particles to a particular orientation suitable for the tape or film being made (which differs between audiotape and videotape as well).

The velour effect manifests itself in different recording sensitivity dependent on the direction of the tape. Recording from head to tail will produce different results, especially at high frequencies (short wavelengths), than when recording from tail to head. So just turning the tape around can affect the high-frequency response! This effect is unnoticeable on many stocks but happens on enough of them to highlight here. Naturally, cassettes that are meant to run in both directions are optimized for no velour effect.

After oxide has been applied to the base, using a variety of techniques to get an even coating, the tape or film is processed. Depending on the purpose of the tape or film, postcoating treatments can include:

- Magnetic alignment of the particles in the oxide with a strong magnet arranged between coating and drying.

- Surface treatment of various types. One is called *calendaring*, which is a process of rolling the tape or film between two precision cylinders and literally smashing the oxide flatter. A smoother oxide coat is the result, and more magnetic material comes into intimate contact with the heads, with the bumps in the oxide having been smacked flat.

  If this process is taken to the extreme, the tape can be made so flat that it potentially sticks at guide rollers and heads through molecular adhesion. Therefore, there is an optimum surface flatness that produces the best tape-head contact, but not so much as to cause sticking problems.

- Back coating. Coating the face opposite the oxide with a separate coating has two advantages: It produces better winding properties, that is, less scatter between layers when wound at high speed because of a slightly rougher surface, and the coating is made electrically conductive to dissipate static charges which can cause snapping or clicking sounds in fast wind or even playback because the film may discharge a static buildup from winding at the (conductive metal) heads. The only difficulty with back coating is that it is sometimes impossible for the user to know which is the oxide side and which is the base when looking at a new stock, but all open-reel formats in the United States are supplied wound with the oxide in. (This is not true of open-reel tape in Europe, some of which is used oxide out.)

Years ago it was easy to distinguish the sides of a piece of tape visually: The oxide was the dull side, and the base was the shiny side. With today's back-coated tape and with surface treatment of the oxide, it is more likely that the reverse would be true! Mixing up the faces is a potentially fatal error to a recording, because the spacing loss in attempting to record through the base is enormous, and no usable recording for any purpose can be made if the oxide and base are reversed.

Playback equalization

Direct analog magnetic recording is not a system for which the frequency response is automatically flat; it must be made so.

This is due to the fact that the process of "reading" the magnetic flux on the tape or film with a conventional playback head is *differentiating*, that is, the head responds to changes in the field strength, not to the absolute value of the magnetic field. In other words, there is no output at all from a head if the tape is stopped, and as a given sine wave recording is moved faster, both the frequency and the output level increase, demonstrating the nonflatness of the inherent frequency response. The output level from the head rises with frequency at 6 dB/octave until a particular high-frequency limit is reached that is different for each tape type, tape head, tape speed, etc.

To overcome this inherent lack of a flat frequency response in the medium, the playback preamplifier in the recorder or dubber[4] is, also, not flat. Instead, it has a frequency response that is complementary to that of the tape-head system, yielding an overall flat response. The reason that it is the playback response equalization that must be standardized is that it is important to be able to play any tape made to a given standard without having to adjust the playback frequency response for that particular tape.

---

4. A *dubber* is a film term for a playback-only film transport, found in much greater profusion than film recorders, because many more tracks must be played than recorded during a mix.

Unfortunately, the details of how this is to be done were worked out on tape differently in Europe than in the United States, so tapes interchanged across borders do not necessarily meet the local *playback equalization* standards. This can lead to large errors in international productions when one sound crew is working with equipment set to European standards and another set to U.S. standards. It also may not be clear from where they are working which set of standards are being followed, because a location crew hired in Borneo could be set to either standard.

The U.S. standard is called *NAB equalization* (for the National Association of Broadcasters, which first standardized them), and the European standard was formerly called *CCIR equalization* which is still in widespread use as a name, but the name has been superseded to IEC. If one ignores the error, it amounts to 6 dB at the lowest frequencies and 3 dB in the opposite direction at high frequencies, a very significant amount. The message is clear: You must know the equalization standard to which the recorder is set to be able to correctly playback tapes made on it.

Ultrasonic bias

At the dawn of tape recording, we said earlier that the Germans had made a "discovery" that made high-quality recording possible. This discovery, as distinguished from invention, came about accidentally in a research lab where one researcher was working on tape recording and another in an adjacent room on high-frequency radio. They discovered that each time the radio transmitter was on in the next room, the tape recordings they made were much better! Tracking down what was going on led to the universal use of ultrasonic bias in direct-analog magnetic recording.

Tape recording depends on the ability of oxide to store magnetic fields, unchanged between recording and playback. If it were possible to alter the stored field with small amounts of magnetism, then even the Earth's magnetic field could have an effect on recordings, and this would make it an impractical medium. So for very low amounts of magnetic field from an outside force, no change is rendered in the state of the particles, called *domains*, that make up the magnetic material. As the level of an external magnetic field increases, then some of the domains change magnetic state (north and south poles interchanging), and a recording is beginning to be impressed on the medium. As this process continues at higher and higher levels of magnetic field, more and more of the domains change state, until all the available magnetic matter reaches the same state of organization (e.g. all north poles). This point is called *saturation* because no matter how much more magnetic field the oxide is exposed to, it cannot produce any higher level of "organization"; all the domains already point the same way.

In the absence of bias, trying to record a voice to tape would sound like an extremely poor connection that drops out at low levels, only responding when the performer is speaking loudly and dropping all lower level sound. Adding a strong ultrasonic sine wave that is about ten times greater in level than normal audio gets the audio signal up over that initial area where no recording occurs, which is why it is named bias. We say that bias "linearizes" the medium, because to try to work without it leads to enormous distortion.

The amount of bias needed varies depending on the oxide, the speed, and the record head gap.[5] The amount of bias affects many parameters: sensitivity (level), frequency response, and distortion. Tape machine manufacturers generally specify the way that their particular machine is to be set with a given tape for best overall performance.

Bias is to audiotape what film speed (exposure rating) is to camera film: It must be accounted for in order to achieve the right exposure. This factor

---

5. The *gap* is seen as the sharp line on the face of the head where the magnetic field deliberately "leaks" out onto the tape in the case of an erase or record head. In the case of a playback head, this is the place where the magnetic field is captured by the head.

means that tape is not as interchangeable as probably believed by most consumers. Professionals use only one tape type for a given setup of a recorder and must alter the setting of bias and other adjustments in order to change tape.

In cassette recording, this process was given attention in the form of the different Type numbers, I, II, and IV (III is obsolete).

Conventional Type I tape uses a "regular" level of bias and 120 µs playback equalization, as described earlier, while Type II uses "high" bias, and Type IV even greater bias level, both with 70 µs playback equalization. The attempt with this system was to better match tapes and recorder setups by using categories. Unfortunately the range within each category is fairly large, especially in Type I and II tapes, so it is only a relatively crude adjustment to set the recorder for the tape type (and, more recently, holes in the back of the cassette shell tell the machine which type it is, rather like the coding of 35mm still film canisters that has been introduced in recent years to tell the camera the film speed), but having only this crude adjustment is better than the open-reel situation where basically nothing is predetermined in the tape-machine interface. For important original recordings, users of cassette tape should use a tape type of the highest grade specified for the machine they are using.

Appendix II Table 2. Cassette Types

IEC Type no.	Oxide	Playback equalization time constant	Bias level
I	"Standard" iron oxide, γ-Fe_2O_3	120 µs	Regular
II	"High bias" cobalt-doped γ-Fe_2O_3	70 µs	High
III	Obsolete designation		
IV	Metal	70 µs	Highest

Record equalization

Once playback equalization has been set for flat response for the standards in use, and the bias has been set according to the needs of the particular format and tape, the remaining major parameter that must be adjusted is the record equalization. Record equalization is basically arbitrary: It is set to whatever it needs to be to make the machine have a flat frequency response. Generally record equalization is used to make up for losses in re-

cording, not playback. This varies quite a lot depending on the format. For example, 35mm film generally uses very little record equalization, whereas cassettes use up to 20 dB of high-frequency boost to overcome losses.

This factor, interacting with bias, is what most audibly distinguishes the faster analog media from the slower ones. The greater high-frequency boost needed at slower speeds reduces high-frequency headroom. A cassette deck and a 35mm film transport may have a similar frequency response at low levels, but the higher speed 35mm film can handle much more high-frequency signal without over-load. Thus, a cymbal crash recorded at reasonable levels will sound very different in the two media: probably clean on the 35mm film and distorted on the cassette.

Appendix II Table 3. Reference Fluxivities

Reference fluxivity (nW/m)	Where used
100	Videotape longitudinal audio tracks
185	Magnetic film, sound effect libraries, some music
250	Common music studio level
320[*]	Mono Nagra
355, 370	Elevated music studio levels
510[*]	Stereo Nagra

[*] The fluxivity levels of 320 and 510 are used on Nagra recorders with quasi-peak meters. The other reference fluxivity levels are either used with VU meters, or if quasi-peak meters are used, the reference fluxivity is set to a level well below full scale. For instance, in BBC usage, the reference fluxivity is set to 4 on a scale of 7, where each "point" equals 4 dB. Thus, the reference fluxivity is set 12 dB below the typical peak level of program.

Reference levels

Some common reference fluxivities are given in Table 3 along with where they are used.

There are two approaches to take in maintaining the reference level from one reel to the next over time on analog tape. As tape gets better, it is natural for the reference fluxivity to move up to account for the improvement; thus the reference level is a moving target. In music studios it has changed from 185 to 250 to 355 nW/m in the last 15 years for users of the best available tapes and maintaining the same head-room. That is not a problem in music libraries, where older tapes can be adjusted for when they are taken from storage for new uses, but it is a problem in sound-effects library, where random access to any sound in the library is desirable.

The second approach is to keep the reference level constant across time and to either take all of the improvement as a reduction of distortion or to record to a higher maximum level while keeping the reference level constant

AFM tracks

The sound recording is distinguished from the video one by three means: carrier frequency, head azimuth, and depth of recording in the oxide. *Head azimuth* is the angle of the head to the track. It differs between picture and sound

carriers to reduce interference between sound and picture on videotape AFM formats. The different depth of the recording comes about because the higher the frequency being recorded, the closer to the surface of the oxide the recording resides. In this case, the audio carrier is recorded underneath the video because it uses a lower carrier frequency.

Level setting

As magnetic oxides have improved there are two ways that have developed to handle the improvement. In music recording what has generally been done is to adjust the reference fluxivity upwards to account for improvements, keeping distortion performance more or less constant, while improving the signal-to-noise ratio. So reference levels that were 185 nW/m 15 years ago are today 320 to 370 nW/m. This is fine *as long as there is no intercutting of older and newer material.*

Sound-effects libraries are large, are added to continuously, and are used continuously. Here, changing reference levels would drive operators crazy, because each transfer would have to be done to the standards of the date of making the original recording. To prevent this, it is more common to keep the reference level, such as 185 nW/m, constant over a whole library but to employ peak meters set with a great deal of headroom above the reference level so that ongoing improvements in oxides can be accounted for by allowing higher peaks over time.

These considerations are disappearing as libraries are converted to digital forms. The abrupt and dramatic overload upon clipping a digital medium means that there is an optimum level that will not change over time. The optimum level for digital is the level that just exercises all of the bits but does not require more bits. In order to be sure that the peak level does not exceed the maximum coding range, it is useful to leave a few deciBels at the top of the range unused.

The problem with this approach is that although it maximizes the signal-to-noise ratio for each piece of program material, it also means that the loudness of the program material varies with each recording. The loudness varies because all sources have had their peak level adjusted to approximately the same value, but loudness is only tangentially related to peak level. Thus, if we put various compact discs into a player, we find that they all play at a different loudness, or at different settings of the volume control for the same loudness. This may be acceptable in some media, but the need for a constant volume-control setting in film and television sound is a major problem.

Source materials such as production sound recordings, music recordings, etc. should thus use the scheme described earlier to maximize signal-to-noise ratio among sources, modulating to within a few deciBels of the top of the medium, but in subsequent post production it is more valuable to use a standard playback reference level and volume-control setting so that the loudness of the program is the final loudness of playback. The two approaches are fundamentally different because one seeks to maximize signal-to-noise ratio for each portion of the program, while the other seeks to represent all portions of the program material in correct proportion.

For this reason, the Nagra modulometers are adjusted to read 0 dB at high reference levels, 320 nW/m in mono, and 510 nW/m in stereo measured to the DIN standard.[6] To help ac-

count for this difference, Nagra internal generators are not adjusted to read 0 dB. In the case of mono machines, the tone at –8 dB on the modulometer equals 118 nW/m at the U.S. standard, about 4 dB below the film reference level of 185 nW/m. For the stereo machine, the tone at –10 dB re 510 nW/m equals 188 nW/m U.S., sufficiently close to 185 to be interchangeable.

Much the same thing goes on in a cassette deck, but some cassette decks have dual capstans, one before and one after the head stack in the tape path, arranged to run at slightly different speeds to maintain head tension. Although potentially an elegant solution to keeping smooth motion and constant tape tension, it is complicated and expensive to get right. The dual-capstan principle has also been applied to a few models of open-reel tape recorders.

Film transports are available with capstan-type drives, with a method to "read" the perforations to control the absolute speed, but this does not appear on many transports in the United States. More commonly the Davis loop drive is seen, wherein the film passes by a toothed roller on its way to the head stack, and back again past the same roller on its way from the head stack. This *closed-loop* drive has the advantage of isolating the film within the head side of the loop from any disturbances outside the loop. Either of these forms, capstan or closed loop, can be used to make a good transport, but the closed loop probably has an advantage with less than perfectly wound reels and splices because the isolation between reels and heads is higher.

Print through

Print through was discussed earlier. It is a primary cause for concern in production sound recording, because that type of recording so often offers opportunities for it to become audible, having its silences interspersed with lines of dialog. The dialog prints through onto adjacent layers of the tape, and, over silence, becomes the most audible noise. Special tapes have been available in the past to minimize print through, which are especially useful in production sound recording, ADR, and Foley recording, although these types are scarce today. These tapes may raise the signal-to-print ratio by as much as 15 dB.

Companding systems

One of the major steps taken in the history of tape recording was the introduction of companding systems in the late 1960s. Companding might be called an enabling technology, because it surely had

---

6. The U.S. and European standard methods of calibrating fluxivity are different so that when measuring the same source tape, the two differ by 0.8 dB in their recording, with tapes recorded on European standards and played on U.S. machines reading low.

a strong impact on film and television production. As the complexity of sound tracks grew over the years, films began to mix down from a greater number of tracks. With each increase in the number of tracks came increased noise. It was the widespread use of companding systems in filmmaking starting in the middle 1970s that allowed for more sophisticated productions, without sacrificing signal-to-noise ratio performance. The first system to find widespread use in the film and television industry, Dolby A type, gave a 10 to 15 dB improvement in signal-to-noise ratio (depending on frequency), the equivalent of being able to more than triple the number of tracks in use while maintaining the same noise floor.

The word *compander* is made up from combining the words compressor and expander, processes which are described in Chapter 10. Companders have two halves, one half placed before a medium, and one after. The basic idea behind a *compander* is fairly simple but there are a lot of problems in precise implementation that make this an area of great specialization. The idea is generally to decrease the volume range of a source signal so that it can be recorded within the dynamic range capability of a medium, then increase the volume range upon playback to restore the program material to its original range.

For low levels, companding "turns the volume up" to get the signal above the noise floor of the medium, then "turns the volume down" upon playback, restoring the program signal to its original level. Noise added in between the halves of the compander only "sees" the second half, the part which "turns down the volume," thus reducing noise.

At the other end of the dynamic range, some systems also decrease the highest level signals upon recording and increase them an equal amount in playback in order to increase the available headroom.

Matching record and playback reference levels is a necessity with many companding systems. Consequences of not playing back the film or tape with the correct companding system, or of mismatching levels, include *pumping*, an effect in which it sounds like someone is randomly moving a volume control in the system, causing unnatural swells and diminutions, and frequency-response errors. Because these systems are proprietary, they will be described in terms of the companies that supply them and their offerings.

Dolby

Professional uses are made of three different companding systems, Dolby A, Dolby C, and Dolby Spectral Recording (SR) (Table 4). These systems are characterized by use of multifrequency bands and by relatively complex processing of the signal to achieve the noise-reduction and signal improvement goals with minimum audible side effects. Dolby A was introduced in 1969 and was used primarily for improving analog tape recording, although other uses were also known. It employed four fixed frequency bands and only operated on lower levels of the signal, leaving higher levels alone. Widely used in post production, in recent years it has been largely replaced by Dolby SR, but it is still used on most optical sound tracks for theatrical release, discussed in Chapter 11.

Dolby SR, with a more sophisticated approach using both fixed and sliding frequency bands, was introduced in 1989 and is widely used on analog multitrack tape machines and on film recordings. The noise reduction is highly adapted to human hearing, reducing the noise greatly in the most sensitive regions of the spectrum, by as much as 26 dB. In addition to low-level signal processing, specialized high-level processing improves the headroom at the frequency extremes. This is particularly useful at the low-frequency end, because it is here that higher levels are needed to sound equally as loud as the midrange.

Consumer noise reduction systems have progressed from Dolby B through Dolby C to Dolby S over the years. Applied generally to compact cassette recordings, these noise-reduction systems helped to make the cassette medium into a very widely used vehicle for music. Another application area for Dolby C type is for the longitudinal tracks of professional cassette videotape, such as Betacam and MII, where they are an important ingredient in the performance of these fairly low-speed systems.

Most prerecorded cassette software is made using Dolby B noise reduction, wherein a single high-frequency sliding band compander is used to produce about 10 dB of audible noise reduction. Dolby C and S are systems of increasing sophistication. They offer greater noise reduction than Dolby B, and thus provide a very wide dynamic range medium at low cost. This has attracted documentary filmmakers, some of whom use the Sony Pro Walkman with a special modification that uses one of the normal audio channels to carry a crystal sync signal. While this uses one audio channel for sync, the system consisting of the Pro Walkman with Dolby C noise reduction and Type IV metal tape makes an inexpensive system capable of wide dynamic range and high-enough quality for many practical professional purposes.

A system for improving high-frequency headroom, especially of low-speed recordings, is called *Dolby HX* (for Headroom eXtension). This system, licensed through Dolby Laboratories but designed at Bang & Olufsen, uses the fact that high audio frequency signals provide the equivalent of ultrasonic bias for low audio frequency signals, and thus in the presence of strong high-frequency signals, media such as the compact cassette recording become overbiased. Thus, the headroom is increased if the ultrasonic bias is turned down dynamically during passages having strong high audio-frequency content, with consequent greater high-frequency headroom.

Appendix II Table 4. Dolby Companding Systems

Type Designator	Area of Application	Maximum noise reduction (dB)[*]
A	Older professional 2- and multi-track recorders, magnetic film; current optical sound tracks	10–15, depending on frequency
B	Compact cassette, prerecorded software, some VHS machines on longitudinal tracks	10
C	Compact cassette (less popular than B type), longitudinal professional Betacam, Betacam SP, MII, U-Matic	20
HX Pro	Compact cassette, not a companding system[†]	0
SR	Professional recording tape and film, some optical sound tracks, adds headroom, especially at frequency extremes, as well as noise reduction	26
S	Compact cassette, some prerecorded cassettes	20

* This is of necessity a gross simplification of the effect of these various systems, which range in sophistication in a number of ways, such as their capacity for dealing with misadjustment, improvements to headroom, and tolerance for wide ranges of program material without audible artifacts.

† "Headroom extension" improves high-frequency level handling capacity by making the ultrasonic bias dynamic, controlled by the high frequencies in the audio signal.

In general, it is impossible to mix various types of companding noise reduction systems: Each Dolby A encoder located before a recorder should be matched by a Dolby A decoder on playing back that tape. No mixing or level changes are permitted between the encoder and decoder, or the equal and opposite effect of the companding cannot occur. On consumer machines and cassette videotape this is not a problem, because the Dolby companding is built in, but on open-reel formats of tape or film, especially given interchange from studio to studio, it is important to note the type of companding in use and the reference level in order to be able to play back a tape or film properly.

AFM recording

A primary functional drawback to FM recording on videotape is the inability to separately record audio and video. The recordings must proceed simultaneously, so this makes an awkward medium for use in post production. It is used widely, however, at two places in the production chain, in camcorders, such as Betacam, and on the consumer formats VHS, S-VHS, 8 mm, and Hi 8.

In the area of technical specifications, AFM on paper is better in every way than the longitudinal tracks on the same videotape format: Headroom, signal-to-noise ratio, frequency response, and wow and flutter are greatly improved. Audio recorded in the same region as video on tape suffers from crosstalk from the video signal. *Crosstalk* has been greatly reduced statically by the application of a strong companding noise reduction system, described later in this chapter. The problem is that the noise caused by the video signal grows when an audio signal is present. While the audio signal itself provides frequency masking which helps to obscure the changing noise level, it may not do so completely effectively. Furthermore, small alignment differences from machine to machine in the rotating head assembly cause huge variations in the amount of noise when a recording from one machine is played on another. In mass-produced VHS tapes found in rental stores, it is not uncommon to hear a nasty buzz that comes and goes with the audio signal from the AFM tracks. In the later formats that use the process, and especially the higher speed professional ones, this problem was greatly reduced through tighter manufacturing controls and higher tape speeds, so that AFM tracks on professional media are basically free of this problem.

Digital recording

In Chapter 3 it was pointed out that digital recording depends on delivering a copy of precisely the same digits from one part of the chain to another. To the extent that this is achieved, copies can be considered clones of the original source. If precisely the same bits cannot be delivered throughout the chain, this failure will result in errors. Powerful error codes provide a means to completely correct for many errors that arise, but in the presence of excessive errors the error coding may be overwhelmed, resulting in the need for interpolation. In extreme cases, where even interpolation fails, the output is muted for the duration of the error.

Digital audio-only recorders meant for professional use not only employ error codes but also may resort to relatively large bit sizes for improved reliability. The Nagra D digital machine, for example, uses large bits for long-term reliability. Some formats write the audio data more than once to be certain it can be read back at least once, and most use some kind of interleaving, spreading the data out over the tape to be certain that localized defects do not cause failures. At least one digital videotape format records audio data in the center of the tape, leaving the video to the more error-prone edges, because dropouts and clicks in the audio are more annoying than similar drop outs in the video.

In cascading generations a chain needed to produce a finished consumer DVD is, for example:

1. audio is delivered "double system" separately from the picture; this is because there may be multiple 5.1- or 2-channel language tracks and it takes a lot of channels to hold all those tracks

2. the audio is imported into an authoring computer and there synchronized with the picture (editors say "I am going to sync the track," "I already sank the track," "it has already been sunk.")

3. subtitles, closed captioning, chaptering and so forth are added in authoring

4. the output is recorded on a high-capacity digital format computer tape

5. then recorded onto the optical disk master at the pressing plant.

The audio transparency of most of this chain, despite the number of generations, is perfect, because all of the generations are bit-by-bit copies of the preceding. The audio has remained in digital form from the original source through all these generations and is only converted back to analog in the end-user's equipment.

Appendix III: Magnetic Film Editing

An example of traditional production is recording production sound on $1/4$-in. mono tape and transferring it to 35mm stripe coat film. Increasingly today nonlinear editing systems are in use to accomplish the same post production editorial jobs at greater speed, but traditional film editing is still occurring so it is described here.

Usually it is an assistant picture editor who prepares dailies by:

- Removing picture and sound out-takes if they have been printed but not "circled" on production logs. (Some productions print all negative footage, others print circled takes only.)

- Preparing head leaders so that the picture and sound can be threaded in sync. These consist of an SMPTE countdown leader, or an Academy one, on the picture. The SMPTE leader countdown is in seconds, the Academy one in feet. The frame of sound leader opposite the 2 frame of the SMPTE is replaced with a one frame of magnetic film consisting of a 1 kHz tone recording, to form a "2 pop" that lets viewers know that the threading is correctly in sync.

- "Syncing" the dailies, usually by cutting and splicing the sound track so that it is identical in length with the picture. This involves, for each scene, running the picture down to the point where the clapperboard slate just comes closed, then finding the corresponding frame in sound by *scrubbing* the mag film back and forth over the head to find the moment when the slate comes closed. The picture and sound frames corresponding to each other are then placed in a *sync block*, a mechanical device for carrying several strands of film along in sync with each other by mechanically engaging teeth on the synchronizer with the perforations in the film. The assistant then rolls back to the head of the shot and splices the sound and picture to the leader. Each take receives the same treatment and is spliced onto the tail of the preceding take. Dailies are usually shown in the order in which they were shot, because this helps diagnose problems, for example, if there is a camera defect.

Following dailies, a picture editor cuts the scene, keeping what is now called the *A track* (the original production sound transfer) in sync with the picture, probably using a Moviola® or flat-bed editing table. Throughout rough cutting usually just one track is used for simplicity, but the picture editor may "build" more than one sound track, calling the next the *B track*, if that is needed to produce, for example, dialog overlaps essential to a scene. Once the scenes constituting a reel (about 10 minutes in length for film; 20 minute lengths are common today on other systems) have all been cut,

243

screened, and approved for *picture lock*, meaning that no further adjustments to the picture are expected, the cut work print is sent to a lab to have *dirty dupes* made—low grade black-and-white copies needed for editorial purposes only.

The sound-editing team receives picture dirty dupes, or video copies, the production A track or tracks, and a log of scenes and takes used in the cut. Note that the production A track is likely to be in poor shape by this time because it will have been run so many times. It also lacks *handles;* that is, each sound cut corresponds to a picture cut typically, with no additional sound footage available from before or after the picture cut. This may well cause problems in post production because abrupt cuts may ruin the sound continuity. For these two reasons, the dialog editor starts over building the original production tracks, now in probably at least two *units* or cut reels of film. The sound film is *checkerboarded* between the two reels, with shot 1 in reel 1, shot 2 in 2, shot 3 in 1, and so forth. This method gives subsequent post production mixing all of the available good material to deal with because every shot boundary is covered. It is not essential to do this if everything, including especially the background sound (called *presence* or *room tone*), matches precisely across the picture cut, but perfect matching is rare, so the checkerboard method comes into use. Sound editors say that they spend more time matching backgrounds than they do on what is said!

While sound editing has started, picture editing often does not stop. Both before and after picture lock, a picture editing assistant keeps track of the length of each of the reels (and even scenes within a reel) in feet and frames, and in time. The director frequently asks the current running time of the show, and the picture assistant must know this time for the current state of the cut. The term *LFOP* means Last Frame of Picture, which is the length of the reels in feet and frames. This information is given to the sound editors upon delivery of the locked picture, and at many times thereafter, acting as a kind of reality check on whether the current state of the various sound units conforms to the current state of the picture edit.

Following the same methods described in Chapter 9, the dialog editor uses wild lines, out-takes, and ADR to build the dialog tracks, employing the same track splitting sensibility as discussed there.

Working in parallel with dialog editing, sound effects editors build units. There may be some modification of the sound possible in transfer, such as off-speed transfers to make a sound lower pitched and thus seem bigger, but by and large sound editors cutting mag film do not modify sound; that is left to mixers.

Music editors also work in the manner described for digital audio workstations. However, each analog generation of the mixing process involves some loss. To prevent the accumulation of losses becoming audible on music, a generation used for sound effects or dialog is skipped. It is the music mixdown on film from the scoring stage that is edited like a unit but used as a premix, thus saving a generation.

Film editing mechanics

Diagonal and butt splices are both possible and widely used, with the diagonal splices more common where sound is edited to sound, and butt splices used for cutting in silence (like cutting in a piece of magnetic film containing a Foley effect before the effect starts, and then after it is over) and for "hard" edits such as the middle of words in dialog. Also, an indelible marker should be used on mag film, not a grease pencil. These are easy to mix up because a film editor needs both, the grease pencil to mark the picture and the indelible marker for the sound track.

There are three different methods used in editing to hear sound off mag film. The first of these, sync block editing, although primitive in appearance and sound quality, nevertheless is very widely used because the equipment is so cheap and does the job at one level of necessity—it allows sound editors to hear the sound and to cut it with respect to a picture. In *sync block* editing an editorial device called a *synchronizer*[1] is used to carry multiple strands of film along in synchronization, by using metal teeth to engage the perforations of the film. Sync blocks also measure feet and frames, and thus, are useful in logging the activity to produce the cue sheets necessary for mixing. Usually in sound editing the black-and-white dirty dupe work print is placed in one "gang" of the synchronizer, and sound tracks occupy the other gangs. The sound may be heard right at the sync block by running the mag film oxide side up and dropping a magnetic head on a small arm down onto the film. The head is traditionally connected to a *squawk box*, which is a small set of playback electronics and a loudspeaker (headphones may be substituted for the speaker).

Once an edit point has been found by scrubbing the film back and forth past the head, the head assembly is flipped up out of the way and the film is marked for splicing. Note that the film is oxide side up, so it is useful to make any marks necessary in between the perforations, rather than over the whole surface of the film. If more extensive writing is necessary for identity of a certain cut, then the base side should be used.

---

1. Not to be confused with an electronic synchronizer used for SMPTE time code.

The second method is editing on an upright Moviola®. The Moviola is a machine that has a *picture head* and a *sound head*,[2] which can be locked to one another, or unlocked, as need be. One runs the picture down to a place where a sound effect is needed. Leaving the picture and sound sides disconnected from one another, mag film is then played to find a place that should correspond to that picture. Locking the picture and sound together, the sound can then be heard in a trial synchronization with respect to the picture, and when a satisfactory synchronization is found, the effect is spliced into the sound unit, usually using a sync block for the actual editing.

The third form is the flat bed editing table. These *flat beds* have one or more picture heads and one or more sound heads, all of which can operate independently or in synchronization. The trade-off between upright Moviola and flat-bed editing is that the Moviola is quicker to thread because it has a simpler film path, but it also has worse sound quality. Flat-bed editing tables have more complicated threading paths, which in general makes the film motion smoother and, therefore, results in less wow and flutter. Flat beds are good enough that it is possible to produce temp mixes on them to be recorded on an external recorder.

All three methods also require a splicer. Sound splicers come in a number of forms. Some use preperforated splicing tape, and others perforate the tape themselves on making a splice. Some permit both butt and diagonal splices, and others are dedicated to one type. All must be in good repair to prevent excessive damage to the film base, particularly if polyester base film is to be cut.

Film editorial operations

Head and tail leaders

Regarding head and tail leader markings, the sound editor must observe both the conventions of the format (35mm or 16mm) and the requirements of the dubbing stage to which the tracks will be delivered. Traditionally there are different requirements for leaders in post production and laboratory work which can sometimes be confused. In post production, the most common leaders have one unambiguous sound start mark coincident with the picture start frame of the Academy or SMPTE leader (they both have a start frame, but they are a different length from the first frame of the picture because the Academy leader,

2. The use of the term *head* is to be distinguished from the idea of a tape or film playback head, a much smaller device. In a projector, the whole assembly that plays back sound is also called a *sound head*. So the term *head* is used to denote many things.

used for theatrical release, is footage oriented, whereas the SMPTE leader is time oriented). It is traditional to cut a single frame of tone into all the units corresponding to the frame marked 2. This *2 pop* provides a means on the dubbing stage to know that all of the units have been threaded in sync, because by listening to all the tracks at once, one single (loud) beep should be heard, not beep-beep-beep, on playing the tracks.

Fill leader

Sound tracks are often filled with many feet of what is intended to be silence, interspersed with recorded sound. It would be possible to use unrecorded mag film for the silent segments of the track, but that would be needlessly expensive and the dubber playback head would be "reading" hiss from the unrecorded mag continuously. Fill leader is inserted instead. This fill leader or spacer usually consists of old release prints, which are probably worn, but are supposed to be undamaged insofar as the purposes of a leader are concerned. Also, fill leader should not be too dirty or have damaged perforations so that it will run cleanly through the machines.

There is one difficulty in using old, cheap release prints for fill leader. The picture fill leader has an emulsion side and a base side. The emulsion is relatively soft and can be scratched off as it is dragged over playback heads. If this occurs, the buildup of emulsion on a playback head will quickly cause a spacing loss, losing high frequencies most rapidly. *So it is essential to cut fill leader so that the base of the leader faces the playback heads.*

There are two ways to distinguish the emulsion from the base of printed picture film. One is based on the fact that they reflect light differently. When looking at the emulsion side, the reflectance of the area outside the picture is different from the picture, and the different color layers can sometimes be seen to have different reflectance as well. The base side appears more uniformly shiny. Also, on licking the film you will find that your tongue sticks to the emulsion side but not to the base side. This trick is useful in a darkroom with raw negative if the "wind" (emulsion position) is unknown.

It would be confusing in head-and-tail leaders to have picture going by and it would be difficult to read writing on the leaders, so it is customary to use white *light struck* or other colored leader for heads and tails. Light-stuck leader, which is a slightly creamy color, has a particularly soft emulsion, so the rule about emulsion position must be observed here as well as with fill leader. Some editors use different colored leaders for the head and tail so that one can tell by looking from a distance whether a wound-up spool of mag film is heads or tails out.

Edit sync vs. projection sync

Throughout post production, one kind of synchronization is used among the various tracks and in relationship to the picture. At this point in the process, the sound tracks are said to be in *edit sync*, short for editorial synchronization, that is, "level" in the sync block with the corresponding picture. When picture and sound are "hung" for playback in the dubbing stage, the start marks on the elements are placed in the picture aperture or on the magnetic head of the dubber, and played in sync.

In laboratory processes that follow post production, a different form of synchronization is necessary, with the sound track offset from the picture. The reason for this offset is that the sound head in a projector is not in the same position as the picture aperture; they are displaced. So the sound track must be "pulled up" or "pushed back" from edit sync to account for the offset between picture and sound. One of the problems with marking head and tail leaders is the potential confusion between what is needed in post production and what is required by a laboratory to sync the picture and sound track in the dark on the printer. Sound editors rarely deal with laboratory sync points used for printing, and confusion levels are lowered if only one sync mark appears on the head leaders throughout post production—edit sync.

Track breakdown

Now let us say that the sound editor has ordered up a number of sound effects from transfer, and that they have been delivered sequentially on a reel. In this case, the sound editor *breaks down* the mag film into separate cuts and rolls them up base out, without reels. The resulting *donuts* each contain one sound effect, and it is easy to get to an individual sound if they are all well organized on a shelf. The editor usually proceeds from the head to the tail of a reel while preparing one or two units at a time, doing this process over until the required number of units for the project have been cut.

Saving and organizing trims and outs

When a sound is cut in, the mag film will be longer than the portion of it that is actually used. The portion before the head cut in is called the *head trim*, and the trailing unused portion is called the *tail trim*. After the used portion has been cut into the sound track, the unused head and tail trims are not discarded; they are rolled up as donuts or hung in a *trim bin*. This permits returning to them in case the picture is changed by a scene extension so that they

can be cut in as needed. For this process to work, of course, it is essential to know the correspondence between the trim and the pieces of film that have been cut in. Therefore, the trims must be properly labeled.

Conforming to changes in the picture cut

If the picture changes after sound editorial work has begun, of course the sound tracks must be changed to match. In the case of mag film editing, this is done by one of several processes:

- When a shot is added to the picture, fill leader of the same length as the shot has to be added into all of the cut units, thus resynchronizing all sounds coming after the shot insertion. Then new sounds are cut in for the new shot.

- When a scene or shot is removed, equal footage is removed to keep tracks in sync. The edit point might not be at the same place in the picture and sound, due to possible sound overlaps with scene boundaries, but the same footage of sound that came out of the picture must also come out of the tracks to maintain sync.

- When a shot is extended at the head or tail, the sound-editing requirement depends on the sound. A *hard effect*, such as a car door closing, will just need to be adjusted to remain in sync with the corresponding picture. On the other hand, more or less continuous sounds, such as ambience, will need to be extended to cover the new footage. If the proper head or tail trim can be found, it may simply be inserted as required; if not, then a new transfer is needed.

Impact of companding noise reduction

The playback standards of squawk box and Moviola editing are pretty low grade, but the flat-bed editing system is better, good enough for temp mixes. Sound editors must deal with a situation caused by listening to sound tracks that contain companding noise reduction compression without having the corresponding expansion available. The sound that editors hear over their systems is quite compressed, up to 26 dB of compression in the case of Dolby SR. This means that low-level sounds have been raised as heard by editors to be nearly three times as loud as they are when decoded. Sound editors have come to understand that the sound they are hearing in such cases is highly compressed, and not representative of the final sound.

Appendix IV: Working with deciBels

deciBel is a means to express logarithmic relationships across levels. For voltages, or sound pressure levels, the equation for a dB relationship is:

$$dB = 20 \times \log(V/(Vref))$$

where *Vref* is the reference and log is to the base 10. There are several reference voltage values used in audio shown in Table 1.

Appendix IV Table 1. Reference Voltage Levels used in Audio

Level	Voltage, Vrms
+4 dBu	1.228
0 dBu	0.7746
−10 dBV	0.316

To use these, let's calculate the voltage level for the specified input noise voltage of a microphone preamplifier having a rating of −127 dBm, a rather commonly seen number. The first thing we need to know is that dBm equals dBu in voltage. dBm is deciBels relative to 1 mW of power, an older method of measuring level that originated with the telephone company (the villain in one of the Flint films, called TPC there).

The dBm measurement method used matching impedance conditions, but today we virtually always use bridging conditions, explained in Chapter 3. We hang onto the tradition of referencing to the voltage that corresponds to 1W in 600 ohms though, and that is 0.7746Vrms. Root mean square is a method of measurement of ac waveforms that is equivalent to their dc value in terms of heating up a resistor. It is not the peak, nor peak-to-peak voltage, but instead for a sine wave is 0.707 times the peak voltage.

So −127 dBm = −127 dBu.

and

$$-127dBm = 20 \times \log \frac{V}{0.7746Vrms}$$

Solving for V means:

1. dividing −127 by 20,

2. taking the antilog (10^x),

3. multiplying by 0.7746.

The answer is 0.35 µVrms.

For reference sound pressure level in acoustics, 20 µN/m² is used for 0 dB SPL.

When it comes to power, whether it is electrical power or acoustical power, a different equation is used.

$$dB = 10 \times \left(\frac{P}{Pref}\right)$$

where the most common P_{ref} is 1 W. Watts are not rated in rms (although you'll see that happen everyday, it is incorrect), but rather in average Watts.

So twice as much voltage is about 6 dB (actually 6.02 for pedants), twice as much power 3 dB (3.01). Psychoacoustically however, to sound twice as loud the sound pressure level must be increased on the average by about 10 dB, although answers can be gotten anywhere from 6 to 11 dB, depending on the experiment.

Table 2 allows you to estimate voltages and powers from deciBels and vice versa quickly.

Appendix IV Table 2. deciBels versus scale factor for Voltage and Power

Power multiplier	dB	Voltage multiplier
100	+20	10
10	+10	3.16
4	+6	2
2	+3	1.41
1	0	1
0.5	−3	0.71
0.25	−6	0.5
0.1	−10	0.316
0.01	−20	0.1
0.001	−30	0.0316

Appendix IV Table 2. deciBels versus scale factor for Voltage and Power

Power multiplier	dB	Voltage multiplier
0.0001	−40	0.01
0.0001	−50	0.00316
0.00001	−60	0.001
1×10^{-6}	−70	0.000316
1×10^{-7}	−80	0.0001

Many dB ratios can be determined from the table by adding and subtracting deciBels, and multiplying or dividing correctly. For instance, a voltage gain of 46 dB is 20 + 20 + 6 dB, so it's $10 \times 10 \times 2$ or a factor of 200 in voltage.

The ultimate noise floor of a system is controlled by the impedance at its source. That's because there is an irreducible noise due to the random motion of electrons in any impedance that occurs at any temperature above absolute zero. This is called Johnson noise, after its discoverer at Bell Labs. A typical electrodynamic microphone has an impedance of 200 ohms. The Johnson noise of a 200 ohm impedance is:.

$$e_n = \sqrt{4kTBR}$$

where k is Boltzmann's constant (1.38×10^{-23}), T is the temperature in degrees Kelvin (293°K at room temperature), B is the bandwidth in Hz, (20 kHz), and R is the impedance in ohms (200). This voltage is 0.25 µVrms.

Interestingly, now we can calculate how much more noise the microphone preamplifier specification calculated above is greater than the thermal noise of this microphone, in deciBels. Such a comparison is used widely in radio frequency engineering, but not much in audio, and it is called the noise figure.

$$dB = 20 \times \log((0.35 \mu Vrms)/(0.25 \mu Vrms))$$

The noise figure of this microphone preamplifier is 3 dB, that is, when you turn it up, the noise you hear as hiss is within 3 dB of the theoretical noise floor that you could possibly have for this microphone.

Calculating dB gain

A calculation can be made of how much gain is needed in a mixing console so that the loudspeakers produce the same SPL as was picked up by the microphone. Let us say that a performer is speaking at an average 65 dB SPL, 1 m from the microphone. The microphone sensitivity is 6 mV at 94 dB SPL, and its output voltage will thus average 0.2 mV, since this is 29 dB (94 − 65 = 29) below 6 mV. In order for the loudspeaker to produce 65 dB SPL at our listener's ears, we need about 0.4 V (85−

65 = 20 and 20 dB below 4 V is 0.4 V from the preceding performer example). Thus the gain needed in the electronics is 0.4 V/0.2 mV = 2000 = 66 dB.

A more typical case would call for more amplification, since movie sound tracks for speech are on average 10 dB louder than face-to-face speech. Thus 76 dB is necessary, overall, divided among the microphone preamplifier, the rest of the mixing console, and the loudspeaker power amplifier. Since a typical power amplifier gain is 30 dB, the console must provide about 46 dB gain in this instance.

Bibliography

Altman, Rick, ed. *Sound Theory Sound Practice,* Routledge, New York, 1992.

Berger, Eliot, ed., et al., *The Noise Manual,* Fifth Edition, American Industrial Hygiene Association, 2000.

Bregman, Albert S., *Auditory Scene Analysis,* MIT Press, Cambridge, 1990.

Chion, Michel, *AudioVision, Sound on Screen,* Columbia University Press, New York, 1994.

Chion, Michel, *The Voice in Cinema,* Columbia University Press, New York, 1999.

Eargle, John M., *The Microphone Book,* Focal Press, Boston, 2001.

Eargle, John M., *Handbook of Recording Engineering,* 3rd ed., Chapman Hall, New York, 1996.

LoBrutto, Vincent, *Sound-On-Film, Interviews with Creators of Film Sound,* Praeger, Westport, CT, London, 1994.

Moore, Brian C. J., *An Introduction to the Psychology of Hearing,* 4th ed., Academic Press, 1997.

Murch, Walter, *In The Blink of an Eye,* Silman-James Press, Los Angeles, 1995.

Pasquariello, Nicholas, *Sounds of Movies: Interviews with the Creators of Feature Sound Tracks,* Post Bridge Books, San Francisco, 1996.

Pickles, James O., *An Introduction to the Physiology of Hearing,* 2nd. ed., Academic Press, London, San Diego, 1988.

Seeberg, Wolf, *Sync Sound for the New Media,* available from www.coffeysound.com, and www.locationsound.com, frequently updated information about specific equipment time code issues.

Tannenbaum, James, *Using Time Code in the Reel World,* 3rd ed., available from www.opamp.com.

Taub, Eric, "Production–Sound Mixer, Boom Operator, Third Man" in *Gaffers, Grips and Best Boys,* St. Martin's Press, New York, 1995.

Yewdall, David, *The Practical Art of Motion Picture Sound,* Focal Press, Boston, 1999.

Glossary

AC (alternating current): applies to the power derived from commercial power generators as a 60 Hz sine wave in the U.S., as opposed to dc power derived from batteries or dc generators.

A chain: that part of a theater sound system including reproduction of the print with the sound head on the projector, preamplification, noise reduction or Academy filtering, digital decoding, and matrix decoding, each where used. The A chain is the part of a system that is identified with a particular format, such as *Dolby Digital,*[1] *DTS, SDDS,* etc. See *B chain*.

A track: an term used in editing for the production sound that is cut in sync with the picture.

Absorption: the property of materials to turn incident acoustical energy into heat. Absorption of the materials on the surfaces of a room is usually the only factor available to control reverberation time, because absorption and room volume (three-dimensional size) are the only classical factors affecting reverberation time. Also used to describe losses that occur during transmission through a medium, such as *air absorption*.

Academy mono: a conventional monaural optical sound-track format intended to be used with a rather strong high-frequency rolloff in playback. The rolloff is necessitated by the need to suppress audible noise due to grain of the motion-picture print. The rolloff is accomplished in two possible ways: in a conventional monaural theater it is due to loudspeaker and screen high-frequency losses, as well as a possible *low-pass filter*, while in a stereophonic-equipped theater playing a monaural print, it is a (different) *low-pass* filter. The distinctions are explained in the standards SMPTE 202 and ISO 2969. The effects of the rolloff are partially overcome by boost *program equalization* applied by the post production mixer during dubbing, but this process has limitations because boosting high frequencies may lead to noticeable distortion.

Acetate (tri-cellulose acetate): basically wood pulp. A material used for the base of motion-picture film. Usually chosen for its ease of cutting in editing situations, despite the fact that it is not as stable as *polyester* base. Acetate base is hygroscopic (absorbs water from the atmosphere), so temperature and humidity conditions of storage are more critical than for polyester-based films.

---

1. All italicized words are themselves defined within this Glossary.

ADR: automated dialog replacement. A system of equipment and a controlled recording studio or stage that permits watching and listening to a performance through headphones and repeating the performance for recording without the background noise and reverberation of location shooting. Also known as looping.

AES: see *Audio Engineering Society*.

AFM recording: a method of recording by way of heads on the scanning drum of helical scan video tape formats. The recording is buried underneath the corresponding video, and is at a different azimuth angle, which permit separation from the video. Cannot be separately recorded subsequent to video recording.

Air absorption: losses in propagation beyond those expected from considerations of sound spreading out over distance; greater at high frequencies than at low frequencies, and changes with humidity.

Ambience: generally speaking, ambience is widely used as a synonym for *ambient noise*. In film and video sound production, the term is used more specifically to mean the background sound accompanying a scene, whether present in the original production recording (in which a better term for it is *presence*) or deliberately added in *sound-effects editing* in order to provide an acoustic space around the rest of the dialog and sound effects. Ambience helps establish the scene and works editorially to support the picture editing by, for example, staying constant across a picture cut to indicate to the audience that no change of space has occurred, but rather only a simple picture edit. Conversely, if ambience changes abruptly at a picture cut, an indication is made to the listener that the scene has also changed.

Ambient noise: the acoustic noise present at a location (which includes a set) without considering the noise made by the production. A preferred term is *background noise* so that ambient noise and *ambience* (which may be deliberately added) are not confused.

American National Standards Institute: the U.S.'s supervisory standards body. AES and SMPTE standards may become American National Standards.

Amplification: see *Audio amplification*.

Amplitude: the size dimension of a waveform, usually represented graphically in the vertical plane. The size represents the strength of the unit being measured.

Analog audio: any signal representation in which the signal waveform is transmitted or stored in direct 1:1 correspondence with the sound wave. The means of representation may be electrical, mechanical, magnetic, electromagnetic, or optical. The amplitude dimension of the audio *signal* is represented by means of a direct analogy between a voltage, displacement of position (such as for the phonograph or an analog *optical sound track*), or strength of magnetic flux (analog *tape recording*), for example, and the signal. Analog systems may also employ modulation and demodulation such as frequency modulation (FM), in which audio is imposed on a carrier frequency, such as a radio frequency by means of modulation; despite the modulation/demodulation cycle, the audio remains in analog form because no digitization has occurred.

Analog audio is distinguished from digital audio by the fact that analog systems do not use quantization (see *Digital audio*). This means that the representation is intended to be continuous in the amplitude domain. On the other hand, analog audio may be sampled, which is generally considered to be a digital audio process, but if the audio remains unquantized it is not digital audio. An example of a device that uses sampling but not quantizing is the bucket brigade analog delay line, often used in the past for inexpensive audio delay.

General areas of advantage for analog audio over digital include some specialized applications, such as most transducer-associated amplifiers (for microphones and loudspeakers), and the fact that analog audio is a mature technology, with good economy for a given level of sound quality. Disadvantages include the fact that because each stage of analog audio involves making an analogy between the actual signal and its representation, inevitably noise and distortion accumulate across generations because the analogy fails to completely replicate the signal; the signal is not a clone but a more or less good representation of the signal. This process is manageable with care and has led to some great sounding sound tracks. The capabilities of digital audio grow daily, especially considering that many of the possibilities are driven by a much larger industry, computer manufacturing. On the other hand, the viewpoint that film and television "would sound better if it were just all digital" is naive, because "sound better" depends on a great many factors, the most important of which is probably the sound design.

ANSI: abbreviation for *American National Standards Institute.*

ASA: 1. abbreviation for Acoustical Society of America. 2. (obsolete.) abbreviation for American Standards Association, the forerunner of the *American National Standards Institute.*

Atmos (British usage): abbreviation for *atmosphere.*

Atmosphere (British usage): synonym for *presence.*

Audible frequency range: usually considered to be between 20 Hz and 20 kHz, although these are not rigid limits. Below 20 Hz sound is less well perceived as tonal than above 20 Hz, degenerating at lower frequencies into individual pulsations. Sound at high levels and infrasonic frequencies is more likely to be perceived as vibration than as sound. Above 20 kHz the hearing of sound in air of even the best young listeners rapidly rolls off. Below 20 Hz sound is called *infrasonic,* while above 20 kHz it is called *ultrasonic.*

Audio: a broad term covering the representation of sound electrically or on a medium: "audiotape" is better usage than "sound tape," although *sound track* persists in the film industry to describe audio accompanying a picture.

Audio amplifier: audio amplifiers take a number of forms. First are input transducer preamplifiers such as microphone preamplifiers, intended to raise the output of the transducer to a higher nominal level for processing by further circuitry. Specialized preamplifiers in this category include phonograph and magnetic film and tape preamplifiers, which have both a gain function and an *equalization* (definition 1) function to compensate for the transducers and the *frequency response* used on the medium to optimize dynamic range.

Second are line-level audio amplifiers, which raise the signal level further. Third are specialized audio amplifiers for processing the signal usually having unity gain but offering features such as *equalization* (definition 2). Fourth are amplifiers used principally for buffering, that is, for preventing unwanted interactions among components. Fifth are summing amplifiers used to add together multiple signals, without interactions among them. Finally, there are audio power amplifiers intended to drive loudspeakers.

Major concerns with all audio amplifiers include the dynamic range capability which means both the maximum signal handling capability versus frequency and noise versus frequency; linear *distortion,* such as *frequency response* errors; nonlinear *distortion*; and input and output conditions, such as nominal levels and impedances.

Audio bandwidth: generally considered to be the range 20 Hz to 20 kHz, although these are not hard limits.

Audio cassette: any system that uses tape housed in a generally continuous outer shell designed to be interchanged from machine-to-machine, offering physical tape protection. By far the most popular is the *compact cassette,* standardized by Philips. Under this broad definition also falls an endless-loop cartridge used in broadcasting and some film applications, known as the NAB cartridge.

Audio Engineering Society (AES): a U.S.-based international group of professionals in audio that includes standards-making among its activities.

Audio frequency: usually considered to be the frequency range between 20 Hz and 20 kHz, based roughly on the limits of human perception.

Audio mixer: an ambiguous term applied to both audio mixing consoles and the persons who operate them. Generally speaking, the functions of an audio mixing console can be broken into two broad classifications: processing and configuration. Among audio processes are *audio amplification*, control of levels by way of *faders, equalization*, and control over program dynamics by means of *limiters, compressors*, and *expanders*. The configuration part of console design has to do with arranging the audio processes in certain preferred orders, combining signals, and routing the signals throughout the console. Issues included in configuration include signal routing (e.g., which microphone input goes to what channel of a multitrack recorder), *buses, auxiliary sends*, and *pan pots*.

Azimuth: see *Head alignment*.

B chain: the part of a theater sound system following the *A chain* from the top of the volume control, through *one-third-octave equalization*, electronic crossovers where used, power amplifiers, loudspeakers, and their acoustical environment, both local and global. The B chain encompasses every factor having an aural effect on the listener after the processes occurring in the A chain.

Background noise: the acoustical noise present on a location or set without the presence of the production.

Backgrounds: synonym for ambience.

Bandpass filter: an electrical filter designed to pass only a certain range of frequencies while suppressing signals at frequencies outside the range. Bandpass filters are often adjustable as to frequency, and may be composed of a combination of a *high-pass filter* and a *low-pass filter*. An example of the use of a bandpass filter is in limiting the frequency range of a speech recording to a narrow band to simulate speech heard over a telephone.

Bandstop filter: an electrical filter designed to pass only frequencies lying outside a defined range; both lower and higher frequencies are passed, while frequencies lying within the range of the filter are suppressed. A bandstop filter is usually used to suppress unwanted noise that lies in only one frequency region. It is similar to a *notch filter*, but has a broader frequency range of suppression than a notch filter.

Bandwidth: the frequency range, usually stated from low to high frequency, over which a system has a stated uniform *frequency response*. Usually, if left unstated the bandwidth is the frequency range over which the output does not fall more than 3 dB from its midrange value, thus, a specification such as "bandwidth from 30 Hz to 20 kHz" probably means ±3 dB from 30 Hz to 20 kHz. Clearly, it is far better when both the frequency range and the response tolerances over the range are given.

Barney: a generally soft motion-picture camera cover meant to reduce the acoustic noise of the camera for sync sound shooting.

Beat: in music, the beat is the underlying meter or rhythm. In sound in general, however, it has an additional meaning. Whenever tones of two or more frequencies are passed through a device exhibiting nonlinear *distortion*, new tones will be created at new frequencies corresponding to sums and differences of the form $f_2 + f_1$, $f_2 - f_1$, $2 \times (f_2 - f_1)$, $f_2 - (2 \times f_1)$, etc. out to higher orders. These new tones are called beat notes. Often the term is applied to the first-order difference tone at $f_2 - f_1$, because it may be well separated in frequency from f_2 and f_1, and thus be audible because it is not subject to much *frequency masking*. The term also applies to, for example, multiple piano strings used for one note that are not perfectly tuned to one another; the resulting amplitude modulation leads to an audible "wobbling" in time.

Bias: to employ bias is to add an inaudible dc or ac signal to a desired audio signal in order to overcome nonlinearities of amplification or the medium. In the case of amplifiers, bias is, for example, the dc idle current that is present in the circuit in the absence of a signal. Here the bias serves to place the particular stage of the audio amplifier at an operating point where it can most accommodate the range of signals expected.

Ultrasonic ac bias is used in analog tape recording to linearize the tape medium, which would otherwise be highly distorted. Bias in this case is a high-frequency sine-wave signal supplied by a bias oscillator that is added to the audio signal, usually after the last stage of amplification and before application to the record head. The bias frequency is usually from 100 kHz upwards in professional machines. The level of ultrasonic bias is important in analog tape recording because it has an impact on many important parameters, including medium- and high-audio-frequency sensitivity, headroom versus frequency, and noise of various kinds. Choice of a bias operating point is made by considering the characteristics of the tape medium, tape speed, and the record head gap in use. Usually the manufacturer of a tape or film machine will supply a procedure for best results, but a common example would be to operate at a certain amount of overbias, such as 2 dB, at 10 kHz. This means finding the bias operating point having the highest sensitivity by adjusting the bias level up and down while measuring the effect on the level of a 10-kHz tone and then adding more bias until the desired degree of overbias is achieved.

Bilateral: a term applied to analog variable-area optical sound tracks to describe a sound track that is symmetrical and a mirror image about its centerline. The advantage of a bilateral sound track is that its use helps to cancel out variations in output level and the accompanying distortion occurring due to non-uniform illumination across the sound track area; if one side is moving into an area of less illumination, then it is likely that the other side is moving into an area of greater illumination, the effects of which cancel. In order to accommodate stereophonic information, two bilateral sound tracks are placed side by side, and the whole track is called the "dual-bilateral stereo variable area."

Binder: a group of chemicals that, when combined with magnetic oxide form a complete magnetic coating for film and tape. The binder has multiple purposes, including long-term binding of the oxide to the base, lubrication to prevent stiction at tape and film heads and guides, and reduction of the electrical resistivity of the oxide to prevent the buildup of static electricity, which can discharge at heads and cause crackling noises.

BKSTS: see *British Kinematograph Sound and Television Society.*

Black track print: A motion-picture prerelease print format with picture elements generally complete, but printed black in the optical sound-track area. The black-track procedure is often used for early answer prints before an optical sound track is available.

Blimp: a more or less solid, continuous, camera cover meant to reduce the acoustic noise of a motion-picture camera for sync sound shooting. See also *Barney.*

Bloop: in production sound recording, the term bloop is a shortened form of bloop slate. The bloop slate consists of a pushbutton and light connected to an electronic oscillator supplied in portable tape machines to indicate synchronization points between picture and sound. It is most often used in documentary film production, where the use of the traditional clapperboard slate may be intrusive to the subject. The bloop oscillator is at a different frequency and has a different timbre from the reference oscillator so that they may be easily distin-guished by listening. In optical sound recording, the term bloop refers to making the sound track either transparent or opaque, as called for on a negative or positive recording in order to prevent hearing a transient noise, such as a click or a pop, particularly at splices.

Boom: a mechanical device for holding a microphone in the air, manipulating it in several dimensions by swinging the boom arm and rotating the microphone on the end of the boom. Booms are generally floor-standing, fairly heavy devices. Booms are preferred in fixed-set situations, but their size and weight makes them more problematic for productions shot on location, where the *fishpole* is perhaps more often used.

Board: synonym for *console.*

Boom op: *boom operator.*

Boom operator: the user of a microphone boom, whose other duties often include operation of *fishpoles*, planting of hidden microphones on the set, and placement of radio microphones and their transmitters on actors. The boom operator often has a sophisticated job to do in balancing among the actors in order to get the best recording of each of them.

British Kinematograph Sound and Television Society (BKSTS): a British-based professional group with interests in film, video, sound, and television.

Bulk eraser: see *Degausser.*

Bus: an electrical interconnection among many points, so called because it can be viewed as a bus line, with stops (connections) along its way. Signal buses include main buses, often called mixdown buses; buses intended to send signals to a multitrack tape recorder, called multitrack buses; and buses to send signals from input channels to outboard devices, called auxiliary buses. Auxiliary buses may be named for their purpose: reverb send (signals sent to a reverberation process) and cue send (signals sent to performers in order to cue them).

Buzz track: a special type of recorded *optical sound* test film used in the alignment of the area scanned by optical sound heads (playback devices). It consists of two recordings made outside the usual sound-track area, with their maximum peaks just touching the outer edges of the area to be scanned, each at a different frequency. The optical sound head is adjusted correctly for lateral position when essentially no sound is heard, while adjusting to one side results in hearing one frequency and to the other side a in hearing different frequency.

Cinema Audio Society (CAS): a U.S. based group of recording professionals with interests in film and television sound.

Cable boy: the third man on a *production sound* crew responsible for cable handling and maintenance of sound equipment.

Calibration tape or film: a magnetic tape or film prepared under laboratory conditions with recordings having prescribed characteristics. In audio, these characteristic include the absolute level of reference *fluxivity* sections at a standard frequency, such as 1 kHz, and the relative level of different frequencies according to the standard in use. Specialized test tapes or films also are available recorded with low *flutter* so that flutter due to transports can be measured.

In video, the prescribed characteristics include reference levels for white and black, and reference level and phase for color, among many others.

Cans: slang for *headphones.*

Capacitor microphone: see *Electrostatic microphone.*

Capstan: the rotating cylindrical shaft against which tape is pressed by a *pinch roller* in order to impart the correct linear speed to tape or film. The average thickness of the tape must be accommodated in the design in order to produce the correct linear speed.

Typical professional tape speeds are 30, 15, and 7 $\frac{1}{2}$ in./sec, while film speeds are 22$\frac{1}{2}$ in./sec (70mm film), 18 (35mm film), and 7.2 (16mm film) in./sec.

Cat. 43: a single-ended noise-reduction device, used during playback without any corresponding encoding during recording, manufactured by Dolby Laboratories under catalog number 43. It consists of four frequency bands of downward *expansion*, allowing 10 to 15 dB of noise reduction with a minimum of other audible artifacts, based on *Dolby A* noise reduction.

Cat. 430: a single-ended noise-reduction device similar to the Cat. 43, but based on the more sophisticated multiple fixed and floating-frequency band capabilities of *Dolby SR.*

CCIR: a European standards organization after which a set of *equalization* time-constant curves used for analog magnetic audiotape recording were named. The name of the organization has changed to the International Telecommunications Union, but CCIR is still a term in use.

CCIR equalization for all speeds uses an infinity low-frequency time constant (using no low-frequency record boost nor corresponding playback cut) and high-frequency time constants, which vary with tape speed: 15 in./sec uses 35 μs, 7 $\frac{1}{2}$ in./sec uses 70 μs.

Channel: an audio term specifying a given signal path. When audio is physically recorded on film or tape, the term applied to the physical representation on the medium is *track*. Thus, the input of a tape machine may be labeled in channels, while the recording it makes on tape is made on tracks. In console terminology, the term applies to both input channels and output channels. Input channels usu-

ally represent various single sounds coming into a console for mixing, while output channels represent various combined sounds, for example, all sounds destined for the left loudspeaker represent the L output channel.

Clapper: *clapperboard.*

Clapperboard: the traditional device used to synchronize sound and picture starts by banging a board down on top of another within view of the camera so that a reference mark is made in both sound and picture.

Click track: a sound track, usually prerecorded on one track of a multitrack medium, to guide musicians and others in making recordings in synchronization with the picture and other sound tracks, consisting of clicks at the correct intervals to correspond to the beat. Use of the click track requires using *Sel-sync* (playback off the record head) to ensure synchronization.

Cochlea: the inner ear. The organ that converts mechanical sound energy, delivered by way of the outer and middle ear, to electrical impulses for detection by the brain. The fundamental mechanism is a spatially dependent spectrum analyzer, with one end of the membrane stretched in the cochlea responding to high frequencies and the other end to low frequencies, with the membrane covered in hair cells and nerves, which make the transduction from mechanical to electrical energy.

COMMAG (Common Magnetic): refers to a married motion-picture release print having magnetic sound on the print, as opposed to *SEPMAG*, in which the sound is on a separate piece of film.

COMOPT (Common Optical): a married motion-picture release print incorporating an optical sound track. Because the optical sound track may be of a number of forms, including *Academy mono*, stereo variable area, and digital, additional information is required.

Compact Cassette: one specific *audio cassette* that is one of the most widely used and familiar audio media in the world. It uses a standardized outer cassette shell for protection of the tape and generally standardized recorded characteristics, such as speed, track format, *equalization*, and noise-reducing companding (see *Dolby*) for good interchangeability.

The majority of the higher fidelity prerecorded tapes are made at 1$\frac{7}{8}$ in./sec in two-channel stereo with the choice of one of two equalization time constants (120 and 70 μsec; see *equalization*) and with *Dolby B* noise reduction.

Tape used in the compact cassette shell has been categorized by the standards organization IEC into four types, designated Types I, II, III, and IV. Type I is usually used with 120 µs time constant *equalization* and its most salient feature is economy. Type II are the "high-bias" type tapes, such as those using chromium dioxide particles and others compatible with this increased level of *bias*, generally using 70 µs time-constant equalization. Type III is an obsolete designation. Type IV uses metal particles, offering potentially higher performance, along with the highest bias level requirement and cost, using 70 µs time-constant equalization. The most important user advice is to use tape for which the particular machine is intended because the amount of *bias* and record equalization are best optimized with tapes for which the machine has been set up.

Compact disk audio (*Compact Disc*, Philips): the popular standardized audio disk format using optical recording to encode two channels of 16-bit linear pulse code modulated audio information of up to approximately 72 minutes in length.

Companding: a system of compressing a signal before recording and expanding it on playback in a precise complementary way. The object is to restore the signal exactly, but any noise that intervenes between encoding and decoding will be subject only to decoding—the tape noise will only be expanded downward and thus be reduced.

Compression driver: an electro-acoustic transducer designed to be coupled to the throat of a *horn*. The operating principle of most compression drivers is similar to a conventional loudspeaker, with a coil of wire, called the "voice coil," suspended in a strong magnetic field and supplied with audio current from a power amplifier, often by way of a crossover network. Application of electrical current to the voice coil produces corresponding motion. The voice coil is attached to a suspension to keep it mechanically centered in the magnetic field, and to a diaphragm, which moves air in and out of the throat. Due to the differing path lengths from the outer diameter compared with the center of the diaphragm down the throat, which would cause high-frequency cancellation as the sound waves from different parts of the diaphragm arrived at the throat at slightly different times, it is customary to insert a "phasing plug" into the throat, with multiple paths machined through the plug designed to time the sound waves so that they arrive at the throat simultaneously.

Compressor: a special kind of audio amplifier arranged so that equal level changes in the input result in smaller level changes at the output, often used to help fit a wide *dynamic range* program into a narrower dynamic range channel.

Condenser microphone: synonym for *electrostatic microphone*.

Console: a piece of audio equipment designed to amplify, combine, and otherwise process multiple inputs. See *Audio mixer*.

Contact microphone: a specialized microphone designed to pick up vibration directly from a solid body. Contact microphones have been used to record items as diverse as a violin and a bridge structure stimulated by traffic.

Container: a specialized *limiter* designed for use in preparing master recordings used especially for transfer to analog optical sound tracks, respecting the headroom limitations of the variable area sound track versus frequency.

Crosstalk: undesired audio signals coming from adjacent sources or tracks is known as crosstalk. The sources of crosstalk include inductive and capacitive coupling among, for example, the various channels of a tape head.

Crystal sync: the term used generally to describe a method for synchronizing tape recordings with film cameras. A separate recording derived from an accurate quartz-crystal-based oscillator is made as a reference on conventional nonperforated tape simultaneous with audio recording. Crystal sync relies on accurate motor speed control of the camera and an accurate frequency of the reference oscillator in the recorder.

Cue tone: any system in which a tone is used to cause an action. An example is a slide-change system based on tones on one track of a tape recorder, while other tracks may contain program material intended to be heard.

Cue track: the track of a multitrack recorder assigned to cue tones, or a track with incidental information, such as editing information.

DC (direct current): The power derived from a battery or a specialized generator, as opposed to *ac*. dc refers to power delivered at 0 Hz.

DM&E (Dialog, Music, and Effects): master that is intended to be used with the three stated elements summed together in the proportions 1:1:1 but kept separate in case the primary language or balance must be changed. Useful only for monaural work because each source track is only mono, but the idea may be extended to stereo through the use of multiple channels for each of the elements.

DDL: abbreviation for *digital delay line*.

deciBel (dB): literally, one tenth of a Bel. The use of the term deciBel means that logarithmic scaling of the amplitude of a quantity divided by a reference amplitude has been used. Such scaling is useful because the range of amplitudes encountered in sound is extremely large and because hearing generally judges the relative loudness of two sounds by the ratio of their intensities, which is logarithmic behavior. Differing factors are used when applying deciBels to various quantities so that the number of deciBels remains constant: A 3 dB increase is always 3 dB, although is represents twice as much power but only 1.414 times as much voltage.

For reference, 3 dB is twice as much power, 6 dB is twice as much voltage, and 10 dB is twice as loud. Thus, approximately nine times the sound power is required to make a sound twice as loud. Because the use of the term dB implies a ratio, the reference quantity must be stated. Some typical reference frequencies are as follows:

dB SPL	Referred to threshold of hearing at 1kHz
dBm	Reference 1 milliwatt, usually in 600 ohms
dBV	Reference 1 volt
dBu	Reference 0.7746 volts
dBFS	Reference Full Scale

Degauss: to demagnetize. When done deliberately in a degausser, this means first applying a strong ac magnetic field that can continuously reverse the state of all magnetic domains in the object being demagnetized, and then decreasing the field strength in an orderly way to zero. This process leaves the state of the various magnetic domains utterly random, and thus demagnetized.

De-emphasis: rolloff of a frequency range of an audio signal, usually corresponding to a pre-emphasis applied earlier in the audio chain. The object of the pre-emphasis/de-emphasis loop is generally to trade off *headroom* against *signal-to-noise ratio*, both versus *frequency*. That is, a strong high-frequency boost applied to audio before transmission of FM radio signals is counteracted by a equal and opposite high-frequency rolloff in reception, with the advantage of reduced high-frequency noise but the disadvantage of equally reduced high-frequency headroom.

Desk (British usage): synonym for *console*.

Diffraction: the property of sound that permits it to be heard around corners; sound encountering an edge will reradiate into the space beyond the edge.

Diffusion: the property of acoustical barriers to provide usually desirable scattering in reflected sound. An example of a lack of diffusion is the flutter echoes arising between two flat, parallel, hard walls. Good diffusion promotes smooth-sounding reverberation, without discrete audible events such as echoes.

Digital: a signal that has been converted to numerical representation by means of *quantizing* the amplitude domain of the signal (putting amplitudes into bins, each bin denoted by a number). This means that for each amplitude a number is derived for storage or transmission. This process must be done frequently enough to adequately capture the signal through *sampling*. The advantage of digital is that to the extent that the numbers are incorruptible by means of error-protecting coding, the signal will be recovered within the limits of the original quantizing process, despite the number of generations or transmission paths encountered by the signal.

Digital audio: the use of *digital* techniques to record, store, and transmit audio. Audio, once digitized, may also be processed in a huge variety of ways in the digital domain, some of which are impossible or impractical to do in the analog domain. Digital reverberators, for example, which construct models of acoustic spaces mathematically through a variety of tactics, may produce a very convincing sonic illusion of space.

Digital delay line: a method of producing a time delay of an audio or video signal, by analog-to-digital conversion at the input of the device, delaying by means of digital memory, and subsequent conversion from digital-to-analog representation at the output. Delay lines have many uses in both audio and video signal processing. In audio, the output of the delay is added together with the original signal to produce a range of effects from "thickening" a voice to discrete echoes. In video, one-line delay lines are used for many purposes, including color decoding of composite video signals.

Digital recording: any method of recording, be it on tape, disk, or film, that uses digital *sampling* and *quantization*.

DIN: the German standards organization.

Dip filter: an electrical circuit having one, usually tunable, frequency that is suppressed, while passing audio at both lower and higher frequencies. A dip filter is most useful for removing tonal noise from recordings, such as hum or certain whistles.

Direct sound: that sound that arrives by way of the shortest path from source to receiver within line of sight.

Directional microphone: a microphone exhibiting any *microphone polar pattern* other than omnidirectional.

Directivity: the factor describing a preference for one direction of sound propagation over another; a highly directional sound source is said to have high directivity or high Q.

Distortion: any undesired alteration of the signal that is related to the signal (this definition excludes noise). Distortion is separable into two types, linear and nonlinear. Linear distortions include *frequency response* and phase errors, and are characterized by reversibility by equal and opposite signal processing. Nonlinear distortions involve the generation of new frequency components not present in the original and are thus not generally reversible.

The simplest nonlinear distortion is harmonic distortion. With harmonic distortion, a sine wave, passed through a distorting device, appears at the output with added frequency components at harmonic intervals above, and potentially below, the original input frequency. Thus, if a 1-kHz sine-wave input suffers harmonic distortion, there will be an output of at least one of the following: 2 kHz, 3 kHz, 4 kHz, etc. Total harmonic distortion is often used in the measurement of audio equipment and is the root mean square sum[2] of the amplitude of all of the harmonics in the output of a device, often expressed as a percentage of the amplitude of the sine wave that appears at the output.

All other distortions are called "intermodulation distortions" because they involve the input of more than one sine wave (or, sometimes square waves combined with sine waves) into a device under test, and the examination of the output for the amplitude of energy at new frequencies not present in the input. One type is called "SMPTE intermodulation distortion" and involves the combination of a low-frequency sine wave such as 60 Hz, and a high-frequency sine wave, such as 8 kHz. The output is examined for the level of distortion components at $f_2 + f_1$ and $f_2 - f_1$, which is basically a measure of how much amplitude or frequency modulation the high-frequency tone undergoes during a cycle of the low-frequency tone. Another intermodulation distortion test involves using two high-frequency sine waves and examining the output for the distortion product at the frequency $f_2 - f_1$. This is called "difference-tone intermodulation distortion."

Dolby: a set of technologies introduced by Dolby Laboratories with applications in professional and consumer audio. Professional companding noise-reduction and general signal-improvement systems, the company's first activity, are Dolby A and Dolby Spectral Recording (SR), which both are characterized by use of multifrequency bands and by relatively complex processing of the signal to achieve the noise-reduction goals with minimum audible side effects. Dolby A was introduced in 1969 and was used for improving analog tape recording and optical sound track recording. Dolby SR, with a more sophisticated

approach using both fixed and sliding frequency bands, was introduced in 1989 and is widely used on analog multitrack tape machines, on magnetic film recordings in post production, and on optical track release prints.

Consumer noise-reduction systems have progressed from Dolby B through Dolby C to Dolby S over the years. Applied generally to *compact cassette* recordings, these noise-reduction systems helped to make the cassette medium into a very widely used vehicle for music. Most prerecorded software is made using Dolby B noise reduction, wherein a single high-frequency sliding band compander is used to produce about 10 dB of audible noise reduction. Dolby C and S are more sophisticated systems used less widely. With their greater noise reduction than Dolby B, they offer a very wide dynamic range medium at low cost. This has attracted documentary filmmakers, some of whom use the Sony Pro Walkman with a special modification using one of the normal audio channels to carry a *crystal sync* signal. While this gives up one audio channel for sync, the system consisting of the Pro Walkman with Dolby C noise reduction and Type IV metal tape makes an inexpensive system capable of producing a wide dynamic range and high-enough quality for many practical professional purposes.

For motion-picture-based program material, the use of the Dolby 4:2:4 amplitude-and-phase coding matrix has made practical widespread use of four-channel stereo, with left, center, and right screen channels, and a surround channel. In this system, four channels of information are encoded into the two available tracks on the medium, such as the two tracks of an analog optical sound track, or the two tracks on a "hi-fi" VCR. Suitable decoders in the theater or home can then decode the signal into four channels for application to appropriate loudspeakers. This process uses the trade name on the film program material of Dolby Stereo or Dolby's double-D logo, and is decoded with either Dolby Surround or Dolby Pro Logic decoders, the Pro Logic version being the more sophisticated.

Dolby is also active in the area of low-bit-rate *digital audio* coders, with increasingly sophisticated systems and greater bit-rate-reduction from Dolby AC-1, AC-2, and AC-3. AC-1 is used for digital audio radio services, with very low decoder cost and moderate bit-rate reduction. AC-2 is based on Fourier transform coding using a multiband filter bank, and is used in more recently introduced broadcast and computer disk-based systems, with excellent quality at one-half the bit rate of AC-1. AC-3 produces another doubling of bit-rate efficiency in the context of 5.1-channel audio for use on digital optical sound on film and in video applications. All of these systems

---

2. The square root of the sum of the squares.

have discrete audio channels and are an improvement on matrixed analog sound.

When recorded on release prints as SR-D, AC-3 code is used at 320 kbits/sec for 5.1 channels, recorded as blocks of data in the area between the perforations on the sound-track side of the print. This area is not used by any other process, so permits recording along with an analog track, and either one or both of the other digital sound for film formats, DTS and SDDS.

The use of the term *Dolby* may be confusing in some contexts, because more than one of the systems described earlier may be used together for one application. For conventional Dolby Stereo analog optical sound on film for example, Dolby A or SR type noise reduction is used, and the 4:2:4 matrix is also used.

Doppler effect: the effect on frequency caused by the source or the receiver of sound moving, similar to the pitch drop of a train whistle as it passes an observer. The Doppler effect is put to good advantage during post production of motion pictures by using a digital pitch shifter to simulate objects in motion.

Double perf: abbreviation for double perforation, used to describe 16mm film perforated along both edges.

Double system: a system wherein the picture and sound elements are on separate strands of film or tape, designed to be synchronized during reproduction by mechanical or electronic means. The separate pieces of film to be synchronized must be unambiguously marked with edit sync marks so that they may be threaded up in sync. Usually double system is used until nearly the end of post production, when married answer prints become available, with sound and picture on one piece of film.

Dropout: a momentary loss of signal, usually applied to audio or video signals recovered from a medium or transmission path. The signal loss may not be complete but may result only in a change in level.

Drum (aka impedance drum, inertial roller): a cylindrical rotating element in the path of a film or tape transport having substantial mass. The tape or film wraps around the element, whose inertia helps to reduce speed variations and thus to improve *wow and flutter* performance. In the Davis loop drive design used on many film sound transports, the tape path through the head assembly is immediately preceded and followed by such drums.

DTS (Digital Theater Systems): method of recording sound on a CD-ROM format disk and following a custom time-code track on release prints, placed between the analog sound-track area and the picture. This space is used for no other purpose, so prints may contain an analog track, and either one or both

of the other two competing digital sound for film formats Dolby SR-D and SDDS.

Dub: see *Dubbing*.

Dubber: a playback-equipped only motion-picture film transport designed to play various sound-track formats as required.

Dubbing: 1. The process of re-recording sound tracks. This occurs when the *elements* or *units* cut by sound editors are dubbed into *premixes*. Subsequently, a final mix is prepared by dubbing the various premixes to make the final mix *stems*. Then the stems are used in preparation of the various *print masters* needed for all the release media.

Dubbing uses a wide variety of processes, including equalization, filtering, dynamic range control such as expansion and limiting, noise-reduction devices such as the *Cat. 43*, reverberation, pitch shifting, panning, and many others to produce a desired mix from the individual elements. Subsequent processing includes limiting to the capabilities and desires of various media: A digital theatrical release both has greater dynamic range capability and a larger desired range than, say, a mix for broadcast television.

2. Any copying operation, particularly applied to videotape.

Dubbing mixer (British usage): synonym for re-recording mixer.

Dummy: synonym for *dubber*.

Dynamic microphone: a transducer that changes acoustical energy into electrical energy by the motion of a conductor in the field of a magnet. A typical construction involves a diaphragm exposed to a sound field and allowed to move. Attached to the diaphragm is a voice coil, which in turn is suspended in the field of a magnet. Motion of the diaphragm moves the voice coil in and out of the field, thus cutting the lines of magnetic force with a conductor. Dynamic microphones have a reputation for high reliability and ruggedness, and may be built using most of the common *microphone polar patterns*. A special case of the dynamic microphone is the *ribbon microphone*, using the same principle for electroacoustical conversion, but with a different construction.

Dynamic range: the range stated in deciBels from the background noise level to the overload level of a medium. Dynamic range may be stated in terms of audio-band-wide noise to midrange overload, or in a variety of other manners. A complete description would include a graph of the headroom and of the noise versus frequency.

Early reflections: sound arriving at a receiver by way of one, two, or a few reflections off the environment.

Distinguished from reverberation because the individual reflections can still be discriminated, at least by instruments. What is generally considered the psychoacoustically useful part of early reflections for live sound events usually lie between 0 and 50 ~ 80 msec of the direct sound, while later arriving discrete reflections may be heard as echoes. On the other hand, for reproduction systems, early reflections can alter timbre, location, and spaciousness of a sound event, and may be regarded in this role as detrimental to reproduction of a sound track.

EBU: European Broadcasting Union, a standards-making body of European broadcasters.

Echo: a discrete repetition of a source signal, distinguished by its separation from reverberation by its greater level. To be defined as an echo, the repetition must be late enough (>50 to 80 msec) to not be integrated into the source sound by the ear and high enough in level to be distinct from reverberation. A special case of echo is the "flutter echo," occurring when two parallel surfaces reflect acoustical energy back and forth between them. The result is a characteristic patterned reflection.

Echo unit: an older term generally used to describe what is thought of today as a reverberator. *Echo* means specifically what is heard as a discrete repetition of a sound, and that is not generally what is meant when the term echo unit is used. On the other hand, a *digital delay line* can be used to produce a discrete echo.

Eigentones: synonym for *room modes*.

Eight track: see *Track formats for tape recording*.

Electret microphone: an *electrostatic microphone* type in which the insulator is made of a plastic material that can be permanently charged electrostatically so that the microphone needs no externally applied polarization voltage. Electret microphones are often less expensive than air-condenser microphones due to their greater simplicity.

Electro-acoustic response: the *frequency response* of a complete sound system, including loudspeakers and the effects of room acoustics measured with microphones. The electro-acoustic response is usually measured with either a *real-time analyzer* or a time-domain-based analyzer, such as time-domain spectrometry, maximum-length sequence, or fast fourier transform analyzers. For use during original design, the utility of the time-domain-based analyzers cannot be denied, but in day-to-day use as an alignment tool for sound systems, the use of the RTA predominates. The electro-acoustic response for both kinds of analyzers is made much more reliable and repeatable by spatial averaging, and the output of an RTA is made more repeatable when used with computed temporal averaging.

Electrostatic microphone: a transducer capable of changing acoustic energy to electrical energy by means of measurement of the small changes in electrical capacitance that result as one or more diaphragms move with respect to a fixed back plate. Both the diaphragm(s) and the back plate are made electrically conductive and are separated by air. In one type, the capacitance is measured by applying a bias voltage, usually between 48 and 200 Vdc, between the diaphragm(s) and back plate, and measuring the ac voltage resulting from motion between the elements. Alternately, in the rf (radio frequency) electrostatic microphone (not to be confused with the radio microphone, which radiates the output of a microphone on radio waves for pickup at a distance), the varying capacitance is used to frequency modulate a radio-frequency oscillator, and a frequency-modulation detector is used to demodulate the audio, all within the microphone body. Due to its lack of a bias voltage, the rf radio microphone is claimed to have high reliability in the field. In a third type, called electret microphones, the back plate is permanently polarized with an electrical charge during manufacture, and electronics convert the changing capacitance with diaphragm motion into a voltage. Electrostatic microphones may be built having many different polar patterns: omnidirectional, bidirectional, cardioid, hypercardioid, and superdirectional microphone configurations are all possible. See *Microphone polar pattern*.

Element(s): a single strand of film cut by a sound editor to synchronize with the picture for use in *rerecording*. The original elements are broken down by discipline into dialog, music, and sound effects. Within each category there is further breakdown, particularly with sound effects, into, for example, *ambience, Foley,* and principal effects. The breakdown is done so that the process of premixing the elements can be accomplished readily. Many elements contain a large amount of fill leader used as spacing between sounds just to maintain synchronization with the picture.

Envelop: to surround or immerse oneself in a sound field, as in, "the surround sound of the jungle in the tiger scene in *Apocalypse Now* envelops the listener."

Erase head: a tape head, addressing one or more tracks at a time, that subjects the magnetic domains on the tape to a strong magnetic field adequate to saturate them. As the oxide moves away from the gap in the direction of travel, the gradually diminishing field leaves the oxide with no net magnetization, and thus no signal. The source of high-frequency ac current for the erase head is usually the *bias* oscillator.

Equal-loudness contours: a set of curves plotting amplitude versus frequency characterizing the sensitivity of human listeners across the audible frequency range at various levels. The lowest curve is the minimum audible sound field versus frequency, and it shows that human hearing is most sensitive to midrange frequencies centered around 2–4 kHz, with less sensitivity at lower and higher frequencies. The curves also show that at no sound-pressure level does human hearing have a flat *frequency response*. While the best known of these curves are named after the original researchers who found the effect, Fletcher-Munson, more recent work is more widely accepted and has been standardized as an ISO standard.

Equalizer: a device to produce *equalization*. The device may produce fixed equalization, as in compensating for deliberate response variations (such as RIAA equalization used on phonograph records) or it may be adjustable. Among adjustable types, some are designed as *program equalizers* for users to adjust by listening, and others are designed to be set using the results of instrumented measurements, such as *one-third-octave equalization.*

Equalization: generally, equalization means to adjust the *frequency response* of audio by means of either fixed or adjustable devices. 1. Fixed equalization consisting of standardized frequency response alterations (bass boost or cut; treble boost or cut) is usually used to correct an audio system for overall flat response from input to output, where it may be impractical or undesirable to have flat response on the medium itself. Examples include phonograph records, all analog tape and film audio formats, and the compact disc when using the optional "emphasis." Equalization may be applied both before and after a medium: In the first case it is called "record equalization" or *pre-emphasis*, and in the second "playback equalization" or *de-emphasis*. The purpose of the process is to tailor the capabilities of the medium to the needs of the signal. Thus, for example, if there is little energy in expected signals at high frequencies, it is useful to boost highs on record and to cut them correspondingly in playback. The result is a reduction in noise of the medium because it only encounters the playback cut. The downside of the process occurs if an occasional signal violates the assumptions under which the equalization was developed: If strong high-frequencies should occur along with treble-boosted pre-emphasis, then distortion would result.

2. "Program equalization" is any deliberate frequency response alteration, such as the use of tone controls or equalizers to improve sound.

European Broadcasting Union: a standards-making body of European broadcasters, concerned especially with the interchange of audio and video programs.

Exciter lamp: the light bulb, which, together with optics, provides the illumination for playing optical sound tracks.

Expansion: the opposite of compression; any device or process that increases the volume range of source material. An "expander" is an amplifier whose gain is deliberately controlled by the signal, effectively turning the volume down in low-level passages, and turning up the volume in high-level passages. A special case of the expander is a downward expander that expands the signal only below a threshold, usually adjustable. The purpose of a downward expander is to reduce noise by adjusting the threshold level to be set between the level of the desired program material and the level of the noise. Then only passages in which the only content is the noise will be subject to downward expansion and a useful noise reduction occurs.

Fader: a level control, also known as a "pot" (for potentiometer), a gain control, or a volume control.

Feedback, acoustic (aka howl round): the familiar sound system squeal occurring when an open microphone output is amplified and applied to a loudspeaker with sufficient gain. It seems to always precede a line from a character who is speaking through a sound reinforcement system in movies—one of the silliest movie clichés.

Filtering: removing a part of the frequency spectrum, usually performed to reduce the effect of undesired sound lying within the rejected frequency range in favor of the desired sound lying within the passband of the filter. Categorized by high-pass, low-pass, bandpass, bandstop, or notch filters, depending on shape and what range is rejected. Note that a *high-pass filter* is one that "passes" highs; it rejects lows. The term "high filter" usually means, in contrast, that it is the highs that are being filtered, so a "high filter" is really a low-pass filter.

Final: see *Final mix.*

Final mix: the outcome of mixing together the various component parts of a sound mix. In a preceding stage, individual sound *elements*, cut by sound editors, were re-recorded to form *premixes*, such as dialog, music, ambience effects, Foley effects, and principal on-screen sound effects. In final mixing, these are combined to produce the final mix *stems*, which are the number of tracks and strands of film or tape needed to completely represent the mix, while still keeping various kinds of sound separate so that they can be replaced for specific purposes, such as for foreign language mixes.

The final mix stems usually remain broken down into at least separate dialogue and combined music and effects component parts. In addition, stereo mixing calls for separate tracks for at least left, center, right, and surround, with two separate surrounds left and right and an extra low-frequency only enhancement channel gaining acceptance. Stereophonically related program material must lie on one piece of film because otherwise the small time variations on different pieces of analog film would cause potential cancellations.

The final mix thus represents everything that is intended to be heard, mixed in proper proportion, but separated enough so that it is easy to prepare alternative versions. The final mix stems are mixed once again to the various *print masters* to represent the sound just as it will appear on the final motion-picture prints or video releases.

Fisher boom™: a brand-name microphone *boom*.

Fishpole: a lightweight, hand-held microphone pole widely used to get a microphone close to actors but out of the shot being filmed.

Fletcher-Munson curves: the first measured *equal-loudness contours*, now considered obsolete, replaced by international standards.

Flutter: see *Wow and flutter.*

Fluxivity: the strength of a magnetic field stored on a tape or film usually given in units nanoWebers/meter (nW/m). Reference fluxivity is the level recorded on a *calibration tape* used in aligning tape and film recorders.

FM sync: a synchronization method used with stereo ¼-in. tape recording; see *Crystal sync*. A narrow track is added between the two audio tracks carrying the sync-tone frequency modulated on a 13.5-kHz carrier. The use of the high-frequency carrier to carry the tone is helpful in preventing crosstalk from the sync signal into the audio tracks.

Foley: a kind of sound effect that is made in a sound studio while watching a picture. The most well-known Foley effect is footsteps, but many other sounds are also recorded in this manner. The use of Foley effects started with the need for such kinds of sounds in pictures that were dubbed into foreign languages and lacked any of the other sound picked up on the set during *production sound recording*. The need grew as the field became more specialized and production sound mixers concentrated more on recording dialog; in these cases, it has been found expeditious to add many low-level kinds of sounds with the Foley process in order to make the sound seem more real.

Free-field microphone: a measurement microphone calibrated for use with sound fields in which one principal direction of the field is predominant, such as in an anechoic chamber. Usually such microphones are used with the diaphragm perpendicular to the incident sound field.

Frequency: for a sinusoidal wave, the number of occurrences of one complete wave per second. The unit for frequency is Hertz (Hz), equal to one cycle per second. For a complex wave consisting of many sinusoids, typically the lowest occurring is the fundamental frequency, which, along with its harmonic overtones (also called "partials," such as 2nd, 3rd, 4th. . .), together form the waveform.

Frequency is related to wavelength and the speed of sound through the mathematical relation:

$$f = \frac{c}{\lambda}$$

where *f* is the frequency in Hertz, *c* is the speed of sound in the medium, and λ is the wavelength in the medium.

Frequency masking: see *Masking, frequency*

Frequency response: the amplitude output with respect to frequency characteristic of a system under test. One method of measurement is to drive the system with a sine wave that sweeps from one end of the desired frequency range to the other while measuring the amplitude of the output. The resulting curve of amplitude versus frequency, usually plotted in deciBels of amplitude versus logarithmic frequency, is a "frequency-response curve."

Full coat: 35mm perforated film coated with magnetic oxide across at least the full area between the perforations. It may be recorded in track formats accommodating three, four, or six tracks. (Nothing prevents recording just one track, but these recordings are generally made on *stripe coat* film.)

Futz: to deliberately distort for a desired effect.

Galvanometer recording: one of the methods of producing a variable-area optical image to represent sound. The galvanometer is a voltage-sensitive coil of wire placed in a magnetic field and connected to a mirror. Current through the coil moves the coil and, thus, the mirror, which, with a light source and appropriate lenses and masks, produces the varying area needed to expose the sound negative.

Graphic equalizer: an audio *equalizer* having a multiplicity of controls arranged so that in use they draw out a visual representation of the *frequency-response* curve that they produce.

Harmonic distortion: when a pure sine wave is applied to a system, the output of the system may contain the original sine wave accompanied by sine waves at harmonic frequencies of $2 \times f$, $3 \times f$, etc. Harmonic distortion is caused by a lack of perfect replication of the original sine wave.

Head alignment: a term applied to film and tape recording of analog or digital, and to audio, video, or other signals meaning the correct positioning of the head with respect to the tape or film. Important considerations include the need for continuous intimate contact between the tape or film and the head, or else severe spacing loss will occur. Head alignment terms include *azimuth, footprint, gap, height, rotation*, and *zenith*.

Azimuth: the angle formed between the reference edge of the film or tape and the recording. It is 90° in analog audio recording, but other angles are used for other purposes, particularly on helical-scan analog and digital videotape, to permit closer spacing of the tracks.

Footprint: the area of the tape or film that is in contact with the head. It is typical to check that the footprint produces an area that is centered on the gap.

Gap: a mechanical straight-edged line in a magnetic head structure in which two parts (usually halves) are joined to deliver or receive magnetic fields from the tape or film.

Height: refers to the position of the head gap or recorded area relative to the reference edge of the film or tape.

Rotation: a head adjustment provided in some head-mounting arrangements that permits centering the footprint of film or tape contact on the magnetic gap.

Zenith: a head adjustment provided in some head-mounting arrangements that ensures uniform contact across the width of the head gap; perpendicular to the azimuth.

Headphones: small electroacoustic transducers meant to be worn by individual users and classified according to whether they are worn with contact around the outer ear, sit on the outer ear, or are inserted in the ear canal.

Headroom: the amount of signal-handling capacity above a reference level before reaching a specified distortion. For example, "the headroom of magnetic film at 90 feet per minute is +17 dB for 3% total harmonic distortion above a reference level of 185 nW/m."

Headset: see *Headphones*.

Hertz: the unit of frequency in cycles per second. kHz is thousands of Hz, MHz is millions of Hz.

Hi-fi tracks: audio recording recorded to and replayed from the tape by heads on the video-scanning drum of VHS, S-VHS, Betacam, and other video recorders. Kept separate from the video by the use of a different carrier frequency (rather like tuning into a different station on a radio), a differing azimuth (see *Head alignment*) from the video, and other tricks. Better quality than longitudinal recording because the relative tape to head speed is much higher (the heads are rotating). Uses a specialized companding noise-reduction system that can sometimes be tricked by video, with the result of hearing a video-based buzz coming and going with the audio.

High filter: a source of unending confusion, this is a term used in consumer audio for a filter that rolls off high frequencies. The corresponding professional term is "low-pass filter" because the standard used by engineers is to define what is passed rather than what is rejected in the name of the filter.

High-pass filter: an electrical filter that passes frequencies above a specified and usually adjustable one while rejecting frequencies below the cutoff frequency. High-pass filters are most often used to reduce the effects of background noise, which often has predominant low-frequency content, while minimally disturbing the desired signal, such as voice. For example, a high-pass filter set to 80 Hz, with a steep rolloff below cutoff, can be very useful in reducing the impact of traffic noise, while minimally affecting a voice recording. In consumer and semiprofessional applications, this may be called a "low filter."

Horn: an acoustical amplifying device known since antiquity (the megaphone is an example, or even cupping one's hands to shout) whose principal purpose is to provide better coupling between an acoustical source and air. The basic configuration of a horn is to control the expansion of sound waves from a small source at the throat of the horn to a larger end radiating to the air, called the "mouth." Horns come in many different shapes as progress over half a century has dictated ever higher levels of performance, particularly with respect to uniformity of output coverage over differing output angles. Early exponential horns, while still in use, were known by the 1930s to be not very uniform with frequency, collapsing their output to smaller angles while moving upwards in frequency. The 1940s brought "multicell horns," with dividers placed in the mouth of the horn to better "steer" high frequencies across the desired output angles. These horns, while an improvement over the simplest ones, suffered from non-uniform coverage because different sources from the different cells interfered with one another at high frequencies. The most recent development of horns is the constant directivity type, which is non-traditional in shape, but better performing than earlier types for most purposes. The drivers coupled to the throat of a horn are called *compression drivers*.

Howl round: synonym for acoustic feedback, see *Feedback, acoustic*.

Hz: abbreviation for Hertz.

IEEE: see *Institute of Electrical and Electronic Engineers.*

Infrasonic frequency range: The region below the audible frequency range, from extremely low frequencies associated with slow changes in air pressure up to 20 Hz. Very high levels of infrasonic acoustic energy, especially around 12 Hz, can lead to discomfort and nausea.

Institute of Electrical and Electronic Engineers: a U.S. association of engineers.

Intensity: Among acousticians, used precisely—the complex characteristics of sound propagation, quantifying both amplitude and direction of sound. Slang—used interchangeably with amplitude, but applied usually to sound pressure. Street slang—loudness.

International Electrotechnical Commission (IEC): an international standards-making body located in Geneva, Switzerland with activity in audio, electroacoustics, video, television, and photography, among others. It is probably best known to the lay public as the organization that standardized the categorization of Compact Cassette™ tape types in four types, numbered I, II, III, and IV (See *Compact cassette*), and film speeds. Its standards are generally available within each country from the local standards-making body, such as ANSI in the U.S. and B.S. in England.

International Standards Organization (ISO): an international standards-making body located in Geneva, Switzerland with activity in acoustics and cinematography, among others. It is probably best known in audio as the organization that standardized the electro-acoustic response curve of motion-picture theaters (the X-curve). Its standards are generally available within each country from the local standards-making body, such as ANSI in the U.S. and B.S. in England.

Intermodulation distortion: see *Distortion.*

Inverse square law: the property of sound waves to spread out from a point source as a function of distance leads to a decreasing intensity of sound with distance. The "law," or rule that the fall-off follows is a "square-law," that is, for twice the distance the amplitude is reduced by four times.

Iron oxide: one of several possible active ingredients in a magnetic coating for audiotape and videotape or film.

kHz (kiloHertz): see *Hertz.*

Layback: the process of copying audio from a sound-only master "back" to a video master tape. The processes of *laydown* and layback together permit sound post production to be done on media especially well suited for audio.

Laydown: the process of copying audio from the sound tracks of an original videotape onto the post production audio recording medium.

Layover: any audio copying stage in post production, especially in television post production.

Limiter: an electronic device that acts to keep the amplitude of signals from exceeding a usually adjustable maximum amount. The limiter "turns down" the signal by the amount by which it exceeds the maximum as required so that the output contains no higher level than the maximum.

Limiting: the process of applying a *limiter.*

Logarithmic: scaled along an axis where equal intervals are related by powers of 10: 1, 10, 100, 1,000, 10,000, 100,000, etc. lie equally spaced.

Logs (production sound): see *Production sound logs.*

Longitudinal: 1. Generally, any recording that occurs along the length of a piece of tape, used with video recording to describe recordings made with other than the rotating head assembly.

2. An audio recording made along the edge of a piece of videotape by conventional direct analog magnetic recording methods. Limited in quality by the nature of the tape (optimized for video recording) and by the low tape speed.

Loudness: subjective strength of a sound field, a complex function of sound pressure level, spectrum, duration, and other factors.

Loudspeaker: an electro-acoustic transducer that takes an electrical input and converts it to sound meant to be heard by a number of people.

Low filter: see *High-pass filter.*

Low-pass filter: an electrical filter that passes signals at frequencies below a cutoff frequency while attenuating frequencies above cutoff. The term is used by electrical engineers and by professional audio personnel, but note that the term used for the same thing in the consumer marketplace is *high filter.*

Lt Rt (literally, Left Total Right Total): two-track recording format that embeds information content from four channels—left, center, right, and surround—through the use of an amplitude-phase matrix. Also used to describe a *print master* recorded in this format.

Magnetic: pertaining to the property of certain materials observed in antiquity to attract one another and one of the fundamental forces of nature. Magnetism may occur naturally or may be induced by means of electromagnetism arising from, say, a coil of wire energized from an electrical source.

Magnetic film: a magnetic recording medium consisting of a base film coated with an *oxide* and *binder* and optionally coated on the opposite side with a conductive backing. The base is perforated according to the standard in use and made of tricellulose *acetate* or *polyester*, in the range of 0.003 to 0.0055 in. thick. The oxide is magnetically "hard" material, designed to be magnetized under certain conditions and then to hold the magnetic field for a very long time. Common types include *full coat* and *stripe coat* in 35mm, and 16mm *single perf.* and *double perf.*

Magnetic head: an electromagnetic device designed to erase, record, or reproduce magnetic film or tape. It is made of magnetically "soft" core material on which is wound a coil or wire. (Magnetically soft material inherently does not retain a magnetic field. One of the largest difficulties in head design is finding magnetically soft materials that are also mechanically hard for long wear.) The core is gapped so that magnetic flux may leak out in the case of erasure and recording, and be received by the core material in the case of playback. A current through the coil of wire sets up a magnetic field in the core, which then leaks out to the tape or film by way of the gap in order to record; for reproduction the process is reversed.

Magnetic sound recording: recording of signals on magnetic tape or film by means of *magnetic heads*.

Magnetic stripe: a magnetic oxide coating in a stripe along the length of a piece of film. The film may contain a picture in the case of magnetic release prints, in the 70mm, 35mm, and 16mm film gauges. Super 8 also used a magnetic stripe for audio recording, generally after processing.

Magnetic tape: a strand of material intended for magnetic recording that contains two essential ingredients, a base and a magnetically responsive coating. Tape is distinguished from film by the lack of perforations on tape. The base consists of *polyester* or *acetate* (historically), usually between 0.0005 and 0.0015 in. thick. The coating consists of a magnetic *oxide*, along with a *binder*, lubricants, and antistatic agents. Optionally, the tape may be back coated with an antistatic backing intended to also improve winding characteristics. Note that with backcoated tapes, the oxide side may not be immediately obvious because both sides are coated.

Magoptical: refers to motion-picture prints containing both a magnetic sound track and an optical sound track. Magoptical printing was used historically for some 35mm prints and some 16mm prints.

Married print: any motion-picture print that contains an integral sound track.

Masking, frequency: the property of hearing that makes one frequency cause another to be inaudible to human listeners. Masking is more effective close to the masker tone or noise than further away in frequency, is more effective towards high frequencies than low frequencies, and is more effective at higher levels than at lower ones.

Masking, temporal: the property of hearing that causes one sound to audibly suppress another, despite their not being precisely simultaneous in time. Divided into premasking, in which the sound covered up occurs very slightly before the masking sound; and postmasking, in which the sound covered up occurs after the masking sound. A use by filmmakers of premasking is in close cutting of dialogue. An editor will cut a plosive "p" with a butt splice to make it produce premasking, which will tend to hide the edit.

Microphone: an electro-acoustic transducer responsive to sound pressure, velocity, or intensity, producing an electrical output.

> **Microphone polar patterns:** the directional character of a microphone traced out by varying the angle between a free sound field and the microphone body.
>
> **Bidirectional microphone:** a microphone directivity pattern that responds to sound energy from two sides, in a figure-eight-shaped pattern. Bidirectional microphones are most likely to be ribbon or condenser types.
>
> **Cardioid microphone:** a microphone directivity pattern that responds to sound energy in a generally heart-shaped pattern, with a null point located to the back of the microphone. Useful because by aiming the microphone at a source, the relative pickup of the source compared with noise and reverberation in the room is enhanced over omnidirectional microphones. In addition to pointing the sensitive side of the microphone at the desired source of sound, another useful property of the cardioid is that one can "point" the null point at the rear of the microphone at an offending noise source.
>
> **Hypercardioid microphone:** similar to the cardioid microphone but having a narrower front angle of acceptance, two symmetrical nulls rather than one straight to the rear, and a small "lobe" showing sensitivity to sounds from the rear of the microphone.
>
> **Interference tube (shotgun or rifle) microphone:** a microphone with a strong frontal sensitivity and with all other directions de-emphasized. It has the highest ratio of direct to reverberant sound energy of all normally used microphones, but suffers from changing directivity with frequency when used in any practical length. Also, most models show strong off-axis frequency

response coloration. Still, probably the most often used production sound microphone.

Omnidirectional microphone: a microphone directivity pattern that responds to sound energy nearly equally well from all directions. Omnidirectional microphones are most likely to be dynamic or condenser types.

MIDI (Musical Instrument Device Interface): a popular interconnection bus for synthesizers, drum machines, and other musical instruments capable of electronic control. May be interfaced to SMPTE time code to synchronize the action of the MIDI bus with film or video.

Mike: slang for microphone.

Mix: used both as a noun and as a verb to describe the activity required to produce a complete sound track from the various different sources required. Mixing activities may be further broken down into premixing, final mixing, and print mastering. In premixing, the original cut sound *units* or *elements* are hung on *dubbers*, which run many strands of film in synchronization. Each of the outputs of the dubbers forms an input to the *console*. The output of the console is recorded on a new piece of film, called a *premix*. Sound editors and sound designers usually break down the premixes first into dialog, music, and sound effects, and often further into the type of sound effects such as *Foley*, *ambience*, and conventional cut effects. Following premixing, the various premixes are hung on dubbers and the console is used to produce a *final mix*. The final mix may still be recorded on many tracks, and even across multiple strands of film, forming the final mix *stems*. Then, *print masters* may be prepared for each of the different release formats. Keeping the dialog separate from the other parts of the sound in a separate stem makes foreign-language dialog mixing simpler because the dialog stem may simply be replaced one prepared in the new language, and then new print masters made for the foreign-language dub.

Mixdown: synonym for *mix*.

Monaural: having only one audio channel.

Monophonic: synonym for *monaural*.

Multitrack: pertaining to audio formats using more channels than the release format used for flexibility in mixing. The usual professional multitrack analog recorders have 4 tracks on $1/_2$ in. tape, 8 tracks on 1 in. tape, and 24 tracks on 2 in. tape. Digital multitrack recorders usually have 24 or 32 tracks on 1 in. tape.

Mute: silent, especially a control to turn off an audio signal.

Mylar ™ : a tough plastic material used as the backing for magnetic films and tapes.

NC curves: a set of curves used to rate the background noise of spaces in terms of human perception of noise. The NC curves permit a higher measured sound pressure level of low-frequency noise than of high-frequency noise because human hearing is less sensitive to low-frequency noise than high. Some typical ratings are as follows:

Recording studios	NC 10
Dubbing stages	NC 20
High-quality theaters	NC 25
Maximum permissible in theaters	NC 30

In particular, the NC-10 rating for studios is lower than historical ratings given for these spaces. This is because of the advent of improved recording methods, with their wider dynamic range.

Neo-pilottone: see *Pilot tone*.

Noise: technically a sound is said to be noiselike when the signal cannot be distinguished as having tonal properties. Examples include a waterfall, most jet-engine noise, and most air-conditioning background noise. In more common usage, noise is any undesired signal.

Noise filter: usually a *low-pass filter*, sometimes made dynamic by responding to the high-frequency content of program material. The idea is that if there is high-frequency program material it will mask high-frequency noise, so that there should be no filtering, but in the absence of high-frequency program, the filter should be applied to attenuate noise that often takes on the audible character of high-frequency hiss.

Notch filter: an electrical filter arranged to produce generally sharp attenuation in a fairly narrow frequency band, passing frequencies both lower and higher than it without attenuation. Notch filters are particularly useful in attenuating tonal noise, such as hum or whistles, while having minimum audible effect on the program material.

Omnidirectional: see *Microphone polar patterns*.

One-third-octave equalization: adjustment of the *frequency response* of a sound system, which usually includes loudspeakers operating in a room, in order to produce a standardized or desired octave-to-octave spectral balance. Equalization typically is performed by means of a set of boost or cut *equalizers* located on center frequencies uniformly spaced at intervals of approximately one third of an octave over the frequency range of interest, such as from 25 Hz to 20 kHz. The frequency centers are usually taken from the ISO series: 25, 31.5, 40, 50, 63, 80, 100, 125, 250, etc., rationalizing the strictly calculated center frequencies to nearby round numbers. The one-third-octave spacing was chosen by the marketplace as close enough to the critical bands of human hearing (which are closer to one-fifth octave above 200 Hz) to do productive work without excessive cost and is the most popular spacing in use. For aligning sound systems in real rooms, the use of multiple microphones for spatial averaging and computed temporal averaging is dictated for reliability of the results.

Open reel: any tape recording format that does not use a cassette, which generally implies that it must be threaded by the user. The tape may be supplied either on reels or on a *pancake*.

Optical sound recording: the process of recording sound photographically by means of an optical camera recording a sound negative, usually using a variable area to represent the waveform of the sound, and subsequent development of the negative, printing, and print developing. The result is an economical means of supplying large quantities of release prints with sound, which can be printed in the same printer as the picture negative. Thus, its costs are much lower than magnetic sound recording and its use predominates on the 35mm and 16mm formats.

Overdub: the process of using a *multitrack* recorder for recording different parts at different times, *playing* back already recorded sounds from the *record head* as a synchronization reference. In this way, a prerecorded click track, for instance, can be played into headphones on musicians who then play their parts for recording on other tracks. Synchronization in time is assured by playing from the same head that is recording on separate tracks. See also *Sel-sync*.

Oxide: magnetically responsive material forming the basis of magnetic recording. It comes in a variety of types with different recording properties, especially suited to the needs of audiotape or videotape recording at a variety of densities of recording.

Pancake: audio magnetic tape wound on a core without flanges.

Parametric equalizer: an audio *equalizer* with added controls that include such factors as center frequency of equalization, and Q (relative sharpness of the *frequency response* curves) along with the boost/cut level controls available on other equalizers.

Peak meter: a level meter that responds quickly to incoming signals. Peak meters are generally used to avoid audible distortion; they are not particularly useful for determining *loudness*, for which even the primitive *VU meter* is superior. A typical response time for a peak meter to reach full indication is 10 msec.

Phase: pure sine waves can be described by only their amplitude and frequency. Most useful *signals*, on the other hand, are constituted of a multiplicity of sine waves simultaneously that change in time. For periodic waveforms, those with repeating waves, an additional element is needed beyond amplitude and frequency to completely describe the signal, and that element is phase. Phase is the relative starting point of the various component sine waves in a composite waveform. Thus, when a 1-kHz sine wave is mixed with a 3-kHz one, and the 1-kHz sine wave crosses zero amplitude going in the positive direction at a point in time, but the 3-kHz sine wave is at its crest, the 3-kHz sine wave is said to have a phase relative to the 1-kHz reference wave of +90°.

Phasing: the process of making certain that the various paths in a sound system have identical polarity, that is, if presented with a positive-going increase at the input of the system, a positive-going signal will appear at all accessible points within the system. If sound systems are not phased correctly, undesirable cancellations of sound may occur.

Phon: a unit of subjective loudness. By plotting a point at a frequency and sound-pressure level on an equal-loudness contour graph, one can determine where such a point lies with respect to the equal-loudness contours. The loudness in phons for such a tone is the nearest loudness contour that can be drawn through the point. The reference for phons, which are given in deciBels, is a sinusoidal tone at 1 kHz and 40 dB SPL.

Pilot tone: a synchronization method for $1/4$-in. magnetic tape (see *Crystal sync*). Using pilot tone, a precise 60-Hz tone (in the U.S.) is recorded to correspond to 24 fps. The recording is made with two small gaps out-of-phase with one another, and in the same *azimuth* as the main recording, so that the net sum of the two at a full-track playback head is zero, but a head having matching gaps, and wired with the correct phase, can play the tone back.

Pink noise: a random signal having equal energy in equal logarithmic units of frequency. Thus pink noise has equal energy in each one-third-octave band, for example, making it useful as a source in testing sound systems with a *real-time spectrum analyzer*.

Pinna: the external ear parts. Sound fields approaching the ear from different angles encounter various reflections and shadowing from the head and outer ear. The resulting frequency-response changes can be detected as locational and movement information.

Pinch roller: in tape transports, a disc of elastomeric material such as rubber that pushes the tape against the *capstan* so that the tape takes on the speed imparted by the capstan.

Pitch: the sensation of a tonal sound ascribed as lower or higher; affected mostly by the frequency of the sound, but also by *sound-pressure level* and *timbre*.

Play head: a tape head intended to recover recorded flux available from a magnetic oxide and to convert it into an electrical signal. Mechanically it is similar to a record head, although there are differences that optimize heads for either record or play use. Some machines are still produced that have only two heads—an erase head, and a combination record and play head—with a necessary compromise between the characteristics of each type.

Playback equalization: the frequency response correction applied on playback of a medium. See *Equalization*.

Polyester (Mylar™): a tough plastic base material for motion-picture film. Although more difficult to cut than acetate, its greater dimensional stability makes it desirable. In sound recording films, it is used especially in premixes, final mixes, and print masters, which are infrequently cut.

Post: slang for *post production*.

post production: the phase of making motion-picture and television programs that occurs after principal photography or recording has been accomplished; includes picture and sound editing, special effects production, and sound mixing.

post production sound: the phase of making motion-picture and television programs that occurs after shooting of the production sound, including editing, mixing, and print mastering. The outcome of the process is a set of *print masters*, which represent the sound-track formats needed to produce all the various release formats desired.

Pot (potentiometer): see *Fader*.

Precedence Effect (aka Law of the First Wavefront, and Haas Effect): localization in the direction of the first-arriving sound despite later reflections. It can be overcome if the later reflections are of sufficient amplitude.

Predub: synonym for *premix*.

Pre-emphasis: the process of applying *equalization* before a medium, combined with *de-emphasis* to form a complete system.

Prelay: the term is applied in television applications, both to a room and to the equipment used to re-record sound effects from a sound library to an editorial medium, such as a Digital Audio Workstation.

Premix: one of the stages of preparation of sound tracks for film and television programs during which individual edited *units* of like kind are mixed together to form one complete component part of a final mix. Examples of premixes include *dialog*, *Foley*, and *ambience* premixes.

Presence: (atmos. and room tone) background noise recorded during *production sound* recording meant to match the production sound track so that it may be intercut with the track and provide a continuous-sounding background.

Pressure microphone: a microphone whose output is proportional to varying air pressure caused by a sound field. Pressure microphones generally consist of a diaphragm enclosing a sealed chamber. It is the changes between the externally applied varying sound pressure and the fixed internal air pressure that the microphone converts into electrical energy.

The term is used specifically with measurement microphones to indicate microphone types that are calibrated in such a way that the high-frequency response rises on axis due to the buildup of pressure in front of a barrier, which becomes increasingly true at higher frequencies in the case of microphone-size objects. Pressure-calibrated measurement microphones generally measure sound fields having a strong predominant single direction component with the best flatness when used at grazing incidence, with the sound field passing across the diaphragm rather than perpendicular to it.

Principal photography: that part of a motion-picture production in which the main actors are photographed and sound recorded.

Print master: a complete sound track containing all sound elements, such as dialog, music, and sound effects, recorded in a format compatible as to number of available tracks with the needs of mass production of prints or video discs or tapes.

Print-through: a defect of analog magnetic tape recording wherein a recording made and wound onto a reel affects the adjacent layers, causing noticeable pre- and post-echoes. Print-through is exacerbated by time and increasing temperature.

Production sound: sound recorded during *principal photography*.

Production sound logs: written notes in prescribed form recording the content of each production sound tape. Usually included are scene and take information, printed take information through the convention of circling the printed take numbers, and other production and technical information needed to locate information and playback the tape correctly.

Production sound mixer: the person in charge of recording on the set, who generally controls the microphone technique, operates the *audio mixer*, often in portable form, and operates the recorder.

Program equalization: *equalization* deliberately added by a mixer to make the program better balanced in octave-to-octave response for the intended purpose, as opposed to "fixed equalization," which is used around media to compensate for deficiencies.

Propagation: the process by which sound is distributed through a medium, by molecules nearer the source progressively imparting energy to ones further away through mechanical vibration.

Punch-in/punch-out: to begin and end recording, especially while rolling to record just one section of tape or film.

Quantizing: in digital representation of a signal, the process of "binning" or measuring the amplitude of each sample in order to represent it as a set of numbers. Then, the numbers are combined with additional numbers used to provide protection against errors and to tailor the stream of resulting numbers for a specific purpose, such as for a medium before recording or transmission. Some issues relevant to this process are the basic method, the number of "bins," the regularity of the bins, and the deliberate addition of a small amount of noise, called "dither," which acts to smooth the transitions across the bin boundaries.

The most widely used method for audio today is 16-bit linear pulse code modulation, used for professional audio recording and the compact disc medium. This method uses a straight, uniformly stepped ramp to compare the amplitude of the signal against, producing one 16-bit binary number each sample period for each channel. Thus, the compact disk, for example, uses 16 bits/sample × 44,100 samples/sec × 2 channels = 1,411,200 bits/sec, not counting error overhead, etc.

Radio frequency: any frequency that may be used for electromagnetic modulation of a carrier by a signal, extending from near audio (for transmission underwater) to many millihertz.

Radio microphone: a microphone system using a radio transmission link. Usually the transmission link will be by means of frequency modulation of a high-frequency carrier with noise-reduction companding for professional quality. Optionally, "diversity reception," that is, reception at more than one antenna with the receiver constantly examining the inputs and switching to the strongest one, helps to reduce the influence of multipath. Multipath results in distortion caused by a drop in signal level as the main path is interfered with by other radio frequency paths, which may cause complete signal cancellation at some positions of the transmitter and receiver.

Real-time spectrum analyzer: a device for measuring the amplitude versus frequency response characteristic of a device or system under test that measures all parts of the desired frequency range simultaneously. Real-time analyzers generally use a bank of frequency-selective filters and a means of measuring the output levels from the bank of filters that is displayed as a graph of amplitude versus frequency.

Record equalization: an *equalization* applied before recording to be complemented with a *playback equalization*. The purpose of the record and playback equalization cycle is to produce the best trade-off of *headroom* versus *signal-to-noise ratio* of a medium for its intended use.

Recording galvanometer: see *Galvanometer.*

Record head: a tape head intended to leave a magnetic recording on a tape, consisting of thin metal laminations around which an electrical coil is wound. Electrical current injected into the coil then produces a corresponding magnetic field in the laminations. The laminations are stacked together, and the whole assembly is cut with a gap. At the gap a magnetic field extends out from the head that is able to record on the *oxide* layer of *tape* or *magnetic film.*

Reference fluxivity: a standardized level of magnetic flux, measured in nanoWebers/meter (nW/m) recorded on a tape or film, for use in calibrating tape and film recorders. Common reference fluxivities values include 100, 185, 200, 250, 320, and 355 nW/m.

Reflection: sound encountering a barrier may be reflected off it. A flat barrier will reflect sound with a "specular reflection," just like a billiard ball encountering a bumper at the edge of a pool table. A shaped barrier can either concentrate or diffuse sound, depending on its shape. One example of a deliberately shaped barrier to capture sound energy is a whispering gallery, which has two points of focus, many feet apart, that conduct sound between them very well.

Reproducing head: a tape head designed for playback of a signal stored on tape or other magnetic media. Reproduce heads are made similar to *record heads*, but the process is reversed with the flux from the tape or film being "captured" by the gap and is delivered to a coil of wire wrapped around the metal laminations.

Re-recording: the process of sound post production in which sound elements are combined into premixes, then again into final mix stems, and then finally into print masters. Because these processes do not involve live recording typically, the process became known as re-recording to distinguish it from original recording.

Reverberation: acoustic reflections from the environment occurring so frequently at such close spacing in time that the individual reflections making up the ensemble can no longer be distinguished. Reverberation time is the amount of time for an interrupted steady-state sound field to decay away to 60 dB below its original sound-pressure level.

Reverberator: a device that by mechanical or by computer-calculated means supplies the effect of *reverberation*.

Ribbon microphone: a microphone type that converts acoustical energy into electrical energy by means of a fine, lightweight metal ribbon suspended in the field of a magnet. The ribbon moves in the magnetic field corresponding to the sound energy, and a voltage is obtained between the ends.

Rifle microphone: a slang name for an interference-tube microphone having a club-shaped *microphone polar pattern*.

Room modes: see *Standing waves*.

Room tone: see *Presence* definition 1.

Room synthesizer: a specialized digital audio reverberator especially designed to simulate room acoustics. Room synthesizers are often used in post production to add spatiousness to "dry" recordings. The system of adding reverberation in post production is often preferable to recording the right amount in the first place on many sound elements because it is difficult to judge the effects of reverberation on only a single element of a complex sound track. Also, it is difficult if not impossible to reduce the amount of recorded reverberation, and simple to add it, leading to the method of making generally "dry" recordings, and then adding reverberation during mixing.

RTA: abbreviation for *real-time spectrum analyzer*.

Sampler: a device that can store audio by means of *sampling* a waveform, digitizing it, and storing it away using a variety of means. A term prominent among musicians, not to be confused with definition 1 of *sampling*.

Sampling: 1. The process of capturing the amplitude of a signal at regular intervals quickly enough that the desired audio signal is completely represented. The sampling theorem states that this process must occur at least somewhat more frequently than twice each cycle of the audio to be represented, so popular sampling frequencies have become 32 kHz (some broadcast links, especially in Europe), 44.1 kHz (consumer audio, including compact disk), and 48 kHz (professional audio). Because frequencies higher than one-half the sampling frequency would be misrepresented as aliases, that is, as frequencies other than themselves, much like wagon wheels when photographed at 24 fps may appear to run backward, anti-aliasing filters are used to strip off any ultrasonic components of the audio signal before sampling in order to prevent this effect. The sampling process also produces an aperture effect as the input frequency approaches one-half the sampling frequency, and this effect is compensated by adjustment of the frequency response with an equalizer.

2. Colloquial: the action done by a *sampler*.

SDDS: abbreviation for *Sony Dynamic Digital Sound*.

Sel-rep or **Sel-sync™:** a mode of multitrack recorders that permits using the record head for listening purposes rather than the playback head, selectable on a per channel basis. Use of the record head for playback ensures synchronization when sound is not all recorded at the same time, but instead is built up in layers. As a time reference for recordings to be added after the initial recording, performers can listen to reference channels off the record head in headphones while recording to other channels simultaneously. The entire process is called "overdubbing," and was invented by guitarist Les Paul so that he could play multiple parts on a recording.

SEPMAG: literally, separate magnetic, otherwise known as *double system*.

Shotgun microphone: see *Microphone polar pattern*.

Signal: the desired information content of a program. Used as a term to distinguish the desired program from the undesired added effects of noise, or distortion.

Signal-to-noise ratio: the amount that noise of a medium or transmission path lies below the reference level in the medium. For example, "the signal-to-noise ratio is 65 dB re 185 nW/m." This is an incomplete specification because many conditions affect the measurement of signal to noise: Is the measurement weighted for human perception or measured flat? What kind of measuring voltmeter was used? A better specification is "the signal-to-noise ratio is 65 dB re 185 nW/m, measured with flat weighting and an rms meter."

Single perf: abbreviation for single perforation, used to describe 16mm film that has been perforated along only one edge.

Single system: a method of recording both picture and sound on one piece of film. The sound recording may be by either photographic or magnetic means, used to describe the type of sound camera often used for, for example, newsreel shooting, where simplicity of setup is paramount in use.

SMPTE: see *Society of Motion Picture and Television Engineers*.

Snake track: a special analog optical sound-track recording used for testing the uniformity of illumination across the sound-track area. The film consists of a small tone signal riding slowly back and forth across the sound-track area. Uniformity of illumination is important in analog optical sound tracks because a fall-off of illumination to one side, for example, will cause that side to be under-represented in the output, which leads to distortion.

Society of Motion Picture and Television Engineers (SMPTE): the U.S. group having standards-making activity in film and television. Certain of its standards are adopted as American National Standards.

Sone: an alternate unit of subjective loudness. In addition to accounting for equal-loudness contours such as the phon, the sone goes one step further and scales the logarithmic measures so that twice the number of sones represents twice as loud. 40 dB SPL at 1 kHz = 1 phon = 1 sone; 50 dB SPL = 10 phons = 2 sones.

Sony Dynamic Digital Sound: a method of recording digital audio in the 5.1- or 7.1-channel formats (7.1 adds left center and right center front channels to the 5.1-channel standard) in the area outside the perforations on motion-picture release prints. It may appear simultaneously on a print with an analog optical sound track, and with either one or both of the competing digital audio formats, Dolby SR-D and DTS.

Sound: motion of particles in a medium (air, water, steel) about a mean position.

Sound camera: a motion-picture camera that is either inherently made quiet or is equipped with a noise-reducing *blimp* or *barney* so as to make the recording of sound possible without excessive camera acoustical noise interference.

Sound design: the process of selecting sounds, editing them, and mixing them together to form a desired artistic effect, usually used as a term when sound is accompanying the picture.

Sound drum: a mechanical cylinder having mass located in the path of film or tape transports used to impart greater stability of speed to the film or tape.

Sound-effects editing: in traditional motion-picture production, the process of choosing sounds, then cutting sound *elements* or *units* into synchronization with the picture, and delivering them with the cue sheet to the dubbing stage for *premixing*. In television production, it is more likely that sound-effects editing involves choosing sounds then re-recording them to multitrack tape or to a digital audio workstation.

Sound head: in production and post production, the term applies to the general class of tape or films heads, including erase, record, or playback heads. In cinema usage, it means the whole assembly used to recover sound from the film, including mechanical devices for guiding the film and stabilizing its speed, light sources needed for photographic sound tracks,

and a pickup device, such as a solar cell for photographic sound or a magnetic playback head for magnetic sound tracks.

Sound-level meter: an instrument for measuring sound-pressure level. Sound pressure is referenced to a small pressure variation near the threshold of hearing.

Sound log: a record kept by a production sound recording corresponding to each reel of tape used, noting scene and take information and including notes regarding any wild sound (not shot with the picture) recording. On sound logs it is conventional to circle the take number of takes that the director wants printed so that only those takes will be transferred for dailies, saving magnetic film in transfer.

Sound mixer: an ambiguous term equally applicable to a sound *console* and to a production sound recordist.

Sound pressure: the primary factor used to assess the amplitude of sound waves. Although sound particle velocity, intensity, and power can all be measured and indicate the strength of a sound field, sound pressure is usually preferred because it is the simplest to measure.

Sound pressure level: measured sound pressure, usually given in deciBels re a reference pressure corresponding approximately to the threshold of hearing of young adults. The dynamic range of human hearing at frequencies near 1 kHz is from the minimum audible sound around 0 dB SPL to the threshold of a sensation of tickle in the ear, approximately 120 dB. Common alternative reference levels used for microphone sensitivity specifications are 1 microbar = 74 dB SPL and 1 Pascal = 94 dB SPL.

Sound track: often used to describe the physical sound placement on a motion-picture release print containing sound. Also used to describe the recording contained on a motion-picture release print, and sometimes to describe the musical score of a motion picture available in another medium.

Speech mode: the idea that the brain separately distinguishes speech from other sounds and processes it in a different part of the brain reserved for speech. The presence of a speech mode helps explain otherwise disparate observations about human hearing.

Speed of sound: 1130 feet per second in air at 72°F. For the range −22° to +86°F, the speed is given by $c = 1052 + 1.106F$, where c is in ft/sec and F is in degrees Fahrenheit.

Standing waves: a term in room acoustics used to describe the effects of sound interacting with multiple enclosure surfaces in ways that tend to strengthen or diminish the sound field at various frequencies, measured at a point in the space. Standing waves occur because sound waves cover a range of wavelengths that include wavelengths wherein integral ratios of waves fit precisely between the boundaries. At these frequencies, mutual reflection of the waves back and forth between two surfaces or among more surfaces produces points in space where the sound pressure varies greatly (at the maxima) and where it varies very little (at the minima). Standing waves generally lead to a lack of uniformity of sound fields in enclosures, being worse in the bass frequencies and in small rooms.

Stems: the constituent parts of a final mix. The various channels may be used to represent direction, such as left, center, right (corresponding to the picture), and surround; and to represent the various kinds of sounds, such as dialog, music, and sound effects. The advantage of keeping the final mix as a multitrack representation is that it makes the preparation of subsequent special versions, such as foreign language release, simpler because all that need to be done is to substitute only a new language element for the dialog, and then new *print masters* may be made as needed in the new language.

Stereophonic: pertaining to any of a number of sound systems that can represent sound spatially, starting with conventional two-channel home stereo, up to multichannel sound systems often used to accompany pictures in large-scale presentations. For conventional film sound, what is usually meant today is at least four channels: left, center, right, and surround. More often, 5.1-channel sound is used, with two surround channels and a dedicated low-frequency channel added to the front channels. The opposite of the single-channel *monaural* sound, whose only spatial capacity of which is the depth dimension along one line radiating away from the listener.

Stereophony: synonym for *stereophonic.*

Sticks: colloquial for *clapperboard.*

Stripe coat: the alternative to *full coat.* Magnetic film that is coated with oxide in a stripe meant for recording a single channel. A "balance stripe" is applied near the opposite edge to produce better winding characteristics. Stripe coat is a term that typically applies only to such 35mm magnetic film stock.

Sub dub: synonym for *premix.*

Surround sound: any of a series of *stereophonic* sound systems that uses at least left, center, and right screen channels and one or more surround-sound channels. One popular variation uses L, C, R, left surround, right surround, and a dedicated extra low-frequency channel. This system is called 5.1-channel sound.

SVA: (*Stereo Variable Area*): generic name applied to the Dolby Stereo format wherein two different bilateral sound records, side by side, carry Lt Rt information that can be decoded in a theater to in L, C, R, and S channels.

Sync sound: sound recorded in conjunction with a picture, either *single system* or *double system.* In the case of double-system sync sound, a means must be provided to keep the picture and sound media in sync, such as *crystal sync.*

Tape: see *Magnetic tape.*

Tape speed: one of a series of nominal rates of tape velocity past tape heads. For analog sound recording the speeds range across 30, 15, 7 $\frac{1}{2}$, 3 $\frac{3}{4}$, and 1 $\frac{7}{8}$ in./sec, with the 15 and 7 $\frac{1}{2}$ in./sec speeds being the most common.

Tape recorder/player: a device for recording picture and sound or sound only on a moving strand of magnetic tape. Tape recorders represent the signals to be recorded as either analogs of the signal (such an analog being the strength of the magnetic field used to represent sound in direct analog magnetic recording, or the instantaneous frequency of an FM carrier in analog video recording) or as digits in digital recording of audio or video. The essential ingredients of a tape recorder are a transport to move the tape past the *magnetic heads* and record and playback electronics, usually used with record and playback equalization to tailor the signal.

Temporal masking: see *Masking, temporal.*

Test tape: a carefully prepared tape containing test signals for the alignment of playback on audiotape and videotape recorders. Most adjustments on tape machines start with making playback fit a set of standards so that when the record side is adjusted, it is done under a known set of playback conditions.

THX: a set of technologies licensed by Lucasfilm first developed for the cinema and subsequently for the home. In the theater, this means a specific electronic crossover, choice of power amplifiers and loudspeakers, local acoustical environment around the loudspeakers, global acoustical environment of the theater, and tuning of the theater sound system in accordance with standard SMPTE 202. In the home, both electronic- and loudspeaker-design tactics are used to better translate the program material prepared in a dubbing stage into the home environment.

Timbre: the sensation about a tonal sound that cannot be described by loudness or pitch. Related to the strength of the various harmonics and the fundamental, and how they change across time.

Time code (SMPTE time code): a method of encoding position into hours, minutes, seconds, and frames, along with other information, so that unsprocketed media, such as videotape, open reel tape, etc., can be run in frame-accurate synchronization by use of an electronic synchronizer. Time code occupies the space of one audio channel typically but may be recorded to a dedicated time-code channel or embedded with the video by means of a vertical interval time code placed in the video lines above the active picture area.

Tone: a sound is said to be "tonal" when the constituent sine waves of which it is made can be distinguished. Tonal sounds usually can be assigned a pitch. Examples include an organ pipe, sine-wave oscillator, square-wave oscillator, and whistle. Also used to describe the reference sine wave used for level and response adjustment, as in "send me the 1 k tone."

Track: the physical area or other space on a medium such as film, tape, disc, etc. within which the record of the sound, picture, or data are recorded or printed.

Track formats for film recording:

Stripe (one track), three-track, four-track, six-track: names applied to the track layouts describing 35mm magnetic film containing sound only. Stripe-coated stock is usually used for one-track recordings. Three-, four-, and six-track formats are recorded on *full-coat* 35mm film stock with magnetic oxide across the full width.

Edge track, center track, EBU stereo: names describing various formats of 16mm full-coat magnetic film containing no picture. Edge and center track are what their names imply and are not interchangeable. EBU Stereo consists of one edge and one center track, which may be used for stereo program material or for different language presentations.

Track formats for tape recording: full-track; half-track; two-track; quarter-track; 4-, 8-, 16-, 24-track formats: names applied to the track layouts describing open-reel nonperforated tape, over the range from $^1/_4$ in. wide to 2 in. wide. On $^1/_4$ in. tape, the following are possible: Full-track is recorded across the entire width. Half-track implies two recordings, one made from heads to tails, and one from tails to heads with the tape being "turned over" when the tail is reached (this is a radio-station format, not a film format). Two-track is two-channel recording, usually stereo, with both records inline across the width of the tape. Quarter-track is an obsolete consumer format for four tracks on $^1/_4$ in. tape, usually used two at a time for stereo going from head to tail and tail to head. 4-track is a format for $^1/_2$ in.

tape. 8-track is a format for 1 in. tape. 16-track (obsolete) and 24-track are formats for 2 in. tape.

Transfer: the process of recording from one piece of tape or film to another, applied widely in audio and video.

Tweeter: a high-frequency loudspeaker, combined with a *woofer* in a complete loudspeaker system for full-frequency range coverage. In theater usage it is more common to use the term horns to apply to the combination of a *compression driver* and *horn* that emits high frequencies.

Ultrasonic frequency range: the region above the audible frequency range, above 20 kHz. The region is of interest to dogs, bats, and burglar alarms but not to people unless the amplitude is extremely high.

Unblooped: pertaining to a motion-picture sound-track negative wherein the discontinuities due to splices have not been minimized by making opaque the area near the splice with "blooping" tape or ink.

Unit: synonym for *element*.

Unmodulated track: an optical sound track containing no deliberate signal. For variable-area sound tracks, unmodulated track is made narrow when there is no signal present to reduce the noise caused by the optical grain of the film.

Variable-area sound track: an optical sound track for motion-picture prints that uses variations in the area of the recorded track to represent the amplitude of the audio signal.

Variable-density sound track: an optical sound track for motion-picture prints that uses continuous gradation from black to white to represent the amplitude of the audio signal. These tracks are generally of historical interest today, with the wider dynamic range of variable-area sound tracks having made obsolete the variable-density track.

Volume range: the range in deciBels of a program, from the loudest passage to the softest. Hopefully, the volume range fits within the *dynamic range*.

VU meter: a meter intended to read the level of dynamic program material in a standardized fashion, used by audio mixers to improve the interchangeability of programs, and to avoid audible distortion. The VU meter standards were originally designed so that a meter movement could be used directly without electronics to read the program level, and, thus, VU meters are relatively slow, requiring about 300 msec to rise to 0 VU from rest. This makes the VU meter a better indicator of *loudness* than a *peak meter*. Although rigorously standardized in ANSI C16.5, many meters marked as VU meters do not meet the standard.

Wave: a disturbance in a medium that progresses through *propagation*. Transversal waves are perpendicular to the direction of travel, and longitudinal waves are in the direction of travel. Water waves are typically transversal; sound waves are longitudinal.

Waveform: variation in amplitude of a quantity versus time, such as sound pressure versus time, voltage versus time, etc.

Wavelength: for a sinusoidal pressure wave, the distance from peak to peak of the wave. The wavelengths corresponding to the audible frequency range cover from more than 50 feet to less than 1 inch.

White noise: a random signal containing all frequencies containing equal energy for equal increments of frequency. In sound, reproduced white noise sounds quite "bright" because it contains as much energy between the high audio frequencies of 10 and 20 kHz as between 0 and 10 kHz. See also *Pink noise*.

Wild sound: sound recorded without a camera rolling. The term is used for sound gathered independent of a picture, such as a close-up sound of an effect that is going to be photographed, for use by sound editors in post production who must match a sound to what is seen on a picture.

Woofer: a low-frequency *loudspeaker*. It is generally combined with a *tweeter* (in consumer terminology) or with a *compression driver* and *horn* (in typical theatrical usage) to cover the full frequency range.

Worldize: to re-record sound through a channel that includes a loudspeaker and a microphone, generally in an acoustical space. The purpose of worldizing is to make the sound seem as though it came from the space in question, rather than being a direct electrical recording. See also *Futz*.

Wow and flutter: any change from absolutely constant speed during direct analog recording or playback results in corresponding frequency changes, which can be audible. Slow changes are called "wow" and faster ones "flutter," but both represent the same phenomena.

X-copy: a copy made as closely as possible to a 1:1 match. This applies to "equal flux" copying, wherein a copy is made at the same flux levels as the master.

X-curve: one particular *electro-acoustic response* curve having a prescribed high-frequency rolloff. Its use in motion-picture dubbing theaters, screening rooms, and exhibition theaters helps greatly to standardized what is heard by the audience. It is specified in SMPTE Standard 202 and ISO 2969.

Zenith: see *Head alignment*.

Instructions for Accompanying CD

The CD accompanying this book may be played on virtually any sound system, and most of the demonstrations will work. However, the better the sound system, the better some of the more subtle effects will be demonstrated. While most of the demonstrations are monaural, some use the two channels for two different, but related, recordings. The best means for playing the two separate recordings is noted individually in the description of the tracks.

The last track provides a means to set the level with a sound level meter, if one is available, so that repeatable demonstrations can be made. The track consists of band-limited pink noise recorded at −30 dBFSrms (although it will read higher on peak meters). This track may be set to 85 dB sound pressure level (although a lower reference of 75 dB SPL is used in film post production for this recorded level, setting to 85 dB is typical for studio playback of conventional CDs).

Track No.	Description
1	Level setting. Set the playback monitor level of your sound system for 75 dB SPL C weighted and slow reading for each channel in turn. This signal is band limited pink noise recorded at −30 dBFSrms.
2	Demonstration of level of direct sound vs. distance
3	100 Hz, 1 kHz, 10 kHz sine wave tones alternating, illustrating frequency range
4	400 Hz tone with a variety of waveforms: sine, square, triangle, and synthesized waves
5	Radiation pattern of voice demonstrated by recording at various angles
6	Doppler shift is an important part of a pass by
7	The addition of one strong reflection at 10 ms
8	Reverberation illustrated
9	Frequency boinks covering the 10 octaves of the audible frequency range
10	Noise played at 10 dB increments over an 80 dB range
11	Loudness effect: bands of noise at various center frequencies and levels
12	The rise of loudness with time
13	Frequency masking
14	Temporal masking
15	Timbre I: Harmonic structure of various instruments helps us identify them
16	Timbre II: The importance of onset transients
17	Microphone proximity effect demonstration. A pressure mike and a pressure-gradient mike (bi-directional) are compared at a close distance. A pressure-gradient microphone boosts the bass when the sound source is near the mike.
18	Demonstration comparing pressure and pressure-gradient microphones on very low frequency response. Due to its method of operation, the pressure microphone responds to lower frequencies in the sound field than do directional microphones. For this demonstration, the sound system you use must have extended bass response for the effect to be audible.
19	This track has the same program material as track 6, but the outputs of the two microphones types being compared are intercut. This may make the effect more audible. The microphone with the greater low-frequency output is the pressure type, and is the first heard. The level of the two microphones has been set to be equal for mid-range sounds.

Track No.	Description
20	Demonstration making a cardioid microphone by adding a pressure and a pressure-gradient microphone together by summing their outputs.
21	Microphone polar patterns illustrated. This track is a "walk around" of five different microphone types: omni-directional, bi-directional, cardioid, hypercardioid, and interference tube. The microphones are all at the same distance from the talker (2 m), and the room is moderately reverberant. The effect of on- and off-axis microphone responses for the various types is clearly audible.
22	This track is similar to track 21, only the presentation order is different, with the microphones intercut at each primary angle so that they can be more directly compared. The angles are 0° (on axis of the front of the array of microphones), 45°, 90° and 180°.
23	Microphone wind susceptibility demonstration. A pressure mike and a pressure-gradient mike are compared by blowing into them. Due to the diaphragm tension and method of measuring the sound field, a pressure microphone is less wind susceptible than a pressure-gradient microphone. The pressure microphone is on the left channel, and the pressure-gradient on the right channel, so listening either in stereo, or to one channel at a time, is necessary. An inadvertent "pop" appears on the word "pressure" in the pressure-gradient mike, showing a related difference between the types.

Tracks 24 through 30 compare seven different microphones, used at distances and angles that are typical of different types of film and television production. Also, the distances used correspond to the relative pick up by each of the microphones of direct and reverberant sound, so the direct-to-reverberant ratio stays approximately constant among the tracks. This is in contrast with track 1, where the microphones are at a fixed distance. The microphones were recorded simultaneously to a multi-channel recorder, and copied here to the left channel only of each of the cuts. One channel only was used to prevent interference effects in loudspeaker reproduction that occur when two channels are used. The words used constitute a list that is phonetically balanced, that is, which represents typical English language incidence of the various speech phonemes.

Track No.	Description
24	Omnidirectional measurement microphone used as a reference. A Bruel & Kjaer model 2230 sound level meter set for flat response to direct sound, used at about 2 ft. in front of the seated talker on the axis of his mouth. This microphone serves as a reference since it has flat frequency response.
25	Omnidirectional recording microphone with a slight high-frequency emphasis, usually used at a distance to compensate for air loss, but used here to demonstrate the difference due to the microphone response (which is fairly small). The microphone is next to the sound level meter, and has a Schoeps MK2S capsule.
26	A bi-directional pressure-gradient microphone at 1.7 times the distance of the omni types and practically on the axis of the talker. A Neumann U89 adjustable pattern microphone set to the figure 8 pattern.
27	A cardioid microphone at 1.7 times the distance of the omnis, also nearly on axis. A Schoeps MK4 capsule.
28	A hypercardioid microphone at 2.0 times the distance of the omnis, mounted on an overhead fishpole at about 45° above the talker, and on axis viewed from above, aimed at the talker. A Schoeps MK41 capsule.
29	An interference tube shotgun microphone used at 3.0 times the distance of the omnis, mounted on an overhead boom at about 40° above the talker, and on axis viewed from above, aimed at the talker. A Sennheiser MKH815.
30	A lavaliere microphone clipped to the shirt of the talker about 8 in. below his mouth. This microphone exhibits a greater direct-to-reverberant sound ratio than the others due to its placement. A Tram microphone.

Track No.	Description
31	Dynamic range of analog vs. digital. The same recorded speech appears on the two channels, with the left channel recorded digitally, and the right one recorded in analog before being transferred to the digital master. Note that each recording should be played alone, one at a time, and preferably over the same loudspeaker system. The analog recording is more audibly distorted at normal levels, but less than the digital when the headroom of the two media is exceeded. Also, the over-recorded analog sounds quieter than the digital due to tape saturation. The noise level is much more audible on underrecorded analog than on digital. If the two recordings are added together in an external mixer, they "flange," that is, produce a comb filtered frequency response due to the imperfections in the speed of the analog machine, and the consequent frequency response additions and subtractions. The amount of flanging heard when summing is typical of good quality synchronization of film sound tracks when they are checked for sync. Length 1:06.
32	Edit demo 1. A picture editor usually cuts sound between two close ups at the picture cut, but a sound editor may delay the cut until just before the first word of the incoming speech. The sound editor is using the principle of backwards masking (Chapter 2) to cover up the edit, and others of the Gestalt principles to produce a convincing whole. Length 0:38.
33	Edit demo 2. When a cut across a scene boundary may become noticeable due to the "bump" at the edit, sometimes a smooth crossfade produces a better effect. This is an effect which was commonly done on mag film by using chemicals to remove the oxide in a long stripe in order to produce a fade in. Today it is much more common to use such smooth crossfades in digital audio editing. Length 0:37.
34	Edit demo 3. A common problem in cutting between two shots is that one of them will contain only part of a sound which we expect to be complete, such as having only one half of a "car by." Extending the car by, usually by using the trim off the head or tail of the appropriate shot, works to make the scene seem whole. Length 0:27.
35	Edit demo 4. Another common problem is shooting towards dusk, with crickets becoming louder in later setups. In this case the editor has take a snip of sound from the louder take, looped it, and extending it over the quieter take, so the cricket level stays constant after editing. The crickets in the softer take are masked in the edited version. Length 0:37.

Editing demonstration: Roger Pardee

Recording interns: Ai Fujisaki, Benny Ho, Mike Baiocchi, Cheryl Uyehara

Additional test signals are available on the Test Disc Series from The Hollywood Edge, 37 Commercial Blvd., Novato, CA 94949, USA, www.hollywoodedge.com.